God's Funeral

By the same author

The Laird of Abbotsford (1980)
A Life of John Milton (1983)
Hilaire Belloc (1984)
Tolstoy (1988)
C.S. Lewis. A Biography (1990)
Jesus (1992)
Paul. The Mind of the Apostle (1997)

Fiction
Wise Virgin (1982)
The Vicar of Sorrows (1993)
Dream Children (1998)
etc.

God's Funeral

A.N. WILSON

W. W. Norton & Company
New York   London

For information about permission to reproduce selections from this book,
write to Permissions, W. W. Norton & Company, Inc.,
500 Fifth Avenue, New York, NY 10110.

Composition and manufacturing by the Haddon Craftsmen, Inc.

Library of Congress Cataloging-in-Publication Data

Wilson, A. N., 1950–
God's funeral / A. N. Wilson.
p.   cm.
Includes bibliographical references and index.
ISBN 0-393-04745-8
1. Religion and science—History—19th century. I. Title.
BL245.W66   1999
200´.94´034—dc21   99-21306
CIP

W. W. Norton & Company, Inc., 500 Fifth Avenue, New York, N.Y. 10110
www.wwnorton.com

W. W. Norton & Company Ltd., 10 Coptic Street, London WC1A 1PU

2 3 4 5 6 7 8 9 0

Contents

Illustrations

28. William Gladstone
29. Lord Queensberry
30. Annie Besant
31. Eleanor Marx
32. Sigmund Freud
33. Samuel Butler and Henry Festing Jones
34. Alfred Loisy
35. George Tyrrell
36. Baron von Hügel
37. William James and Josiah Royce

The author and publisher would like to thank the following for permission to reproduce illustrations: 1, 2, 4, 5, 9, 16, 19, 20, 23, 25, 26 and 30, Mary Evans Picture Library; 3, Gemälde von Gottlieb Doebler, 1791/Photo: AKG London; 7, 11 and 15, Hulton Getty; 8, photograph by Julia Margaret Cameron, 1867, The Royal Photographic Society Collection, Bath, England; 10, University College/Image Select; 12, Tate Gallery, London; 14, 21 and 24, Illustrated London News Picture Library; 17, National Portrait Gallery, London; 18, 27 and 28, Ann Ronan at Image Select; 22, 29 and 32, AKG London; 31, Alfortville, Frédéric Longuet Collection/Photo: AKG London; 33, The Master and Fellows of St John's College, Cambridge; and 35 and 36, James Crampsey, SJ, Provincial of the British Province of the Society of Jesus, from original photographs in the provincial archives.

Preface

THE GOD-QUESTION does not go away. No sooner have the intelligentsia of one generation confined the Almighty to the history books than popular opinion rises against them. We see this in our own time, and the spectacle is not always pleasant: Ayatollahs call out in the name of God for holy war, or evangelical Christians make their own comparably intolerant, though less murderous, contributions to public debate on such subjects as abortion, the modern marriage and politics. The majority of people in the Western world still claim, when asked by opinion polls, that they believe in God. Politicians, anyway in the United States, invoke God when they want to reassure the electorate that they are good guys. To a European eye President Clinton's Prayer Breakfast in September 1998 at which he confessed his sins and expressed a belief in divine grace was one of the most bizarre episodes of that colourful gentleman's career. Yet at the very least he clearly supposed that it would do no harm to demonstrate to television audiences his belief in the 'old, old story of Jesus and His love.'

Why not? For many people, the old story still counts, and still 'works'. Religion has what an American philosopher of the late nineteenth-early twentieth century called 'cash value'. This is an unhappy phrase in some ways, but what he meant by it is that, irrespective of whether you can prove the existence of God, you can demonstrate the effectiveness of religious practice. The person who finds himself in disgrace can call for Divine Mercy, and receive the sense that it has been vouchsafed. In the actual business of life, in grief, fear and sorrow, men and women and children say their prayers and find themselves comforted. This continues, whatever the unbelievers may wish to say about the sheer irrationality of the practice.

But even a fervent religious believer must, if honest, confront problems in relation to faith which were not necessarily present for those of earlier generations. The Renaissance popes reacted furiously to the notion that the earth was not the centre of the universe, nor man the most important being on earth. There was logic in torturing Galileo, who first began to make this known, since these beginnings of what we call a 'scientific' viewpoint shook the foundations of an old religion which believed that God had put Adam in charge of all His earthly creation, and made Man in His own image and likeness; even, when Man had disobeyed Him, this self-same God had Himself become Man, and come down to earth to redeem Him of His sins. You could not have a more anthropocentric view of things than this, and any factual discovery which began to weaken this belief had to be resisted.

The truth can't be resisted, of course. Eighteenth-century sceptical philosophers could ask what possible reason there was for supposing there to be a mind behind the Universe, but few read their words, and those who did could fall back on the argument that a Universe of such intricacy and order must have had a designer. What kind of a designer? Geologists in the opening decades of the nineteenth century began to realize, not only that the world had taken aeons to evolve, and that it was not all created in the six days of Genesis: but, much more disturbingly, that it was a pitiless universe. Whole species had been evolved, and then allowed to become extinct: that was the message of the fossils. If such a thing could happen in one generation to the brontosaurus, what was to stop it happening in a much later generation to humankind? A belief in God as a loving, benevolent and omnipotent Creator came to be seen as in fact depending upon a man-centred view of Nature which was increasingly hard to sustain.

Hence the disturbingness, for many minds in the middle decades of the nineteenth century, of discovering that Nature, with its evolving species, has no discernible purpose, certainly not a loving purpose, or an anthropocentric purpose. In other words, if you pressed the argument from Design too far you might infer a God who was curious about a multiplicity of life-forms, entirely unconcerned about the bloodiness and painfulness with which so many of these forms sustained life while on this planet, a God who was no more demonstrably interested in the human race than He was in, say, beetles, of which He created an inordinately large variety.

The nineteenth century, in other words, began to confront the human consciousness, not simply with new *ideas*, but with demonstrable new facts which challenged religious belief. Once the cold eye of modern scholarship had been cast on the Bible itself, even that looked a less solid bulwark than had once been supposed.

In some parts of our world, particularly in the United States, the battles which raged more than one and a half centuries ago have not gone away. Against patient scholars with no axe to grind who would like to point out this fact or that about the Bible (the high improbability, for instance, that the Gospels contain the actual words of the historical Jesus) the believers can always reply with their unshakeable knowledge that the Bible is the inspired word of Truth, the voice of Almighty God Himself. The Darwinian who points to the mid twentieth-century discovery of DNA as a confirmation, beyond reasonable doubt, that the theory of natural selection was correct, can do nothing to alter the beliefs of the Creationists.

That is a story in itself – the twentieth-century religious conflict. This book, however, returns to the origins of that conflict, and attempts to make sense of it by getting to know the men and women who were caught up in it. This is not a work of science, though scientific ideas are mentioned in its pages. Its author is no philosopher, but he has made some attempts to explain the underlying philosophical background to the story. This is not a theology textbook, but it shows the qualities of strife which afflicted women and men who found themselves honourably at war with theology. Periodically in the course of the century, they proclaimed that God was dead; and that is how it appeared to many of them who lived through those times.

GOD'S FUNERAL

Thomas Hardy

I

I saw a slowly-stepping train –
Lined on the brows, scoop-eyed and bent and hoar –
Following in files across a twilit plain
A strange and mystic form the foremost bore.

II

And by contagious throbs of thought
Or latent knowledge that within me lay
And had already stirred me, I was wrought
To consciousness of sorrow even as they.

III

The fore-borne shape, to my blurred eyes,
At first seemed man-like, and anon to change
To an amorphous cloud of marvellous size,
At times endowed with wings of glorious range.

IV

And this phantasmal variousness
Ever possessed it as they drew along:
Yet throughout all it symboled none the less
Potency vast and loving-kindness strong.

V

Almost before I knew I bent
Towards the moving columns without a word;
They, growing in bulk and numbers as they went,
Struck out sick thoughts that could be overheard:-

VI

'O man-projected Figure, of late
Imaged as we, thy knell who shall survive?
Whence came it we were tempted to create
One whom we can no longer keep alive?

VII

'Framing him jealous, fierce, at first,
We gave him justice as the ages rolled,
Will to bless those by circumstance accurst,
And long suffering, and mercies manifold.

VIII

'And, tricked by our own early dream
And need of solace, we grew self-deceived,
Our making soon our maker did we deem,
And what we had imagined we believed.

IX

'Till, in Time's stayless stealthy swing,
Uncompromising rude reality
Mangled the Monarch of our fashioning,
Who quavered, sank; and now has ceased to be.

X

'So, toward our myth's oblivion,
Darkling, and languid-lipped, we creep and grope
Sadlier than those who wept in Babylon,
Whose Zion was a still abiding hope.

XI

'How sweet it was in years far hied
To start the wheels of day with trustful prayer,
To lie down liegely at the eventide
And feel a blest assurance he was there!

XII

'And who or what shall fill his place?
Whither will wanderers turn distracted eyes
For some fixed star to stimulate their pace
Towards the goal of their enterprise?' ...

XIII

Some in the background then I saw,
Sweet women, youths, men, all incredulous,
Who chimed: 'This is a counterfeit of straw,
This requiem mockery! Still he lives to us!'

XIV

I could not buoy their faith: and yet
Many I had known: with all I sympathized;
And though struck speechless, I did not forget
That what was mourned for, I, too, long had prized.

XV

Still, how to hear such loss I deemed
The insistent question for each animate mind,
And gazing, to my growing sight there seemed
A pale yet positive gleam low down behind,

XVI

Whereof, to lift the general night,
A certain few who stood aloof had said,
'See you upon the horizon that small light –
Swelling somewhat?' Each mourner shook his head.

XVII

And they composed a crowd of whom
Some were right good, and many nigh the best ...
Thus dazed and puzzled 'twixt the gleam and gloom
Mechanically I followed with the rest.

I

God's Funeral

'Religion … its time is up …'
Morrison I. Swift
(nineteenth-century American anarchist)

THE ENGLISH POET Thomas Hardy, some time between 1908 and 1910, wrote a poem[1] in which he imagined himself attending God's funeral. It is one of his most extraordinary poems, and it expresses in the most cogent form some of the issues which will be explored biographically in the following pages. It starts – what a good film-sequence it would make – with the Wessex pessimist seeing the macabre procession as a 'strange mystic form' is carried to Its, or His, last rest.

> And by contagious throbs of thought
> Or latent knowledge that within me lay
> And had already stirred me, I was wrought
> To consciousness of sorrow even as they.

What was being carried away from the people was something which had 'symboled' a 'potency vast and loving kindness strong'. God is seen in this poem as a great projection of human fears and desires.

> 'Framing him jealous, fierce, at first,
> We gave him justice as the ages rolled,
> Will to bless those by circumstance accurst,
> And long suffering, and mercies manifold.
>
> 'And, tricked by our own early dream
> And need of solace, we grew self-deceived,
> Our making soon our maker did we deem,
> And what we had imagined we believed.
>
> 'Till, in Time's stayless stealthy swing,
> Uncompromising rude reality
> Mangled the Monarch of our fashioning,
> Who quavered, sank; and now has ceased to be ...'

The 'myth's oblivion' is not a cause for crowing in this poem, nor even particularly for agnostic, lofty point-scoring. Quite the contrary. When 'some in the background', 'sweet women, youths, men' exclaim 'Still he lives to us!', Hardy has nothing but sympathetic feeling for these gallant believers who persist in worshipping a dead God:

> I could not buoy their faith: and yet
> Many I had known: with all I sympathized;
> And though struck speechless, I did not forget
> That what was mourned for, I, too, long had prized.

Hardy wonders how 'to bear such loss' and 'who or what shall fill his place'. Unlike many of the high-minded liberals of the previous century, beguiled by a 'religion of humanity', Hardy knew that the first of the Ten Commandments contained an objective truth. Ersatz substitutes for God are not God. 'Thou shalt have no other Gods before me.'[2] Hardy is left merely 'dazed and puzzled' by the funeral.

Perhaps only those who have known the peace of God which passes all understanding can have any conception of what was lost between a hundred and a hundred and fifty years ago when the human race in Western Europe began to discard Christianity. The loss was not merely an intellectual change, the discarding of one proposition in favour of another. Indeed, though many intellectual justifications were offered by those who lost faith, the process would seem to have been, in many cases, just as emotional as religious conversion; and its roots were often quite as irrational. In all the inner journeys which ended with 'God's funeral' for the believer, there was potential for profound agony, whether the intellectual justifications for religious faith-loss were to be found in the fields of science, philosophy, political thought, biblical scholarship, or psychology. This is the story of bereavement as much as of adventure.

Unlike so many European atheists, Thomas Hardy had no hatred of the faith which he discarded. His continued fondness for ritual, music and even for the teachings of the Church, long after faith itself had departed, would have puzzled many a hard-line Continental atheist. When he was elected to an honorary fellowship at Magdalene College, Cambridge he discussed with the dons there the ceremony by which he would be sworn in. The diarist A.C. Benson was one of the Fellows.

4

The Master was afraid [Benson wrote] that Hardy might dislike a religious service. But Hardy said that he wasn't afraid of a service or a sur-
plice; he used to go to church three times on a Sunday; it turned out that
he often went to St Paul's and other London churches, like Kilburn, and
knew a lot about ecclesiastical music and double chants. He had ordered
a complete set of robes, too – bonnet, gown and hood. This restored the
Master's confidence. We sate and talked and smoked; and the old man
wasn't a bit shy – he prattled away very pleasantly about books and
people. He looks a very tired man at times, with his hook nose, his weary
eyes, his wisps of hair; then he changes and looks lively again. He rather
spoiled the effect of his ecclesiastical knowledge by saying blithely, 'Of
course, it's only sentiment to me now!'[3]

It is in some ways paradoxical that so intensely churchy a man as Hardy,
whose profession before he wrote novels was that of ecclesiastical architect and whose written work betrays not merely a knowledge but also a
love of church services, church music, church gossip, should have suffered a fate which might more fittingly have been reserved for the belligerent blasphemer. His last novel, *Jude the Obscure*, was burned by a
bishop, no less a man than the Bishop of Wakefield, William Walsham
How, who wrote the popular hymn 'For all the saints, who from their
labours rest'. One of the details about the incident which particularly
hurt Hardy (ever the parsimonious countryman) was that, since the
Bishop chose the height of summer for his gesture of casting *Jude the
Obscure* into his grate, he must have had to order a fire to be specially
(and wastefully) lit for the purpose.

Hardy suggests in his own account of the matter that it was the
Bishop's intolerance which drove him out of the Church; that he would
have been only too happy to continue with occasional church while
keeping his own counsel about the verifiability of doctrine. This position, which came to be known loosely (in the Roman Catholic Church
especially) as Modernism, was one which was most vigorously detested,
both by the ultra-orthodox and by the bigots of the sceptical view. If
one stretches the net wide, it would seem to have been the view of
Carlyle, Ruskin, Matthew Arnold, Tennyson ... But those professional
seekers after truth who attempted to justify such positions within the
churches were vilified (F.D. Maurice, George Macdonald) or in the
Roman Church actually suppressed (Abbé Loisy, Father Tyrrell). No
wonder, then, that when Hardy confronted 'that terrible dogmatic
ecclesiasticism'[4] of the Bishop of Wakefield, he should have decided to

define his own religious position in terms of negatives – 'only a sentiment'. God's funeral pyre, as far as Hardy was concerned, had been
stacked by the Church. 'The only sad feature in the matter to Hardy was
that if the Bishop could have known him as he was, he would have found
a man whose personal conduct, views of morality, and of the vital facts
of religion, hardly differed from his own.'[5]

Like many who lost faith (like many who retained it), Hardy was not
completely consistent. He was a human being, not an automaton.
Anyone who has read his work (think of that other poem of his, 'God's
Education') would know what his old friend Edmund Gosse meant
when he asked why Mr Hardy should have 'shaken his fist at
Providence'.* The cumulative effect of watching the characters of his
novels being buffeted by misfortune makes some readers weary of
Hardy's manipulative pessimism. More sympathetic readers of the
Wessex novels, however, would wish to say that, though Hardy's plots
are melodramatic, the stories are fundamentally truthful. The lives of
many human beings on this planet are indeed scarred by the repeated
onslaughts of disease, financial anxiety, unhappy matrimonial entangle-
ments, or a miserable combination of these and other misfortunes. Most
readers of Hardy's best-known novel will end the story in love with Tess:
and that will affect their feelings about God – anyway, about Hardy's
God. ' "Justice" was done', the narrator tells us, 'and the President of the
Immortals, in Aeschylean phrase, had ended his sport with Tess.'[6]

It is the simple unfairness of life which makes this phrase powerful
and novelistically appropriate. Hardy depicts suffering which is not so
much 'innocent' as pointless. He is more Homeric than Hebraic, closer
to the *Iliad* than to Job. The reader finishes a novel of Hardy's knowing
that stoicism is not its own reward; nor will it be rewarded by some
sympathetic external agency. Many church Christians, particularly the
clergy, must have tried to hide this from themselves when they read
Hardy's novels, and seen his 'pessimism' as a distorting lens; they had
to wait until they were exposed to the shrapnel and gunfire on the
Western Front before their imaginations were exposed to such pitiless
Homeric reality, which Hardy could see relentlessly at work in the
country villages of Dorset.

---

* They would not necessarily share Gosse's bizarre view that *Jude the Obscure* was 'the most inde-
cent novel ever written'. Presumably the works of Cleland, Diderot and the marquis de Sade
were not on the shelves at the House of Lords, where Gosse worked as the librarian.

The anarchist American writer Morrison I. Swift, arguing against what a great philosopher calls 'the airy and shallow optimism of current religious philosophy', cited a newspaper article which could, with very little alteration, have translated itself into one of Hardy's sadder tales:

> After trudging through the snow from one end of the city to the other in the vain hope of securing employment, and with his wife and six children without food and ordered to leave their home in an upper east-side tenement because of non-payment of rent, John Corcoran, a clerk, today ended his life by drinking carbolic acid. Corcoran lost his position three weeks ago through illness, and during the period of idleness, his scanty savings disappeared. Yesterday, he obtained work from a gang of city snow shovellers, but he was too weak from illness and was forced to quit after an hour's trial with the shovel. Then the weary task of looking for employment was again resumed. Thoroughly discouraged, Corcoran returned to his home late last night to find his wife and children without food and notice of dispossession on the door. On the following morning, he drank the poison.[7]

Swift lambasted those contemporary philosophers known as Idealists (figures such as F.H. Bradley and T.H. Green in England, and Josiah Royce in the United States) who dared to say that 'The Absolute' (roughly, their word for an impersonal God-substitute) 'is the richer for every discord, and for all the diversity it embraces'. Swift writes of the philosopher who

> means that these slain men make the universe richer, and that is Philosophy. But while Professors Royce and Bradley and a whole host of guileless thoroughfed thinkers are unveiling Reality and the Absolute and explaining away evil and pain, this is the condition of the only beings known to us anywhere in the universe with a developed consciousness of what the universe is. What these people experience *is* Reality ... These facts invincibly prove religion a nullity. Man will not give religion two thousand centuries or twenty centuries more to try itself and waste human time; its time is up, its probation is ended. Its own record ends it. Mankind has not aeons and eternities to spare for trying out discredited systems ...[8]

It is surely sentiments such as these which underpin Hardy's carefully and gloomily plotted narratives. His love of the cult, country churches, metrical psalms, High Church ritual in the bricky suburban churches of London, surplices, cannot disguise his deep core of scepticism, his fundamental atheism. Hence, we may feel, the appropriateness of a symbolically powerful scene, one with its own reverberations in the History of English Literature, which took place when Thomas Hardy was thirty-five years old. He was summoned (the year was 1875) to the house of the editor of *The Cornhill Magazine* in London.

Leslie Stephen, eight years older than Hardy, is best known today for the two literary monuments which he bequeathed to the world: the *Dictionary of National Biography*, of which he was the editor, and the novelist Virginia Woolf, of whom he was the father. He had been ordained as a clergyman in the Church of England, lost his faith, and then made his way in the world of journalism and letters. (His first wife was the daughter of Thackeray.)

In the spring of 1875, then, he asked Thomas Hardy to visit him in his study, no matter how late the hour. The evening was far spent when Hardy climbed the stairs to the top of a tall house, to find Stephen pacing up and down the room. The only light was a solitary lamp on the reading-table. 'The dressing-gown which Stephen was wearing over his clothes accentuated his height, so that he looked like a seer in robes as he passed in and out of the shadows, the lamp illuminating his prophetic face each time he passed the table. On it, lay a document.' It was a legal deed, by which Stephen renounced his holy orders, and Hardy had been called to witness his signature.[9] This was years before Hardy wrote *Jude the Obscure* or 'God's Funeral'; yet, of all Stephen's acquaintance, which must have included many of the more eminent agnostics of the day, Hardy was chosen, surely aptly, to be the witness for the final severing of his links with the Church.

Seventeen years before, Stephen had been ordained priest in Cambridge. True, like many a clever young man who wanted to become a don, he had taken orders because it was a professional requirement. Offered a job as college tutor at Trinity Hall, he needed to become at least a deacon. But it would seem as though Stephen entered upon his priestly life with seriousness and piety, determined to inculcate in young men the principles of 'fearing God and walking a thousand miles in a thousand hours'.[10] In 1860, his mother considered that he read the service in 'an impressive and beautiful manner'. But within two years the Victorian disease, Doubt, had struck. By 1862 he felt quite unable, in conscience, to conduct any services at all.

It is all fairly mysterious – the life of Stephen to this extent having been completely typical of so many Victorian spiritual journeys. These young men in the Church of England were not in the same position as their Continental counterparts who, in their Catholic seminaries, were kept in genuine ignorance of biblical scholarship or of the developments in modern philosophy which might have been injurious to faith; and who therefore suffered easily explicable crises when, in later life, they started to read books or to think for themselves. True, there were very few men in the Victorian Church of England who had confronted the contradictions in maintaining as strong a loyalty to faith as to reason; and true, Stephen, like many other men in his position, was very young when he was ordained. But it is hard to believe that he was not aware of the difficulties, even if he had not read as much sceptical literature as he was to in middle age.

One of the formative influences on Stephen as an undergraduate was Henry Fawcett, destined much later in the century to become Postmaster-General in Gladstone's government of 1880. Fawcett, an out-and-out radical, was a Utilitarian, a follower of John Stuart Mill and, even more, a follower of Mill's father James, and of his great mentor Jeremy Bentham.

The influence of Bentham and the Mills and of the system of thought known as philosophic radicalism we will return to in the pages which follow. It was through Fawcett that Stephen began to read philosophy – Hobbes, Locke, Kant, Berkeley, Hume – all writers whose works had been in print for decades (centuries, in the case of Hobbes) before Stephen learnt to read. Hume's overt scepticism had been generally known for the better part of a century. Utilitarianism and philosophic radicalism had been discussed for decades before Stephen's *crise*. 'The average Cambridge don of my day', Stephen wrote,

> was (as I thought and think) a sensible and honest man who wished to be both rational and Christian. He was rational enough to see that the old orthodox position was untenable. He did not believe in hell, or in 'verbal inspiration' or the 'real presence'. He thought that the controversies on such matters were silly and antiquated, and spoke of them with indifference, if not with contempt. But he also thought that religious belief of some kind was necessary or valuable, and considered himself to be a genuine believer. He assumed that somehow the old dogmas could be explained away or 'rationalized' or 'spiritualized'. He could

9

accept them in some sense or other but did not ask too closely in what sense. Still less did he go into the ultimate questions of philosophy. He shut his eyes to the great difficulties and took the answer for granted.[11]

We for our part probably take for granted the idea that this position was inevitable, that intellectual honesty compelled Stephen and his generation to avoid the intellectual cowardice of the position he describes. Distinctively of his time, place and generation, Stephen was unable to distinguish between *religious life* and experience, and the intellectual positions advanced at certain periods of human history either to bolster or destroy metaphysical assertions. His biographer Lord Annan attributes Stephen's loss of faith to a relentless need to apply the strictest Utilitarian factual principles of verifiability to the Bible stories. When he had done so, he discovered that he had never had any 'faith' to give up.[12]

Those born at different periods, or in different traditions, can afford to be aghast at such a crude definition of 'faith'; but this is a battle, broadly speaking, which was fought in and out of the churches throughout the second half of the nineteenth century, often with the most surprising results. 'The Oriental style misled certain minds inclined to seek before all things scientific rigour, or too much accustomed to logical formalism. They failed to distinguish between parable and history; they thought they saw astronomical and geological theses in pages destined to develop the religious and moral life of the soul.'[13]

If the literalism and the idolatrous (to a mind of a later generation) attitude to 'science' are characteristic of the Victorians who lost their faith, so too is their terrible, pitiable unhappiness, their sense of metaphysical isolation. Since we are aware of how she met her own end, there is something chilling about the footnote added to this unhappy period of Leslie Stephen's life by his daughter, Virginia. According to the testimony of his friends, she tells us, they feared Leslie Stephen would commit suicide. His 'state of mind was such that Fawcett entertained serious fears that he might cut his throat during the night'. Read Mrs Humphry Ward's *Robert Elsmere*; or the diaries of Arthur Clough; or the mental agonies chronicled in Edmund Gosse's *Father and Son*. The story of God's Funeral drifts continuously between the disciplines of psychology and philosophy. Scepticism in the nineteenth century was, as often as not, allied not with the sunny good cheer of Gibbon or Hume, but with profound depressions, self-hatred and melancholy.

Psychology as a discipline cannot explain belief or unbelief; nor can a vague appeal to the *Zeitgeist*, though this somehow inevitably, and not always unhelpfully, must be made. Which came first? The sense of lassitude and misery, the belief that the universe is godless and without purpose, the generalized sense, expressed so forcefully by Morrison I. Swift, that God had been given the benefit of the doubt for long enough and that the hour demanded the discarding of creeds? In *The Diary of a Writer*, in 1876, Dostoevsky wrote:

In truth, we do observe a great number of suicides (their abundance is also a mystery *sui generis*) strange and mysterious, committed not by reason of poverty or some affront, without any apparent reasons and not at all because of material need, unrequited love, jealousy, ill-health, hypochondria or insanity – but God only knows why. In our day, such cases constitute a great temptation, and since it is impossible to deny that they have assumed the proportions of an epidemic, they arise in the minds of many people as a most disturbing question. Of course, I am not venturing to explain all these suicides – this I cannot do – but I am firmly convinced that the majority of suicides *in toto*, directly or indirectly, were committed as a result of one and the same spiritual illness – the absence in the souls of these men of the sublime idea of existence.[14]

Nineteenth-century unbelief seldom limits itself to an expression of specific uncertainty about, let us say, the literal truth of the Bible, or the existence of angels. It accompanies wider symptoms of disturbance, a deep sense (personal, political, social) of dissolution. Dostoevsky is only one of the most eloquent proponents of the idea that society had lost, not merely its sense of the sublime, but also a hold on morals, a common purpose, a cohesion and unity. For him, the Death of God was a symptom of a sickness which had infected Russia as a result of espousing Western materialism and the scientific outlook. In his later years he blamed the liberalizers, the Westernizers, the St Petersburg radicals, and allied himself, not always with convincing ease, with the conservative, slavophil believers in the Orthodox Church. But what had happened to the nineteenth-century mind if it was forced to choose between giving up intellectual honesty, or abandoning that spiritual and religious dimension to life which, as far as we can discover from the historians and anthropologists, is so fundamental a part of all previous human experiences? Was it really enough, as Dostoevsky said it was, to denounce science and progress and liberalism and come to kneel at the feet of Jesus? In some moods he thought it was. But the dramas of all his novels, as of his own life, reveal him to have been truly an exemplar, a thermometer of his age, an underground man cut loose from the old roots and staring despair and emptiness in the face. *The Possessed*, as it is known in the West (more accurately, *The Devils*), sees society as in demonic possession, the idiotic liberals merely leading the way over the Gadarene cliff. Without God, there was none to help them.

As Dostoevsky made so clear in that terrible prophecy, and as Thomas Hardy and Leslie Stephen and Morrison Swift would probably all in their different ways have agreed, the nineteenth century had created a climate for itself – philosophical, politico-sociological, literary, artistic, personal – in which God had become unknowable, His voice inaudible against the din of machines and the atonal banshee of the emerging egomania called The Modern. The cohesive social force which organized religion had once provided was broken up. The nature of society itself, urban, industrialized, materialistic, was the background for the godlessness which philosophy and science did not so much discover as ratify.

After a hundred years, a century in which the human race has done more damage to itself and to the planet than in any previous aeons, we still seem no nearer to an understanding of the implications of what the Victorians passed through. Discussions of religion, its meaning and truth, would seem in the close of the twentieth century to be as loud and as ill-informed as they were a hundred years ago. The spiritual hunger of men and women does not merely disappear because so many, in the churches and the universities, seem incapable of understanding what is really at stake. That is why it seems appropriate, as our century comes to an end, to revisit the Victorian experience of faith and doubt.

Chou En-lai famously thought it was too soon to say what the effects of the French Revolution had been. Perhaps, by the same token, it is too early to gauge the effects of nineteenth-century religious scepticism on the history of the twentieth century. Has it been a story of religious people continuing to practise their faith while the majority were, in Ivy Compton-Burnett's phrase, 'perfectly sensible agnostics'? Not so. Religious institutions, and in particular the Christian churches, have been enormously affected by the Victorian crises of faith. So, too, has that part of the secular world which for the first time in European history has been untouched by any overt religious dimension.

In any generation, individuals will move in this direction or that, just as in any human life there will be phases of greater or lesser piety, greater or lesser sympathy with the things of the spirit. Perhaps there are fewer men and women now than in the last century who make the mistake of supposing that 'Religion' is primarily a theory to explain the origin of the Universe. *Factorem coeli et terrae* never was, nor could have been, a rival to the Big Bang Theory set to Gregorian chant. But many Christians, including popes, thought that it was, which was why so much effort was expended on both sides to defend literally nonsensical positions. 'Science', equally, could no more explain the Universe than a clock, left to itself, could tell the time.

God's funeral was not, as many in the nineteenth century might have thought, the end of a phase of human intellectual history. It was the withdrawal of a great Love-object. Why is this an important story, a story of reverberant significance to us, to the men and women of the late twentieth century, whose inner lives and perspectives, whose personal and political aspirations, seem so different from those of our nineteenth-century forebears? Perhaps its importance is found in two spheres especially: no doubt in many others, too, but in these two most significantly.

First, it must be of importance to individuals whether or not they pray and, in turn, whether those prayers are part of an ages-long conversation between humanity and the Deity, or whether they are, as Hardy suggests in his poem, mere projections of our own private fears, aspirations, longings. Is our personal religion that which links us to the ultimate reality, or is it the final human fantasy, the most pathetic demonstration, in a spiritually empty, spatially limitless universe, of human aloneness? Is prayer the last existential pathos? No system of thought, no philosopher, no theologian will ever solve this question for individuals. It is a question they must answer, each and every one, for themselves. The ways in which our nineteenth-century forebears confronted this, the most basic of questions, will, however, always have implications and echoes in our generation. They were not so very different from us.

If the first sphere of importance is intensely personal – is there anybody there? – the second is of general application. Many human beings, both sceptics and believers, wish that the great metaphysical question were cut and dried. 'Is He there', or isn't He? Is 'religion' true, or false? Is there a world of value outside ourselves, or do we, collectively and individually, invent what we call The Good? Is there an objective transcendent truth in these areas, as we believe there is in physical science, or is there only an inner mystical 'truth', where inverted commas are always to be needed if we are not to proclaim lies?

This remains one of the most important areas of human inquiry in the modern world. And if war is too important a matter to be left to the generals, then this metaphysical inquiry is certainly too important to be left to the theologians and metaphysicians.

When religion becomes unbelievable or untenable, intelligent and sensitive human beings will reject it. *Écrasez l'infâme!* was Voltaire's rallying-cry, to wipe out the iniquity of superstition and mumbo-jumbo together with the unjust aristocratic system which the Church had supported. But would Voltaire himself have wanted the Terror; would the agnostic liberals who are lampooned in Dostoevsky's *The Devils* have been able to believe the accuracy of his ferocious and immoderate prophecy of a future dominated first by atheist anarchy, then by something worse? If some religion, or all religion, is 'just a projection' ('our making soon our maker did we deem'), then would it not be the projection of the most fundamental of our concerns? Would not the discarding of this projection have calamitous psychological effects? And what if the analysis was in any event wrong? What if the literalists or the fundamentalists of both sides were the false guides, and the truth lay elsewhere, in those mysterious and linguistic areas which the simple-minded would like to dismiss as wishy-wash or fudge? In the Roman Catholic Church, for instance, what if Pius X had been ludicrously wrong, and those whom he condemned for 'modernism' right, to dismiss early Christian history as mythology while continuing to revere *Le Grand Mystère?* 'Let us seek to fathom those things that are fathomable, and reserve those things which are unfathomable for reverence in quietude.'[15]

The words are Goethe's, but Wittgenstein is famous for articulating a similar submission of silence. Yet there is a different silence – and that is part of the drama. It is the silence of God Himself. The Bible is full of it, so the Victorian doubters were not the first to wonder at the difficulty of apprehending the Divine. What they were especially good at, however, was articulating their bereavement. The individual journeys of modern men and women show that none of the compelling questions raised by the Victorian crisis of faith received finished answers – else the matter would not continue to haunt us today. Modern believers tread warily, knowing that the ground can easily open before them, revealing only emptiness and darkness.

> Yet it is a long pursuit,
> Carrying the junk and treasure of an ancient creed,
> To a love who keeps faith by seeming mute
> And deaf, and dead indeed.[16]

2

Hume's Time-bomb

Durch Vernünfteln wird Poesie vertrieben
(Ratiocination drives Poetry away).

Goethe

THE IDEAS WHICH undermined nineteenth-century religion took shape in the eighteenth century. The coterie-atheism of the French *philosophes* of the Enlightenment, the scepticism of the Continent, were perceived, particularly in conservative England, to have led to such horrors as Robespierre, the Guillotine, the Terror and the Napoleonic wars. No wonder atheism was associated in many minds with social anarchy. And yet the two books in the English language which have done more than any other, perhaps, to undermine faith were written by an English Member of Parliament of impeccably conservative taste, and by an equally conservative (from a political viewpoint) Scottish aristocrat. They are Edward Gibbon's *The History of the Decline and Fall of the Roman Empire* (published in three instalments between 1776 and 1788; that is, neatly sandwiched in time between the American and French Revolutions) and David Hume's *Dialogues Concerning Natural Religion*, published in 1779, three years after his death. The former work made it difficult to admire many of the greatest saints, popes and doctors of the universal Church; the latter made it more than difficult to enter into their beliefs.

For religious-minded men and women of the nineteenth century Gibbon represented a huge difficulty, not least because for those whose only language was English he represented not the principal but the only source of information about the first thousand years of Christian history. 'It is notorious', Newman lamented, 'that the English Church is destitute of an Ecclesiastical History; Gibbon is almost our sole authority for subjects as near the heart of a Christian as any can well be.'[1]

For Samuel Taylor Coleridge, to whom so many looked in the early years of the nineteenth century as the white hope of Christian revival, it was primarily Gibbon's style which was 'detestable'.[2] Gibbon's supreme achievement as an anti-Christian propagandist was that style did all his work for him. It enabled the historian to suggest, without once stating it either as an opinion or as a fact, that nearly all the early Christians, the martyrs, the doctors and the council fathers, were, when not totally contemptible, then morally absurd. The ironical tone said all. The puppet-master never needed to come out from behind the toy proscenium, or tell the affronted audience what he actually believed. When he was stung into doing so, by an impertinent reviewer, he hotly repudiated the picture of himself as an infidel.[3] Nor was this an entirely hypocritical pose. The passage in *The Decline and Fall* about the character and achievements of Pope Gregory I, for instance, was clearly written by a man who was no atheist.[4]

Gibbon was (is) destructive of faith, not because of any metaphysical arguments kept hidden up his sleeve, but in his blithe revelation, on page after page, of the sheer contemptibility, not only of the Christian heroes, but of their 'highest' ideals. He writes from a position of urbane civilization which, as the style alone indicates, is demonstrably superior to the barbarism which he depicts. Imagine, his style seems to state, Saints Polycarp or Simeon Stylites or Bernard of Clairvaux at a dinner table with my Lord Sheffield, with Mr Adam Smith or Sir Joshua Reynolds or Dr Burney! Need anything more be said? It is not merely in the repeated and hilarious identification of individual Christian wickedness that Gibbon reaches his target.* Rather, it is in his whole attitude, which resolutely refuses to be impressed by the Christian contribution to 'civilisation'. Even the devout, after an exposure to Gibbon, would hesitate to use the word Christian as a term of approbation.

As he tells us in that quasi-Romantic, quasi-Augustan passage in his *Autobiography*, 'It was at Rome, on the 15th of October, 1764, as I sat musing amidst the ruins of the Capitol, while the barefoot friars were singing vespers in the Temple of Jupiter, that the idea of writing the decline and fall of the city first started to my mind.'[5]

The Capuchins singing vespers in the classical ruins provide a scene which could have inspired a landscape by Claude, or the habitat of a late

---

* Almost any chapter of the *History* would yield amusing examples. Consider the conversion of the Emperor Constantine: 'As he gradually advanced in the knowledge of truth, he proportionably declined in the practice of virtue; and the same year of his reign in which he convened the Council of Nice [Nicaea], was polluted by the execution, or rather murder, of his eldest son' (chapter xx). Or, of the theological factions of Constantinople: 'Day and night they were incessantly busied either in singing hymns to the honour of their God, or in pillaging and murdering the servants of their prince' (chapter xlvii); etc., etc.

eighteenth-century gentleman – one in which, from the classical proportions of his library or saloon, a landowner could look down upon a
Gothick Folly inhabited by a paid hermit. The *Autobiography* tells us
that the friars, or rather, the religion which they professed, had been so
seductive to the young author that he had actually (and to his father's
disgust) become a Roman Catholic:

> The marvellous tales, which are so boldly attested by the Basils and
> Chrysostoms, the Austins and Jeromes, compelled me to embrace the
> superior merits of celibacy, the institution of the monastic life, the use
> of the sign of the Cross, of holy oil, and even of images, the invocation
> of saints, the worship of relics, the rudiments of purgatory in prayers for
> the dead, and the tremendous mystery of the sacrifice of the body and
> blood of Christ, which insensibly swelled into the prodigy of
> Transubstantiation.[6]

The reader of the *Autobiography* senses that the pious believer whom
Gibbon was most intent upon scotching was his earlier self.* To his
adult eye the chanting, medievally-clad figures in the Capitol represented not a romance, but a hideous tableau of folly and barbarism. They
are not decorative, but destructive of all that the Capitol in its pre-
ruined state had represented, and which the Whig aristocracy of mid
eighteenth-century England did their best to reconstruct. We recall the
devastatingly effective peroration at the end of his chapter in *The Decline
and Fall* about monasticism, a relentless catalogue of superstition, wickedness and folly, culminating in the ludicrous career of St Simeon
Stylites (390–459), who excited the admiration of the Christians, not
by living a useful or charitable life but by the feat of spending thirty
years on top of a sixty-foot column in the desert east of Antioch.

> If it be possible to measure the interval between the philosophic writ-
> ings of Cicero and the sacred legend of Theodoret, between the charac-
> ter of Cato and that of Simeon, we may appreciate the memorable
> revolution which was accomplished in the Roman empire within a
> period of five hundred years.[7]

---

* Consider the moment when, under pressure from his father, he renounced the 'Romish creed':
'On Christmas Day 1754, I received the sacrament in the (Protestant) church of Lausanne. It
was here that I suspended my religious enquiries ...' He is writing (aged 52) of his 17-year-old
self. The notion that between the ages of 17 and 52 no further inquiry has been made in the
area of metaphysics is itself eloquent.

The contrast between the evident wisdom of pre-Christian civilization and the superstitious barbarism of the monks, hermits and their
devotees is in its way quite as damaging to Christian faith as the robust
and ironical assaults of the famous fifteenth chapter, 'The progress of the
Christian religion, and the Sentiments, Manners, Numbers and
Condition of the Primitive Christians', in which Gibbon cast irremovable doubt in any reader's mind, not merely upon the veracity but upon
the impressiveness of the Christian claims. In the no less damaging sixteenth chapter, he demonstrated that the persecutions under Diocletian
and other emperors were not nearly so severe as pious history would have
had us believe: '... on the subject of martyrdoms, it must still be
acknowledged, that the Christians, in the course of their intestine dis-
sensions, have inflicted far greater severities on each other, than they had
experienced from the zeal of infidels.'[8]

All the evidence would suggest that Gibbon was sincere in his rejection of the charge of outright atheism against himself. His claim to be a
Deist makes perfect sense of his work, as of his life. It is from the Deist
point of view that his history was written. Deism was the most widespread religious creed among eighteenth-century intellectuals – it was
the view of Voltaire, for example; namely, that this universe, with its
physical and moral laws, is verily the creation of the Deity, but that this
Godhead does not choose, or has not chosen in recent or recorded history,
to intervene in His Creation. Like a Divine Clockmaker, He has set the
machine in motion, and now allows it to work of its own accord. (In this
book, I use the word Deist to refer to this specific belief in a remote
Deity, and the word Theist to refer to anyone who believes in [a] God.)

Some readers of the eighteenth-century Deists assume that their lofty
and blasé position is a code for atheism. Certainly, while many readers are
prepared to accept Gibbon's claim to have been a Deist, there are those
who have assumed that Hume's comparable profession, in his *Dialogues
Concerning Natural Religion*, must be taken with a pinch of salt.[9] Perhaps
the truth is that Hume did not maintain a consistent position, preferring
for most of his life to put metaphysical considerations out of his mind.
His remarkable conversation with James Boswell, which took place
shortly before his death, reveals him still the good-humoured agnostic,
amiable – Hume is surely the most amiable British philosopher? – flip-
pant, but disinclined, merely because death was imminent, to embark
upon any Pascalian wager. He told Boswell that he had 'never entertained
any belief in Religion since he began to read Locke and Clarke'.[10] But he

admits that he was religious when young (a Presbyterian). Perhaps this accounts for his later distrust of Enthusiasm, and his impatience with follies to which he himself as a youth had been a prey. Yet we should be wrong to describe him as an atheist if by that we mean a man who insists upon the non-existence of any Deity of any description. Famously, when dining in a large group with baron d'Holbach in Paris, Hume wondered whether there really were any atheists, properly speaking. '*Je n'en ai jamais vu* (I've never met one)', he said. To which the baron replied, '*Vous avez été un peu malheureux; vous voici à table avec dix-sept pour la première fois* (You've been slightly unfortunate, for now here you are for the first time in your life surrounded by seventeen of them)!'[11]

Perhaps the anecdote tells us more about the differences between France and England than it does about Hume's state of mind? Certainly going to France quickened his hostility to superstition and to the many follies of human religious expression. When he was in Paris in 1765, Hume looked back across the Channel and observed that the English were relapsing fast 'into the deepest Stupidity, Christianity and Ignorance'.[12]

In the works published during his lifetime Hume contented himself, however, with asking devastating questions rather than supplying, without qualification, negative answers. His Essay on Miracles had scandalized Christian opinion (and most notably that of Dr Johnson) by its insistence that the miracles of Jesus be judged precisely like other historical reports: they are subject to the criteria of credibility. 'No testimony is sufficient to establish a miracle, unless the testimony be of such a kind, that its falsehood would be more miraculous than the fact, which it endeavours to establish.'[13] Whenever the subject of 'natural religion' arises in his writings, Hume makes no secret of his view that he does not believe religion to have any rational foundations at all.

This is the area which he tackles head-on in his *Dialogues*, a version of which he had completed by 1751 or thereabouts, when he was forty years old, but which he continued to rewrite until shortly before he died – the final revision belonging to the very year of his death, 1776.[14] One modern commentator goes so far as to say that the *Dialogues* are not so much a lethal weapon against religion as 'a death certificate'.[15]

The narrator of the *Dialogues* is a young figure called Pamphilius: it is he, strictly speaking, and not Hume, who commends to the reader the Deist position which in the *Dialogues* themselves is represented by a figure named Cleanthes. The view of Christian piety is argued by one Demea, while that of absolute scepticism is argued by one named Philo.

Philo's most destructive assaults are on the very arguments from Design and Cosmology which were the cornerstones of Deist belief. Of the three foremost traditional proofs for the existence of some Deity, it is often supposed that the Argument from Design is the most plausible; this is why the Argument from Design was so important to those late seventeenth- and eighteenth-century philosophers who accepted Descartes's system. The Deist did not claim knowledge of mysteries. But when he contemplated the intricacies of Nature's laws, and the pattern of things, it made sense to him to believe in a Designer.

In Hume's *Dialogues*, it is left to Philo to enunciate two great metaphysical principles which, once they have been admitted to the consciousness, can never quite leave it. On their own terms they are irrefutable. Those who struggle, for whatever reason, to resist the empirical scepticism of Hume will never be able completely to banish the rhetorical and emotional effect of these arguments, which lead inexorably to that grand expression of the agnostic viewpoint: 'a total suspension of judgment is here our only reasonable resource.'[16]

The first devastating question is to ask why 'mind' should be our anthropomorphic model for looking at the universe. 'What peculiar privilege has this little agitation of the brain which we call thought, that we must thus make it the model of the whole universe?'[17] Subsidiary to this line of inquiry is the disturbing question (to which there could not possibly be any answer) why we should suppose, if such a mind there be, that it is *one* mind? Doesn't the evidence of the plurality of the universe suggest pluralities of intention and designs? And if so, would we not 'behold then the theogony of ancient times brought back upon us'?[18]

The second question is similar to the question why we should suppose that 'mind' was a good piece of picture-language for the way that the universe might be supposed to work. 'For aught we know, *a priori*, matter may contain the source, or spring, of order originally, within itself, as well as the mind does.'[19] This is an absolutely crucial piece of argument. It was first written down over a hundred years before Darwin published his *Origin of Species*. It lays the groundwork for the devastations caused in the Victorian Age by 'science'. There were, as it happens, many scientists who continued to be Christian believers after Darwin's theories were published. There is perhaps nothing inherently injurious to faith about any *factual* discovery. There is, however, something quite incompatible with Christian or perhaps any religious faith in Philo's picture of the Universe as a system without mind, without purpose, and which contains within itself its own morally pointless methods of movement, progress and survival.

Gibbon and Hume were widely read as historians. Hume felt quite confident that his metaphysical speculation would only be comprehensible to the few. One of the great differences between their generation and that of Darwin was the size of the educated classes. The generation who lapped up Hume's History of England (he eventually covered the whole story, from Julius Caesar to the Stuarts) enjoyed it on the same level that they could savour Gibbon on the *Decline and Fall of the Roman Empire*. Both authors were incapable of dullness. They were urbane, vigorous and, above all, funny. It required a generation devoid of humour, perhaps, to make them dangerous. The Victorian Catholic revivalists who built pseudo-Gothic abbeys and revived monks, nuns, rosaries and incense also attempted the more difficult task of imitating the thought-processes of Gibbon's chanting Capuchins. They hoped to hold at bay the subversive ideas of Gibbon and Hume, but in fact these authors had planted time-bombs to explode in the faces of the Victorians. For fifty or sixty years they sat on the shelves of college or vicarage libraries, giving delight to the discerning. Only when serious religion began to revive, first among evangelicals, then among Anglicans and Catholics, did the destructive business of thinking about religion begin.

What Hume had done was remove any philosophical *necessity* for believing in God. Being himself a sunny, cheerfully-disposed individual, he appears to have felt no particular sorrow that we live in an empty, Godless universe, devoid of purpose. The world was really awaiting, after Hume, some empirical demonstration of his metaphysical inquiries. They were supplied in the nineteenth century, not by one scientist, but by a cluster of men any one of whose theories and discoveries would injure faith in the goodness of God or the purposes of God. Lamarck's evolutionary theories, Lyell's geology, Darwin's species relentlessly striving for mastery, make more sense to a universe like Hume's than to one where God made all things bright and beautiful.

'Are God and Nature then at strife', Tennyson asks,

> That Nature lends such evil dreams?
> So careful of the type she seems,
> So careless of the single life; ...
> 'So careful of the type?' but no:
> From scarped cliff and quarried stone

> She cries, 'A thousand types are gone:
> I care for nothing, all shall go ... '[20]

Compare Hume on the possibility of Immortal Life, when asked by Boswell if he believed in a Future State:

> He answered It was possible that a piece of coal put upon the fire would not burn; and he added that it was a most unreasonable fancy that he should exist for ever, that immortality, if it were at all, must be general; that a great proportion dies in infancy before being possessed of reason; yet all these must be immortal; that the trash of every age must be preserved, and that new Universes must be created to contain such infinite numbers ... [21]

For Hume himself there was no virtue in 'sincerity', if that meant spilling the beans to stupid people. Having grown up in the bigoted atmosphere of Presbyterian Scotland (his own grandfather a Martyr for the most bigoted form of that faith),[22] he knew how human beings who had no capacity for logical argument delighted in theological controversy. South of the border, he fully supported the candidacy of a young friend for preferment in the Church since that was a perfectly sensible way of self-advancement for someone without means in Lord North's England.

> It is putting too great a respect on the vulgar, and on their superstitions, to pique oneself on sincerity with regard to them. Did ever one make it a point of honour to speak truth to children or madmen? If the thing were worthy being treated gravely, I should tell him, that the Pythian oracle, with the approbation of Xenophon, advised everyone to worship the gods. I wish it were still in my power to be a hypocrite in this particular. The common duties of society usually require it; and the ecclesiastical profession only adds a little more to an innocent dissimulation, or rather simulation, without which it is impossible to pass through the world. Am I a liar, because I order my servant to say, I am not at home, when I do not desire to see company?[23]

But if you want to test the effects of Hume's late eighteenth-century ideas on a mid nineteenth-century high-minded liberal, consider the reaction to Hume's rhetorical question of John Morley – later Lord Morley – best known to posterity as an energetic journalist (editor of the *Fortnightly* in its heyday: that is, when it had become a monthly) and the biographer of Mr Gladstone, in whose third administration of 1886 he was Chief Secretary for Ireland.[24] Morley, who was a great friend of Leslie Stephen, had a journey which was very similar to Stephen's, though he may be said to have paid for it with greater financial sacrifice. Born in 1838, he was the son of a doctor in the northern industrial town of Blackburn – a real Coketown. Morley *père*, a convert to (low-) Church of England from Wesleyanism, had a high social conscience, and John's political convictions were always coloured by the injustices and poverty of which his middle-class childhood had been the witness. But, alas, when he went to Lincoln College, Oxford in 1856 as an undergraduate, destined for a career in holy orders, he suffered doubts. He got a second in 'Mods', and then made the mistake of coming clean with his father. Poor Morley was obliged to leave Oxford with only a pass degree and, with no further financial help from home, he had to earn his living in Grub Street. We shall meet him again in the company of George Eliot, Huxley and all the others – he was at the very centre of Victorian intellectual journalistic and political life.

Given the way Morley's own life was shaped by what he took to be the necessity for a clean confession of unbelief, it is perhaps not surprising that he should have been disgusted by Hume's cynicism. Interestingly enough, in his own discussion of whether it is ever permissible to dissemble about one's religious unbelief, he considers that the only occasion where such cloaking of the truth could be morally justifiable is in the matter of sparing the feelings of parents – the one area where he himself had inflicted grievous pain by his honesty: 'one relationship in life, and one only, justifies us in being silent where otherwise it would be right to speak. This relationship is that between child and parents ...'[25] Morley thinks it is perfectly permissible, indeed desirable, that husbands and wives should torture one another with displays of frankness in this area.

Hardy, whose own poor wife was so upset and aggrieved by his unbelief that she wholeheartedly sided with the Bishop of Wakefield in the matter of the burning of *Jude the Obscure*, would have been a good case study for Morley's premiss. Hardy's robust, peasanty mother would probably have been able to laugh off his impiety, whereas Emma Gifford (the niece, as Hardy took the trouble to inform readers of *Who's Who*, of an archdeacon) was rendered miserable by what she thought were his blasphemies. Hardy took the view that Morley 'could have been the Gibbon of his age'.[26]

Perhaps Hardy was influenced in Morley's favour since it was Morley who, as a publisher's reader, recommended Macmillan to take on

Hardy's novels.[27] Certainly Morley's was a prolific pen, both in the periodicals and in those works of popular improvement, the 'English Men of Letters' – a series which he edited and to which he contributed the volume on Burke. As well as his three-volume life of Gladstone (for which his name remained famous for two or three generations) Morley also wrote popular works on Voltaire (1872), Rousseau (1873), Diderot (1878), Walpole (1889) and Cromwell (1900).

To an eye less favourably disposed to Morley than Hardy's these works, estimable as they are, have a whiff of the very worthy public lecture, the evening class at the Workers' Educational Association. Above all, they lack any of the bubbling irony of Gibbon's prose. Hume could languidly state that honesty is a waste of time in the company of people who are on the same intellectual level as children or madmen. Morley was of a different generation and a different character. He considered what it would have meant for himself in practice had he pursued a career as a parish clergyman, perhaps in some Coketown such as the place where he grew up, surrounded by just such children and madmen as Hume would have despised. Such hypocrites in holy orders

> have a hell of their own. It is no light thing to have secured a livelihood on condition of going through life masked and gagged. To be compelled, week after week, and year after year, to recite the symbols of ancient faith and lift up his voice in the echoes of old hopes, with the blighting thought in his soul that the faith is a shadow, and the hope no more than the folly of the crowd; to read hundreds of times in a twelve month with solemn unction, as the inspired word of the Supreme, what to him is meaningless as the Abracadabra of the conjuror in a booth; to go on to the end of his days administering to simple folk holy rites of commemoration and solace, when he has in his mind at each phrase what dupes these simple folk are, and how wearisomely counterfeit the rites: and to know through all that this is really to be the one business of his life, that so dreary a piece of play-acting will make the desperate retrospect of his last hours – of a truth here* is the very abomination of desolation of the human spirit.[28]

---

* Typical of Morley to have used a phrase from the Gospels (Mark xiii. 14) to enforce his point. The *DNB* remarks: 'agnostic though he remained to the end, Morley cared less and less about religious polemics, and his attitude towards religion revealed a sense of piety, holiness and of the mystery of life and death not always found among orthodox church-goers' (*DNB*, 1922–1930). 'Cut him open', said George Meredith, 'and you will find a clergyman inside.' This is true of a great many nineteenth-century sceptics of both sexes.

The picture drawn by Morley of the parish clergyman trying to conceal his unbelief from himself could have been drawn from the pages of Mrs Gaskell's *North and South*, or Mrs Humphry Ward's *Robert Elsmere*, or many another Victorian rehearsal of the theme. Hume, one suspects, would have echoed Oscar Wilde's view of such productions of 'the *genre ennuyeux* ... It reminded him of the sort of conversation that goes on at a meat tea in the house of a serious Nonconformist family.'[29]*

Had David Hume, however, said the last word on the religio-metaphysical question? Like Gibbon, he claimed to be a Deist. Hume died thirteen years before the storming of the Bastille. Burke would have wanted to remind him that the French Revolution showed what happened when frank atheism took to the streets, and Hume would probably have agreed. Safer to say you are a Deist, and not rock the boat. The Deist position kept God happily in His place. So long as He was far away, there was no need to kill Him off, this mechanical Deity. Besides, like President Coolidge in Dorothy Parker's famous quip, it would have been difficult to know whether the Deist God were dead or alive. The Deist Universe after all is the product of a God who has abandoned His toy; or, as is said in Hume's *Dialogues*, 'it is the production of old age and dotage in some superannuated Deity; and ever since his Death, has run on at adventures, from first impulse and active force, which it received from him.'[30]

Here the Death of God, rather than being shrieked about by Nietzsche, is only considered worth mentioning in parentheses. For Gibbon and Hume, God had become like a constitutional monarch of the Hanoverian dispensation: whether He had any influence or not, whether He was mad or not, whether He was there or not, did not make as much difference to the scheme of things as it would have if He were an absolutist Bourbon King. Hume, with rather less generosity than William James towards the close of the nineteenth century, attempted to demonstrate that religious belief rose 'from a concern with regard to the events of human life, and from the incessant hopes and fears, which actuate the human mind.'[31]

The trouble with this assertion, from a strictly philosophical viewpoint, is that it is non-verifiable. To one human mind Hume's arguments, lucid, witty, restrained, will make perfect, even desolating, sense. To another, they will seem like the attempts of a blind man to

---

* The judgement is of *Robert Elsmere*.

describe colour. He never touches on those deeps which have enabled intelligences quite as acute as his – Pascal, or Augustine, or Simone Weil – to believe themselves to have known God.

Religion, and religious experience, continue to confound the empirical philosopher, and to remind him that there is not, or need not be, anything which makes it easier or harder to believe in God in one century rather than in another. And yet, it is in the nineteenth century that we watch the House of Cards collapse.

Hume had delivered some mortal blows against the old arguments for the existence of God. Religion could choose to turn a blind eye to the calamity, or to rail against it, or to say that it did not, perhaps, matter. But if the process of human reason is the primary arbiter of truth, and if the strictures of empiricism rightly limit our criteria of what may be known to impressions created by 'sense impressions', then Hume's destruction of the religious position would seem to be absolute. Truths which had been taken as self-evident for fifteen or sixteen hundred years were about to be demolished.

Hume and the eighteenth-century *philosophes* constituted a tiny proportion of the population; many of them must have shared Hume's opinion that no good would be served, when metaphysics were in question, by letting the cat out of the bag to the population at large. Within a hundred years, however, their coterie-doubts had become a universal orthodoxy. One could compare the manner in which the ideas of Marx (how outlandish they would have seemed to a visitor to his tobacco-infested study in the 1850s, how essentially a minority-view!) were destined, within a generation or two of his death, to be the creed by which half the known world was governed.

But Hume and the other British empirical philosophers of the eighteenth century have left a question in the air: *how do we know anything?* By what criterion can we claim that this proposition is verifiable, and that not? Is there any infallible means of distinguishing truth from falsehood, or even of knowing what we mean when we say *I know* or *I think?*

These are very basic questions, and it would be as well not to disappoint any hopeful reader. No one in the history of philosophy has ever found satisfactory answers to them. All that they have ever done is posit more or less plausible world-views, based on their responses to these questions. And the cleverest and most interesting philosophers have been able, if not to answer these questions to their satisfaction, then to see the kind of questions they are – how far they relate to language alone, how far they relate to the composition of the human mind; how far they may be said to relate to a reality *out* there, a reality in itself.

There is perhaps no philosopher who has devoted a more agile or patient attention to the very bases of epistemology – that is, of how we can claim to know anything, the way that knowledge *works* – than Immanuel Kant (1724–1804).

Kant, who is a thinker of immense intricacy, and whose mind was an astonishing combination of accuracy and audacity, set up various profound epistemological problems which, in the terms in which he posed them, would appear to be insoluble. No slapdash summary could explain those problems. He was working on them to the end of a long life, as the posthumous notebooks, not published until the twentieth century, reveal. Since few if any of Kant's readers have been as clever as he was, nor as patient (a fact which is almost as important), there have been three obvious responses to his philosophy.

The first is to ignore it altogether. This was largely the response of the English Utilitarians – as indeed, of course, of the great majority of the human race. The second is to stress the empiricist aspect of Kant's thought – this, if one can say so (at the risk of distorting a life's work), is the approach of modern British Kantians such as Professor Strawson.[32]

The third and much the most influential, because much the easiest, response to Kant is to stress the Idealist aspect of his thought. This is, of course, to use the word Idealist not in the sense of one who follows some ideal view of life or humanity, but in its philosophical sense. Philosophical Idealists have felt the need to distinguish between Appearance and Reality; they have sometimes gone so far as to limit 'what is real' to 'what is in our minds'. Kant undoubtedly had an Idealist strand to his thinking, as the mainstream of nineteenth-century philosophy did – they made him the forerunner of Hegel, the great Idealist. This perhaps is why so many empiricist philosophers of the British and American schools have been biased against Kant, wanting to make of him something windier and barmier than he was.

The Cartesian system had thrown up two theories for explaining how the human mind may be said to understand the realities outside itself. The rationalist explanation saw the mind as conceiving the way things

had to be, working out the inner logic of natural science and of metaphysics by what appeared to them to be the self-guaranteeing nature of
Reason; whereas the empiricists of the British school believed Locke's
idea of the mind as a *tabula rasa*. For them, the mind was a bit like a
cinema screen on to which reality was projected. The sense impressions
were received by it passively.

But, said Kant, we know that human perception is not quite like
that. Think of Isaac Newton's theory of optics. If Newton was right (and
every *savant* in the eighteenth century assumed that he was), the faculty
for colour-perception exists in the optic nerve of the human being which
views the object. The apple is not red in itself. If a dog looks at an apple,
he sees a smudge of greys. It is the human being (assuming he is not
colour-blind) who sees it as red. Does that mean that apples 'aren't
really' red? Or does it mean that the 'redness' is all in the human capacity to invent what it sees? Not really, because any (not colour-blind)
human eye will see red when it sees the apple. There is an inevitability
about this. It is in this mysteriously double-edged fashion – of the
human mind inevitably perceiving reality in a particular way; but none
the less being itself an essential ingredient in bringing the perception
to pass – that human beings build up their picture of reality. Hence
Kant's view that it would not be possible for statements descriptive of
space or *time* to make any sense unless the human mind had an innate and
pre-existent concept of time and of space by which to organize perceptions according to a spatio-temporal frame.

It does not matter, for the purposes of this argument, that the empiricists have always rejected Kant's arguments about Time and Space; nor
whether you, the reader, find them any more convincing than his belief
that the Categorical Imperative (our sense of right and wrong) is just
such a pre-programmed piece of instant knowledge – that we both
shape and immediately recognize the difference between good and evil,
in a manner which is comparable with our immediate recognition of
time differences or spatial relations. The point, for our purposes here, is
that this was the way Kant thought that reality should be envisaged:
namely, as gaining its order from the mind that observes it. This was his
'Copernican revolution'. However little you regard this great thinker,
you have to recognize that, in the history of Western philosophy, this is
a moment of stupendous historical importance. It is hard to tell with all
great thinkers whether they are responsible for a change in the way a
whole generation thinks, or whether they are merely the most articulate

spokesmen for the *Zeitgeist.* But it is no accident that the great Romantics saw Kant as 'their' philosopher. The human mind had never been quite so important, quite so central to the scheme of things, quite so inventive of the world in which it found itself, while at the same time so passively receptive to the world in all its objective and scientific reality as when Kant wrote his three great Critiques. Science and Goethe – Darwin and Wordsworth – the objectivity of Lyell's *Geology* and the mysterious man-centredness of the haunted landscapes of Caspar David Friedrich – all seem of a piece with Kant's *Weltanschauung.*

If you haven't read Kant before, I should strongly recommend that you avoid summaries or introductions to his work until you have given yourself a few weeks, let us say, to catch the quality of his mind at first hand. Even a desultory reading of the man himself will show you, when you do turn to the commentaries or books about him, how very difficult it is to convey his true flavour. Of course, anyone could sit down and write a textbook account of Kant's theory of knowledge and reason; what he had meant by saying that David Hume had awakened him from his dogmatic slumber; how he posited the differences between the knowable and the unknowable; how he classified areas of knowledge into Categories; how he distinguished between Phenomena – things which could be discerned empirically – and Noumena – things-in-themselves which we knew to be, but which we could not claim to discern empirically. And yet, having made such a textbook analysis of Kant and worked out its implications, you might still not catch the extraordinary quality of freshness, of being alive, which is contained in the rococo chess puzzles which he set up.

Enter the land of Kant, then, before you read any summary – for he engages us here precisely because of the 'feeling of life' which he engenders. Over the specific question which concerns this book, the great question of God which human beings were asking themselves throughout the last century, Kant gives out important but ambivalent signals, which is why he is enlisted by both sides of the argument, the believers and the unbelievers (compare the position 150 years later of Wittgenstein, in many ways the Kant or neo-Kant *de notre époque*). Furthermore, Kant himself would seem to have hovered between two distinct positions about God. And these two distinct positions are themselves going to keep recurring in our story. You could call them the Immanentist and the Transcendental ways of thinking. For the Immanentist, God is an inner reality; in so far as He is real, and we can truthfully say that we believe in Him, we are really saying that we hold sacred the God Within. The Transcendentalist, on the other hand, will want to say yes, while God may be *known* within, it is ultimately atheistical to say that this is the only way in which He is known. If God is no more than something or some feeling within ourselves, then He has no objective reality. We can only truly say that we believe in God if we believe in something, some value system, some possibility of 'things in themselves', outside ourselves, indeed outside the empirical world altogether.

Kant's published, early writings are Transcendentalist. His later writings and his notebooks suggest that he became an Immanentist verging on atheism. Kant shared Hume's view that there was no more mileage left in any of the three conventional proofs for the existence of God. He very specifically rejected the Ontological Proof, that is, the idea that God is a 'necessary' truth. He also made short work of the Cosmological Proof, the idea that facts are contingent, must have causes, and of the related Arguments from Design, all for reasons which would be familiar to readers of Hume's *Dialogues Concerning Natural Religion*.

It was in the sphere of Ethics that Kant at some periods of his life seemed to believe that he had found an area which, in terms of practical belief, suggested to most of us the existence of something outside ourselves. The categorical imperative, the sense of duty to a set of moral laws which are not of our own invention, implies the existence of a lawgiver. 'The realism of the Idea of God can be proved only through the duty-imperative ... A being which is capable of holding sway over all rational beings in accordance with laws of duty (the categorical imperative) and is justified in so doing, is God ...'[33] This was the proof of God's existence which Kant had advanced in the *Critique of Practical Reason* (1788).

'Kant was a deeply religious thinker.'[34] While this is obviously true of the philosopher who wrote in the *Critique of Practical Reason*, 'Two things fill the mind with ever new and increasing admiration and awe, the more often and steadily we reflect upon them: *the starry heavens above me and the moral law within me.*' At the same time, Kant's whole life would be seen as a reaction against the pietism of his upbringing; he hated psalm-singing and hymns; on the only occasions when university duty required him to preside at religious ceremonies or to preach, he made excuses and avoided them; he certainly did not maintain orthodox Christian belief; and it is necessary to remember that 'no thinker ever placed greater emphasis on reason's boundaries than Kant; at the same time, none has ever been bolder in asserting its unqualified title to govern our lives'.[35] He was single-minded in his philosophical pursuits. Indeed, it is hard, from a biographical viewpoint, to think of any great philosopher whose life-story was duller.

It was so dull as inevitably to invite jokes: Heine's remark that no one could write Kant's life-history since he had neither a life nor a history; Bertrand Russell's crueller gibe: 'Hume, by his criticism of the concept of causality, awakened him from his dogmatic slumbers, so at least he says, but the awakening was only temporary, and he soon invented a soporific which enabled him to sleep again.'[36]

One sees the point of Heine's joke, but Russell's dismissal, admittedly written at a time when it was politically and financially profitable to mock all things German, is grotesquely unfair. We can read the outwardly uneventful story of this tiny man (his nose scarcely visible above the lectern when he delivered his discourses), who for most of his eighty years never left Königsberg in East Prussia; never married, never varied his daily routines.* But this life of Kant's was also the progress of a mind which, *pace* Russell, moved considerably. In the magisterial trilogy of Critiques (*Critique of Pure Reason, Critique of Practical Reason* and *Critique of Judgment*), and in *Religion within the Limits of Bare Reason* (1793–4), which could be read as a theological coda to those three great works, Kant makes the distinction which is the hallmark of all his metaphysics, between things which can be known empirically and things which can be posited by Reason but which are not subject to proof. He *allows* such concepts as God, Soul, Immortality, but demonstrates that such concepts can never be proved: they belong to the realm of the unknowable. But as his posthumously-published writings show us, he had by no means, in this area of speculation or any other, invented a soporific which would enable him to sleep again. Unshakeable in his belief in the Categorical Imperative, our innate sense of duty, our idea that there is such a thing as right and wrong, Kant was, to put it mildly, ambivalent about the transcendent reality of the Deist God. Theism, to which in various ways he clung in the privacy of his notebooks (more, really, than

---

* The people of Königsberg set their clocks by the time he passed their doors on his 'constitutional', the only two days when this unfailing system broke down being when he was unable to stop himself reading Rousseau's *Émile*.

in the outward observances of his blameless life), became inseparable for him from his own inner life, his own inner sense of The Good. This impersonal sense of Duty (much derided by the Cambridgey philosophers of Russell's generation: they associated it with the dull, Victorian agnosticism of their parents' generation) seems to have replaced the notion of the externally 'real' Creator.

'God is not a being outside me, but merely a thought in me. God is the morally practical self-legislative Reason. Therefore, only a God in me, about me, and over me.' And again, 'The proposition: There is a God says nothing more than: There is in the human morally self-determining Reason a highest principle which determines itself, and finds itself compelled unremittingly to act in accordance with such a principle ...'[37] Such thoughts, often in scraps of unfinished sentences, are found in the private notebooks of Kant as he approached his eightieth year, and his end. The categorical imperative remains, but the Deist God has indeed become an unnecessary hypothesis.

In a sense, though, we distort Kant if (as Coleridge did) we scan his works for evidences of what he thought about theology, and ignore their major substance. He was attempting the North Face of the Eiger: hardly surprising, then, that all the alpinists who followed him slithered down one side of the mountain or the other without reaching the peak. For Kant had been attempting to describe the process of knowledge itself. He was trying to marry the twin truths: namely, that by the very process of perceiving and knowing, we invent our world; and also that this world has a reality of its own.

Kant is not an 'influential' thinker in the sense that Marx or Freud were influential: that is, he isn't a thinker of whom the man in the street has necessarily heard or whose central idea, in however simplified a form, has passed into folk-knowledge. Nevertheless, he is a toweringly important figure in Western intellectual history, arguably the most important of all modern philosophers. It is precisely because he asked questions to which no completely satisfactory answer can be given that he remains so interesting.

From the European point of view, he is important in two areas. First, he was (not entirely through his fault) the father or grandfather of the system of philosophy known as Idealism which was to dominate metaphysics for the next century and more. He made possible Fichte, Hegel, and all those who either followed or reacted against Hegel. Basically, this was a way of doing philosophy which concentrated on Kant's insight that the 'world' is only the picture flashed onto the magic lantern screen of our own imaginings. The Hegelians discarded Kant's austere belief in things-in-themselves and in their differing ways discovered that history, time, religion itself were all human constructs that had no meaning outside the sphere of human thought.

Secondly, and quite differently, Kant had an effect on science. Among sober thinkers and persons of common sense it became clear, after Kant, that some of the problems of philosophy were unanswerable. There had to be another way than metaphysics of understanding the world. Inevitably, this was physical science.

Much of Kant's writing, particularly in the *Critique of Judgement*, is taken up with teleology; that is, with explanations of the end (*telos*) or even the meaning of things. Is it possible, from looking at Nature, to discern any purpose in it all? The old optimistic Leibnizian view of Nature and her purposes was as simply anthropocentric as the medieval Thomists. By spelling this view out, Kant almost satirizes it. What is the purpose of vegetation? Why, to feed herbivores. And of herbivores? To be a prey to carnivores. And of carnivores? To serve Man, who is the centre of the universe. Yet, as he says of man,

> Nature has not taken him for her special darling and favoured him with benefit above all animals. Rather, in her destructive operations – plague, hunger, perils of waters, frost, assaults of other animals great and small, etc. – in these things she spared him as little as any other animals.[38]

The state of knowledge in Kant's day about how the species evolved was still primitive. He took the view, which from a post-Darwinian perspective seems strange, that the 'bosom of mother earth, as she passed out of her chaotic state ...' had 'given birth in the beginning to creatures of less purposive form, that these again gave birth to others which formed themselves with greater adaptation to their place of birth and their relations to each other; until this womb became torpid and ossified, limited its births to definite species *not further modifiable*' (my italics).[39]

It was the destruction of the idea that species could not modify any further which caused such anger in the post-Darwinian controversies: that, and the idea, which Darwin seemed to confirm, that teleology had no place in the scientific outlook. The universe was without purpose. Kant toyed with these bleak notions, wondering how they matched our innate moral and aesthetic senses. He certainly cleared the way for the development of scientific study. Science was thereby given the blessing of the greatest and most influential of all European academics. Though Kant reminded scientists of the limits of their scope – they could understand how nature worked, but not why – he not only sanctified science as a respectable university discipline, he made it more or less inevitable (given the limits and definitions which he had placed on the boundaries of human knowledge) that science would become *the* dominant discipline of the future. When it was established that the *noumena* were unknowable, it would follow as the night the day that the intelligent mind would concentrate upon *phenomena*, with a consequence equally ineluctable: that 'scientific proof' would become, not *a* but *the* legitimate criterion for verifying the truth of propositions.

3

The Religion of Humanity

'Who ever heard the like of it – in the nineteenth century, mind; in an age of progress, and in a country which rejoices in the blessings of the British constitution? Nobody ever heard the like of it, and, consequently, nobody can be expected to believe it.'

Wilkie Collins, *The Moonstone*

'ON YOUR MARROW bones, sir!' These were the instructions shrieked out by Jeremy Bentham to James Mill as they approached the cottage at the bottom of the garden at Barrow Green, near Oxted. To demonstrate that he was serious, the great sage of Utilitarianism waved his walking stick (which he nicknamed Dapple) until James Mill actually fell to his knees in the presence of this garden-temple dedicated to the greatest English republican: 'Sacred to Milton, Prince of Poets', an inscription on the wall said.

The Mills were for a period accommodated in that poky cottage near Oxted, until the dark and the damp made Mrs Mill and the children unwell. The upbringing of John Stuart Mill, the 'saint of rationalism', is one of the great paradoxes of the nineteenth century. Few men were more altruistic in their desire to better society, and yet almost none can have passed a less social childhood. The Utilitarians were responsible for many of the great reforms which made Britain, little by little, a saner and more tolerable place to live in than many of the autocratically-governed countries of the European continent. Prison reforms, parliamentary reforms, social reforms, of a kind which a later generation would deem eminently sensible as well as humane, all owed their origins to men who were by any standards deeply odd. Bentham, who in the last twenty years of a long life was more or less a hermit in Westminster, was eccentric as only the very rich, perhaps, can be. Wearing his hair down to his waist, and crowning his head with a battered straw hat, this father of modern democracy (an idea to which he was only converted in his seventies) would be seen pottering around Queen's Square Place for what he called his 'ante-jentacular' (pre-breakfast) or post-prandial walks. The casual observer could have been forgiven for believing he was a lunatic, and yet all over the known world he was revered as a radical, not merely in the sense of someone who took (eventually) a progressive view of politics, but as someone who had read and pondered through all the Laws of England, and who – whether he was giving his mind to prisons, or the Poor Laws, or the ballot-box (his idea and invention) – thought down to the very roots of things. Lampooned by Dickens as the philosophy of Gradgrind, Utilitarianism did indeed deal in *Facts*, and it had small time for religion. The 'marrow bones' might be bent for Milton, but not for the Almighty.

Bentham's work is marked by an obsessive attention to detail. When he invented the Panopticon, and lost £23,000 of his own money (which the Government eventually paid back), he was trying to reduce violence and deaths in prisons by a hideously intrusive spying device into the day-to-day, hour-by-hour life of prisoners. When drawing up plans for new Poor Laws, he even specified what type of straw bed the paupers should be given. Anything which could not be stratified, classified, labelled and explained in good empirical fashion (Hume was his philosophic mentor) was a waste of time in Bentham's book.

So it is not surprising that he was impatient with religion. As a very young undergraduate at Oxford in the 1760s (he was only twelve years old when he went up, and still sufficiently Tory in those days to refer to Charles I as The Royal Martyr) he showed some hesitation about assenting to the Thirty-nine Articles of the Church of England, and his uneasy guilt about having done so left him with a perpetual grudge against the Established Church. Years later (in 1818, when he was seventy) he was to publish his *Church of Englandism and its Catechism Examined*: 'He who has entered into that fold cannot have entered into it without having sold himself to the practice and service of vice ...'[1]

The undermining of the Established Church was, quite unashamedly, part of the agenda of the early nineteenth-century radicals, and it was to have widespread effects. The emancipation of the Catholics in 1829, for example, came about, as the High Church followers of Keble were not slow to recognize, because Parliament no longer believed the Church of England to have any unique or sacred claims. It was merely a department of state; and it was not tolerable, this being the case, to grant to it a unique status. From this comparatively esoteric point could be said to spring the whole Liberal impetus for Irish Home Rule and independence, a long, slow, bloody story which was in itself a metaphor for many other disentanglings – the dissolution of the British Empire itself. Everyone in the early decades of the nineteenth century, though, agreed that the Established Church was weak, so Bentham enjoyed himself demolishing the easiest Aunt Sally who ever sat in his sights:

> In the sight of Jesus, if any credit be due to Gospel history, all men are equal. The claim of the poor was, in the eyes of Jesus, superior to that of the rich. Not so in the eyes of Dean Andrewes ... In his stall at Canterbury, chief of a set of idlers, paid for doing nothing under the name of Prebendaries ... To the sportive genius of this Receiver of the Holy Ghost, ... by this Dignitary of the *Daughter* church ... men who are neither so rich, nor so wedded to wine as to loath all cheaper liquors will be seen marked out as the objects of scorn, and their health as an object of just regard, under the name of Ale-drinkers ...[2]

Bentham, who liked to drink his own home-brewed ale, would of course seize upon this offensive epithet. The contrast between the Son of Man who had not where to lay his head, and the fat Anglican dean or prebendary with his enormous state revenues, tells its own story.

The modern reader of *Church of Englandism* will not need to be convinced that Dean Andrewes was corrupt. But he might notice that when Gradgrind/Bentham goes into Canterbury Cathedral (in actuality or in mind), the fat prebendary is all he sees; his eye does not swoop up above the prebendal stalls to the beauty of Gothic tracery, the richness of stained glass. Nor does he ask himself (as would Carlyle) what we had lost since the days when the Cathedrals of England were built; nor (as would Ruskin) what we continue to lose, if we do not open our hearts to these Gothic sermons in stone.

The life of John Stuart Mill himself reveals a casebook study of the effects of Gradgrindism on the soul. The opening chapter of his *Autobiography* recounts how at the age of three he began to learn Greek, sitting at the same table as his father, who was engaged in writing *The History of British India* (the book which was to lead to James, and eventually John, Mill's lucrative appointments in the East India Company). Since in those days there were no Greek–English lexicons freely available, the child had to interrupt his father's work and ask the meaning of any word he did not understand as he struggled through Aesop's Fables, and then Xenophon's *Anabasis*. The whole of Herodotus, Xenophon's *Cyropaedia*, Diogenes Laertius, some Lucian, and Isocrates' *Ad Demonicum* and *Ad Nicoclem* were read in this fashion. At the age of six or seven he read six Dialogues of Plato, and began to master mathematics. In his eighth year he began to learn Latin, and to read Homer, as well as to embark on a wide programme of historical reading, and of Hobbes's 'Computatio sive Logica'.

> I was constantly meriting reproof by inattention, inobservance and general slackness of mind in matters of daily life. My father was the extreme opposite in these particulars: his senses and mental faculties were always on the alert; he carried decision and energy of character in his whole manner ...[3]

This strange childhood, devoid, as far as we can see, of ordinary boyish friendship, of games, of fantasy or fairy-tales, was also rigidly secular. James Mill 'found it impossible to believe that a world so full of evil was the work of an Author combining infinite power with perfect goodness and righteousness'.[4]

The younger Mill was basically loyal to his father's Benthamite creeds, and we can be sure that, in some strange way which it is difficult to analyse but which is incontrovertible, the many liberal and democratic reforms for which John Mill as a Parliamentarian campaigned would not have made much progress in a religious society. Hence, perhaps, his arguing so passionately for national education to be wholly secular in character ('To say that *secular* means irreligious implies that all the arts and sciences are irreligious, and is very like saying that all professions except that of the law are illegal ...)'[5] He noted as a very young man that in Catholic Europe there was no civil liberty; and liberty, as he made clear in his most famous essay, was the beginning and end of his *credo* ('In all countries where they could get civil power to side with them, [the clergy] have succeeded in their nefarious purpose and mankind are still grovelling at their feet').[6]

But, as Mill was aware, the rigid secularism and utilitarianism of his upbringing, although they trained his mind to its lofty hatred of hypocrisy, its high moral purpose, and its love of freedom, were also oppressive. The first symptom that all was not well came in the autumn of 1826, when he was twenty. He had not at that stage read Coleridge, but in after-time he felt that the quatrain from the poet's 'Dejection: An Ode' exactly described his own state of mind:

> A grief without a pang, void, dark and drear,
> A drowsy, stifled, unimpassioned grief,
> Which finds no natural outlet or relief
> In word, or sigh, or tear.

The feelings of emotional desiccation, spiritual dryness and depression which overwhelmed the young John Stuart Mill were relieved by reading the poetry of Wordsworth, an unlikely remedy by Benthamite standards, particularly in the mid to late 1820s, by which time Wordsworth had abandoned his early radicalism and become a Tory die-hard and a churchman. 'What made Wordsworth's poems a medicine for my state of mind, was that they expressed not merely outward beauty, but states of feeling, and of thought followed by feeling, under the excitement of beauty.'[7]

The conversion to Wordsworth did not lead to any religious conversion in a serious sense of the word, but it did lead to a break with the rigidities of Benthamism. Moreover, it led to the blossoming of friendships which were of particular refreshment to a young man who had had no conventional schooling, no university education, and no companionship of coevals in all his childhood. Coleridgean Christians who were wrestling with the doubts and difficulties of Christian faith, young men such as John Sterling and Frederick Maurice, became friends with Mill at this period. 'With Maurice I had for some time been acquainted through Eyton Tooke, who had known him at Cambridge, and though my discussions with him were nearly always disputes, I had carried away from them much that helped to build up my new fabric of thought.'[8]

It is hard to imagine two men whose views of the religious question were more different. Maurice – destined to be a friend of Tennyson, Ruskin and Carlyle – was deemed a dangerous liberal, even a heretic, by some orthodox churchmen for his views on eternal punishment, yet nevertheless had a completely orthodox view of God and His existence. For Mill, even in his new fabric of thought, such talk must have been very largely meaningless. The fact that his posthumously-published *Three Essays on Religion* came as such a shock to his unbelieving liberal friends and disciples shows that they had always regarded him, in life, as soundly agnostic.

The *Essays* came down very, very tentatively in favour, not of Christianity, but of some kind of Theism. 'I think it must be allowed that, in the present state of our knowledge, adaptations in Nature afford a large balance of probability in favour of creation by intelligence.'[9]

Mill rejected the idea that this 'intelligence' would or could choose to intervene to disrupt the Laws of Nature. He would seem to have embraced a watery version of Deism; that is, the Universe probably was invented by God, but He made no efforts to speak to the human race and they could only infer His existence by viewing the pattern of Creation or contemplating their certainty of moral truth. Religion, as far as Mill was concerned, was to be explained in broadly Utilitarian terms: it was a system which helped men and women to be more moral. In defiance of early Christian history, he held the view that the first believers followed Christ as a moral reformer. In a sentence which encapsulates the 'liberal Protestant' view – to the point of caricature – Mill condescendingly observes, 'When this pre-eminent genius of Christ is combined with the qualities of probably the greatest moral reformer and martyr to that mission who ever existed upon earth, religion cannot be said to have made a bad choice in pitching on this man ...'[10]

This is hardly Dostoevsky, falling in tears at the feet of the Redeemer. Certainly Mill endorsed no formal creed, belonged to no Church, and did nothing in his earnest and unselfish life to promote views even as faintly religious as these posthumous thoughts. The essence of the Utilitarian contribution was secular, and in the pattern of Victorian society which it helped to bring about – greater democracy, a discussion of the rights and freedoms of women – the secularism was a necessary, even an inevitable part. It was no accident that so many of the liberals were unbelievers, and so many of the unbelievers political. If Gibbon appeared to have said the last word on Church History, and Hume on metaphysics, if Kant had demolished the traditional proofs for the existence of God and left a moral imperative in the place of a spiritual enthusiasm, then the English Utilitarians wrote an agenda for change which was very largely followed in the nineteenth century. Religion, as popularly practised and understood for fifteen hundred years in Europe, was sent the way of pocket boroughs and inadequate drains. By damning religion with faint praise, Mill had on one level been inconsistent; but on another, it could be said that the Essay on Theism barely amounts to an endorsement. It is hard to imagine anyone praying to, let alone dying for, the 'intelligence' which Mill deemed to be a 'probability'.

This, then, is the background to the religious history of the nineteenth century – for the first time in Europe a generation was coming to birth who had no God, or no God of any substance, and who found it difficult to justify religion except in the most basic of Utilitarian terms.

This very self-consciousness of the early nineteenth century, its belief that it was different, its awareness of modernity as a concept and its idea of progress, is itself part of the story. Indeed, you could say that it was the central nineteenth-century idea, the idea of progress. It underlies Georg Wilhelm Hegel's (1770–1831) view of history. At first sight, Hegel's historiography would seem to be as religious as that of the authors of the Bible itself.

> The truth is inherently universal, essential and substantial; and, as such, it exists solely in thought and for thought. But that spiritual principle which we call God is none other than the truly substantial, inherently and essentially individual and subjective truth. It is the source of all thought, and its thought is inherently creative ...[11]

Hegel uses language in such an exuberant and imprecise way that it is sometimes difficult to make out whether God is for him a being with any objective reality, or whether He is a product of the collective mind. On the one hand, he speaks of the study of history as 'a theodicy, a justification of the ways of God (such as Leibniz attempted in his own metaphysical manner), but using categories which were as yet abstract and indeterminate.' On the other hand, his famous doctrine of the three phases of history, culminating in the apogee – the German phase – makes no bones about the fact that the collective imagination of humanity is stronger than its gods – that they are, indeed, the product of this faculty: 'And thus Zeus, who set limits to the depredations of time and suspended its constant flux, had no sooner established something inherently enduring than he was himself devoured along with his whole empire.'[12] If this was true of Zeus, that he was swept away with the Greek civilization of which he was a mere expression, was it not equally likely that the Protestant God of the Germans would one day be seen as no more than a part of their *Geist,* their imperium? A household god, in short, and not an objective reality underpinning all reality, a subjective truth, and not a truth underpinning all truth.[12]

The God of Hegel is the prevailing mood, and the prevailing mood is God. Hegel greets *now* with more exuberance than any previous philosopher, seeing history as an unfolding, purposive series of majestic rollers, making their way to the shore of his own generation, his own thought processes. Hegelianism is mass-egomania on the grand scale. It is the belief that history has been moving in our direction, that we now are evolving or discovering systems of thought, of political government, of education and science which entirely supersede the wisdom and experience of previous ages. They had their place and time – but we are different. This thought underlies the whole of Hegel. It is what made him by far the most exciting and influential nineteenth-century philosopher, almost all European metaphysicians being influenced by him, or choosing to react against him.

What was Hegel's influence on the decline of religious belief in the nineteenth century? The windy language sounds, and indeed *is*, so religious that it would be possible to make out a case for Hegel being one of the great defenders of religion. 'The Christian religion is the religion of truth', he proclaimed in his lectures.[13] But he immediately added, 'but if by "the truth of the Christian religion" we mean that it is historically accurate, this is not what is intended here'.[14] The Christian religion, and Christ Himself, were the products of the communities of faith which produced the Gospels. From this idea of Hegel's and his belief that religion manifests itself in myth, sprang the modern critical Germanic school of biblical criticism, centred largely upon the Tübingen School of Divinity. And if any one phenomenon may be said to have been responsible for the destruction of ordinary Christian faith in the nineteenth-century Protestant world (and in the Catholic world, when they allowed themselves to become aware of it), it was this critical approach to the Scriptures.

Equally, Hegel's philosophical influence, particularly in England and the United States, would appear to have been very religious. The Idealists wrote much of Absolutes and Spirit and used language which at first sight looks like the old language of religion. When examined, however, it is usually the case that their use of terms like *Absolute* was as a substitute for God. Most of the Idealists (and they were by far the most influential academic philosophers from the closing decades of the nineteenth century well into the twentieth century in England and America) were agnostic or actually atheist when it came to the big question of whether they believed in the objective reality of a personal God.

Hegel's influence, then, is so widespread that it is difficult to quantify, but it is questionable whether he, with his grand idea of history as an unfolding progress, a tale with a meaning which we can read (or which we can impose upon it), invented the nineteenth-century idea of progress or was himself part of it.

In England, a philosopher who was of far greater influence over such figures as John Stuart Mill or George Lewes (eventually George Eliot's life-companion) was Auguste Comte (1798–1857). The essence of his system of thought, known as *Positivism*, was comparable to Hegel's.

Comte divided history into three phases. In the first stage, the theological stage, it made perfectly good sense for medieval men and women to explain their intellectual and scientific problems in terms of spirits, miracles and divine force. After the Reformation and the coming of Descartes, Newton and company, humanity entered the second phase, the metaphysical stage, in which it made sense to see the universe (as had Leibniz, for example) as a machine governed by unseen forces. But the third phase, the Positive Stage, saw this world as the possession of the human race. Science now enabled us to understand that we were the lords of creation. There was no need to bow down before non-existent deities, to accept political tyrannies or physical hardships as inevitable. We had it in ourselves, as Humanity, to make society better. Sociology is a word invented by Comte and the Positivists.

It is easy to see why this heady collection of thoughts should have made such appeal to Mill's generation. Here was something based entirely on the material world which an empirical, Utilitarian philosopher would agree to be *the case*. And yet here was something a little more inspiring than Benthamism with its *fact, fact, fact*. Here was what Comte called The Religion of Humanity.

But Comte was a strange individual. Indeed, it would not be stretching language to say that he was mad; and the English Positivists had a hard time of it at the hands of their French master.

The phrase 'religion of humanity' was not a metaphor. Comte did in fact institute a new 'church', with special humanist saints such as Adam Smith and Frederick the Great. He had hopes that Notre Dame in Paris could be converted into a Temple – the central church of the Occidental Republic. There were sacraments and rituals: the presentation of an infant, the initiation into humanity at fourteen, corresponding to Confirmation, full admission at twenty-one, destination at twenty-eight, marriage before thirty-five, maturity at forty-two, retirement at sixty-two and, finally, the sacrament of 'transformation'. He invited the General of the Jesuits, the Tsar of Russia and Mehemet Ali to join his new church, but they appear to have declined.[15]

Comte's own slightly rocky emotional-cum-sexual history was also projected and generalized to a point where it became part of the universal Religion. When he was in his early twenties Comte had walked into a bookshop and recognized the girl behind the counter as someone with whom he had once slept. Before long they had set up a ménage together, which threatened to break up when she was arrested, in a restaurant where she was having dinner with Comte, on the charge of being a registered prostitute. This was technically the case: it was how she had met Comte in the first instance.

A civil marriage made an honest, but not perhaps a happy, woman of Caroline Massin. Comte's first attack of madness occurred in 1826 (he was twenty-eight) and she faithfully nursed him through it rather than allow him to be incarcerated in an asylum. While Comte formed the impression that he was one of the heroes in Homer, and began hurling knives in their small Parisian apartment, his old mother materialized from Montpelier and explained that it had all happened as a punishment from God for marrying outside the Church. Young Mme Comte even consented to be remarried to her lunatic husband by a priest. Her reward was persistent vilification from Comte, who filled his voluminous political and philosophical pamphlets with paranoid denunciations of his wife, and embarrassingly explicit rehearsals of her earlier career.

They eventually split up, and Comte was destined to form his second important emotional attachment to Mme Clothilde de Vaux, a young woman some fifteen or sixteen years his junior who – when they met in 1844 – had been abandoned by her husband, a petty government official. She died two years after they met and was buried in the Père Lachaise cemetery on 7 April 1846.

If Clothilde died without allowing the philosopher his desires, it was not for the want of trying on Comte's part. The fact that his attempts on her virtue (many and frequent) were all unavailing did not diminish his love – indeed, it positively increased it. If poor Mme Comte was the Scarlet Woman of the Religion of Humanity, Clothilde was its Blessed Virgin. The faithful were treated to annual printed confessions to this Virginal Deity. Her empty red plush chair was officially designated the Altar of his church. Around his neck Comte – or, as he now signed his circulars and encyclicals, Le Fondateur de la réligion universelle, Grand Prêtre de l'Humanité – constantly wore a medallion containing Clothilde's hair.

Furious denunciations were heaped on the heads of his English disciples, particularly Lewes and Mill, for their unwillingness to use these titles in full when communicating with the Master. They on their part, resolutely men of the left (Mill moving from Liberalism to Socialism towards the end of his life), were disconcerted that Comte, who had begun his career as a political philosopher meditating on the power which was invested, as of right, in organized labour, should have ended it as a champion of royalism, with the Emperor Napoleon III as his hero.

Perhaps Mill viewed the progress, or decline, of Comte's world-view with cautious dismay, and asked himself whether there was any echo, in the lunatic ravings of the French philosopher, of his own endearing but irrational devotion to Mrs Harriet Taylor, the woman whom after years of chaste but passionate wooing he was able to marry in 1851. The *Autobiography*, which credits her with, for example, having contributed the better part of *On Liberty*, praises Harriet in terms of which Comte himself would have been proud in writing of the Blessed Clothilde. Those who would mock her like to remember the sixth chapter, where he compares her to Shelley, adding, inevitably, that 'in thought and intellect, Shelley, so far as his powers were developed in his short life, was but a child compared with what she ultimately became'. She ultimately became, of course, a paragon; and when her daughter (who had been the constant companion of Mill's last years) thought of publishing the *Autobiography*, she was warned by their friend Alexander Bain: 'I greatly doubt the propriety of your printing [Mill's view that] ... Harriet ... [was a] greater poet than Carlyle ... [a] greater thinker than himself ... [a] greater leader than his father. I venture to express the opinion that no such combination has ever been realized in the whole history of the human race.'[16]

Clearly, it never occurred to Mill in any part of his conscious mind that his Harriet-worship was absurd, any more than he or the other believers in Positivism questioned the notion that they had definitely *moved on*, that society as at present constituted, and the human race in its present high level of enlightenment, had grown out of religion.

The old Nobodaddy of Deism had been dissected and destroyed by Hume, just as, on the Continent, the *philosophes* were held partially responsible for that *écrasez l'infâme* which had destroyed the Church and placed the Temple of Reason, and the Terror, in its place. In the post-Revolutionary situation of the 1830s and 1840s the Church made its comeback, and the pious revivals in England – with their Clapham Sects, their evangelical reformers, their Puseyism and their Irvingism, their resurrection of the Church of Rome, their Cardinals Wiseman and Manning – had their Continental counterparts. But as far as the *intelligentsia* were concerned (and their attitude was undoubtedly shared by many of the periodical-reading, middle-class public) the Church, together with the ideas and stories which it enshrined, was out of date. The future lay with radicalism, feminism, parliamentary reform, suffrage, education.

'The old opinions in religion, morals and politics, are so much discredited in the more intellectual minds as to have lost the greater part of their efficacy for good', Mill opined in his *Autobiography*. 'More recently a spirit of free speculation has sprung up, giving a more encouraging prospect of the gradual emancipation of England ...'[17]

It is very largely owing to Mill and his friends that these emancipations came to pass; very largely owing to them and their prosaic and practical attitude to political questions that England weathered 1848, the Year of Revolutions, and did not experience a Paris Commune of 1870, a Russian Revolution of 1917, or a large Fascist uprising after the First World War. The fact that their political ideas were so benign and so sensible is not diminished by the touching elements of irrationality in John Mill's nature. As his encomiums of Harriet Taylor remind us, the human race can easily deprive itself of Christianity, but finds it rather more difficult to lose its capacity for worship.

4

Carlyle

Wer darf ihn nennen
Und wer bekennen:
Ich glaub Ihn!
Wer empfinden
Und sich unterwinden
Zu sagen: Ich glaub Ihn nicht!

(Who can presume to name him, and to declare
  'I believe in him'?
And who can feel and dare to say, 'I do not believe
  in him'?)

Goethe, *Faust*, I

'CARLYLE HAS A hairy strength which made his literary reputation a mere chance,' observed his percipient American friend Ralph Waldo Emerson. Meeting him after a gap of fourteen years, in 1847, Emerson reminded himself that Carlyle 'is not mainly a scholar, like the most of my acquaintances, but a very practical Scotchman, such as you would find in any saddler's or iron dealer's shop, and then only accidentally, and by a surprising addition, the admirable scholar and writer he is.'[1]

This must go a long way towards explaining why Carlyle appealed to his contemporaries. He was, as Emerson saw, 'unique, here, as the Tower of London' and 'no mortal in America could pretend to talk to Carlyle'.[2] This was partly because of his out-and-out condemnations of almost all and each. 'His sneers and scoffs are thrown in every direction. He breaks every sentence with a scoffing laugh "windbag", "monkey", "donkey", "bladder" and let him describe whom he will, it is always "poor fellow" ...'[3] Yet Emerson could also discern the paradox (for he had first met Carlyle when that most Scotch of Scotch writers was still resident at the remote hamlet of Craigenputtoch): 'he is the voice of London – a true Londoner with no sweet country breath in him'.[4] Carlyle, in other words, for all his extreme oddity, and the acerbity of his humour, spoke for the post-industrial generation of men and women who, in the 1830s and 1840s, gazed bewildered on a new world. Emerson observed that in so far as efforts were being made to educate the working classes in England in the 1840s through schools and Mechanics' Institutions, the inspiration derived almost entirely from Carlyle. If there was any question bigger in people's minds than what Carlyle had called the 'Condition of England question', it was the possibly related one of the Condition of God or the Condition of Religion question. He had 'the utmost impatience of Christendom and Jewdom'[5] – Emerson again, but how we hear Carlyle's voice in the coinage! – and he believed that the Christian religion had lost 'all its vitality'. More urgently, it had lost its credibility. And that was something which everyone had begun to feel in their bones, and that was why Carlyle was so important to them.

For the Victorians, it was Carlyle's ordinariness and not his extraordinariness which appealed. We, perhaps, approach him as a highly eccentric historian; it would be better to think of him as a journalist of genius, peculiarly in touch with the *Zeitgeist* which he so abominated and deplored. He was indeed an embodiment of the Victorian dilemma about God. He wished to believe – in a Supreme Lawgiver, in Duty and Morality, in a personal Guide to life. But he had looked into Christianity and found it to be false. His heart could not subscribe to it. The God and the religion of Revelation being incredible to him, Carlyle could not rest in mere unbelief. Such a thing was horrifying to him. So he spoke and wrote *as if* God were true, manifesting Himself less in the miraculous and unbelievable tales of religious mythology than in the inexorable workings of History itself.

It is difficult for the men and women of our generation to get Thomas Carlyle right. There are too many red herrings to confuse us. For a start, there is his prose style, an extraordinary cocktail of bombast and jokes, half-Scotch, half-German in its blend of allusiveness, puns, hilarity and savagery. Then again, there are the friends, in life and death, to confuse us. In life he was, seemingly, revered by anyone who was anyone. John Mill, Dickens, Tennyson, F.D. Maurice, Leigh Hunt, Ruskin – they all at various stages befriended Carlyle and his wife. Almost from the beginning of his life in London, this penniless young man and his clever wife Jane attracted not merely the famous writers and thinkers, but many of the *bien-pensants*. True, liberals such as Mill and Matthew Arnold were dismayed by some of the later utterances of Carlyle, but even when they were dismayed, they would have agreed with George Eliot's often-quoted

> It is an idle question to ask whether his books will be read a century hence; if they were all burnt as the grandest of Suttees on his funeral pile, it would be only like cutting down an oak after its acorns have sown a forest. For there is hardly a superior or active mind of this generation that has not been modified by Carlyle's writings; there has hardly been an English book written for the last ten or twelve years [Eliot was writing in 1855] that would not have been different if Carlyle had not lived.[6]

This is the view of Carlyle's friends in life. But the friends he made in death are of a different kind. It is impossible to forget the fact that during the last days in the bunker beneath the Potsdamerplatz, as the Allied armies brought the Third Reich to its fiery end, Dr Goebbels read aloud to his beloved Führer from Carlyle's *Frederick the Great*.

The discrepancy shocks our contemporaries, but they do not often trouble themselves to read Carlyle's works to see if there might be any explanation: how could the friend of dull, virtuous John Mill,* the author of *On Liberty*, be the hero of the Nazi dictator? When a new book about Carlyle is published, most late twentieth-century observers are prepared to blame Carlyle for his posthumous German admirers, but they look for no answer. These are often the reviewers who consider his complex and heart-rendingly unhappy marital journey to be a cause for ribald and intrusive speculation. Therein lies another reason for our age (erotically obsessed, as Carlyle's was religiously obsessed) to deplore him: impotent!

No one would deny that Carlyle had his faults – as an historian, and as a man. But the modern literary journalists who throw a stone through the old sage's window and then run away up the street do not only him an injustice, but also his Victorian admirers. Carlyle's was a tragic life. His house in Cheyne Row breathes a solemn misery. It is a place of suppressed gloom and rage, of unfulfilled desire and of affection which could not be rightly directed.

Who among those who have read it will ever forget the moment in his *Reminiscences* when he recalls the visit of John Stuart Mill, coming 'pale as Hector's ghost' to break the terrible news? Mill had borrowed the manuscript, the only manuscript, of the first volume of Carlyle's *French Revolution*. The years of writing that book, the poverty of them, the anxiety, the sheer grind, had taken their toll on the health and happiness of both the Carlyles. It had stolen their youth, as Carlyle, a former liberal, now more despondent than any Tory about the possibility of any scheme for political improvement increasing the sum of human happiness, contemplated the French Revolution, a great event which lay at the back of all nineteenth-century reflections on religion, politics and society. With one part of himself Carlyle had contemplated the rotten aristocratic system, the moribund church-creeds, the indefensible injustice of the *ancien régime* and considered that if any rotten wood had

---

* Of Mill's conversation: 'Talk rather wintry' ... 'Sawdustish as old Sterling once called it' (*Reminiscences*). These perfectly-chosen epithets give a taste of Carlyle at his best.

deserved to be burnt to the roots it had been this. And yet, the burning had been terrible; the anarchy and sheer evil unleashed by that revolution both horrified and fascinated Carlyle, and he had written about it, not with the cold, analytical, 'wintry' mind of sawdustish Mill, but with his own blend of grotesque oratory, comedy and bombast. Mill had helped him, by giving him money and lending him books (just as Carlyle was to help Dickens with barrow-loads of books on the Revolution when Dickens came to write *A Tale of Two Cities*). So it was inevitable that Mill should have wanted to read *The French Revolution* as soon as it was finished. He came round to deliver the most unwelcome verdict that any author can ever have heard: the manuscript, the only manuscript, had been accidentally burnt.

> It was like half sentence of death to us both, and we had to pretend to take it lightly, so dismal and ghastly was his horror at it, and to try to talk of other matters. He stayed three mortal hours or so; his departure quite a relief to us. Oh, the burst of sympathy my poor darling then gave me, flinging her arms round my neck, and openly lamenting, condoling, and encouraging like a nobler second self ...

In his Journal, Carlyle cried out at the time: 'Oh, that I had faith! Oh that I had! Then were there nothing too hard or heavy for me. Cry silently to thy inmost heart to God for it ...'[8] Heroically, he sat down and wrote the volume again. It is one of the most extraordinary and courageous stories in the history of nineteenth-century literature.

The burning was an accident, but one of those emblematic accidents which seems fitting. Mill both loved and loathed Carlyle. Carlyle both loved and loathed the Revolution. And the essence of all his *saeva indignatio*, both on the page and in life, is encapsulated in those five desolate words in the Journal – 'Oh, that I had faith!' The point was, though – faith in *what*? Faith, for Carlyle and his contemporaries, was not a virtue in itself. Wintry Mill put it well in his *Autobiography*: 'The old opinions in religion, morals, and polities, are so much discredited in the more intellectual minds as to have lost the greater part of their efficacy for good, while they still have life enough in them to be a powerful obstacle to the growing up of any better opinions on those subjects.'[9] Carlyle, as his disciple and biographer Froude wrote,

> believed that the fate of France would be the fate of all nations whose hearts were set on material things – who for religion were content with

decent unrealities, satisfying their consciences with outward professions – treating God as if he were indeed, in Milton's words, 'a buzzard idol'. God would not be mocked. The poor wretches called mankind lay in fact under a tremendous dispensation which would exact an account of them for their misdoings to the smallest fibre.[10]

Hence, for his contemporaries, the electrifying importance of Carlyle. His *French Revolution* – still a marvellously readable, indeed a compulsive book, if you can only accustom yourself to his idiosyncratic prose manner – made him famous. It was published in 1837, the year that Queen Victoria came to the throne, a little less than fifty years after the events it so violently and vividly described. No wonder that it enjoyed a quite phenomenal success.[11] Dickens never travelled without a copy in his pocket. Southey read it more than six times. The great Whiggish liberal historians – Macaulay, Hallam, Brougham – recognized that, inimical to everything they stood for, Carlyle had enunciated uncomfortable truths. For the human race did not, as the Whigs hoped, progress in a bland upward spiral towards greater and gentler enlightenment. It lurched from one form of blind folly to another, from one superstition to another, from one tyranny to another. Faith was not something which could be gradually eliminated from the human scene. It was a vital component in the human make-up – personal and collective. If it was not directed towards the true God, it would be directed towards idols. Hence Carlyle's view – as we can now see, a fatal though perfectly accurate one – that the human race, having discarded belief in the unseen God of Israel, would always look towards an *Übermensch* or Superman as its God-substitute.

There is no accident about the fact that he who was once the friend of Mill should (posthumously) have become the friend of Hitler. The answer to Mill's question is that the 'old opinions in religion', once replaced, would not be satisfied by non-religion, only by false religion. Carlyle would have derived no satisfaction at all from contemplating the National Socialists, their garish vulgarity, their cruelty, their hypnotic power over the masses; but nor would their torch-lit processions, their persecutions of the Jews, their warmongering, their self-destructiveness, have caused any surprise to the author of *The French Revolution*. It is facile to say that we would all prefer to live in a world where the ideas of Mill and Arnold and George Eliot prevailed, rather than those of the Heroes and Hero-worshippers. Carlyle is a prophet without honour because his prophecies were disgracefully true.

His contemporaries could not see as clearly as he what would happen to the human race. They could not see the ghastly firebrands flickering in his crystal ball, they could only hear the hypnotic Scottish accent of their prophet. There is no doubt that Carlyle saw himself not merely as a writer, but as someone who in his very life and person could embody the needs and spiritual aspirations of his age.

There is a remarkable passage towards the end of his essay on Boswell's *Life of Johnson* in which he contemplates two of the great men of the eighteenth century, David Hume, the relentless sceptic, and Samuel Johnson, the High Church Tory. The one was a Puller-Down, the other an Edifier and Repairer. The tragedy of European civilization – this is the theme of *The French Revolution* – is that the things which deserved to be pulled down and the things which deserved to be repaired and built up were one and the same; or, rather, they were entangled together.

> To Johnson Life was as a Prison, to be endured with heroic faith: to Hume it was little more than a foolish Bartholomew-Fair Show-booth, with the foolish crowdings and elbowings of which it was not worth while to quarrel; the whole would break up, and be at liberty, so *soon*. Both realized the highest task of Manhood, that of living like men; each died not unfitly in his way: Hume as one, with factitious, half-false gaiety, taking leave of what was itself wholly but a Lie; Johnson as one awestruck, yet resolute and piously expectant heart, taking leave of a Reality, to enter a Reality still higher. Johnson had the harder problem of it, from first to last ...[12]

Johnson had the harder problem, of course, because the Christianity in which he so devoutly believed was not true, or not true in the way that in his most rigorously conservative moods he would have liked to make it. And yet, life without humility and piety and awe is lacking something. A world which was all Humeish, and with no element of the Johnsonian, would be tinny and empty. Carlyle saw Johnson and Hume as 'the two half-men of their time: who so should combine the intrepid Candour and decisive scientific Clearness of Hume, with the Reverence, the love and devout Humility of Johnson, were the whole man of a new time.'[13] The review belonged to 1832, when Carlyle was still in his thirties. We can't doubt that this was how he saw his own vocation, to bring together the two eighteenth-century half-men and make the perfect man of the nineteenth.

Too many obstacles stood in his way, besides the rather obvious one that Carlyle was not remotely like either Johnson or Hume in personality. He could, like both those men of an earlier age, be good company – he could be hilarious and convivial when the mood took him. His inspired oratory drew huge audiences to his public lectures. But there was something, for all his greatness, his undeniable greatness, unconsciously a little comic about him, too. If he strove to become a combination of Hume and Johnson, the effect for much of the time was that of A.A. Milne's Eeyore. His famous domestic irritability, his hypochondria, his obsession with noise, loom as large in the biographies as the grand themes of his works; and though there is injustice in this, it is understandable that they should, for the plaintive petulance, the dyspepsia and irrational gloom and rage are present in his pages as well as in his character.

Nevertheless, he was the first great Victorian prophet to enunciate their difficulty. The old idols of the *ancien régime* had deserved to be destroyed. But how could we live without the truths which these gimcrack shrines had housed?

Carlyle's famous lie to his Presbyterian mother only seems like one to us; to him, it was really a struggling after a kind of truth, a yearning for its falsehood to be true. This was his claim that, *au fond*, he did not differ from her in religious faith. She believed it to be a lie, he hoped it wasn't. That is, he hoped that his Immanentism – his belief in a certain something inside us, in a Divine Voice speaking to our conscience – was the same *really* as the God of Abraham and Isaac and Jacob. Her anguished letter, written shortly before a mental breakdown, and when Carlyle was a student at Edinburgh University and beginning to wrestle with Doubt, makes everything plain: 'Oh, Tom, mind the golden season of youth, and remember your Creator in the days of your youth. Seek God while He may be found. Call upon Him while He is near. We hear that the world by wisdom knew not God. Pray for His presence with you, and His counsel to guide you.'[14]

Profound as his devotion was to his 'old Minnie' – Froude calls it 'the strongest personal passion which he experienced through all his life'[15] – it was not enough to expunge the effects on him of reading Gibbon and (an author who disgusted him) Rousseau. 'I first read Gibbon, and then first clearly saw that Christianity was not true ...' Gibbon had caused 'the extirpation from his mind of the last remnant that had been left in it of the orthodox belief in miracles'.[16]

You can't get more uncompromising in unbelief than this, and in his gaunt heroic way Carlyle remained true to this unbelief – in Christianity. He longed to continue, however, to believe in Providence, in History, in Moral Absolutes, in personal conduct – the essence, as he saw it, of the Calvinism in which he had been reared. Hence the 'lie' to his mother. This great drama – how to live without lying, and yet without rejecting God – is the drama of his life. This – not the secret of his marriage chamber – is the real impotence of his thought: it is the acknowledged impotence of the prophet who wants to speak in the name of a God of whose presence he is not really sure.

> Historical religions, Christianity included, he believed to have been successive efforts of humanity, loyally and nobly made in the light of existing knowledge, to explain human duty, and to insist on the fulfilment of it; and the reading of the moral constitution and position of man, in the creed, for instance, of his own family, he believed to be incommensurably truer, than was to be found in the elaborate metaphysics of utilitarian ethics ... To Carlyle the Universe itself was a miracle, and all its phenomena were equally in themselves incomprehensible. But the special miraculous occurrences of sacred history were not credible to him.[17]

So urgently however did Carlyle wish to continue his belief in the essence, in the anti-materialist interpretation of history and human behaviour, that he felt it necessary to disguise, from his own very self – never mind his mother, or his readers – the implication of what he was saying. If he rejected the revealed religion which brought him Christianity and the Bible, it was hard to see by what logical criterion he could accept an idea of God or Duty which was not, in fact, very similar to that of Mill's Utilitarianism or Rousseau's Romanticism, creeds which on the surface of things, and at some deeper psychological level, Carlyle found uncongenial. He was by temperament a prophet of the Old God: 'Oh, that I had faith!'

We can see his face change in the various likenesses which have come down to us. The youngest survives in a print of 1832, when he was thirty-six, a dark-eyed, deep-eyed, dark-haired, angular Scotsman. He is saturnine and handsome. There is satire too in the unbearded face which looks at us from the portrait painted by Tait in the 1850s. But as he moved into what he and his wife came to call the Valley of the Shadow of Frederick – those long gloomy years in Chelsea when he was writing the Life of Frederick the Great – something descended upon his face which was more than the beard and the wrinkles. It is deep sorrow. Julia Margaret Cameron's is the most inspired portrait, a photograph showing a prophet half in focus, tormented, wild. Had photography existed in the days of the prophet Jeremiah or the philosopher Diogenes ...

Two of the friendships in Carlyle's early, or earlyish, life stood out for him in later years as emblematic of the intellectual tragedy to which the godless nineteenth century was pre-ordained: that with Edward Irving, and that with John Sterling. He wrote extensive and highly personal biographical studies of them both, and since their names have faded in our own day even more than that of Carlyle himself, it is perhaps ne-cessary to record them briefly.

If Johnson and Hume were the two half-men of the eighteenth century, Irving and Sterling were perhaps the two half-men of Carlyle's younger days. Irving represents the path of intellectual suicide – of an acceptance of a wildly irrational religious creed which, in the minds of many intelligent observers, crossed the borders of absurdity. Sterling represented that Honest Doubter whose doubts and intellectual honesty were their own form of heroism, but which paralysed him, made him in effect useless for anything else.

Carlyle met Irving, who was three years his senior, when they were both poverty-stricken schoolmasters in Fife; though, as Carlyle reflected, they had probably often been in the same church together in their boyhood in Annandale. The fact that they hied from the same part of Scotland and were both away from home quickened their intimacy. Both came from roughly similar social backgrounds: Irving was the son of a tanner in the tiny town of Annan, and his mother's people were yeomen farmers in a very small way near Ecclefechan, where Carlyle was born and grew up and where his father James was a stonemason. James Carlyle was, his famous son averred, among Scottish peasants what Samuel Johnson was among English authors. 'I have a sacred pride in my peasant father and would not exchange him, even now, for any king known to me.'[18]

There were three things about Edward Irving which were to mark him out as a figure of peculiar importance in Carlyle's personal history. The first was that Irving – very tall, markedly handsome, and from the earliest times mellifluous – was the first real friend Carlyle ever had.

Carlyle as a youth was painfully shy, moody, dyspeptic, frightened. Irving's extension of friendship to him made him 'the sun in my firmament where all else had become so wintry. Such a friend as I never had again or before in the world.'[19] Carlyle, who had got through college in Edinburgh with modest distinction, had made no true friends there. He was twenty-one before he met this striking figure of a man, so much more at ease with the human race and able to take him around, in Edinburgh and St Andrew's, escort him to lectures, lend him books.

It was from Irving's extensive library that Carlyle obtained and devoured Gibbon. 'It is inconceivable to me now with what ardour, with what greedy velocity, literally above ten times the speed I can now make with any book. Gibbon in particular, I recollect to have read at the rate of a volume a day (twelve volumes in all) ...'[20]

Irving had become engaged to Isabella Martin, the daughter of a clergyman. He had initially been hired as her tutor, and he was subsequently to get one of his first engagements as a licensed preacher in the Church of Scotland in Dr Martin's parish: two facts which made it difficult to retreat from the relationship when, as happened, little by little, his ardour for her cooled. 'She was very ill-looking withal; a skin always under blotches and discolourment; muddy grey eyes, which for their part never laughed with the other features; pockmarked, ill-shaped triangular kind of face, with hollow cheeks and long chin ...'[21] It was all the more unfortunate for Irving that after his engagement to Isabella, he should have fallen in love in earnest with someone else.

And here is the second and the supremely important reason why he played such a role in Carlyle's personal myth. In 1810 Irving had secured the mastership of the so-called Mathematical School at Haddington, and it was here that he began to teach a little girl, a doctor's daughter, Jane Baillie Welsh – animated, clever and certainly a good deal prettier than Isabella Martin. He did not marry Isabella until 1823. In the course of that time, Jane Baillie Welsh grew up into a very charming, witty young woman, with whom by 1821 Irving was profoundly in love. He tried to extricate himself from the engagement with Isabella, but these were the days when Breach of Promise was a criminal offence, and the Martins (perhaps aware that their daughter was not a very saleable proposition) were unwilling to release him. Jane herself was certainly very fond of Irving, too. In 1821 he introduced her to his friend, the shy irascible dominie from Ecclefechan.

By now, Jane's mother was a widow. Jane herself, aged twenty, was 'extremely pretty', by the account of her friend Geraldine Jewsbury, 'a graceful and beautifully formed figure, upright and supple, a delicate complexion of creamy white with a pale rose tint in the cheeks, lovely eyes, full of fire and softness, and with great depths of meaning'.[22] Carlyle, too, at this date, was of outstanding handsomeness. The courtship was not rapid, and she had other suitors (so many that she sometimes signed her letters Penelope). But the pair were married eventually, in 1826. The morning after their wedding night has passed into legend – when Carlyle was seen 'in a fit of ungovernable fury'[23] destroying the flower-garden at Comely Bank. What had or had not happened in the previous few hours, what would or would not happen in the next forty years of gratingly incompatible and yet hideously well-suited partnership, remains quite largely a matter of speculation.

If the first two reasons for Irving's importance in the Carlyle personal myth were his offer of friendship and his introduction to Jane Welsh, there was surely a third element. Carlyle was hypnotized, as a whole generation in London were to be hypnotized, by Edward Irving's rhetorical fluency; Carlyle was fascinated by it, envious of it.

Irving was not on Carlyle's intellectual level, though he was clever in a superficial way. But once he had received a licence to preach, it became apparent that he had the power to excite the crowds. After a spell in Glasgow he was appointed, when only twenty-seven, to be the minister in charge of the Caledonian Chapel in Hatton Garden in London, a Presbyterian outpost in the English capital. Very soon the little chapel was packed to bursting with fashionable sermon-tasters and upper-class ladies, and Irving had become famous. Canning made complimentary references to him in the House of Commons. Irving was a star. Hazlitt, who wrote about him in his *The Spirit of the Age*, thought his appeal largely sexual: 'his very unusual size and height are carried off and moulded into elegance by the most admirable symmetry of form and ease of gesture; his sable locks, his clear iron-grey complexion and firm-set features, turn the raw, uncouth Scotchman into the likeness of a noble Italian picture ...'[24] At this stage, Irving was still within the mainstream of Presbyterianism. This 'new Peter the Hermit', as Hazlitt called him, 'would get rid of all we have done in the way of improvement on a state of barbarous ignorance, or still more barbarous prejudice, in order to begin again on the *tabula rasa* of Calvinism, and have a world of his own making'.[25]

Carlyle's own journey, by this stage, had taken him far from Calvinistic orthodoxy. *Sartor Resartus*, his first published work, which he wrote between October 1830 and July 1831 in the solitary marital confinement of Craigenputtoch, pays testimony to that. (It must be the oddest literary début in our history, being at the same time a skit on the German philosophy and history which was Carlyle's favourite reading, a commentary on his own times, and in part, like most first books, an autobiography.) It purports to be a thesis on clothes by a German professor, Teufelsdrockh. 'In all speculations,' he wrote, 'philosophers and historians had written about man as a clothed animal, whereas we know him to be a naked animal.'

> Many a deep glance, and often with unspeakable precision, has he cast into Mysterious Nature [says Teufelsdrockh's 'editor'] and the still more mysterious life of Man. Wonderful it is with what cutting words, now and then, he severs asunder the confusion; shears down, were it furlongs deep, into the true centre of the matter; and there not only hits the nail on the head, but with crushing force smites it home, and buries it. On the other hand, let us be free to admit, he is the most unequal writer breathing.[26]

It is extraordinary, preternatural, that Carlyle should so presciently have reviewed his own life's work before he wrote it. The reader (if many such apart from myself there still be) of *Sartor Resartus* can be in no doubt that the author has left Christianity behind, as one of the many illusions with which humanity has tried to clothe itself, and presses on, with Goethe as his principal guide, towards a rather woolly hope that *awe* in the face of Nature, obedience to a Kantian moral imperative, will somehow cancel out the essential nihilism of the original conception of the human condition. Carlyle's most recent biographer is surely right to read as autobiographical[27] the passage in *Sartor* when he describes himself wandering through the streets of Paris (a trip undertaken with and at the expense of Irving in 1825):

> Perhaps the miserablest man in the whole French Capital or Suburbs was I, one sultry Dog-Day, after much perambulation, toiling along the dirty little *Rue Saint-Thomas de l'Enfer*, among civic rubbish enough, in a close atmosphere, and over pavements hot as Nebucadnezzar's Furnace; whereby doubtless my spirits were little cheered; when all at once there rose a Thought in me, and I asked myself: 'What art thou afraid of? Wherefore, like a coward, dost thou forever pip and whimper, and go cowering and trembling? Despicable biped! What is the sum total of the

worst that lies before thee? Death? Well, Death; and say the pangs of
Tophet too, and all that the Devil and Man may, will or can do against
thee! Hast thou not a heart; canst thou not suffer whatsoever it can be;
and, as a child of freedom, though outcast, trample and defy it!' And as
so I thought, there rushed like a stream of fire over my whole soul; and
I shook base fear away from me forever, I was strong, of unknown
strength; a spirit, almost a god. Ever from that time, the temper of my
misery was changed; not Fear or whining Sorrow was it, but Indignation
and grim fire-eyed Defiance.

Thus had the EVERLASTING NO (*das ewige Nein*) pealed authoritatively
through all the recesses of my Being, of my ME; and then it was that my
whole ME stood up, in native God-created Majesty, and with emphasis
recorded its protest ...[28]

Irving's Rebirths and Reawakenings were on very different lines.
After he moved to London Irving became the object of hero-worship,
first in the Caledonian Chapel (a small and hitherto unregarded place of
worship, only a few yards from the real-life setting of Fagin's lair in
Oliver Twist), then at a larger place in Regent Square – a chapel which
seated over a thousand. It was in 1831 that manifestations began to
occur at Irving's services, screams, hysteria, and the phenomenon known
as 'speaking with tongues'.

'If I had married Irving,' said Jane Welsh Carlyle long afterwards,
'the tongues would never have been heard.'[29] The exact processes by
which Irving came adrift from the parent-stem of Presbyterianism
belong to another book. The Church of Scotland looked askance at what
appeared to be the revival of apostolic manifestations in the congregation of this charismatic and exhibitionistic young man. He was further
accused, by the Annan presbytery, of heresy over the question of Christ's
human nature. Orthodox Christian belief insisted that Christ was of His
essence sinless; Irving declared that Christ had, while actually being
guilty of no sin, inherited the fullness of human nature, that is of sinful
human nature. He was expelled from the Presbyterian Church, and from
1832 until his untimely death at the close of 1834 he was on his own.

But not alone.

Irving is one of those, like Wesley and Luther, whose name is given
to a church. The Irvingites, or the Catholic Apostolic Church, to give
them their other name, are thin on the ground these days, but they
enjoyed some popularity in the decades between Irving's death and
the close of the nineteenth century. The Catholic Apostolic title may

surprise any reader who supposes that Irving was a simple Bible ranter. He was not anything of the kind. He combined the belief that New Testament times had been revived (hence the manifestations of the spirit in his congregation) with a reverence for some of the ritual and outward forms of Catholicism. Moreover, since his move to England he had fallen in with the Conservative Member of Parliament for Albury in Surrey, a pious landowner, Henry Drummond. It was Drummond who presided over the Albury Conferences, whose purpose was to examine the Scriptures for signs that the End of Days was at hand, and that the Church of the Revelations of St John the Divine (with its orders of Angels, Archangels, Elders, et cetera) should be recreated in readiness for the Coming of the Lord. The group included clergy of various denominations and at least two aristocrats – the future Duke of Manchester and the future Lord Rayleigh.[30]

The view of the Albury Conferences was 'that a great period of 1260 years commenced in the reign of Justinian, and terminated at the French Revolution; and that the vials of the Apocalypse began then to be poured out; that our blessed Lord will shortly appear, and that therefore it is the duty of all, who so believe, to press these considerations on the attention of all men.'[31]

People usually sneer at the Catholic Apostolic Church and its adherents and, by implication, at Irving who, if not its founder exactly, was a leading luminary at the time of its origins. The reason that the Irvingites have now dwindled to a tiny number is that they were honest enough, having made a mistake about the dating of the Parousia, not to fudge things. The Coming of the Lord did not occur at the end of the nineteenth century. But the Irvingites did not therefore claim that they now believed in the Coming in some spiritualized sense. They ordained and consecrated no more bishops or elders or angels. Gradually, their sacramental life ceased. The Church of Rome and the Church of England remain committed to the literal truth of the End of the World, while conveniently fudging their commitment to an actual date.

Irvingism is a paradigm of nineteenth-century literalist religion. It follows many of the same psychological patterns and courses as revived Anglicanism (Puseyism or Evangelicalism), revived Catholicism (the pseudo-Italianate Catholicism of the Ultramontane Manning or Faber), or some of the other religions, such as the Plymouth Brethren, which came into existence at about the same time. They all thought it was possible to defy the onslaughts of secularism by what in modern terms would be called fundamentalism; by asserting that you could still take readings of the universe and of human experience by a pre-enlightenment template. Carlyle knew that this was not the case, and that what had been poured forth at the French Revolution was something rather more destructive than the vials of the Apocalypse. It was the dawning of the Modern.

His most eloquent exploration of this theme is in *Past and Present*, where he uses the image of the great blackened medieval ruins of St Edmundsbury in Suffolk as an image of the vibrant medieval faith which has been so irretrievably lost. The faith of the monks is something which Carlyle makes live for us again, in some of his finest writing, by a reading of Jocelin's *Chronica* about the Abbot Samson in the thirteenth century. By contrast with the Middle Ages, 'we' – the moderns –

> have closed our eyes to the eternal Substance of things and opened them only to the Shews and Shams of things. We quietly believe this Universe to be intrinsically a great unintelligible PERHAPS ... There is no longer any God for us! God's Laws are become a Greatest-Happiness Principle, a Parliamentary Expediency; the Heavens an Astronomical Time-Keeper; a butt for Herschel telescopes to shoot science at, to shoot sentimentalities at – in our old Johnson's dialect, Man has lost the soul out of him; and now begins to find the want of it! ... There is no religion, there is no God; man has lost his soul, and vainly seeks anti-septic salt.[32]

If Carlyle hoped, by such extreme putting of a case, to shock his readers into a more 'spiritual' state of mind, into trying to recapture the essence of Abbot Samson's faith while rejecting its clothes, he was not destined to be successful. The extracts just quoted are the very passages copied out by Friedrich Engels in his essay 'Die Lage Englands' of 1844.[33]

It is no accident that Carlyle's greatest disciple, James Anthony Froude, should have been an unbeliever. No pair of thinkers could be less congenial to Carlyle than Marx and Engels. For him, atheism was a symptom of profound sickness in society, rather than being (as it is for Marxism) a precondition for its cure. Yet for Carlyle and the Marxists there was a shared truth, that belief in God was bound to decline in an age so slavishly addicted to commerce.

> Midas longed for gold, and insulted the Olympians. He got gold, so that whatsoever he touched became gold – and he, with his long ears, was

little the better for it. Midas had misjudged the celestial music tones: Midas had insulted Apollo and the gods; the gods gave him his evil wish, and a pair of long ears, which also were a good appendage to it. What a truth in these old Fables![34]

What Carlyle tries to do in *Past and Present*, however, is exactly comparable to what he tries to do in his Reminiscence of his friend Irving. The doctrines in which Abbot Samson believed, and which the medieval religious peddled professionally, are repugnant to Carlyle. And yet he believes that it is somehow possible to remember the spiritual values which their false clothes concealed. 'Their missals have become incredible, a sheer platitude, sayest Thou? Yes, a most poor platitude; and even, if thou wilt, an idolatry and blasphemy, should anyone persuade thee to believe them, to pretend by praying them. But yet it is a pity we had lost tidings of our soul; actually we shall have to go in quest of them again, or worse in all ways will befall!'[35] He sees Abbot Samson (who was the surprise candidate in an abbatial election and who showed qualities of leadership in cleaning up the monastery and reforming its abuses) as an archetype of the Carlylean world-view, the Hero or the Genius. What was wrong with the world was that so often the Genius was at the bottom of society and the buffoon at the top. 'George the Third is Defender of something we call "the Faith" in those years; George the Third is head charioteer of the Destinies of England, to guide them through the gulf of French Revolutions, American independences; and Robert Burns is Gauger of ale in Dumfries.'[36]

It would be interesting to know whether Burns when drunk would have been any better than King George when mad at being the charioteer of the British race, but for Carlyle, this would have been a cheap sneer. 'O ye kind Heavens, there is in every Nation and Community a *fittest*, a wisest, bravest, best; whom could we find and make King over us, all were in very truth well ...'[37] One sees where this would lead, politically, in the history of the nations.

For Carlyle, though, surveying the life of his friend Edward Irving, it is a symptom of the wrong-headedness of the times, and of the personal tragedy of Irving himself. We must not commit the 'blasphemy' of pretending to believe the unbelievable; or, worse, sink into the position in which Irving found himself, of actually believing it. 'How are the mighty fallen' is Carlyle's own verdict on his friend.[38] But while being dismayed that his 'poor Irving' was 'veiled and hooded in these miserable manifold crapes and formulas' (of doctrine), Carlyle could not help seeing Irving as just such a potential Führer: if only he had not fallen a prey to that combination of snobbery and superstition which had been the ruin of lesser beings. 'At the sight of Canning, Brougham, Lady Jersey and Co., crowding round him and listening week after week as if to the message of salvation, the noblest and joyfullest thought had taken possession of his noble, too sanguine, and too trustful mind; that the Christian religion was to be a truth again, not a paltry form, and to rule the world, he unworthy, even he, the chosen instrument.'[39]

In his Life of Irving Carlyle wanted to revisit the most important friendship of his early life, to pay homage to a man he had loved, but also to put the record straight, to reveal (to a public who knew only an Irving speaking with the tongues of men and of angels) a kindly friend, one who read Gibbon and, in latter years, Goethe. 'Very curious,' Irving is quoted as saying. 'In this German poet there are some passages about Christ and the Christian religion which, as I study and restudy them, have more sense about that matter than I have found in all the theologians I have ever read.'[40] Poor old Carlyle. He was well over seventy when he wrote of these things, conscious of his own position as a prophet, but as a prophet who, like Moses, would never himself enter the Land of Promise.

The Life of Irving concerns a man who in his day was very famous; the *Life of Sterling* is otherwise. Though John Sterling, an unsuccessful journalist who died aged thirty-eight in 1844, was known to various important figures in the literary world, he could by no stretch of the imagination be described as distinguished or famous. What was Carlyle's intention in writing his life, beyond the personal devotion which he felt to Sterling's memory? There are two things happening here, perhaps. First, the *Life of Sterling* is a genuine and serious attempt to put the record straight about a man whose memory had been, in Carlyle's view, deliberately falsified. And secondly, as in nearly all Carlyle's writings, there is the need and desire to express what he feels and believes, above all about the God-question.

John Sterling (1806–1844) was the son of a famous journalist, Edward Sterling, whose career as the chief correspondent for *The Times* earned that newspaper its nickname of The Thunderer. A more hesitant and less thunderous voice was that of John the son, who went up to Trinity, Cambridge in 1824, became an Apostle, befriended Frederick Denison Maurice, and was taught – a crucial fact – by Julius Charles

Hare, who was to become the rector of the fat living of Herstmonceux in Sussex. Sterling, an idealistic young man who married early, needed to make his way in the world. He tried some reviewing, he wrote a bad novel, he read a great deal of Coleridge, and he got involved (as did his contemporary Alfred Tennyson) with attempts to aid the liberal Spaniards in their struggle to overthrow the tyranny of Ferdinand VII. Poor health made him accept the unlikely job of going to the island of St Vincent to manage a sugar-plantation. It was a terrible mistake. A hurricane destroyed the crops and he became involved in the distressing plight of the slaves, liberated but with no security and no work. (Carlyle wrote of this in his deliberately offensive pamphlet 'On the Nigger Question'.) Then, it was back to Europe – where he went to Germany and began to study the new German theologians, and to compare what they had to say with what Coleridge had to say. The religious preoccupation was, for Sterling, of paramount importance. Coleridge quoted Kant, and appeared to be offering a thoroughly modern defence of old-fashioned Christianity. He expressed this defence in terms so abstruse that they were all but incomprehensible.

The German theologians of the Tübingen school influenced by Hegel, above all D.F. Strauss, made things only *too* clear: while the myth of Christianity contained many deep truths, of a kind, that was what it was: a mythology. The Gospels were not literal or historical accounts of miraculous events which had actually happened, but the expression of religio-mythical belief systems which just happened to have focused on a first-century Aramaen prophet.

With these troubling thoughts in his head, but no money in his pocket, Sterling came back to England, and was almost immediately offered a job by his old tutor, now Archdeacon Hare of Herstmonceux. In 1834 Sterling was ordained as a deacon in the Church of England and acted as Hare's curate. He was an eloquent preacher and, clearly, a good clergyman – attentive in visiting the poor, the old, the children of the parish; kind to the sick and dying. But after only eight months in the post, and without proceeding to the priesthood, he left the job.

There was some talk of Sterling getting the job of Anglican chaplain in Rome. Nothing came of this, and for the last decade of his short life Sterling was an unsuccessful Man of Letters, churning out reviews and bad poems. All the time, he was wrestling not merely with his own calamitously bad health, but with a series of domestic disasters which included, in the year before his own death, the deaths of his mother and his wife on the very same day. When Sterling had himself succumbed to consumption and been buried on the Isle of Wight, Archdeacon Hare, as an act of piety to his memory, published his 'Remains', as the Victorians would have called them, his *Essays and Tales*, in two volumes. The Tales were prefaced with a memoir by Hare (unlike his grandson, Augustus, he was no prose stylist) in which he claimed that Sterling had been, all along, *au fond* an orthodox Christian believer.

For Sterling's friends who had loved him, and followed his inner struggles, there was something sadly wrong with Hare's account of things. Even for those, such as Tennyson or Maurice, who were and who remained Christians, there was something glib about Hare's judgement. Sterling, very much a man of his age, wrestled before he prayed; he struggled with faith, and was not sure – hence his leaving Herstmonceux for the much less comfortable existence of a free-lance writer – that he accepted the orthodoxies in the sense which was required of a beneficed clergyman.

So, as an act of piety to Sterling's memory, and as a Mr Valiant-for-Truth, Carlyle picked up his pen and wrote what has been called a book 'remarkable for its inversion of the usual proportion between biography, biographer and hero. Johnson for once writes upon Boswell.'[41]

The most memorable and the funniest passages in the *Life of Sterling* are about Samuel Taylor Coleridge (1772–1834), the poet who in the second half of his life had become a sage and a philosopher.

> He was thought to hold, he alone in England, the key of German and other Transcendentalisms; knew the sublime secret of believing by 'the reason' what 'the understanding' had been obliged to fling out as incredible; and could still, after Hume and Voltaire had done their best and worst with him, profess himself an orthodox Christian, and say and print to the Church of England with its singular old rubrics and surplices at Allhallowtide, *Esto perpetua*.[42]

In the drama which Carlyle weaves out of Sterling's life, Coleridge becomes the one, the last, hope of retaining a belief in Christianity without a sacrifice of the intellect. And Carlyle makes him, quite deliberately, into a figure of absurd comedy.

> The good man, he was now getting old, towards sixty perhaps; and gave you the idea of a life that had been full of sufferings; a life heavy-laden, half-vanquished, still swimming painfully in seas of manifold physical

and other bewilderment. Brow and head were round, and of massive weight, but the face was flabby and irresolute. The deep eyes, of a light hazel, were as full of sorrow as of inspiration; confused pain looked mildly from them, as in a kind of mild astonishment. The whole figure and air, good and amiable otherwise, might be called flabby and irresolute; expressive of weakness under possibility of strength. He hung loosely on his limbs, with knees bent, and stooping attitude; in walking, he rather shuffled than decisively stept; and a lady once remarked, he never could fix which side of the garden-walk would suit him best, but continually shifted, in corkscrew fashion, and kept trying both. A heavy-laden, high aspiring and surely much-suffering man. His voice, naturally soft and good, had contracted itself into a plaintive snuffle and sing-song; he spoke as if preaching – you would have said, preaching earnestly and also hopelessly the weightiest things. I still recollect his 'object' and 'subject', terms of continual recurrence in the Kantian province; and how he sung and snuffled them into 'om-m-mject' and 'sum-m-ject', with a kind of sole shake or quaver, as he rolled along.[43]

It was while under the influence of Coleridgean 'moonshine' – Carlyle's word – and fifteen years or so before he reached the end of his life, and some very different conclusions, that Sterling had written those Christian pieces reproduced by Archdeacon Hare. There was nothing wrong, in Carlyle's view, with doing 'what you can with the old Churches and practical Symbols of the Noble; nay quit not the burnt ruins of them while you find there is still gold to be dug there.'[44] But it was quite another thing to submit, as Coleridge and his followers did, to 'hocus pocus'. 'To steal into Heaven, by the modern method, of sticking ostrich-like your head into fallacies on Earth, equally as by the ancient and by all conceivable methods – is forever forbidden. High treason is the name of that attempt.'[45]

The *Life of Sterling*, perhaps more than any other work of Carlyle's, prompts one to ask – where exactly did the Victorian sage stand on the question? Is there a God, or isn't there? Carlyle certainly would appear to claim that there is. He castigates Coleridge for 'skirting the howling deserts of Infidelity', and then burying his head in 'poor wigs and church tippets' for refuge, and fathering 'strange Centaurs, spectral Puseyisms, monstrous illusory Hybrids and ecclesiastical Chimeras – which now roam the earth in a very lamentable manner!'[46]

But was not Carlyle himself guilty of the very sins for which he held Coleridge accountable? Did he not spout 'moonshine' on the subject of religion, to disguise an underlying fear that it might be all vanity of vanities? He said that Coleridge, having skirted the 'howling deserts of Infidelity', 'had not the courage, in defiance of pain and terror, to press resolutely across said deserts to the firm new lands of Faith beyond'.[47] But in what did this 'Faith' consist? Arthur Hugh Clough, one of the more frankly atheistical of a younger generation, complained that he and many of his like in the 1840s had been handicapped by Carlyle's implicit religious teachings. He 'led us out into the desert and he has left us there'.[48]

The real-life Sterling would seem to have been a doubter whose views were an agnostic muddle. Carlyle wants us to think that he somehow found another Faith: 'Theologies, rubrics, surplices, church-articles and this enormous, ever-repeated thrashing of the straw. A world of rotten straw all thrashed into powder; filling the Universe and blotting out the stars and worlds.'[49] Literature is invoked as a substitute for religion. It is a very familiar nineteenth-century transition, but Carlyle does not completely explain how it could be.

It is interesting that he should have so mocked Coleridge for introducing German 'moonshine' into the picture as a substitute for thought, since all his own early essays were on the subject of German literature, just as his last, magisterial biographical work looked to a German king as a deliverer. There is a link between the early essays and the late biographies. In his essay On The State of German Literature (1827) Carlyle quotes the Idealist philosopher Fichte with approval, and his notion that there is a 'Divine Idea' pervading the Visible Universe. From the mass of humanity this idea is hidden; 'to discern it, to seize it, and live wholly in it, is the condition of all genuine virtue, knowledge, freedom'.[50]

The old 'proofs' for the existence of God are, for Carlyle, no more interesting than the God they profess to prove. 'Should Understanding attempt to prove the existence of God, it ends, if thorough-going and consistent with itself [,in] Atheism, or a faint possible Theism, which scarcely differs from this ...'[51]

The German Romantics, above all Goethe, rescued Carlyle from this kind of arid atheism. But the spiritual energy or truth in which he places his faith is not really an objective God. In a paragraph which might have been as baffling to its early readers as Coleridge's 'ommject' and 'summject' he wrote:

Meanwhile, let the Reader be assured, that to the charge of Irreligion, as to so many others, the Germans will not plead guilty. On the contrary, they do not scruple to assert that their literature is, in a positive sense, religious, nay perhaps to maintain that if ever neighbouring nations are to recover that pure and high spirit of devotion, the loss of which, however we may disguise it or pretend to overlook it, can be hidden from no observant mind, it must be by travelling, if not by the same path, at least in the same direction in which the Germans have already begun to travel ...[52]

In his popular lectures *On Heroes and Hero-Worship*, Carlyle traced how Odin was transformed from a human hero into a divinity. In later lectures, as in his *Frederick*, he proposes what is, in effect, a new religion, the worship of the *Übermensch*, the discovery in political hero-worship of what many in the past found in their 'hocus pocus'. His historiography follows the Hegelian pattern, with a rough-and-ready anthropomorphic theory of projection to explain the origins of primitive religion. 'The world of Nature, for every man, is the Phantasy of Himself; this world is the multiplex "Image of his own Dream".'[53]

Carlyle sees his own Nordic ancestors, in what is probably indeed a fantasy, as devising religious language in order to come to terms with 'divineness in Nature' ... 'Sincerity, I think, is better than grace. I feel that these old Northmen were looking into Nature with open eye and soul; most, earnest, honest; childlike and yet manlike; with a great-hearted simplicity and depth and freshness, in a true, loving, admiring unfearing way. A right valiant, true old race of men.'[54]

In the second lecture, Carlyle developed the Kantian theme that 'all Power is moral, that the grand point is the distinction for him of Good and Evil, of *Thou Shalt* and *Thou Shalt Not*'.[55] His subject was Mahomet, for whom he had a profound admiration. Indeed, the Holy Prophet's career, with his absolute detestation of the 'vain janglings' of the 'miserable Syrian Sects', his violence of temper, his disbelief in any of the available creeds of his day, combined with his moral certainties, would seem to have borne a remarkable resemblance to Carlyle's own. Mahomet's creed was, apparently,

a bastard kind of Christianity, but a living kind; with a heart-life in it: not dead, chopping barren logic merely! Out of all that rubbish of Arab idolatries, argumentative theologies, traditions, subtleties, rumours and hypotheses of Greeks and Jews, with their idle wire-drawings, this wild man of the desert, with his wild sincere heart, earnest as life and death, with his great flashing natural eyesight, had seen into the kernel of the whole matter.[56]

The trouble was, Carlyle was not a Moslem. 'These Arabs believe their religion, and try to live by it! No Christians ... have ever stood by their Faith, as the Moslem do by theirs – believing it wholly, fronting Time with it and Eternity with it.' For 'Christians' you have to read 'Carlyle' for the sentence to make sense, since, whether we share their faith or not, we know that history is full of Christians who have been wholly steadfast in their faith. 'This night', Carlyle continues, 'the watchman on the streets of Cairo when he cries, "Who goes?" will hear from the passenger, along with his answer, "There is no God but God", *Allah akbar, Islam,* sounds through the souls, and whole daily existence of these dusky millions.'[57] But not, of course, through the souls of white men any more.

Therein lay the tragedy of Carlyle's life and, as far as he was concerned, the tragedy of the nineteenth century. Human beings are natural adorers. Religion is basic to human character. How it is directed, that is the question. Carlyle believed that in Victorian England it was directed, on the one hand to the soul-destroying gods of Mammon and Commerce, and on the other to incredible, outworn creeds.

It was his belief that somewhere in the dead husk of these creeds there was something called Faith which could be cherished, even in an age of unbelief, and this explains his influence and popularity as a sage.

5

---⫸─●─⫷---

Not Angles but Engels

O son of man, beneath man's feet
  Cast down, O common face of man
Whereon all blows and buffets meet
  O royal, O republican
Face of the people bruised and dumb
And longing till thy kingdom come!
              A.C. Swinburne, 'Before a Crucifix'

THE SHEER INJUSTICE and ugliness of early nineteenth-century capitalism was obvious to everyone. The desire to put it right was universal – on the part of the capitalists themselves, as well as of radicals as different as Fourier, Robert Owen or the Chartists; of benign Tories of the Peel colouring, of Whigs and of liberals. It was only the hot-head minority (of whom Marx was aspirant high priest) who positively wanted a repetition of the French Revolution and Terror. The question remained: in the noise and smell and confusion of the factory-dominated Victorian cities, what religion could be heard or believed?

> In loud thoroughfares, still more unawakened districts, troubled with argumentative infidelity, you make the windpipes wider, strengthen the main steam-cylinder; your parson preaches, to the due pitch, while you give him coal; and fear no man or thing ... Ye blind leaders of the blind! Are we Calmucks, that pray by turning of a rotatory calabash with written prayers in it? Is Mammon and machinery the means of converting human souls as of spinning cotton? Is God, as Jean Paul predicted it would be, become verily a Force; the Aether too a gas! ...'[1]

These gaseous exhalations could have burst forth from only one geyser – a London address which was as famous in its day as Karl Marx's was obscure: Number 5 Cheyne Row, Chelsea.

Rather late in the day, the nineteenth-century Church went into the industrial slums of the Victorian cities and was shocked by what it found. Bishop Walsham How must have felt particularly stung by *Jude the Obscure* because it was a book which reflected something he had seen for himself in his own ministry. Hardy depicts a working-man, a stonecutter, who attempts to educate himself and to get into Oxford. It rejects him, and so does the Church. By implication, the Church is only for the middle classes. It is an institution entirely cut off from the struggles and concerns of ordinary people.

The feelings of How can be imagined, when we remember that he had been especially appointed as a bishop with the task of ministering to the lower orders. 'The church is *nowhere* in East London,' he remarked when he was appointed Bishop of Stepney in 1879.[2] It never had been anywhere, and it never would be anywhere. 'The workers are not religious and do not attend church,' Engels had stated authoritatively in 1844.[3] 'It is not that the Church of God has lost the great towns; it has never had them,' said A.F. Winnington-Ingram in 1896.[4] The scholar and divine Dr Pusey averred that if he had no duties in Oxford, 'I would long ago have asked leave to preach in the alleys of London, where the Gospel is as unknown as in Thibet.'[5]

Even where there was a religious proletariat – in those districts where a large number of Catholic Irish had come to England – there were not always enough priests to minister to them. 'About 40,000 Catholics have not made their Easter "duty" for sheer want of someone to hear their confessions,' a priest reported in 1845.[6]

Of course, this situation was to be modified as the century progressed. The ranks of the Catholic clergy grew – partly because of conversions from the Church of England. The Anglo-Catholic movement took the Gospel where Dr Pusey wanted to preach it – to the alleys of London, often with impressive localized effect. The Salvation Army, a lower-middle-class movement with a mission specifically to the poor, became and remained a feature on the urban British landscape. Those who wanted to find among the English proletariat the anti-clerical fervour or hatred of God which might have been present in the Parisian mob were usually as disappointed as the Christian missionaries in 'darkest England'. Ignorance and indifference were, continued to be, and remain, the English working-class attitude to religion. 'What is St Paul's?' Henry Mayhew asked a costermonger. 'A church sir, so I've heard. I never was in a church.'[7] You would get the same reply from a costermonger in London today. Another costermonger told him, 'Religion is a regular puzzle to the costers. They see people come out of church and chapel, and as they're mostly well-dressed, and there's very few of their own sort among the church-goers, the costers somehow mix up being religious with being respectable, and so they have a queer sort of feeling about it. It is a mystery to them.'[8]

This is not to say that no working-class person ever had a religious impulse in the entire course of the nineteenth century. But it is to say that the nineteenth-century churches – particularly the Methodist Church of the *petit-bourgeois*, the small shopkeepers' church which became that of the well-heeled, the so-called mahogany pulpit; and even more the Church of England, with its lands and rents and endowments and its established position in the nation at large – were faced with an old but also a very distinctively Victorian dilemma: you cannot serve God and Mammon. The sheer size and scale and energy of Britain at the height of its capitalistic power struck the foreign visitor – 'Everything in England bespeaks an immense population. The buildings are on a scale of size and wealth out of all proportion to ours,' wrote the American Ralph Waldo Emerson in 1847. Just the feelings an Englishman, a century later, would have when visiting one of the great American cities. America, thought Emerson, 'is the Paradise of the third class; here everything is cheap, here everything is for the poor. England is the Paradise of the first class; it is essentially aristocratic, and the humbler classes have made up their minds to this, and do contentedly enter into the system.'[9]

Not so in the eyes of a German visitor of about the same date – Engels – who saw in the disparity between upper-class wealth and proletarian hardship the seeds of a revolution, the death of a class, and with it the death of its God.

In 1844 Engels had written, 'All the possibilities of religion are exhausted.'[10] After Christianity, after the absolute and abstract religion, after religion 'as such', no other religion could come. Carlyle sees that Christianity, whether Catholic or Protestant, declines irresistibly. 'If he knew the nature of Christianity, he would see that after Christianity, no other religion is possible.'

Since the collapse of the Berlin Wall, the dissolution of the Soviet Union, and the reported collapse of Marxism as a political system, it is easy to imagine that Marx and Engels were mistaken, not merely in some of their analyses of, for example, the condition of the working classes in England in their lifetime, but in their entire reading of human history. Western readers of Marx have been saying this for years. The editors and translators of the 1958 edition of Engels's *The Condition of the Working Class in England* point out that it is not true to say that industrialization (a word which Carlyle coined) always made working conditions worse. 'Domestic spinners and weavers in the eighteenth century had been "exploited" by the clothiers as ruthlessly as the factory operatives were "exploited" by the manufacturers in the 1840s.' This, it perhaps goes without saying, is to miss the point of what Marx and Engels meant by the word 'exploit'. Unlike many species of radicalism, revolutionism, left-wingery or trades unionism, the Marxist creed, as it was to evolve in the minds of its two great progenitors, saw capitalism itself as a contract which was by definition exploitative. They did not look here for a comparatively enlightened factory which did not exploit the workers, there for an unenlightened one which did exploit them. Rather, they saw that 'capitalism has engendered the contradiction that, whereas man would be the master of the products of his labour, he has become their servant'.[11] The 'value theory' was invented by Adam Smith – the idea that Labour alone creates value and therefore, as capitalists strive to make more and more profit, to lay off as much human labour as possible and to use labour-saving machinery, the threat of unemployment will drive workers into the acceptance of an effectual slavery. This theory, as espoused by Marx and Engels, has been much disputed, some would say discredited; but while it is very easy with hindsight to say that Marx–Engels made specific historical mistakes, it seems foolish to score points while missing the overall sweep of their message. Thus, the English editors of Engels's *The Condition* claim that Engels invented the notion of the 'hungry forties' – and that the purchasing power of wages in the 1840s was in fact much higher than in the Napoleonic period. It is also pointed out that Engels used, as evidence of what was going on in the 1840s, abuses which had been reported to the Factories Enquiry Commission of 1833–4. All this might be true. Nevertheless, if one had to choose between being a comfortably-fed academic making these observations in 1958 or a factory hand in Oldham or Manchester in 1844, it is not difficult to know where one's choice would fall.

No doubt Engels got things wrong, and no doubt he saw England with foreign eyes. He came to be a manager in the Manchester branch of his father's cotton business, and it is a paradox that the money which enabled him to live the life of a gentleman, and to support Karl Marx and his family through thirty years, came from the sweated labour which he so much deplored.

Equally, it must be admitted that Engels had an idealized view of the English proletariat which, however much he claimed it was based on observation, the reader may be prompted to doubt. His assertion that 'Strauss's *Life of Jesus* and Proudhon's book *On Property* are ... read in

84

England only by the workers' is surprising, since the first English translation of Proudhon did not appear until 1876. 'Again it is the workers who are most familiar with the poetry of Shelley and Byron. Shelley's prophetic genius has caught their imagination, while Byron attracts their sympathy ... The middle classes, on the other hand, have on their shelves only ruthlessly expurgated "family" editions of these writers ...'

One takes these observations with a pinch of salt. No doubt 'Red Shelley', the author of *The Necessity of Atheism* (the pamphlet for which he was sent down from Oxford), was popular in some quarters, but the notion that no middle-class enthusiast (such as Tennyson, for instance, who as a boy had run out to the churchyard to carve an inconsolable BYRON IS DEAD on a yew-tree) read these revolutionary poets in their entirety, or that loom-workers or weavers had the time to do so, is surely nonsense.

Equally, the commentators have not been slow to point out that Marx made a completely mistaken analysis of what created revolutions. 'The factory worker wants higher wages and better conditions, not a revolution,' wrote A.J.P. Taylor in his introduction to the Pelican edition of *The Communist Manifesto*.[12] It was in the countries where capitalism was least advanced, argued Taylor, that revolutions occurred. 'Apart from Russia, which had hardly begun to share European developments, two countries paradoxically escaped serious revolutionary disturbance. They were Great Britain and Belgium, the two countries in which industrialization was most advanced.'[13]

No doubt these things have to be said in the interests of truth, but in a sense they miss the point of what Marx and Engels were saying as long ago as the 1840s and went on saying for the remaining decades of the nineteenth century, and why they were destined to be incomparably the most important political prophets of the last century. Trying to dismantle Marxism by pointing out that Engels did not know England as well as he thought, or that Marx is never known to have met a member of the working class, is rather like trying to shake the faith of a Christian by saying that human bodies which attempt to walk on water invariably sink. Marx and Engels, but above all Marx, brought to the world something which was rather more than a distillation of all other revolutionary movements at the time. It was something which purported to be a scientific discovery about history itself, therefore about reality itself. It was a discovery which dethroned God more certainly and effectively than the writings of that working-class hero, the Etonian Percy

Bysshe Shelley. It was the discovery that human societies, their culture, their methods of governing themselves – whether as kingdoms or as republics – their rituals of crownings or inaugurations, their laws, their music, their recreations, their art, the stories they tell one another, their domestic patterns and routines, their very gods – are all the product of economic forces.

The notion of freedom – the idea that we can choose to think what we think – is an illusion. We are products of our times, and the times are the products of economics.

It is easy – yet again, on this metaphysical level – to question the plausibility of Marx's theories of value. 'Pearls are not valuable because men dive for them, men dive for them because they are valuable.'[14] Very likely. But determinism is not so easily shaken off by a *mot*. Augustine, drawing the deterministic idea out of St Paul, held intellectual sway over Europe for over a thousand years. And when the essentially deterministic viewpoint of Christianity appeared to be weakening in the sixteenth century, Calvin arose to reinforce the idea. One Determinism can only be replaced by another. 'For bourgeois freedom means nothing more than free trade, free buying and selling' (*Communist Manifesto*).

Marx was one of literature's greatest phrase-makers. We still remember his words, written when he was twenty-six, in the Critique of Hegel's *Philosophy of Law*: '*Religious* suffering is at the same time an *expression* of real suffering and a *protest* against real suffering. Religion is the sign of an oppressed creature, the heart of a heartless world, and the soul of a soulless state of affairs. It is the *opium* of the people.' Of all his great sayings, this is – at least in the Protestant British context – the wrongest. (He wasn't, of course, writing about Britain.) As some of the opening remarks in this chapter make plain, purveyors of opium as different as 'General' William Booth of the Salvation Army, Dr Pusey, Bishop Walsham How and the Roman Catholic Church would have been only too happy to establish a widespread working-class addiction to religion. Mayhew's cheerfully indifferent costermongers were far more typical. But it is in places where the working classes were genuinely religious – Italy, Russia, Spain, Latin America – that Marxism has taken root.

Marx's epoch-making move was to substitute for the God of the Churches (at once one and absolute, but revealing different aspects of his essence at different moments) the movement of history: to stake everything on this, to identify its authorised interpreters, and to make absolute demands in its and their name.[15]

*

This is right, but it does not go far enough. Marx's philosophy is more like art than it is like the dry English empirical way of doing the subject. It is a series of world-pictures. So, in his 'Notes to the Doctoral Dissertation: Reason and the Proof of God', he could see that there is an intimate connection between Western man's attitude to God and his attitude to money. You could say, rather than claiming that Marx saw off God with a Hegelian deification of the movement of history, that he was more like an old Hebrew prophet, exposing the hollowness of the idols of the Gentiles and pointing to the Truth. 'Real dollars' – this is from the Notes –

> have the same existence imagined gods have. Has a real dollar any mode of existence other than in conception, though in man's general or rather communal conception? Take paper money into a country where this use of paper is not known, and everyone will laugh at your subjective concept. Come with your gods into a country where other gods prevail, and people will prove to you that you are a victim of fictions and abstraction.[16]

The future as seen by Marx – that is, the time in which the reader of these pages is now living – is one in which the language of religion will be as useless as toy money. As for the God of the Jews, 'Money is the jealous god of Israel before whom no other god may exist ...' and, 'the God of the Jews has been secularized and become the god of the world'.[17] Marx's self-hating anti-Semitism is a subject in itself, of course. But there is some sense in which one can hear the voice of a long line of rabbi-ancestors in his rant, even though, blasphemously, it is precisely their God whom he professes, before and above all others, to destroy. Having made Money its God, the Nineteenth Century could not turn round and have God as well. It was another Jew, not Marx, who first observed that you cannot serve God and Mammon. Marxism is one way of drawing that gnomic utterance to its logical conclusion.

Marx settled in England as a result of revolutions, or rather counter-revolutions.[18] It was understandable that he should have come with the belief that there were more revolutions on the way. He was expelled from the Rhineland for publishing inflammatory and seditious articles in the newspaper of which he was the editor – the *Neue Rheinische Zeitung*. The final issue was printed in a defiant scarlet. After 'the year of revolutions', Europe was wary of taking in this subversive character. He was not allowed to stay in Paris – where he had witnessed much of the revolutionary activity of the previous year. Switzerland and Belgium were closed to him. So it was that on 27 August 1849 he arrived in London, the city which was to be his home until he died on 14 March 1883.

Marx's early years in the British capital – first in a tiny flat in Soho, then in a series of uncomfortable houses in Maitland Park, on the borders of Kentish Town – were of unmitigated grimness. At first he had no money, and without the help of Engels he would have starved. Then, in 1851, and for the next eleven years, he secured the really rather well-paid (£1 per article) job of European political correspondent to the largest-circulation newspaper in the world, the *New York Daily Tribune*. They were prepared to print two of his articles a week, but since he spent most of his days studying political philosophy and economics in the Reading Room of the British Museum, he had no time to squander on journalism. As it was, of the 500 articles he submitted to the paper, 125 were written by Engels: 'Because my hands are full with my political economy, you really must help me out.'

Almost from the first, Marx was involved with international revolutionaries. Suspected (falsely) of befriending a group who were dedicated to a plot to murder Queen Victoria (code-named Mooncalf), he was investigated by Prussian spies, one of whom has left a vivid description of his domestic arrangements.

Everything is broken, tattered and torn, with a half inch of dust over everything and the greatest disorder everywhere. In the middle of the salon there is a large old-fashioned table covered with an oilcloth and on it there lie manuscripts, books and newspapers, as well as the children's toys, the rags and tatters of his wife's sewing basket, several cups with broken rims, knives, forks, lamps, an ink pot, tumblers, Dutch clay pipes, tobacco ash – in a word, everything topsy-turvy, and all on the same table. A seller of secondhand goods would be ashamed to give away such a remarkable collection of odds and ends.

When you enter Marx's room smoke and tobacco fumes make your eyes water so much that for a moment you seem to be groping about in a cavern, but gradually, as you grow accustomed to the fog, you can make out certain objects which distinguish themselves from the surrounding haze. Everything is dirty and covered with dust, so that to sit down becomes a thoroughly dangerous business. Here is a chair with only three legs, on another chair the children are playing at cooking – this chair happens to have four legs. This is the one which is offered to the visitor, but the children's cooking has not been wiped away; and if you sit down you risk a pair of trousers. But none of these things embarrass Marx or his wife. You are received in the most friendly way and cordially offered pipes and tobacco and whatever else there may happen to be; and eventually a spirited and agreeable conversation arises to make amends for all the domestic deficiencies, and this makes the discomfort tolerable ... This is a true picture of the family life of the Communist chief Marx.[19]

Three of his children – his two sons Guido and Edgar and his daughter Franziska – died in the early years of his London exile, and there is no doubt that the conditions in which they lived shortened their lives. He did not have enough money for Franziska's coffin until a French refugee gave it to him. 'I could not and cannot fetch the doctor', Marx wrote to Engels, 'because I have no money for the medicine.'

Journalism rescued them from these extremes of poverty, and it is hard to think of any other profession in which he could have so brilliantly excelled.* If invective of a crude but often witty and merciless flavour was what an editor wanted, Marx was the man. 'By means of a hidden and artificial sewer system all the lavatories of London spew their physical filth into the Thames. By means of the systematic pushing of goose quills the world capital spews out all its social filth into the great papered central sewer called the *Daily Telegraph*.'[20] Marx was obsessed by this newspaper, and by its editor, a Jew who had changed his name from Levi to Levy. Hardly a very violent change, one might have supposed, and rather less of a transformation than Marx's father effected when he changed his name from Herschel Levi to Heinrich Marx. The anti-Semitic insults which Marx repeatedly rained upon the head of Levy had, like so much of his invective, a demonic fury. There was indeed something of the demon in Marx: his personality and his political philosophy being in this respect expressions, perhaps, not of a purely rational reflection upon the condition of the world, but of some stupendous drama taking place within himself. Proudhon's motto

---

* An application to become a railway clerk was turned down because of his illegible handwriting.

(*Destruam et aedificabo*) could have been Marx's: If I destroy, I shall build.[21] He jocularly signed himself with the name of the devil, 'Old Nick'. Goethe's *Faust* was a book he had almost by heart, and he loved to declaim the verses of Mephistopheles. Pacing Hampstead Heath with his family, Marx would tell the children an interminable story about one Hans Rockle, an obvious self-image, who had sold his soul to the devil. Rockle kept an enchanted toyshop and was always in debt. The shop was full of marvels – men and women made from wood, giants and beasts. Rockle was a magician but his powers were limited, and to meet his obligations to the devil, he was always having to sell off the toys.

In the early days in London when his acquaintance was largely limited to other German exiles, Marx displayed a particularly restless appetite for violence. Once, going up Hampstead Road in a horse-drawn omnibus with Wilhelm Liebknecht, they saw a commotion outside a pub. A woman was screaming 'Murder! Murder!' Marx and his companion alighted from the 'bus at the first opportunity, instinctively drawn to trouble. It wasn't, unfortunately, a murder, nor even a minor riot. The woman was drunk and objected to her husband trying to take her home, but at the approach of Marx she grabbed at his luxuriant beard while her friends, themselves the worse for drink, cheered and booed at the 'damned foreigners'.

Certainly the proletariat – however much he looked forward to their ultimate victory over their bourgeois masters in the world class struggle – were just as likely as anyone else to receive the sharp end of Marx's tongue. During one of his pub-crawls with friends Liebknecht and Bauer they blundered into a public house in Tottenham Court Road where the members of the Order of Oddfellows were holding a reunion. (The Oddfellows were a loosely based mutual benefit society, something between a co-operative and a trades union.) The three Germans were called upon to drink the health of the Oddfellows. Bauer replied with a taunt about English snobbishness. Marx, not to be outdone, launched into a bitter tirade against the lack of culture in Britain and the undoubted superiority of Mozart, Beethoven and Haydn to any British composer. By the time he had warmed to his theme and began to explain why he hated England and the English, the company was becoming rough. Before full-scale fisticuffs erupted, Marx and his friends fled. As they blundered along, by now much the worse for drink, they tripped over a heap of stones. 'Hurrah!' shouted Bauer, 'I have an idea!' Picking up one of the stones he hurled it at the glass panel of a street-lamp. It was two in the morning, and they had managed to smash four or five lamps before the arrival of a policeman resulted in an exciting chase down streets and alleys.

In time, naturally, Marx settled down. His stupendous work, which was to turn into *Das Kapital*, the time he spent involved in helping to organize the First International (1864), and the constant assaults of liver complaints, pulmonary disorders and boils which covered almost every part of his anatomy, compelled a quiet and studious middle age. 'I am plagued like Job, though not so God-fearing', he wrote in 1858. 'Everything that these gentlemen [the doctors] say can be reduced to the fact that one ought to be a prosperous *rentier* and not a poor devil like me, as poor as a church mouse.'[22] The strange, the haunted life reads, if not like that of a tormented patriarch, a little like that of a prophet. It is so easy for modern commentators to point out the many things which Marx got wrong (such as his confident prediction that there would be no Crimean war) and forget the extraordinary fact that for years and years and years he laboured in obscurity, covering thousands and thousands of pieces of paper with his semi-legible handwriting, reading thousands of books, quarrelling with almost every socialist or revolutionary leader whom he met – and this quarrelling was very much part of Marx's political-creative endeavour – and never once, it would seem, lost his sense of himself as a man of destiny, a man who had truly understood the very nature of history itself in a way which had been revealed to no previous inquirer. At the time of the founding of the First International in 1864 he was still known only to a tiny handful of communist conspirators. But in the decade which followed his fame was to grow, and, though in his lifetime he was never very famous in England, he came to be known and revered throughout the world 'as a figure of vast fame and notoriety, regarded by some as the instigator of every revolutionary movement in Europe, the fanatical dictator of a world movement pledged to subvert the moral order, the peace, happiness and prosperity of mankind'.[23]

It was in the house of his friend Dr Kugelmann that Marx became acquainted with the majestic statue of Zeus, known after the Italian village where it was first discovered by archaeologists as the Zeus of Oticoli. It was a statue about which many Germans of the period were inspired to write philosophical fantasies. Marx, who spent much time in Dr Kugelmann's music room, where there was a cast of the god, became amusedly enamoured of it. Dr Kugelmann pointed out the extraordinary resemblance between Marx and the statue, and it is from this period that Marx began to grow his hair over his ears, and to allow his beard to become as luxuriantly bushy as that of Zeus.

On 13 December 1867 an attempt was made to rescue two Fenians, Irish nationalists, imprisoned in Clerkenwell gaol in London. A barrel of gunpowder was blown up on the outer wall of the prison, killing twelve people and wounding about a hundred and twenty others. There was jubilation in the Marx household in Maitland Park, since they supported any armed struggle against the existing authorities. When there was a heavy knock at the front door a few days later, Jenny wrote that she was as surprised as if she had heard the cry 'Fire, fire, the Fenians are here!' In fact, it was the delivery of an extraordinary Christmas present, thundering Zeus himself, or, as Jenny called him, 'Jupiter Tonans in all his ideal purity and colossal magnificence'. The whole Marx family gazed at this life-sized cast of the Oticoli Zeus in awe. It came with the tribute of Dr Kugelmann: to 'the scholar compared to whom all the scholars since Aristotle are no more than pygmies, the thinker who deserves to be called the consciousness of the nineteenth century'.[24]

There is a sense in which this was true, just as Marxism, the greatest alternative to Christianity which has ever been formulated, contained within itself profound truths and half-truths to which a fair-minded person could not but respond. The distribution of wealth between rich and poor in the nineteenth and twentieth centuries was so grotesquely inequitable that no one who had studied, as had Marx, the reports of conditions in industrial England in the Parliamentary Blue Books, or heard the testimonies of revolutionaries the length and breadth of Europe, could fail to believe that history must exact some solution or some recompense.

Vengeance is mine, I will repay, saith the Lord. Marx's atheistic creed thrilled its adherents for a century by its promise that there was an inevitability about the collapse of capitalism, the removal of injustice, and the triumph of the proletarian struggle. 'The classical gods', Dr Kugelmann had remarked to Marx when he discovered the philosopher's obsession with his statues, 'are eternal rest without passion.' 'On the contrary,' Marx replied, 'they are eternal passion without any unrest.'

The energy and violence of Marx's view of the world now seem to us very much of their time. One could easily envisage Marx as a character in Balzac, for example, the fury of his inner passions erupting in a vast, destructive pattern. His vision of the voracious greed of capital, and of the suffering of the toilers and the inequities of society, has the frenzied zeal of some Balzacian exposition of evil in high places, the swirling energy of Berlioz at his most exuberant. His own resemblance to the Zeus of Oticoli seemed to dethrone the deity himself and place Marx – 'the consciousness of the nineteenth century' – on his pedestal.

It is one of the stranger features of the story that, as God or the gods were dethroned in the course of the nineteenth century, the deicides, with their long white beards, came more and more to resemble Blake's Ancient of Days. Marx, Darwin, Herbert Spencer, William Morris, could all have been mistaken for Jehovah in a frock coat.

On the last day of his sanity, it will be remembered, Friedrich Nietzsche saw a horse being whipped in Turin. The horrible sight – it was the beginning of 1889 – triggered something in the brain which in *Thus Spake Zarathustra* had been able to say, 'Behold I teach you the overman. The overman is the meaning of the earth ... Once the sin against God was the greatest sin; but God died, and these sinners died with him. To sin against the earth is now the most dreadful thing.'[25] Once he had seen the suffering of the horse, Nietzsche himself ceased to be human. His madness seems a little like the anti-humanist disgust of Swift's Gulliver who can, after his unhappy experiences of the Yahoos, only be content in the stables; but it is also of course distinctively and utterly Nietzsche's own: 'Sing me a new song,' he wrote within hours of going mad, 'the world is transfigured and all the heavens are full of joy.' He signed himself 'The Crucified'.[26]

Hegel, Marx's master, had taught that 'true humility consists in recognizing and revering God in everything, especially in the theatre of world history'.[27] It would seem impossible to have a more religious view of things than this: that the study of history is a 'theodicy'.[28] But this is until you realize that for Hegel, God is part of the inexorable movement of events. As humanity has moved through its great phases, empires have passed away, and with them, their gods. 'And thus Zeus, who set limits to the depredations of time and suspended its constant flux, had no sooner established something inherently enduring than he was himself devoured along with his whole empire.'[29] God, in other words, is a human construct.

Or, at the very least, He is subject to those mysterious movements of human events, a reading of which we call history. Marx on the one hand created an historiography which claimed to be purely scientific, and based on materialistic dialectic; on the other hand, he wrote about it with a burning, seething passion. He had one of those violent tempers which chews up other people's ideas and spits them out. So, he scalded his way through his Hegelian phase, absorbed a great deal of the materialist outlook from French philosophy, and reserved some of his most vitriolic language for thinkers (such as Feuerbach) whose ideas he had freely borrowed, and whom he revered, while hating.

To describe Marx as 'the consciousness of the nineteenth century' must be to acknowledge that few of his ideas are entirely original. But few of the radicals and revolutionary philosophers in France, Germany or England could rival Marx's fervent and monistic simplicity of outlook. Not only was history to be explained in terms of the class struggle, but the future guaranteed a happy ending to the story.[30] Theoretic Marxists, more than Marx himself, removed any concept of freedom or individuality from our analysis of human motivation. Everyone acts, thinks, creates, composes, writes, in accordance with his economic position and background.

Once embraced, the religion of Marxism became or becomes a worldview which colours and explains everything. It is, rather like the primitive Judaism of those books of the Old Testament which describe the conquest of the Promised Land, essentially violent and ultimately optimistic. The struggle will be a real struggle, with bombs, civil wars, mass slaughter. There is no hiding from that in Marx's pages, and nothing that happened in Russia after the Bolsheviks seized control would surprise a reader of *Das Kapital*. But, like the Bible, the story ends with the chosen people entering their inheritance, with a new heaven and a new earth.

Marx was a prophet but not, in his lifetime, a god. It was left to Lenin, his representative on earth, to see his possibilities as an icon. Lenin hated religion; he called it 'one of the most odious things on earth'.[31] 'Never has the idea of God "linked the individual with society",' he once wrote, 'it has always *tied* the oppressed classes hand and foot with faith in the divinity of the oppressors.' And again, in his *Attitudes of Workers to Religion*, 'Fear made the gods. Fear of the blind force of capital – blind because it cannot be foreseen by the masses of the people – a force which at every step in the life of the proletarian and small proprietor threatens to inflict and does inflict "sudden", "unexpected", "accidental" ruin, destruction, pauperism, prostitution, death from starvation – such is the *root* of modern religion.' After the revolution of 1917, he mocked the peasants for asking for icons when their churches closed; but he was quite cynical enough to oblige them by providing a face on which to focus; and no doubt Marx with his full beard was easily assimilable by souls used to praying to the bearded face of the Byzantine Pantocrator. As early as 12 September 1918 Lenin was writing to the Commissar of Enlightenment: 'I am exasperated to the depths of my soul. There is no outdoor bust of Marx ... I scold you for this criminal negligence.' On 7 November 1918 a huge portrait of Marx was carried in procession through the streets of Moscow, just like the sacred icons which were paraded with the troops in times of national emergency in the days of the Tsars.[32] Even in his lifetime, Lenin himself was perceived by the Faithful as quasi-divine. He did nothing to discourage the editor of the propaganda sheet *Soldatskaya Pravda* from publishing in November 1917 a poem which ran:

> Hail to the Supreme Leader of the People
> Dedicated to the Citizen Ulyanov [i.e., Lenin].
>
> Hail to you, soul of the people,
> Free, pure citizen.
> Hail to you freedom's beauty,
> Invincible giant.[33]

Lenin was in fact rather small. His time in exile, spent stirring up trouble in London and Zurich and doing a deal with the Germans so that he could be smuggled into Russia behind the front line and start the insurrection, was already seen in mystic terms. The parallels between God's decision to arrive in Bethlehem from Heaven and become incarnate, and Lenin's arrival at the Finland Station, St Petersburg are overwhelming:

> You were in a distant land,
> But in spirit you were with us always.
> There great, page by page, grew
> The Holy Bible of Labour ...[34]

Lenin was the

> Invisible messenger of peace
> Crowned with thorns of slander.[35]

As he lay dying of a stroke in 1923, the processes of deification went even further. At the All Russia Agricultural and Domestic Industrial Exhibition they erected an enormous portrait of Lenin made up entirely of plants. In many subsequent exhibitions there was a 'Lenin corner', a shrine exactly comparable to the 'corner' in which an icon would have been placed in the days of Christianity. Schools, factories, mines, collective farms, villages and towns were, many of them, renamed after the messenger of peace who initiated the bloodiest civil war in Russia's history. He died in January 1924. As he lay in state *Pravda* told the people that 'Lenin lives in the soul of every member of Our Party. Lenin lives in the heart of every honest worker.' Among the eulogies over his corpse, one stated that 'Lenin has not died. Lenin lives. There is not a corner in the world where there are working people, oppressed people, exploited people, where Lenin is absent.'[36] Like Jesus, he is with us always, even to the end of the ages.

The Communist engineer and diplomat Krasin was put in charge of constructing Lenin's mausoleum. Krasin was not merely of the view that Lenin lived, in a spiritual sense. He said he was 'certain that the time will come when science will become all powerful, that it will be able to recreate a deceased organism ... to recreate the physical person. And I am certain that when that time will come, then the liberation of mankind, using all the might and of science of technology, will be able to resurrect great historical figures.'[37]

Theodore Dreiser, visiting Moscow in 1928, noted the widespread superstition that so long as the corpse of Lenin remained uncorrupt in its tomb, Communism would be safe. Only while it survived would the new Russia survive. Many believed that, like King Arthur, Lenin only slept in his tomb; he was not truly dead.[38]

> He, having given up his immeasurable burden,
> He has not died, but merely sleeps.
> Our tired leader is resting
> Under his granite tombstone,

as a Siberian poet wrote in 1924. Children in the Soviet Union were taught a creed which stated:

> Lenin, supreme Leader,
> You have not died, you live.
> You have completely merged with immortal glory.

Your thought,
Your gigantic rush,
Pours its lava into the millions,
To bear them in the decisive battle.[39]

As late as the 1960s Lenin was speaking directly to the Faithful. When Stalin fell from favour with the Party, delegates of the 22nd Party Congress of 1961 heard this testimony from Comrade Dora Lazurkina: 'I always carry Ilich in my heart, comrades, and have survived the most difficult moments only because Ilich was in my heart when I took counsel with him. [*Applause.*] Yesterday I took counsel with Ilich and he stood before me as though alive and said: "It is unpleasant for me to be beside Stalin, who brought such misfortune to the Party".' [*Stormy prolonged applause.*][40] Even when translated to immortal glory, it would seem, Lenin enjoyed stabbing his colleagues in the back. We can only imagine what Marx and Engels would have made of such utterances; their thoughts, presumably, would be comparable with those of Jesus if He could witness High Mass at St Peter's.

The Communist Manifesto foresaw the power of consumerism and knew it was more powerful than ideology. It might not have surprised Marx that in our generation the citizens of Communist states could be so envious of those with freezers, washing-machines, CD players and take-away food that they were prepared to overthrow the state for them. The ugly and exploitative side of capitalism created a slave class whom Marx wished to enlist in a cosmic battle. But it was capable, equally, of creating an opiate more addictive than religion: prosperity, on a scale undreamed-of in the nineteenth century, for the great majority of those living in a capitalist state.

Those in our century who like Solzhenitsyn have been most eloquent in their denunciations of the cruelties and blasphemies of the Marxist state have also been loudest in their condemnation of the frivolous materialism of the West, its cellophane-wrapped and pampered godlessness. To such serious observers, it would seem that Marx at least took the human condition seriously, at a date when millions walked and suffered in darkness.

6

Living in a Lumber-room

'The subject Mr Casaubon has chosen is as
changing as chemistry: new discoveries are
constantly making new points of view. Who wants
a system on the basis of the four elements, or a
book to refute Paracelsus? Do you not see that it is
no use now to be crawling a little way after men of
the last century . . . living in a lumber-room and
furbishing up broken-legged theories about Chus
and Mizraim?'

'How can you speak so lightly?' said Dorothea,
with a look between sorrow and anger.

George Eliot, *Middlemarch* (Book II, Chapter xxii)

O F ALL CARLYLE'S visitors and disciples none, perhaps, was to be more important to his subsequent reputation than James Anthony Froude (1818–1894), who made the *haj* to Cheyne Row in 1849, shortly after the publication of his own notorious and transparently autobiographical novel, *The Nemesis of Faith*. The title is self-explanatory.

Froude had particular and personal reasons for his spiritual battle with orthodoxy. When he went up to Oriel College, Oxford his elder brother, Richard Hurrell Froude, was only four months dead.[1] Hurrell Froude had been one of the founders of the Tractarian revival and his *Remains*, put together by John Henry Newman after his death, were to cause scandal by revealing the extent of his popish observances and his almost bitter contempt for Protestantism. The younger Froude was welcomed with particular relish by Newman (still a college tutor at Oriel), and it was a welcome of which he was chary. He felt uncomfortable in Newman's 'reading set' but allowed himself to remain something of a protégé of the great man, while not actually attaching himself to Newman's inner ring as he gradually withdrew from University life in 1843–4 and became a Catholic in October 1845. Several things disquieted Froude about Newman, as he makes clear in *The Nemesis of Faith*. Chief of them was Newman's teaching that reason must be surrendered to faith. 'As I began to look into what he said about it, the more difficult it seemed to me. What did it mean? Reason could only be surrendered by an act of reason. Even the Church's infallible judgements could only be received through the senses and apprehended by reason.'[2]

Newman had asked Froude to contribute to his series of Lives of the English Saints, with a monograph on St Neot. By then, 1844, Froude had taken deacon's orders with a view to getting a fellowship (Exeter

College); but the task of chronicling St Neot was too much for his flimsy faith. The tales of the miraculous which had made other men Catholic struck Froude as palpable 'nonsense'.[3]

Newman described his sensations on entering the Roman Church as 'like coming into port after a stormy sea'. Hugh Walker adds:

> Doubtless it was. The sea was the sea of truth, and the storms were the storms of doubt which inevitably sweep it for those who boldly spread their sails and steer towards the sunrise. Those storms could blow no longer in the still haven sheltered all round by the breakwaters of authority. But what a false idea of life, what a pitiable conception of duty as contrasted with the conceptions of the other great intellects of the time?[4]

Certainly Froude made no such surrenders. As *The Nemesis of Faith* reveals, his hero was not Newman but Carlyle. He saw Carlyle and Newman as holding opinions 'as far asunder as the poles',[5] which was what drew him to Cheyne Row in the middle of June 1849.[6] They first sat in the small flagged court between the house and garden, where Carlyle was smoking his after-dinner pipe, and they (Froude had been brought along by a friend, James Spedding) talked of Ireland. Then they were escorted into the dining room, where Mrs Carlyle gave them tea. At this date Froude was thirty and Carlyle fifty-four.

> He was tall (about five feet eleven), thin, but at that time upright, with no signs of the later stoop. His body was angular, his face beardless, such as it is represented in Woolner's medallion, which is by far the best likeness of him in the days of his strength. His head was extremely long, with the chin thrust forward, the neck was thin; the mouth firmly closed, the under lip slightly projecting; the hair grizzled and thick and bushy. His eyes which grew lighter with age, were then of a deep violet, with fire burning at the bottom of them, which flashed out at the least excitement. The face was altogether more striking, most impressive every way. And I did not admire him the less because he treated me – I cannot say unkindly, but shortly and sternly. I saw then what I saw ever after – that no one need look for conventional politeness from Carlyle – he would hear the exact truth from him and nothing else.[7]

Carlyle, without immediately recognizing it, had met his Boswell. Froude was to become one of the foremost historians of the nineteenth century, a great Tudor historian, and a fervent champion of truth. Unlike Arthur Hugh Clough (who resigned his own Oxford fellowship at the same time in 1849), Froude was never an out-and-out unbeliever. Indeed, in later years he returned to the practice of a watery variety of Anglicanism. He believed in Carlyle's God – the notion that there was a rightness, a moral fittingness in historical events. It was a sort of impersonal determinism. His hatred of superstition, and of Roman Catholic manifestations of this in particular, shows most clearly in his biased but magnificent *The English in Ireland in the Eighteenth Century*. But his greatest book – surely one of the very great biographies – is his *Life of Carlyle*.

He was much vilified for publishing, first Carlyle's *Reminiscences*, which revealed the extent of the giant's grief and remorse about his unkindness to Mrs Carlyle; and then the biography itself, which certainly depicted Carlyle warts and all. Many disputed the accuracy of his portrait, and deplored its tastelessness. The Victorians were used to hagiography, not to biography which told the full and complex truth. Froude himself was a difficult, intricate character, described by one of his contemporaries as 'the most interesting man I have ever known'. The *Dictionary of National Biography* says, 'His conversation was brilliant and none the less fascinating for its subacid flavour.'[8] His own disillusionment with Christianity had stemmed from what he saw as its intellectual dishonesty and, in many of its manifestations, its sheer silliness. Carlyle's gigantic struggles, his attempt to be honest, to avoid 'moonshine', all appealed to Froude's strong mind. 'How delicate, decent, it is, bless its mealy mouth!' Carlyle had written of English biography.[9] Froude guaranteed that no one would say that of his rugged but, for most readers, desperately disillusioning exposure of the Master's foibles.

'With the exception of Coleridge, Carlyle was the first man of letters of the first rank in Britain, not only to acquire a profound knowledge of the language, but to appreciate the true importance of the German Renaissance which, by 1829, stood out in high relief.'[10] Throughout his life, from the early essays on German literature to the last monumental work of German biography, Carlyle opened his readers' eyes to a world that was larger than their own college, their own Inn of Court, their own narrow parlour. To the twentieth-century reader, perhaps, Carlyle seems little more than a windbag. But the bag released winds which blew his contemporaries about, excited them, wafting towards them names and ideas which were all but unheard-of at home – Fichte's idea, for example, that this mysterious universe possesses a Personality; is, indeed, a Personality, an Ego which speaks to our Ego. Not a bad idea to have blown in your face if the alternatives are Jeremy Bentham on the one hand and the Thirty-nine Articles on the other. It was the instinctive knowledge that these were dead alternatives which led the early Victorians to idolize Carlyle, who 'exercised an influence in England and America that no other did upon the course of philosophical thought of his time'.[11]

Standing so far from Carlyle's influence, our generation can miss an obvious fact about the intellectual climate of early nineteenth-century England: its crippling *narrowness*.[12] Can there ever have been a narrower time, a time in which the choices facing an inquiring mind seemed more Lilliputian, or in which the issues they were debating so hotly seemed so extraordinarily footling? In terms of the great metaphysical problems of the age, the young English person beginning to investigate such matters in the 1830s, let us say, would be faced with a choice, either the rigid materialism of the Benthamites and the Positivists – an intellectual strait-jacket which J.S. Mill himself came to find intolerable; or the theological bigotry of the universities. 'The vice of Bigotry has been so indiscriminately imputed to the religious, that they seem apt to forget that it is a real sin. To the millions of Europe, bigotry has been a confutation of all pious feeling. So unlovely has religion been made by it ... that now, as 2,000 years ago, men are lapsing into Atheism or Pantheism.'[13] That was the opinion of Francis Newman (1805–1897), John Henry's brother, who lost his Christian faith at Oxford in the late 1820s. He was briefly a Fellow of Balliol but, finding himself unable in conscience to subscribe to the Thirty-nine Articles of the Church of England, he resigned, and became a Professor of Latin at University College London in 1846. He was never an atheist, interestingly enough. But the sheer bigotry of Oxford and his colleagues there drove him into an out-and-out rejection of Christianity.

Francis Newman, like many other young men at that date, had become dimly aware that something very exciting was happening in Germany. We can now see – whatever views we form of Hegel – that the nineteenth-century German-speaking world witnessed metaphysical debates of a searchingness and a thrillingness unknown since the Athens of the fourth century BC. Carlyle in his windy way, and Coleridge too, whom Carlyle so mocked, were at least aware that completely new ways of envisioning the universe and the human condition had been aired in the lecture-rooms of Berlin University.

> *God has died – God is dead* – this is the most frightful of all thoughts, that everything eternal and true *is not*, that negation itself is found in God. The deepest anguish, the feeling of complete irretrievability, the annulling of everything that is elevated, are bound up with this thought. However, the process does not come to a halt at this point; rather, a reversal takes place: God, that is to say, maintains himself in this process, and the latter is only the death of death. God rises again to life, and thus things are reversed ...[14]

You were never going to hear stirring words like these of Hegel's in 1827 from a lecture podium in Oxford or Cambridge, or Edinburgh or Glasgow. Here was 'the true philosopher of modern consciousness ... The crisis that Hegel was striving to describe – the crisis of a civilization that has discovered the God upon whom it depended to be also its own creation.'[15]

Here was not an outright rejection of the old creeds. Here was no cynical Voltairean Deism, no atheism of Holbach, but a radical reinterpretation of the very meaning of the word God, and of how it had been used and was being used by those who were truly spiritual and religious. Was Hegel talking nonsense? Or were his words indeed destined to change, not merely the way university professors in Berlin and Bonn and Tübingen spoke about metaphysics, but the way that the human race regarded itself? Was the very world changing – and with it the political institutions, the attitudes to social problems, the concepts of ethics, sexual morality, family life to which to such a large extent religious opinions connect?

These were big things, and as young men of Francis Newman's generation at Oxford discovered, Oxford did not want to know about them. The only Oxford theologian to go to Germany in the 1820s and hear what Johnny German had to say for himself was a brilliant Old Etonian Semitic linguist, Edward Bouverie Pusey. He was one of only two Oxford men (it was said at the time) who knew the German language.

Mr Casaubon, in *Middlemarch*, labours for years on a futile academic endeavour, The Key to All Mythologies. His trusting wife's first awareness of Casaubon's intellectual shortcomings dawns when Will Ladislaw, the man who has fallen in love with her, casually but destructively remarks, 'If Mr Casaubon read German he would save himself a great deal of trouble.'

> 'I do not understand you,' said Dorothea, startled and anxious.
>
> 'I merely mean', said Will in an offhand way, 'that the Germans have taken the lead in historical inquiries, and they laugh at results which are got by groping about in woods with a pocket-compass while they have made good roads. While I was with Mr Casaubon I saw that he deafened himself in that direction: it was almost against his will that he read a Latin treatise written by a German ...'[16]

Early nineteenth-century England, and especially Oxford, had plenty of Casaubons who either could not or would not read the Germans. Pusey, however, was not one of them. For the greater part of two years, first at Göttingen, then in Berlin and Bonn, he studied at the universities – with scholars such as Eichhorn, Schleiermacher and Neander, the kind of figures about whom Mr Casaubon did not want to know. It was partly under the influence of Hegel that the German scholars were able to adopt so radical an examination of the Scriptures. If religion is a human construct then it is allowable, and positively desirable, to examine its historical origins. If it is a divine creation, which has been revealed to the human race by the Almighty, then such probings are profanities. The young Pusey quickly became aware that English divines had absolutely no preparation to enable them even to consider such questions. One part of himself was very excited by the new learning. Another part was terrified: if the Bible is all written down by human beings, whose date and origin and social circumstances obviously determined the way they wrote and felt, then in what sense can it be called a divinely inspired collection of writings? Pusey realized that in order to face these questions, it was going to be necessary that he should make himself a first-rate expert in the fields of Hebrew, Arabic and the other Semitic tongues. And this he did, working prodigiously long hours – eighteen on many days – to master them. On the other hand, of course, he realized that what was at stake was not a matter of dry-as-dust facts about the interpretation of some Hebrew phrases, but the interpretation of the Bible as a whole.

It is not for one generation to pass judgement on its ancestors; but if we felt tempted to do so, we should surely wish to censure the intellectual cowardice and dishonesty which motivated Pusey's spiritual as well as academic life. In 1827 he wrote *An Historical Enquiry into the Probable*

Causes of the Rationalist Character Lately Predominant in the Theology of Germany. He attributed the Rationalist Character to 'dead orthodox-ism', and praised the German Pietist movement which had been so dis-tasteful to Kant. But almost as soon as he had published the book, Pusey saw that even this let-out would not quite do. Many of those who read, and reviewed, the book detected in it an evident sympathy with the German 'Rationalists': and why not? Pusey had after all studied under them, heard their lectures, attended their seminars. He knew that they were not demons with horns growing from their temples, but highly dedicated, honest scholars trying to fulfil the scholar's vocation in any generation: to follow the truth, regardless of where it led; and to tell the truth. So dissatisfied with his book on the German Rationalists was Pusey that he never allowed it to be reprinted. He quickly saw that Pietism was not enough to defend the old orthodoxies. What was needed was a belligerent 'dead orthodoxism' of the kind he had previ-ously attacked, a revival of the early Church Fathers, and an absolute intolerance, amounting to fanaticism, of anything which threatened the entrenched position of Christianity as a Revealed Religion. For if it wasn't a Revealed Religion, Pusey had read enough Hume to fear that it could not then be defended, and enough German to know that its chief bulwark against the infidel – namely the Bible – was being dis-sected in German lecture-halls.

To illustrate the difference between the Christianity of our own day and that of the nineteenth century, consider the following paragraph. It is taken from the New Revised Standard Version of the Bible, and offers an account of how the Pentateuch, the Five Books of Moses – Genesis to Deuteronomy – came to be written.

The heart of the story of the Pentateuch is found in the book of Exodus, which deals with the exodus from Egypt and the sojourn at Mount Sinai. All Jewish tradition reaches back to these 'root experiences', which constitute the people's basic understanding of their own identity and of the identity and character of God. At first these crucial experi-ences were related in story, song and proverb, but in the course of time, as the tradition was handed on in various circles and reinterpreted for new situations, the Torah expanded and took written form. During the monarchy it circulated in Old Epic literature; indeed, some scholars detect southern ('J' or Judean) and northern ('E' or Ephraimitic) liter-ary versions. (These letters, derived originally from the terms for God used in the different sources – 'J' for *Jahveh* or *Yahweh*, 'E' for *'elohim'* –

are conventionally used as titles for these two strands of the tradition, as 'P' and 'D' are used for two other sources.) Eventually the old Israelite epic was edited by Priestly writers ('P') perhaps during the Babylonian exile. Finally the Book of Deuteronomy ('D') which belongs with the Deuteronomic History extending from Joshua through Second Kings, was inserted just after the conclusion of the Priestly version of the Torah, because it purports to be Moses' farewell to the people.[17]

This paragraph is not quoted as a matter of scholarly or academic contention. Let us say (as I am told is the case) that there are some scholars who now believe that the earlier stages of composition here described either need not have taken place, or all took place during and after the period of the Babylonian exile. We are not here concerned with academic questions arising from the dating of Biblical authorship. The reason I have quoted this paragraph, which comes from a version of the Bible widely used and read in Christian churches throughout the United States and the English-speaking world, is that very few Christians would today object to the paragraph *on religious grounds*. Some, no doubt, would do so. But the huge majority of Christians, Catholic and Protestant, whether 'old-fashioned' or 'modern' in their approach, would have little or no difficulty with the idea that the Bible evolved over many years and, whatever the sublime or even 'inspired' nature of its teaching, was very much the product of the cultures and communities which produced it. To say this is a commonplace. And to suggest that the 'inspiration' of Scripture depends, as a concept, on the notion that the Bible was dictated all at one time by the Holy Spirit to a particular scribe or group of scribes – rather in the manner that the Holy Koran was dictated, or the Book of Mormon – would not accord with what, one suspects, most contemporary Christians and Jews actually believe. No doubt there are exceptions to this picture of contemporary attitudes to scriptural inspiration, but I believe that what I have said is broadly speaking true.

And yet think of what happened to John William Colenso (1814–1883), Bishop of Natal, when after patient study of the Pentateuch he came to conclusions which are now, at the end of the twentieth century, absolutely commonplace.[18]

Colenso was a serious, clever man, the son of a mineral agent for the Duchy of Cornwall. He did not have it easy at first, and he had to work hard as a teacher before going up to St John's College, Cambridge as a sizar, where he did well (second Wrangler in 1836, Smith's prizeman –

and a Fellow in 1837). Marrying comparatively early, in the years when Fellows were required to be celibate, he became the vicar of a Norfolk church for seven years and made a name as an author of some notable mathematical textbooks. And then, in 1853, he was appointed Bishop of Natal, in South Africa.

Parting from England was sad, and in particular it was hard to take his farewell of Frederick Denison Maurice, a first-rate theologian and friend of Tennyson, John Sterling and others: by the standards of the age, no bigot.

Having arrived in South Africa, Colenso did all the things which might be expected of a conscientious English churchman of the period. He denounced Kaffir polygamy; he tried to protect their women and children when the Kaffir tribesmen insisted on marrying more than one wife; he wrote a grammar of the Zulu language, as well as a prodigious array of textbooks in that language. He also translated parts of the Bible into Zulu for his flock's instruction. Moderns might deem Colenso highly paternalistic, and consider the whole idea of an English missionary bishop telling Africans how to live as itself a manifestation of the political *mores* of the time. But that was not how his contemporaries regarded Colenso at all.

None of his white coevals objected to Colenso's efforts to impose European sexual practices on the Africans. All commended his zeal in attempting to make the tribesmen and their womenfolk as respectable as the suburban inhabitants of Cheltenham Spa or Tunbridge Wells. But they did object very strongly to the increasing signs that poor, earnest Colenso was a heretic.

Having written a commentary on the Epistle to the Romans which shocked many of his contemporaries by its suggestion that Paul believed that Christ's death cancelled out sin as well as the punishment for sin, that it redeemed the whole world and not merely believers who turned to Christ, the Bishop committed an even worse error of judgement. He began to notice – as had other editors of the Five Books of Moses before him – overwhelming internal evidence that they were the work of several hands. Colenso confronted the literalists by a literal reading of the Pentateuch. A modern clerical historian tries to mock Colenso by dismissing him as 'a writer of text-books on arithmetic' who had 'no sense of history, no idea how to criticize documents, no wide reading, and no profundity of mind'.[19] It was, though, precisely the literalism – or the lack of historical sense – which made the Colenso affair so immediately arresting to the general public. The Mosaic books list the numbers of Israelites in the wilderness. By going through the books with the mind of a calculator, Colenso computed that there would have been 600,000 armed men among the Israelite hosts from the time of the departure from Egypt to the arrival in Canaan forty years later. Reckoning up the required amount of foodstuffs, flocks and herds, and contemplating the sanitary arrangements, Colenso demonstrated that these narratives, supposedly dictated by the Almighty Himself, contained many errors. For the accounts to be literally true, it would be necessary to believe that six men had 2,748 sons between them. By calculating the number of priests mentioned, and the number of pigeons consumed, Colenso showed that (once again, if the narrative were literally true) each of the priests at that juncture would have been accounting for 88 pigeons daily.

So few Jews or Christians nowadays, however old-fashioned, would really worry themselves about whether the accounts in Numbers and Leviticus are exact. And a modern historian believes that Colenso's literalist approach (which was in any event based on a miscalculation) 'played into the hands of the Conservatives'. It would be truer to say that the publicity attracted by the case made 'ordinary people' begin to question the Bible in a way they never had before. Our old friend Bishop Walsham How smugly recounts a timber merchant telling him that he had worked out the size and weight of the Ark; on the basis of this, he had concluded that the Bible was unbelievable. Who now looks more foolish – the smug Bishop or the timber merchant?[20]

It was precisely because Colenso was 'crude', because he 'misrepresented' the subtleties of the biblical scholars, that his case dealt such a blow to the Christian religion. But the blow was self-inflicted, by the church authorities. Their first reaction was to suspend Colenso. The Bishop of Cape Town deposed him for heresy, at a synod of (all white, of course) South African bishops.

Rather than appealing through the ecclesiastical courts, Colenso made a direct appeal to the Privy Council in London. He did not ask the Privy Council to adjudicate in the knotty theological question of whether a levitical hierophant in the desert 1500 years BC had been able to consume 88 pigeons per day. He simply appealed to them as a citizen of the British Empire who had been wronged. Sir Charles Lyell and Charles Darwin were among those who paid Colenso's legal fees. He was vindicated and, much to the horror of the church authorities, he returned to Africa to find a cheering crowd on the docks at Durban. Bishop Gray, who had been fool enough to start the whole process by deposing Colenso, wrote a solemn Sentence of Excommunication which was read out by the dean in the cathedral at Pietermaritzburg. Colenso illegally occupied the cathedral and drove the orthodox out, and there ensued what have been called 'unedifying scenes'.[21]

In his way, Colenso was a hero. When Ruskin, in 1887, presented to the Natural History Museum in South Kensington a fine uncut diamond which had cost him more than £1,000, he stipulated that it was 'not to be called the Ruskin, nor the Catkin, nor the Yellowskin diamond', but should be named the Colenso diamond, in honour of 'the loyal and patiently adamantine First Bishop of Natal'.[22]

The tragi-farce of the Colenso affair was an inevitable consequence of the die-hard attitudes of men like Dr Pusey and his friends, who quite deliberately and knowingly turned deaf ears to the advancement of the new biblical scholarship and simply tried to behave as if nothing had happened. Of course, Colenso's literalism was as ridiculous as theirs. But while it is easy to dismiss him as 'a writer of text-books on arithmetic', it is not easy to forgive men such as Pusey and John Henry Newman who, enormously more gifted than Colenso, committed the sin against the Intellect which is surely, in the world of the university, the equivalent of the sin against the Holy Ghost.

Consider what Francis Newman said about the vice of bigotry (page 104), and then consider these words of his brother, John Henry Newman:

> The Church must denounce rebellion as of all evils the greatest ... I do not shrink from uttering my firm conviction that it would be a gain to the country were it vastly more superstitious, more bigoted, more gloomy, more fierce in its religion than at present it shows itself to be.[23] ... Rationalism is the great evil of the day.[24]

It is strange that the man who wrote these words in the nineteenth century should in the twentieth century be seen as the champion of 'liberal' Catholicism; it is partly because, poor fellow, he was hoist with his own petard. When he joined the Church of Pio Nono and the Irish bishops, he discovered what bigotry and superstition really were. It is simply impossible to believe his claim in Part VII of the *Apologia* that 'I never had one doubt.' It is not compatible with his admission that 'it was not logic that carried me on; as well might one say that the quick-silver in the barometer changes the weather. It is the concrete being that reasons; pass a number of years, and I find my mind in a new place; how? the whole man moves; paper logic is but the record of it.'[25]

This is one of the most memorable paragraphs in nineteenth-century literature; but, fascinatingly, the self-obsessed John Newman, who was able to beguile the young into a besotted love for him which he evidently shared, never gives us a picture of 'the whole man'. His spiritual autobiography swims in and out of two distinct modes. The first is that of an ecclesiastical obsessive who would appear never to have had any thoughts or emotions which were not directed towards church, church, church: church dogmatics, church politics, Low Church versus High Church, the Church of England versus the Church of Rome, the Primitive Church versus the Ultramontane Church of modern Roman Catholicism – these are the preoccupations of Newman's voluminous writings. You will scour his enormously prolix correspondence for much in the way of humour. Unintentional comedy is to be found only in a marvellously long (and vituperative) attack on a fellow-cleric who has failed to take his share of domestic duties, and has left others to make the cocoa of an evening, the closest we get to secular diversion.[26] He hardly ever pauses, even when writing to his mother or his sisters, to comment on affairs of the day, let alone to indulge in humour or small-talk. Even when he discusses Jane Austen it is in terms of 'what vile creatures her "odious" parsons are!' (Is this the right word to use of the charming Henry Tilney? Or Edmund Bertram?) 'She has not a dream of the high Catholic [ethos].'[27]

But in the midst of this fusty ecclesiastical bigotry, there is also the figure who, Lytton Strachey believed, had he only been educated at Cambridge, would have turned into a minor poet. This other John Henry Newman is able, better almost than anyone in the English language, to describe religious belief from the inside: to speak about the actual experience of knowing, and believing in, God. Strangely, after a lifetime of poring over the Apostolic and later Fathers, breaking off friendships because he could not agree with this don or that about baptismal regeneration, assessing when exactly he began to lose faith in the validity of Anglican sacraments, et cetera, et cetera, his inner life of prayer would seem to have been as subjective as that of a total Protestant such as Kierkegaard. As a child, he tells us, 'I used to wish the Arabian Tales were true; my imagination ran on unknown influences, on magical powers, and talismans ... I thought life might be a dream, or I an Angel and all this world a deception, my fellow-angels by a playful device concealing themselves from me, and deceiving me with the semblance of a material world ...'[28] His 'childish imaginations' made him 'rest in the thought of two and two only supreme and luminously self-evident beings, myself and my Creator'. And yet, after a lifetime of searching, and the accumulation of one of the largest private theological libraries in England, Newman was only able to tell us, 'I am a Catholic by virtue of my believing in a God; and if I am asked why I believe in a God, I answer that it is because I believe in myself, for I feel it impossible to believe in my own existence (and of that fact I am quite sure) without believing also in the existence of Him, who lives as a Personal, All-seeing, All-judging Being in my conscience.'[29] He thus appears to make the truth of Catholicism depend on Cartesian logic and solipsism.

When he was in his late sixties Newman wrote a justification for religious belief entitled *An Essay in Aid of a Grammar of Assent*. By now he had been a Roman Catholic for over twenty years. Catholic reviews of the book tended to be hostile[30] whereas the more kindly secular notices pointed out that far from relying on Catholic Scholastic philosophy to justify his arguments, Newman wrote in the tradition of Butler's *Analogy* and the Oriel 'Noetics' – in other words, in intellectual terms, he had not moved on at all since he was in his twenties.

How then do we explain the allure of Newman, and of the so-called Oxford Movement, for so many intelligent young men, and some young women, in the 1830s and the 1840s? When we consider the aesthetic effects of the movement – the restoration of Catholic ritual and worship to the sometimes rather boring liturgy of the Established Church – it is not hard to see why people liked *that*. But the aesthetic improvements consequent upon the Catholic Revival in the Church of England – the Gothic revival churches of Butterfield, G.E. Street, J.L. Pearson and Sedding – all happened years, decades, after Pusey, Newman and friends decided to be as obscurantist as they could in their view of the Church. Similarly, 'High Church' ways – vestments, incense, candles, and the like – formed no part of the worship of the Oxford Movement. That came later. Pusey was an enthusiast for it from the 1850s onwards; so was Gladstone; but in the early days, the worship of the High Church was indistinguishable from that of the Low – though the Oxford Tractarians might have cared more about such devotional customs as fasting before Communion, or going to confession.

So the allure was not that of music or mysterious church interiors. The extreme austerity of the Tractarian ethos appealed to the young. But it does seem chiefly to have been a matter of personal charm – Newman's charm – above anything else. This is the impression we derive from witnesses as different as Matthew Arnold (viewing Newman's early career) and Lord Rosebery (who rushed to Birmingham in 1891 to see Newman lying in state at the Oratory). Neither was a Catholic, but they saw Newman's whole life as a spiritual romance.

Newman's decision to become a Roman Catholic did not lead every High Churchman in that direction; but, as far as Oxford was affected, it lanced the boil or pricked the bubble of the Tractarian agitation. Mark Pattison, one of Newman's most fervent admirers, stood back from the brink. Little by little, as the years passed, Pattison lost his faith. 'Catholicism dropped off me as another husk which I had outgrown,' he wrote, forty years on when, as the crabby old Rector of Lincoln College, he had become one of the most eminent of the reforming dons in the University. Not for him the foolish sacrifice of a comfortable college career for the sake of religious scruple. He simply kept quiet about his doubts, noting that Newman's conversion was

a deliverance from a nightmare which had oppressed Oxford for fifteen years. For so long we had been given over to discussions unprofitable in themselves, and which had entirely diverted our thoughts from the true business of the place[31] ...

A.P. Stanley once said to me, 'How different the fortunes of the Church of England might have been if Newman had known German.' That puts the matter in a nutshell; Newman assumed and adorned the narrow basis on which Laud had stood 200 years before. All the grand development of human reason, from Aristotle down to Hegel, was a sealed book to him.[32]

The battle-lines – High Church versus Broad Church – must seem to some readers of these pages as esoteric and as incomprehensible as the disputes in contemporary Islam between Shi'ite and Sunni Muslims. This is particularly the case since the issues about which they quarrelled – appointments to Irish bishoprics, or the Hampden controversy, when a man was appointed to the Regius Chair of Divinity at Oxford in 1836 and the 'Highs' suspected him of being unsound – really have become old, forgotten, far-off things. Lilliputian as it all seems at times, however, the nature of the controversies turned out, as they emerged, to be quite penetrating. More was at stake than whether the Big-ender or the Little-ender got the Regius Chair or the Bampton Lectureship. It was a question, first, of what the Church was, and who God was and whether He was knowable; ultimately, whether He existed at all. By the most tortuous and tortured of routes, the death of God came to be discussed and aired, even at Oxford.

The leaders of the two camps in the 1830s were Thomas Arnold and John Henry Newman. Newman had started as an evangelical, had then been elected to a fellowship at Oriel, fallen under the spell of the High Church John Keble, and begun to see that, for religion to be true, it had to be a revealed religion. Basically, Newman thought this because the only philosophy he had ever mastered was that of the English empiricists – notably John Locke and Bishop Butler, with a smattering of Hume. Obviously, he fought shy of the out-and-out scepticism of Hume, but he was prepared to use it, once he began to develop as a strong churchman, to expose the inadequacy of the alternative ways of viewing the Church. As he and his friends understood the Church, it had to be a divinely-founded society, or it was nothing. It had to have its origins in the Incarnate God, descending to earth and appointing Twelve Apostles to continue His word and His presence on earth. That meant that for Newman and his friends, the bishops and priests of the Church – even the bishops of the Church of England in the reign of William IV – had to be seen as possessed of this divinely-given apostolic authority. And when it was discovered, little by little, that there were insuperable difficulties about seeing the Church of England in this light – the fact, for example, that most, perhaps all, Anglican bishops of the period did not hold this view of themselves – then Newman and his friends left for the Church of Rome; yet some of them remained, as a puzzled and puzzling but rather beautiful presence in the Church of England, singing the Lord's Song in a strange land.

It was because Newman and friends believed that the Church of England *ought* to be immediately identifiable with the purer church of Primitive Times that they wrote their tracts and evolved their austere system of piety; and they were dismayed by any expressions of infidelity or of unbelief in, for example, the actual power, *ex opere operato*, of the waters of Baptism to cancel out sin; the real presence of Christ in the Eucharist; et cetera, et cetera.

Thomas Arnold was once a Fellow of Oriel and a friend of John Keble also. It would have been difficult to find a man more different from

Newman in temperament. Newman was (constitutionally if not, it need hardly be said, in practice) homosexual, Arnold robustly heterosexual – hence his leaving celibate Oriel early to marry; and to run a school from his country parish, and then become headmaster of Rugby School in Warwickshire.

Arnold was quite as horrified as Newman by the general infidelity of the age. As a public-school headmaster, he came face to face with it very violently. The headmaster of Winchester, Dr Moberly, said of the period that 'the tone of young men at the University, whether they came from Winchester, Eton, Rugby, Harrow, or wherever else, was universally irreligious. A religious undergraduate was very rare, very much laughed at when he appeared.'[33]

From the moment he arrived at Rugby, Arnold determined to change all that. Rather than worrying himself too much about how Christianity or the Church were to be defined, he saw that there was an abundant difference between those who did and did not lead Christian lives. 'I wish to make the point,' he says in one of his letters, 'not [of] the truth of Christianity per se, as a theorem to be proved, but [of] the wisdom of our abiding by it, and whether there is any thing else for it but the life of the beast or of the devil.'[34] He saw things much more as Dostoevsky would, later in the century, when he made Ivan Karamazov say that if God did not exist, anything would be permitted. At Rugby when Arnold arrived he found a great deal was permitted among the boys by schoolmasters too weak or too frightened to alter them – drunkenness and violence and sexual licence on a scale which distressed him. He found what a wit of an earlier generation, the Reverend Sidney Smith, had described as a 'system of premature debauchery'.

As we can read in one of Arnold's chief hero-worshippers Thomas Hughes's novel *Tom Brown's Schooldays*, there were still instances of sadistic bullying even in the Doctor's day. But Arnold very largely transformed the school. Without being homosexual he was that much more unusual person, one who liked boys. He befriended them; so did his wife. The chosen favourites began to absorb his values. Although Arnold is caricatured, most amusingly of all in Lytton Strachey's *Eminent Victorians*, as the inventor of the Victorian Public School with its aim to make Christian gentlemen by means of cold baths, organized games and a smattering of Classical learning, he was primarily an intellectual. He was a good historian, who became Regius Professor of Modern History at Oxford and did an edition of Thucydides. He saw, with an historian's clarity of vision, that Europe as a whole faced a choice: life with or without God. Those who wished to pursue godliness were, as far as Arnold was concerned, on the side of Christ; there was no need, at that critical juncture of history, when so many Europeans had abandoned Christianity altogether, to be tightening the entrance requirements to the Church as if it were a holy club; anyone who professed and called himself a Christian was a member of the Church, by Arnold's definition. And it made no sense at all, from his point of view, to force everyone who went to Oxford, for example, to subscribe to the Articles of the Church of England. Let Methodists and Presbyterians and others come in, and let them be welcomed as fellow-Christians.

The only drawback for Arnold's brighter pupils, when they came up to Oxford, was that they found the standard set by the dons so much lower than their masters' at Rugby. One of his pupils wrote in an American magazine:

> I went to Oxford from the sixth form (the highest class) of a public school. I had at that time read all Thucydides, except the sixth and seventh books; the first six books of Herodotus ... I had read five plays, I think, of Sophocles, four of Aeschylus ... four or perhaps five, of Euripides, considerable portions of Aristophanes; nearly all the 'Odyssey'; only about a third of the 'Iliad', but that several times over; one or two dialogues of Plato ... not quite all Virgil; all Horace; a great deal of Livy and Tacitus: a considerable portion of Aristotle's 'Rhetoric', and two or three books of his 'Ethics' ... No words can express the amount of change which I experienced on entering the lecture-rooms of my college – though confessedly one of the very best in Oxford – and on embarking on the course of University study. Had I not read pretty nearly all the books? Was I to go on, keeping up my Latin prose writers, for three years more? ... The daily lectures now, and the weary re-examination in classics three years ahead. An infinite lassitude and impatience, which I saw reflected in the faces of others, quickly began to infect me ...[35]

The career of this Old Rugbeian, Arthur Hugh Clough, amply demonstrates what happened to a sensitive and intelligent young man caught up in the religious controversies of Oxford in the 1830s. Clough came from a line of parsons and squires on the Welsh borders, but his father, a younger son, became a cotton merchant and took the family out to live in Charleston, South Carolina. When he was ten, they dispatched young Arthur back to England to be educated, and it is clear from his ten-year-old self that his religious and aesthetic sensibilities were already highly developed. 'Were you not grieved', he wrote at this tender age to his sister, 'to hear that magnificent building York Minster had been partly destroyed through the destructive means of fire? What a short time it appears since we heard the sounds proceeding from that majestic organ, since we viewed those elegant arches now a heap of blackened ruins ...' His correspondent was aged eight.[36] In grown-up life the ruins he was to survey were of the faith itself.

Clough was one of Dr Arnold's very favourite pupils and, because his parents were abroad, he befriended the whole Arnold family, including the future poet Matt, Tom (whose own religious journey could fill a book, and has), and the sisters. He used to go for merry walking holidays with the Arnolds, staying at their Lake District home, Fox How. Dr Arnold was his hero; and Clough, by the time he left Rugby, was undeniably a rather priggish figure. His astonishment at the low intellectual level of Oxford can only have been matched by that at his discovery that there were some people who did not regard The Doctor in the rosy light which surrounded him in the eyes of the better sixth-formers at Rugby. Newman, in one of the bitchier passages of his *Apologia*, wrote, 'It was the success of the Liberal cause which fretted me inwardly. At this time I was specially annoyed with Dr Arnold ... Some one, I think, asked in conversation at Rome, whether a certain interpretation of Scripture was Christian? it was answered that Dr Arnold took it; I interposed, "But is *he* a Christian?" ...'[37] Clough's mathematical tutor was the most amiable of the Newmanite bigots, W.G. Ward. He was a good-humoured man (heterosexual, incidentally, and early married) but as 'extreme' as they came in his High Church views. An old clergyman, the Reverend Bloxam (certainly not heterosexual, but that is another, and sad, tale), recollected to Ward's son a dinner party which took place in Ward's rooms at Balliol at which the guests were himself, Oakeley, and Newman and Clough – 'all Tractarians except Clough. Bloxham said that before dinner was over, the strained relations between Clough and Ward became very apparent, and Clough was so evidently pained and distressed by the views of all the others that Ward broke up his party before the usual hour.'[38]

Clough was one of the few Oxford men of his generation to admit, to himself and to others, that he was an out-and-out unbeliever, an atheist.

His Balliol diaries show what a difficult (indeed heroic) emotional journey was involved in forcing his heart to follow his head in this matter. Having made the journey, he was able to write some of the sharpest, best-crafted, and most acerb verse of the nineteenth century.

His friends watched his short career, aghast. When he died at forty-two they were naturally grief-stricken. He had been lovable, sweet-natured, funny; and there was always a feeling about him that his talents had been left unfulfilled. But opinion divided between those who saw, with James Russell Lowell, that 'Clough will be thought a hundred years hence to have been the truest expression in verse of the moral and intellectual tendencies, the doubt and the struggle towards settled convictions of the period in which he lived',[39] and those who more or less accused him of having died of Doubt. Matthew Arnold, who when his beliefs were boiled down really believed as little as Clough in a personal God, asked absurdly in *Thyrsis*, 'Too quick despairer, wherefore wilt thou go?' Clough died, not of despair, but of malarial fever contracted in a cheap hotel in the Pyrenees. It is easy to imagine what the mocking voice of Clough the poet would have made of *Thyrsis*, with its lush and 'poetic' descriptions of Oxford.

It seems paradoxical to describe such a mainstream figure as the Master of Balliol as an unclassifiable original, but this was true of Benjamin Jowett (1817–1893) – as far as we are concerned with the Victorian attitude to God.[40] Today, if we have heard of him at all, it is perhaps as a caricature snob-celibate don, with a high alto voice and a taste for duchesses. He turns up in a thousand nineteenth-century anecdotes. After an excruciating reading of one of Tennyson's poems Jowett advised, 'I should not publish that if I were you'; to which the Poet Laureate replied in his Lincolnshire accent, 'Come to that, Master' – a short *a* – 'the sherry you gave us at dinner was filthy.' We know Jowett as the subject of rhymes – what he did not know wasn't knowledge, and so on. He is important in the history of university reform. The subject known at Oxford as 'Greats' or *Literae Humaniores* – a combination of Latin and Greek Literature, Ancient History, Ancient and modern philosophy – was more or less Jowett's invention. Strings of British prime ministers, foreign secretaries, senior civil servants, barristers, bishops, owe their particular cast of mind, their youthful training, in some measure to the syllabus of Jowett's devising. To this extent, he was an embodiment of the Establishment. And yet, like so many 'Establishment' figures, he was something of an outsider. His father was an unsuccessful furrier, and Jowett was a scholarship boy at St Paul's School. Rather than knowing the public school world of Eton, Rugby or Winchester he spent his adolescence very much alone, since his father was too improvident or unsuccessful to have a fixed abode and throughout his schooldays Jowett lodged, by himself, in the City Road, London. The family religion, to which he adhered on winning the Balliol scholarship, was evangelical, and he never felt tempted to make the switch, once he'd come up to the Oxford of Keble, Newman and Pusey, to the narrow Church parties. Throughout his life Jowett was that rather attractive mixture, a person of profound religious feeling and a sceptical cast of mind. Neither the pious emotions nor the intellectual questions could be satisfied with the mere toeing of some English Church party line, High or Low.

Jowett's great work, when he became a tutor at Balliol and later Regius Professor of Greek – before becoming, for the last thirty years of his life, the Master of the college he loved and adorned – was his translation of the Dialogues of Plato, with his own commentary. He would certainly have agreed with A.N. Whitehead's *mot* that 'the safest general characterisation of the European philosophical tradition is that it consists of a series of footnotes to Plato'. And he was by temperament far more inclined to an idealist than an empiricist view in philosophy. Like other clever boys of his age he was made to read Butler and carefully selected bits of Hume when he came to Oxford. He was able to see that Humean empiricism ended by defeating itself, making knowledge itself, let alone faith, impossible; equally, the demands on obedience made by those who insisted on the reality of a revealed religion were an insult to Jowett's free and inquiring intellect.

Unlike most Oxford men of his age, he knew that there was an alternative. When his friend Arthur Penrhyn Stanley (destined to be Dean of Westminster – he is the little boy Arthur who risks the ridicule of his dormitory in *Tom Brown's Schooldays* by daring to kneel down and say his prayers) had finished his magnificent hagiography of his hero Dr Arnold, Jowett proposed that the pair of them take a holiday in Germany. They set off in the summer of 1844, with Liddell and Scott's enormous and newly published Greek *Lexicon*, and with one copy of Kant's *Kritik der reinen Vernunft*, which they took it in turn to read and analyse. They attended various philological conferences, but the most exciting and important thing Jowett did was to meet Erdmann of

Halle – the meeting took place in Dresden. Erdmann was Hegel's representative on earth. The two young Englishmen were thirteen years too late to meet Hegel himself, but meeting Erdmann was the next best thing.

Jowett never became a full-blown Hegelian. There was always a part of him which, as Geoffrey Faber his biographer says, was 'salty' and empirical; there was an even larger part of him which was so Platonist that it did not need Hegel. A typical Jowettism, this:

> Hegel is untrue, I sometimes fancy, not in the sense of being erroneous, but practically, because it is a consciousness of truth, becoming thereby error. It is very difficult to express what I mean, for it is something which does not make me value Hegel the less as a philosopher. The problem of Truth idealized and yet in action, he does not seem to me to have solved; the Gospel of St John does.[41]

There is a brilliance about this remark. Of course, all the churchy bigots regarded Jowett as a complete heretic, and he spent his life, after he came to fame and prominence, being denounced by them. But he was something of a mystic, so that although he never for a moment believed in the Thirty-nine Articles or the literal truth of miracle-stories in the New Testament, he believed deeply in God and in Christ.

At first glance, certainly, idealism, the German version, seemed like the best approach for an attack on the dead hand of materialism and empiricism. The extent to which Hegel's God – mentioned so frequently in that philosopher's works – is the same as the God of Christianity can always be a subject of debate. Is Hegel's God Personal? The community of the Spirit in Hegel consists in the Spiritual Community, or the Church. But this is not understood as Newman and friends would have understood it in using the word. It is not the laying-on of apostolic hands, still less a sacramental 'magic' which constitutes the Hegelian community. The perfected community of enlightened ones is itself, in Hegel's world, God. And he chose, when describing this community, an impersonal word, *Gemeinde*, 'whose ordinary meaning quite excludes any idea of personal unity'.[42]

Jowett was a great teacher rather than himself an original metaphysician. This is what makes his visit to Germany so important – and so different from Pusey's visit to Göttingen and Berlin nearly twenty years before. Whereas Pusey came back to England and decided that there were storms ahead and it was time to batten down the hatches, Jowett returned with a feeling of liberation.

Intellectual history is distorted, even more than other forms of history, by hindsight. It's a funny sort of memory that only works backwards, as Alice learns. We see ideas coming along, and being adopted with enthusiasm; but we also see them being put into practice and discredited, if they are religious or political ideas; or we see them, if they are theoretical notions, through the lens of the next set of ideas. Calvinism, which was the religion of young people and revolutionaries in the 1540s, becomes the dour backbone of terrifying theocracies in Switzerland. Hegelianism likewise is viewed – still – with the disdain of those materialist or empiricist philosophers of the Moore and Russell generation who tired of the more flatulent, airy effusions of the late British 'Hegelians'. Later metaphysicians laugh at the Hegelian concept that relations cannot be detected empirically; that you cannot understand what a concept is, or would be, unless you can also grasp the nature of its opposite. This fundamental Hegelian principle of thesis and antithesis, which seems so unsubstantial when weighed beside 'common-sense' empiricism, actually arises from a philosophical difficulty which the empiricists never solved – and which is, as far as one can see, insoluble: you cannot detect *relations*, empirically. The concept of thesis and antithesis was a useful tool at a certain juncture of history, to demonstrate this puzzling *lacuna*. The fact that very few thinkers could now be content with Hegelian solutions to metaphysical questions does not mean that the questions go away. Consider Quine's scepticism about modal logic and the doctrine of ontological relativity (by the ontology of any particular theory, we mean the range of objects which must exist in order for it to be true). Quine comes from an empirical position, and holds one which could be said to be the very opposite of Hegel's; what he calls his 'physicalism' or his naturalism insists that the physical facts are all the facts. But about our mode of perceiving facts he has pointed out that there is no non-relative fact, no fact which does not relate to another fact. Hegelianism might have been unsuccessful in the attempt it made to declare this state of things, but it was nevertheless observing a particular difficulty: a difficulty which the English empirical school could not grasp. 'Being both is and is not,' said Jowett one day in a lecture in his duchessy tones. An undergraduate sniggered. 'You may laugh, Mr Dugdale,' said the voice from the podium, 'but you will find it is true.'

Of all Jowett's pupils, the one who did the most to popularize what one could call religious Hegelianism was Thomas Hill Green (1836–1882). A rough straw-poll taken among my educated but non-philosophical acquaintances would suggest that Green is all but unheard-of today; that he has vanished almost without trace, except among historians of philosophy. And yet, if you had asked a young person at university in England in the 1880s who was the greatest British philosopher, they would almost certainly have named Green. Perhaps his prodigious success irritated Jowett; certainly the Master of Balliol became alarmed by the effect of Green's preaching on the young, since in his old age Jowett distanced himself from his earlier enthusiasm for Hegel. The extent to which Green himself was a thoroughgoing Hegelian is perhaps of small interest to a generation barely aware that he existed. On the one hand we have the story – more famous than Green himself, for I find those who know it without knowing who said it – of Green telling Sidgwick, 'I looked into Hegel the other day and found it a strange Wirrwarr'; and on the other there is the recommendation to his English readers to abandon the study of the Empiricists Locke and Hume – 'the anachronistic systems prevalent among us' – for the two great German metaphysicians.[43]

Green's old mentor Jowett watched his intellectual development with the mixed feelings which must often be awakened by the success of a less talented (in general) protégé. Green's writings have a kind of earnest heaviness which Jowett's introductions to Plato, or his essay on 'The Interpretation of Scripture', refreshingly lack. But it was in fact from a religious point of view that Jowett viewed Green askance. By the 1870s Jowett, now Master of Balliol, was complaining that 'metaphysics exercise a fatal influence over the mind'. To an earlier generation, Jowett was a heretic; but he at least held on to a belief in Christ, somehow or another. Green had abandoned even this. The progress of 'liberal' theological thought is always like this. One generation's dangerous liberal seems old-fashioned by the standards of the next, until belief has trickled away altogether and it is time for a hard-line religious revival.

As he grew older Jowett was, in any event, more Platonic than Hegelian, though he did accept in 1884 the gift of a bust of the great metaphysician from Lord Arthur Russell. It was placed in the library at Balliol. 'Though not a Hegelian, I think I have gained more from Hegel than from any other philosopher.' Of the bust he observed, 'Hegel looks quite a gentleman.' Lord Quinton adds, 'we may perhaps see this as a symbol of the satisfactory absorption of Hegelianism into British intellectual life'. And this absorption took place very largely through the influence of Green, who persuaded two generations of undergraduates that philosophy was meant as 'a training for public life'. 'This conviction was common to politicians so diverse in their creeds as Asquith and Milner, churchmen like Gore and Scott Holland, social reformers like Arnold Toynbee. It was under Asquith's government that the foundations of the modern welfare state were laid ...'[44]

In a sense, Green's greatest literary work was not one he wrote himself but the novel written by Mrs Humphry Ward four years after his death – *Robert Elsmere,* a best-seller of the 1880s which revisits the intellectual and spiritual atmosphere of her father Tom Arnold's day. The hero is a young clergyman who starts out full of fervour, but who loses his faith as a result of the cynical conversation of the learned local landowner, Squire Wendover, whose acerb and uncompromising scepticism seems impossible to answer. Mrs Humphry Ward is extremely good at describing the heartbreak of losing faith: 'A month ago, every word of that hectic young pleader for Christ and the Christian certainties would have roused in him a leaping passionate sympathy – the heart's yearning assent even when the intellect was most perplexed' – so feels young Elsmere after listening to an evangelical preacher. 'Now that inmost strand had given way. Suddenly the disintegrating force he had been so pitifully, so blindly holding at bay had penetrated once and for all into the sanctuary! What had happened to him had been the first real failure of *feeling*, the first treachery of the *heart*.'[45]

The late Warden Sparrow of All Souls was not the first to identify Squire Wendover with the crabby old Rector of Lincoln, Mark Pattison,[46] though I should have thought there was as good a case for seeing touches of Pattison both in the the squire and in Elsmere's Oxford friend Langham, who recognizes his own defects of nature and longs to be loved by beautiful women. But whether Wendover is Pattison or not, no one doubts that the saintly 'Mr Gray', who rescues Elsmere from out-and-out cynicism, is a simple portrait of Green. Having exposed himself to 'the speculative ferment of Germany and the far profaner scepticism of France', Elsmere finds his Christian faith is in tatters. He has to resign his Holy Orders. But he discovers in Mr Gray a man who, while rejecting miracles and indeed most manifestations of the supernatural, is guided by a fervent sense of the Mystery, and a rather priggish (to our tastes) religion of humanity. Elsmere finds (self-) satisfaction in working in the poorer parts of London and teaching evening classes to the workers on such subjects as botany, zoology and modern New Testament criticism. Henry James, when implored by Mrs Ward to comment on whether he thought it well written, replied that he did not think her novel was *written* at all. For many readers, though, it certainly hit the spot, selling in its hundreds of thousands. By the mid 1880s the loss of faith which had hitherto tormented only a few of the better-informed had reached the suburbs. Mr Gray's waffle seems to suggest redemption through Hegel – but it is Hegel-and-soda. We must turn away from these late manifestations of English Hegelianism and consider the much more devastating Hegelian import of forty years before: namely, Strauss's Life of Jesus and the critical assaults on the very foundations of Biblical belief.

7

George Eliot, The Word, and Lives of Jesus

'This sublime person, who each day still presides over the destiny of the world, we may call divine, not in the sense that Jesus has absorbed all the divine, or has been adequate to it (to employ an expression of the schoolmen) but in the sense that Jesus is the one who has caused his fellow-men to make the greatest step towards the divine.'

Renan

I am sure this Jesus will not do
Either for Englishman or Jew

Blake

THE PAINTING WHICH came to be known as *Christ in the house of his parents*,[1] by John Everett Millais (1829–1896), would strike many late twentieth-century eyes as almost saccharine in its piety. The boy Jesus, with clean hair parted over his pleasant pink English face, stands centre-canvas beside his father's work-bench. He has injured his hand – a heavy foreshadowing of his ultimate and terrible destiny. His adoring mother is on her knees beside him, offering a cheek to be kissed. Without turning to look at Joseph, Jesus holds up his wounded hand towards the carpenter to be caressed. An actual carpenter sat for the body of Joseph but, thinking it impious to depict the face as that of an artisan, Millais painted the head of his own impeccably bourgeois father as the chaste spouse of The Blessed Virgin. With eyes cast down the other figures in the scene, clearly assistants and servants, pursue their appointed tasks with appropriate humility. Sheep outside the door gaze dotingly towards the Good Shepherd.

But when the picture was first exhibited at the Royal Academy in the summer of 1850, it excited a frenzied controversy. The artist was an astonishing twenty years old when he produced this technically polished work. To the Hanging Committee of the Academy, it had seemed risqué. 'It had few admirers' among the academicians, as the grandest of their number and the painting's first great defender, Mulready, admitted. One Royal Academician protested 'there are many to whom his work will be seen a pictorial blasphemy',[2] and this proved to be the case. The mysteriously named PRB, to which Millais belonged, was an as yet undiscovered group. Few knew that the initials on their canvases stood for Pre-Raphaelite Brotherhood; when once they did, it was not known whether the PRB were crypto-pagan or crypto-Catholic, nor was it easy to decide which would have been worse. *Christ in the house of his parents* seemed to offer a good opportunity to attack the youngest member of the group. *Blackwood's Magazine* led off with 'We can hardly imagine anything more ugly, graceless and unpleasant than Mr Millais's picture of Christ in the Carpenter's shop'.[3] *The Times* warned its readers that 'Mr Millais's principal picture is to speak plainly revolting. The attempt to associate the holy family with the meanest details of a carpenter's shop, with no conceivable omission of misery, of dirt, even of disease, all finished with the same loathsome meticulousness, is disgusting ...'[4]

Charles Dickens, in his own periodical *Household Words*, said the picture was 'mean, odious, revolting and repulsive'.[5] You might think that Dickens, with his keen sense of the ridiculous, would have seen something funny in all these stuffy gentlemen in their clean shirts and frock coats expecting the carpenter's shop at Nazareth to be 'respectable'. Not a bit of it. Even when, a few years later, he met Millais, Dickens felt constrained to write pompously to the young painter: 'My opinion of that point is not in the least changed but it has never dashed my admiration of your progress in what I suppose are higher and better things.'[6]

The painting had touched some raw nerves – nerves which were to remain a-jangle in nineteenth-century Europe for at least another fifty years whenever the subject of the true person of Jesus, His actual nature, was raised.

Dickens's own life of Jesus, *The Life of Our Lord*, written for the edification of his children, follows the Bible story fairly closely, while quietly removing from it the notion that Christ's death was an atoning sacrifice for sin. 'Because he did such Good, and taught people how to love God and how to hope to go to Heaven after death, he was called Our Saviour.'[7] That is not, of course, theology's reason for calling Him the Saviour; and note the capital G for *Good* and the lower case for *he*. Dickens's religion was of a fairly unsophisticated character, and is best summed up by the peroration to his book:

Remember! It is Christianity *to do Good* always – even to those who do evil to us. It is Christianity to love our neighbour as ourself, and to do to all men as we would have them Do to us. It is Christianity to be gentle, merciful and forgiving and to keep those qualities quiet in our own hearts, and never make a boast of them, or of our prayers or of our love of God, but always to do right in everything. If we do this, and remember the life and lessons of Our Lord Jesus Christ, and try to act up to them, we may confidently hope that God will forgive us our sins and mistakes, and enable us to live and die in Peace.[8]

It is probably safe to say that this cheerfully Pelagian viewpoint (which Saints Paul and Augustine, not to mention Aquinas, or Calvin and Luther, would not have recognized as Christianity at all) was the religious outlook of the majority of British Protestants in the last century. Jesus in this view of things need, logically, be no more than a prophet of kindliness, like Traddles or the brothers Cheeryble or many another warm-hearted fellow in Dickens's own fictions. No one, though, should expect logic when human beings start to ask themselves what they think of Christ. Liberal Protestants like Dickens could react just as brittly as full-blown Catholics if they felt that Jesus the Divine Saviour was being treated as if He were 'just a man'. It was the growing sense that this indeed was all that He was or had been – a man, and not a god – which lay at the heart of the nineteenth-century loss of faith. The very attempts to write 'Lives of Jesus', or to treat the Gospels as if they were biographies, were themselves symptomatic of the change which had come upon human sensibility in the period we are considering. There is no medieval *Vie de Jésus*. So long as Jesus was an object of piety, and such an object alone, it was somehow imaginatively impossible to investigate Him as if He were just another historical character. Although theology had always taught that He was *very man* as well as *very God*, there was a hair-fine borderline between acceptance of the humanity and rejection of the Divinity. Hence the edginess caused by Millais's picture. If the crowds who flocked to see it or who wrote 'disgusted' letters about it to *The Times* had been one hundred per cent certain that it was a blasphemy they would have reacted, presumably, as Muslims in the twentieth century have reacted to works of art which they deem offensive to their creed. There would have been riots. Millais's life, perhaps, would have been threatened. As it was, he ended his days full of honour. When they buried him in St Paul's Cathedral in 1896 he was a baronet, a Grand Officier du Légion d'Honneur, and President of the Royal Academy. The nerve he had touched as a youth was not the bedrock of Christian piety but the fear, underlying so much of Victorian imaginative life, that Christianity was not true, or at least not as true as their forefathers had once supposed.

Until the eighteenth century, scepticism in Western Europe had been largely silent when the historical plausibility of the New Testament was in question. The generation of Gibbon and Voltaire was the first openly to cast doubt on the authenticity of stories of a virginal conception, or of a human form which could walk on water. Such profanities continued to shock the pious, but they inevitably planted irremovable worries, and worries which grew to doubts, in the literalist mind. How much of this actually *happened*? Since Christianity purports to be a religion rooted in historical reality, these questions are of more than peripheral concern. The Creeds, as conventionally understood by the huge majority of Christians since the earliest days, had spoken of a Deity who chose to become incarnate at a particular juncture in human affairs, at a particular time and place – in the city of Nazareth, of a woman called Mary. The miraculous birth, as foretold to prophets, took place at Bethlehem, at a definable date – in the reign of Herod the King. These do not at first sight read like Myths. We are not told that Perseus rescued Andromeda at a particular date, when So-and-so was king. The Gospels, in their very rootedness to a verifiable history, entwine into their story not merely narratives about Jesus but thoughts and claims about God Himself. In the Fourth Gospel, in particular, Jesus is quoted as saying that no one comes to the Father, except through Him, that He is the Way, the Truth and the Life. Such claims, if made by an historical personage who subsequently rose from the dead, would compel an awe-struck belief. But supposing such words had not been said? Supposing the Gospels, like every other written papyrus in the ancient world, were products of a purely human and collective endeavour? Supposing they reflected not so much a literalist reality in the year 30 AD as the faith and beliefs of Christian communities in the year 60, 80, 100 AD? Supposing they came from communities which had only the haziest memories of Jesus Himself, and were written from the point of view of people who were deeply immersed in a mystery-cult with 'Jesus' as its focus? Then the historical Jesus might turn out, on impartial historical investigation, to be a figure very different from the Jesus of Faith. And if this were the case, would not Christianity begin to look like all the other religions in human history, a human construct, rather than a divine revelation?

There were many ways in which nineteenth-century men or women could lose their faith, but in the Protestant world, where from childhood the Gospels were the ultimate object of reverence, such an undermining would have a cataclysmic effect. And if there was one book which did more than any other to popularize this destructive work, it was *Das Leben Jesu* by David Friedrich Strauss (1808–1874), published in 1835–6. The Germans, then as now, were the supreme theological geniuses of the Western world. Theology was to all intents and purposes a German subject, as Dr Pusey in England had woefully discovered. The diehard bigot conservatives like Pusey at least perceived one truth which was invisible to the liberal Protestants: that there is very little 'evidence' when these matters are in question, and that anything people say about the Gospels is likely to reflect what they already believe, rather than what they have discovered as a result of research.

The rich old Birmingham businessman and radical politician, Joseph Parkes, believed that Strauss's *Leben Jesu* would yield up a dispassionate, historical account of what 'really happened'.[9] As a Unitarian, Parkes had already made up his mind what happened, but he wanted to read Strauss to confirm his prejudices. The actual result horrified him, because the depths of unbelief in Strauss's work appeared to dismantle the very basis of theism itself.

Strauss's agenda is made abundantly clear in the Conclusion to his *Life of Jesus*: 'There is little of which we can say for certain that it took place, and of all to which the faith of the Church especially attaches itself, the miraculous and supernatural matter in the facts and destinies of Jesus, it is far more certain that it did not take place.' The shift in this sentence, from agnosticism about New Testament evidences to an *a priori* dogmatic assertion that no such evidence could ever exist, is an honest demonstration of Strauss's Hegelian viewpoint. He starts with the belief that the History of Jesus is 'mythical'; he moves, from this premiss, to a demonstration that each episode in the Gospel narrative lacks historical plausibility.

> That the happiness of mankind is to depend upon belief in things of which it is in part certain that they did not take place, in part uncertain whether they did take place, and only to the smallest extent beyond doubt that they took place – that the happiness of mankind is to depend upon belief in such things as these is so absurd that the assertion of the principle does not, at the present day, require any further contradictions.

The key phrase here is 'the present day', since for the Hegelians (and for this purpose Auguste Comte and his followers may be counted as Hegelians) it was axiomatic that the human race *moved on* in its perceptions, so that what was acceptable as a mode of understanding or expression in one age became obsolete merely by the passage of time. In the Hegelian view of things, a proposition could be 'true' if stated in the reign of Constantine, and false if repeated in the reign of Friedrich Wilhelm III. Whereas in earlier ages it was possible to believe in the myth of the Incarnation as if it were an objective reality, for post-Kantian humanity the primary *a priori* starting-point of any intellectual investigation is not the existence of God but the workings of human consciousness.

> This is the meaning of the profound saying of Spinoza, that for the purposes of happiness, it is not in any way necessary to know Christ after the flesh; but that the case is different with that eternal Son of God, namely the Divine Wisdom, which appears in all things, especially in the human mind, and in Jesus Christ appeared in a pre-eminent degree. Without this, he says, no one can attain to happiness, because it alone teaches what is true and false, good and bad. Kant, like Spinoza, distinguished between the historical person of Jesus and the Ideal of humanity pleasing to God, involved in human reason, or in the moral sense in its perfect purity, so far as is possible in a system of the world dependent upon wants and inclinations. To rise to this ideal was, he said, the general duty of men; and though we cannot conceive of it as existing otherwise than under the form of a perfect man, and though it is not impossible that such a man may have lived, as we are all intended to resemble this ideal, still it is not necessary that we should know of the existence of such a man or believe in it, but solely that we should keep that ideal before us, recognize it as obligatory upon us, and strive to make ourselves like it.[10]

The Life of Jesus therefore becomes no more than a myth to embody our understanding of Kant's Categorical Imperative, our innate sense that we have a duty to eschew evil and to do good.

From the perspective of the late twentieth century, untouched by the Hegelian approach either to philosophy itself or to New Testament scholarship, Strauss's position has its own oddness. Empiricist philosophers have seen no grounds for believing in a Categorical Imperative; they have not even been sure what it is. Neo-Thomists have seen that a belief in the *a priori* truth of ethical value has itself a theological purport which Kant himself would probably have wished to deny. Wittgensteinians would want to say that there are areas of human experience of which language can say very little that is really useful or intelligible. The whole Hegelian–Idealist view of things now seems as obsolete, among most academic philosophers, as those mythic views of the world which it sought to displace. Likewise, New Testament scholarship has, since Albert Schweitzer's ground-breaking work on the impossibility of drawing Jesus in the liberal Protestant image, gradually recovered a picture of what first-century Messianic Judaism was actually like. The notion that it had very much to do with generalized concepts of an ideal or perfect humanity (as opposed to a very localized, and, to a modern mind, semi-intelligible Jewish aspiration for redemption and liberation from Roman rule) can have few, if any, followers today.

Meanwhile, there remains the more popular and religious purport of those stories. Even Marian Evans herself (George Eliot, 1819–1880), who had lost her faith before she wrote her translation of *Das Leben Jesu*, found herself psychosomatically exhausted by the Hegelians' treatment of the most sacred point of his narrative. Her friend Cara Bray reported in 1846 that she was 'Strauss-sick – it made her ill dissecting the beautiful story of the crucifixion, and only the sight of her Christ-image and picture [a cast of Thorvaldsen's figure of the risen Christ, and an engraving] made her endure it.'[11]

The new Hegelian religion, in which material events (if they happened at all) were mere manifestations of *Geist*, had so little in common with popular Christianity as actually practised by religious people that it had forgotten, astonishingly, the emotional effect of the story of the Crucifixion. J.A. Froude, who lost his faith at just about the period when George Eliot was translating Strauss, remembered the effect of hearing Newman preach in the 1830s in the University Church at Oxford on the subject of the Sacred Passion. 'Calm and passionless as marble', that hypnotic intellectual man spoke in his rapid and deliberately unemotional tones about the scourging, the crowning with thorns, the carrying of the Cross, the last agonies.

> For a few moments there was a breathless silence. Then, in a low, clear voice, of which the faintest vibration was audible in the farthest corner of St Mary's, he said, 'Now I bid you recollect that He to whom these things were done was Almighty God.' It was as if an electric stroke had gone through the church, as if every person present understood for the first time the meaning of what he had all his life been saying.[12]

Far more accessible than *Das Leben Jesu* of Strauss was Ernest Renan's *Vie de Jésus*, published in 1863 and instantly an international bestseller. Strauss had caused anguish in the Protestant world, but in the great sweep of Catholic Europe his impenetrable Hegelianisms could be safely ignored. It was rather less easy to turn a deaf ear to the sweet music of Renan the runaway seminarian. Renan's life (1823–1892), particularly in its early stages, might have been written by Balzac to exemplify the tensions and divisions in French society. His father's people were fishermen who had made a small fortune out of their Breton smack and built a neat, distinctly bourgeois residence in the port of Tréguier – an ancient diocese which had been suspended at the time of the Revolution. The father was an unbelieving Republican; the mother was a devout Catholic Royalist. Torn between the two opinions, the sensitive and highly intelligent Ernest was sent to the local ecclesiastical seminary where he won all the prizes and quickly advanced to the seminaries of St Nicholas du Chardonnet (patronized by clever scholarship boys, like himself, and the sons of the nobility) and St Sulpice. His ecclesiastical superiors recognized someone of uncommon ability, particularly in the Semitic tongues. He studied Hebrew, a rare accomplishment in the French Catholic Church of that date. He read the Book of Isaiah, and it struck him, as it has struck every patient reader of that text, that the first half – up to and including chapter 39 – is written in a quite different style from the second. The first half belongs to a phase of Jewish piety which predates the Babylonian exile, the second half to post-exilic times. No one now (outside extreme Protestant circles) worries themselves about such things. But until the Second Vatican Council in the early 1960s it was forbidden for any Roman Catholic to state, even in academic exercises, that 'Deutero-Isaiah' is a different author from Isaiah; or that 'the prophet Daniel' is obviously a late, fictitious work. Renan, as long ago as 1845, was shocked by the intellectual dishonesty of this. In October 1845, the very month that Newman became a Roman Catholic, Renan left the seminary, and a few weeks later he broke with the Church altogether.[13] He quickly changed – for in France, much more than in England, everything becomes politicized; or perhaps one should say, more overtly politicized. He discovered science – no one had told him about it in the seminary – and he was very excited. He discovered democracy – even more exciting. And embarked on what was to be his life's work, a study of the Origins of Christianity, and of the customs, languages and history of the Near East.

In 1857 the Chair of Hebrew at the Collège de France fell vacant. No one else in the country was so well-qualified as Renan to fill this post, but the Catholic Royalists were violently opposed to the election of the Spoiled Priest. To enable him to escape the rumpus the Emperor, Napoleon III, paid for Renan to go on a trip to Phoenicia. He extended the trip – undertaken with a beloved sister – throughout the Levant.

The immediate consequence of seeing for himself the 'lilies of the field' growing in Galilee was *La Vie de Jésus*. Though to the rigorous German critics of a later generation *La Vie de Jésus* was pretty-pretty, 'a Gospel in Dresden China',[14] this was not how it appeared in 1863. Whereas Strauss saw the Gospels as mythologies, and fitted them into a grand Hegelian world-view in which Jesus represented conceptions of the Deity current at a particular moment in human history, Renan came at the thing from a different angle. In many respects his Jesus remains the Jesus of Catholic piety. Renan amazes the modern reader, for example, by accepting the unhistorical notion that Jesus 'laid the foundations of a Church destined to endure'.[15] As a lapsed Catholic, Renan sees the Gospels as belonging to a *genre* comparable to medieval saints' lives – crammed with *legendary* material, but not myths. He saw them as basically true, though with liberal additions of magical or miraculous folk-tales in which we need not believe. His Jesus is wholly human.

> Obstacles irritated him. His idea of the Son of God became disturbed and exaggerated. Divinity has its intermittent lapses; one cannot be Son of God through a lifetime without a break. One is so at moments by flashes of illumination, lost amid long intervals of darkness. The fatal law which condemns an idea to decay as soon as it seeks to convert men applied to Jesus. Contact with men degraded him to their level ...[16]

To the pious Catholics of 1863 this was blasphemy. The old division – Royalist Catholic versus Republican atheist – which the Revolution had gouged into the heart of France was once more exposed. An extraordinary flow of denunciation – from pulpits, from right-wing presses and newspapers – descended upon poor, gentle Renan's head. 'Nier la divinité de Jésus-Christ, c'est nier tout,' said one reactionary author. 'C'est nier l'existence de Henri IV, de Louis XIV, ce serait douter de la vie de Napoléon 1er et ses triomphes, et le beau règne de notre Empereur, si remarquable en grandes choses ...'[17] Asseline, who set out in thirty-three ambitious but furious pages not only to denounce Renan but also to prove the existence of God, makes much of the Christian allegiance of kings, princes and governors. 'Si le livre de Renan était un bon livre, tous les grands de la terre, philosophes, magistrats, ministres, princes, les têtes couronnés ... qui mettent leur confiance en Jésus et en sa parole sainte et divine auraient été et seraient encore en butte à l'erreur et au mensonge d'un indigne trompeur.'[18] No mention is made of Jesus's own Jewish religion, nor of His marked preference – as against that of the magistrates and kings so beloved of Asseline – for the company of the poor. For Renan, Jesus preached 'Pure Ebionism – that is the doctrine that the poor (*ebionim*) alone shall be saved, that the reign of the poor is approaching. That was the doctrine of Jesus. "Woe unto you that are rich," said he, "for ye have received your consolation"; ...'[19] It was not long before one French commentator, identifying Renan's viewpoint with that of 'le philosophe juif',[20] Spinoza, helpfully pointed out that Renan had lined himself up with the Jews. Another would see *La Vie de Jésus* as 'Le Nouveau Crucifiement de Notre-Seigneur Jésus Christ'.[21]

Renan's book made a sensation in England, but a sensation of a less overtly political temper. Lord Shaftesbury, the evangelical peer who had laboured so heroically in his Factories Acts to rescue working-class children, and who would probably have been considered communist by most of Renan's French detractors, thought *La Vie de Jésus* was written 'for the most iniquitous purposes'.[22] The literature of English responses to Renan (sometimes linking him with Strauss) is almost as large as the French. Cardinal Wiseman, leader of the English Roman Catholics, preached a feline sermon in which he lamented the silence of the Archbishop of Canterbury since Renan had been translated into English. He implied, or more than implied, that many beneficed clergy of the Established Church perhaps shared the sceptical Frenchman's view of Our Lord and Saviour. Stung by this papistical attack a pious and anonymous layman, calling himself Christianos, wrote *Jesus King of the Jews. A letter to his grace the Lord Archbishop of Canterbury suggesting An English Life of Jesus*.[23] Taking us through the familiar territory – brief allusions to Christ in the Roman historians Suetonius and Tacitus, a possible few lines about Him in the Jewish historian Josephus (perhaps a Christian interpolation into the work, perhaps authentic) – Christianos was distinctly an optimist. What is required in their day, he avers, is a dispassionate Life of Jesus, 'a thick volume of facts arranged without order, expounded without philosophy, but serving as valuable materials to all who come after'.[24] The pamphlet, running out as it does after twenty-eight pages, seems in itself a somewhat sad refutation of its own aims. Where, after all, are the facts which could ever have thickened it out?

Nevertheless, a Professor of Latin from London, Sir John Seeley, attempted to do more or less just this with *Ecce Homo*, published in 1865. Because his father was a noted evangelical publisher, Seeley out of filial kindness published his book anonymously, giving rise to speculation as to its authorship. John Henry Newman, A.P. Stanley, the Duke of Argyll, Louis Napoleon and Gladstone were all proposed as possible authors.[25] *Ecce Homo* is not a Life of Jesus. It is an attempt to see whether the Gospels provide us with enough evidence to write such a book, whether they provide us with enough evidence to retain a belief in the Christian religion. It is an extremely dull, stuffy, even ponderous work, at times laughably so. When Jesus encountered the sinful tax-gatherer Zacchaeus, who was hiding in a sycamore tree, St Luke, as translated in the Authorized Version, has: 'He looked up, and saw him, and said unto him, Zacchaeus, make haste, and come down; for today I must abide at thy house.'[26] With the heaviness of a Victorian alderman, Seeley's Jesus 'informed Zacchaeus of his intention to visit him, and signified his pleasure that a banquet be instantly prepared. Such generous confidence put a new soul in Zacchaeus.'[27] Having weighed the 'evidence' for the most important and what must for some be the more improbable episodes in the Gospel, however, Seeley, while conceding that 'miracles are in themselves extremely improbable things', believed that the stories of the Resurrection of Jesus and His appearance to the Apostle Paul 'cannot be tolerably accounted for by any hypothesis except that of their being true'.[28]

Nevertheless, the very fact of Seeley having sifted the evidence was enough to strike many believers as profane. Lord Shaftesbury did Seeley a good turn by denouncing *Ecce Homo* as 'the most pestilential book ever vomited, I think, from the jaws of hell'. It sold 10,000 copies instantly. Shaftesbury lamented having been the cause of putting money into the pockets of 'an infidel'.[29] But even so theologically conservative a figure as Gladstone gave *Ecce Homo* a cautious welcome. He was never one to say in few words what could be stretched out to many; his review of *Ecce Homo* in *Good Words* was later published as a short book. He was worried at first by Seeley's familiar tone, 'which naturally tends to raise hopes that the history of Him to whom so many lands and so many ages, have bowed the knee, is about to receive a very free handling'.[30] But in the end Gladstone admits the good intentions of his author, while stressing that you can not understand anything about Christ, or the Church, unless you admit at the outset the supernatural nature of the material; in other words, unless you beg all the questions.

It was left until after the close of the nineteenth century for a great and original scholar (German, naturally) to point out that the Quest for the Historical Jesus was itself an extraordinary product of the times. Liberal Protestantism gazed at what it supposed was the Jesus of History and saw only the reflection of its own face. But, concluded Schweitzer, 'The Jesus of Nazareth who came forward publicly as the Messiah, who preached the ethic of the Kingdom of God, who founded the Kingdom of Heaven upon earth and died to give His work its final consecration, never had any existence. He is a figure designed by rationalism, endowed with life by liberalism, and clothed by modern theology in an historical garb ...'[31] Schweitzer concluded,

> The study of the Life of Jesus ... set out in quest of the historical Jesus, believing that when it had found Him it could bring Him straight into our time as a Teacher and Saviour. It loosed the bands by which He had been riveted for centuries to the strong rocks of ecclesiastical doctrine, and rejoiced to see life and movement coming into the figure once more, and the historical Jesus advancing, as it seemed, to meet it. But He does not stay; He passes by our time and returns to His own.[32]

It is a superb piece of rhetoric, this of Schweitzer's, and serves to justify, in his view, the Schweitzer Jesus, a tragic Messianic prophet who died with shrieks of disillusion on His lips when He realized that God had broken His promises to Israel.

Yet even Schweitzer (in this book, though not in his life) ignored another radical approach to the whole question: namely, how far any of the teachings of Jesus have applicability in the modern world. Schweitzer would perhaps have wished to say that Lev Nikolaevich Tolstoy, the author of *War and Peace*, made a Rousseau-esque, Proudhonian Jesus by deriving from the Gospels a message of pacifist anarchism.[33] Nevertheless, Tolstoy's reading of the New Testament is perhaps the most powerful of all, concentrating as it does not upon what can or cannot be known about a Galilean prophet living in the first century AD but upon what anyone living in the nineteenth century chooses to make of those famous injunctions not to hoard up treasure on earth, and not to take revenge upon enemies. Tolstoy was hated (and eventually excommunicated) by the Orthodox Church precisely because he showed that if these texts were acted upon, even partially, European civilization, with its aggressive nation states, its greedy capitalism, its ruthless pursuit of *laissez-faire* economics, its empire-building, its religious conservatism, would collapse.

Tolstoy, who devoted the second half of a remarkable writing career to an exposition of these themes, both did and did not have an influence. In pre-revolutionary Russia he was seen as a far greater threat than the communists. In the world at large his doctrines inspired the dropouts, the lovers of Thoreau and the simple life, with the desire to form folksy communities where everyone shared their lentil soup and homemade felt boots. On a more important level, he inspired the young Gandhi, then a lawyer in South Africa, with the idea that passive resistance was the most powerful possible weapon of civil disobedience. In the matter of the God question, Tolstoy was influential in so far as he threw it back upon the individual. 'There are two Gods,' he once said to his friend and English translator Aylmer Maude. 'There is the God that people generally believe in – a God *who has to serve them* (sometimes in very refined ways, say by merely giving them peace of mind). This God does not exist. But the God whom people forget – *the God whom we all have to serve* – exists and is the prime cause of our existence and of all that we perceive.'[34] On another occasion, Tolstoy read a Russian translation of a German book which attempted to show that Jesus Christ as an historical personage never existed. The Russian disciple of Jesus was delighted.

> They are attacking the last of the outworks [he said], and if they carry it, and demonstrate that Christ was never born, it will be all the more evident that the fortress of religion is impregnable. Take away the church, the traditions, the Bible, and even Christ himself: the ultimate fact of man's knowledge of goodness, i.e., of God, directly through reason and conscience, will be as clear and certain as ever, and it will be seen that we are dealing with truths that can never perish – truths that humanity can never afford to part with.[35]

George Eliot was in her late twenties when she translated Strauss. She was in her mid thirties by the time her next translation from the German was published – Feuerbach's *Essence of Christianity*, another of those books of which it is hard to say whether they changed the mind of a whole generation of intellectuals, or whether they expressed what a whole generation of intellectuals was in any event thinking. Even at the time, there were those who had their doubts about the modish Feuerbach. Reviewing the book in the very periodical of which, for a while, George Eliot herself had been the editor, James Martineau (himself no Christian) wrote:

It is a sign of 'progress', we presume, that the lady-translator who maintained the anonymous in introducing Strauss, puts her name in the titlepage of Feuerbach. She has executed her task even better than before: we are only surprised that, if she wished to exhibit the new Hegelian Atheism to English readers, she should select a work of the year 1840, and of quite secondary philosophical repute in its own country.[36]

Time, in its cruel way, would seem to have sided with Martineau. The late twentieth-century reader will find *The Essence* to be vapid stuff. For unbelievers of the 1850s, however, it must have provided useful ammunition against the siren lures of Newman. By the bright spiritual beacons of Idealism, as by the decent liberal standards of Mill and the Utilitarians, the Bible provided, after all, a sorry spectacle of bad behaviour, with its massacres of Amalekites, its murders of Jael, of Uriah the Hittite, its vengeful plagues and its slaying of Baalite prophets.

'The Bible contradicts morality, contradicts reason, contradicts itself, innumerable times ... How does the believer in revelation elude this contradiction between the idea in his own mind, of revelation as divine, harmonious truth, and this supposed, actual revelation?' Even Queen Victoria herself (had she read such a dangerous book as Miss Evans's translation of Feuerbach) might have felt inclined to agree with this point. It will be recalled that when she was dying, and contemplating the various dignitaries whom she might be expected to receive at her first Levee in Heaven, a clergyman told her that she would be in Abraham's bosom. 'We will *not* meet Abraham,' she pronounced solemnly. The patriarch's behaviour in Genesis, Chapter xii, when he pretended to the Pharaoh that Sarai was his sister rather than his wife, thinking the sacrifice of her virtue to the Egyptian potentate preferable to the offering of his own life, put Abraham decidedly beyond the pale. One could not imagine a man who behaved like that being made welcome at Balmoral.

The more man, by the progress of time, becomes estranged from revelation, the more the understanding ripens into independence, the more glaring, necessarily, appears the contradiction between understanding and belief in revelation ... The believer can then prove revelation only by incurring contradiction with himself, with truth, with the understanding, only by the most impudent assumptions, only by shameless falsehoods, only by the sin against the Holy Ghost.[37]

But Feuerbach was speaking only figuratively, of course. The real Holy Ghost is the spirit of human love: 'If human nature is the highest nature to man, then practically also the highest and first law must be the love of man to man. *Homo homini Deus est*: that is the great practical principle: this is the axis on which revolves the history of the world.'[38]

Herein lies Feuerbach's chief claim to fame in the history of ideas. He took the Hegelian view of God to its ultimate extreme, seeing God not merely as a human construct but as, so to say, the ultimate expression of humanity. When, in the past, metaphysicians have been talking about God, their real subject has been man. Feuerbach was not a simple debunker of religion. He managed to discover, a discovery which is almost akin to the mystical vision of Swedenborg, that God *is* man.

> In place of the illusory, fantastic, heavenly position of man which in actual life necessarily leads to the degradation of man, I substitute the tangible, actual, and consequently also the political and social position of mankind. The question concerning the existence or non-existence of God is for me nothing but the question concerning the existence or non-existence of man.[39]

God has now been entirely demythologized and rediscovered as humanity itself.

The historians of ideas can therefore trace Feuerbach as a stepping-stone from Hegel to Marx. In his *Theses on Feuerbach* Marx was able to wrest Feuerbach's philosophy of *praxis* (the Greek for *action*) from an individual level to a social one. What can be done to change society? That is the question of *praxis*. Whereas Feuerbach believed that the godlessness of his universe created an isolated human individual, Marx seized upon the idea in the paragraph just quoted and was able to say, 'All social life is essentially *practical*. All the mysteries which lead theory towards mysticisms find their rational solution in human practice and in the comprehension of this practice.'[40] Marx could say that 'the real nature of man is the totality of social relations'.[41] It is in the reworkings of Feuerbach — in the *Theses* — that we sense how truly Marxism was to become a religion, the actual objects of reverence — of superstition almost — being no longer the Divine Attributes, but the future consummation of social revolutions. In the context of the 1840s and 1850s this meant, for Marx, an escape from the patterns of revolution and counter-revolution which had marked the years 1789 to 1848, and a completely new, apocalyptic vision of a future society transformed by socialism. 'In order to arrive at its own content, the evolution of the nineteenth century must let the dead bury their dead.' [42] But for Feuerbach's English translator, the implications of the *Essences* took a different channel. She was to look for the 'human face divine' in her incomparable fictional evocations of English provincial life; when she was in the midst of her translating work, however, it was perhaps Feuerbach's reflections on personal life rather than political theory which most arrested her attention.

Feuerbach's headiest moments in this advanced religion of humanity come when he is advocating a loosening of sexual taboos. If what we mean by the word *God* is really the spirit of humanity in its strivings towards virtue and love, then the sexual impulse must be the mysticism of the new creed. 'Why then dost thou shrink from naming the nature of God by its true name?' he asks.

> What is virtue, the excellence of man as man? Manhood. Of man as woman? Womanhood. But man exists only as man and woman. The strength, the healthiness of man, consists, therefore, in this: that as a woman he be truly woman, as man, truly man ... Repudiate, then, before all, thy own horror for the distinction of sex. If God is not polluted by Nature, neither is he polluted by being associated with the idea of sex. In renouncing sex, thou renouncest thy whole principles ...[43]

It is of interest, psychologically, that in rendering this work of 'secondary philosophical repute' into her own tongue Marian Evans put it not into modern English but into a watered-down echo of the Authorized Version, as if *The Essence* were itself a new Scripture. Certainly, for the previous five years of her life this spirited and intelligent woman, destined to be one of the most famous of nineteenth-century novelists, could not have been accused of renouncing sex.

What an extraordinary story George Eliot's was. Nowadays, it is taken for granted that any reasonably well-read young woman in England will want to go to London for a period, work, perhaps in journalism, have love affairs, even with a few married men, before, possibly, settling down with one of them. This was by no means the norm of behaviour for provincial middle-class girls in Britain in the 1840s. Her story is of particular fascination in the context of the present inquiry, since none of it would have happened had she not had Doubts.

The Doubts would seem to have begun early. When she was thirteen, she read Bulwer Lytton's novel *Devereux* and was shocked but excited to discover the character of Bezoni the 'amiable atheist' – 'a believer in the dark doctrine which teaches that man is dust' but who nevertheless lived virtuously and 'lost his life in attending the victims of a fearful and contagious disease'.[44] The Doubts worsened during adolescence, largely as a result of reading, which she did on a prodigious scale: philosophy and science, as well as European literature in five languages. Her devout evangelical family were pained and grieved by the scepticism of this lovable but almost grotesquely plain daughter, with her huge head and gat-teeth, who eventually felt obliged to come clean about her unbelief. 'I wish entirely to remove from your mind', she confided to her grief-stricken father,

> the false notion that I am inclined visibly to unite myself with any Christian community, or that I have any affinity in opinion with Unitarians more than with other classes of believers in the Divine Authority of the books comprising the Jewish and Christian Scriptures. I regard these writings as histories consisting of mingled truth and fiction, and while I admire and cherish much of what I believe to have been the moral teaching of Jesus himself, I consider the system of doctrines built upon the facts of his life and drawn as to its materials from Jewish notions, notions to be most dishonourable to God and most pernicious in their influence on individual and social happiness ...[45]

She stopped going to church in 1842.[46]

It would have been difficult for her to find wounds more grievous to her pious father's heart. Robert Evans, a land-agent who worked in the English Midlands which later formed the background to George Eliot's best novels, died seven years after she had written him that confession. She was a devoted nurse at his sick-bed, but the religious rift meant that she was no longer a part of her own family and therefore found herself, at the age of thirty, having to look round for a substitute. It was via her friends in Coventry's free-thinking set that she had acquired the commission to translate Strauss. And the same group – blamed by the Evans family for Marian's drift into heresy – secured her the introduction to the distinctive household of John Chapman in London – 142, Strand.

Chapman was one of the great conduits of free-thinking in mid nineteenth-century England, and his famous address – part lodging-house, part publishing office, part bookshop – may be seen as one of the cells or power-houses of unbelief and modernity, an atheist's equivalent of the first-century catacombs in Rome. Just as the martyrs of the Church are known to have suffered for their faith by fire and combat with wild beasts, so Chapman, a handsome, semi-plausible rogue, may be said to have been a martyr to his lack of principle.

The money for the enterprise (the year before Marian Evans became a lodger in the house the Chapmans had published J.A. Froude's *The Nemesis of Faith*) came from his much (fourteen years) older wife, Susanna Brewitt, only daughter of a Nottingham lace manufacturer. The children, who included Walter, a deaf mute, were too much for them to cope with, and lived in Nottingham with an uncle, giving Susanna and John unlimited time to conduct the melodrama of modern marriage. When Marian Evans became their lodger, Chapman was carrying on an affair with Elisabeth Tilley, aged thirty, ostensibly employed as a governess (to the absent children) and housekeeper. Before long he was having to put up with jealous scenes from both Elisabeth and Susanna, because of his devoted attentions to the new arrival in the household. Marian played the piano in her room; John Chapman discovered a great devotion to Mosart (*sic*) and went upstairs to hear her play. When, very pointedly, Susanna asked Miss Evans to play the piano in the drawing room rather than in the secrecy of her own quarters, Chapman developed a passionate need for private German lessons – and who better to teach him than the translator of *Das Leben Jesu?* Chapman often found himself playing one woman off against another and making all three unhappy.

> Invited Miss Evans to go out after breakfast, but did not get a decisive answer, E[lisabeth] afterwards said if I did go, she should be glad to go, I then invited Miss Evans again telling her E. would go whereupon she declined rather rudely, Susanna being willing to go out, and neither E. nor S. wishing to walk far I proposed they should go a short distance without me, which E. considered an insult from me and reproached me in no measured terms accordingly, and heaped upon me suspicions and accusations I do not in any way deserve. I was very severe and harsh, said things I was sorry for afterwards, and we became reconciled in the Park.
>
> Miss Evans apologized for her rudeness tonight, which roused all E's jealousy again, and consequent bitterness.[47]

It is astonishing that Chapman had time to do any work, but he did. *The Nemesis of Faith* enjoyed a *succès de scandale* when one of the Fellows of Exeter (the college of which Froude himself had been a Fellow) burnt it in the quad: whether for its frank confessions of unbelief or for its risqué story-line – the hero not only loses his faith, but falls adulterously in love with the wife of his best friend – history does not relate. By the time Marian Evans joined the set-up at Number 142 as one of the lodgers (£2 10*s*. per week for first-class bedrooms, £2 5*s*. for second-class and 3*s*. 6*d*. extra for coals) Chapman was engaged in another ploy, the purchase of the *Westminster Review*, the periodical which had been run by J.S. Mill but which, since his severance from it, had fallen into a decline.

In an age of radio, television, the Internet, and the full variety of chattering which falls under the heading 'media', it is difficult to assess the importance of written journalism. Those who write for the serious weeklies in England or the United States tend to overestimate the effect they have on their readers' minds. Those who merely pick up a Sunday newspaper one week, watch a serious TV documentary or interview the next, would find it impossible to know whether any of their views were shaped or guided by *The New Yorker* or *The Spectator*. In the nineteenth century, written journalism had no rivals, and serious periodicals such as the *Westminster* or *The Nineteenth Century* or *The Fortnightly Review* (which, needless to say, was a monthly) could be found on the library tables of merchants, parsons, landowners, industrialists, academics throughout the kingdom. They were all unbelieving in tone (though, clearly, not relentlessly so) and it was left to rivals such as *The Spectator* or specifically religious papers such as *The Tablet* or *The Guardian** to provide an intellectual counterblast. 'The public hungered for intellectual guidance.'[48]

Chapman was enabled to take over the *Westminster* by an eccentric (absentee) Norfolk landowner, Edward Lombe of Melton Hall, Wymondham. An unbelieving radical of the Shelley–Peacock type, Lombe was much hated by his Norfolk neighbours for, among other outrageous peculiarities, allowing his sixty-eight tenants to shoot the game on their farms and (even odder) to vote as they chose in general elections rather than following the standard practice of handing in a block vote at their landlord's dictation. Lombe lived in Florence, and with a £14,000 inheritance from the father with whom he had not been on speaking terms for years he paid Chapman, not only to revive the

---

* A Tractarian weekly, founded in 1846 by R.W. Church, it ceased publication in 1951, and is not to be confused with the current English daily newspaper, formerly *The Manchester Guardian*.

Westminster but also to reprint various favourites of the unbelieving class – Theodore Parker's *Discourse on Matters Pertaining to Religion*, Hennell's *Inquiry*, and an abridged version of Evans's Strauss.[49]

Chapman could trust himself to bring in, or at the least to approach, some of the best writers of the day to contribute to the *Westminster*. One of Marian's memories of these days was of pacing up and down Cheyne Row while Chapman communed with, and tried to persuade, Carlyle to write an article on The Peerage. Among the other contributors were F.H. Newman (brother of J.H.), Wilkie Collins, Herbert Spencer. What he needed in the background was a dogsbody to do the actual editorial grind, the correction of manuscripts, the marking of proofs, the meeting of deadlines with printers, as well as the commissioning of, occasionally the writing of, the book reviews. These humbler tasks his intellectual superior Marian Evans was more than qualified and, being in love with Chapman, certainly willing to undertake.

Her editorial role was not simply that of a drudge. For instance, when Chapman funked writing a letter to James Martineau specifying precisely in what terms their eccentric proprietor wished him to write about 'Christian Ethics and Modern Civilization', it was Marian Evans who drafted the letter.[50] She would seem to have had a hand in persuading Froude to write about Mary Stuart, and to have kept in work some of the better jobbing journalists of the day, most notably Herbert Spencer, a rising young star at *The Economist*, and – the man with whom she was to spend so many years living as his common-law wife – George Henry Lewes.

It soon became clear that none of the four involved in Chapman's eternal quadrangle – his wife, Marian, Elisabeth, he himself – could stand the emotional pace. Both Susanna and Elisabeth made difficulties about Marian continuing to lodge under the same roof as themselves, which meant that she spent extended periods going to stay with her Coventry friends. Chapman needed her as an editor, but he could not easily bear the weight of her love. Nor was he, it seems, a sensitive man. Of one of their jaunts in rural Warwickshire, he recorded carelessly in his diary, 'As we rested on the grass, I remarked on the wonderful and mysterious embodiment of all the elements of nature which man and woman jointly present. I dwelt also on the incomprehensible mystery and witchery of beauty. My words jarred upon her and put an end to her enjoyment. Was it from a consciousness of her own want of beauty? She wept bitterly.'[51]

Poor horse-faced lady. She continued for some time to work as Chapman's assistant on the *Westminster*, but she turned her emotional attention away from him and in the direction of his contributors. The first object of her adoration was, of all unlikely people, Herbert Spencer. In later life this pompous ass sought to play down the amorous nature of Marian's attachment to him, but in old age he still kept a photograph of the (by now famous) novelist beside his bed, causing the sisters who kept house for him in the 1890s to rib him. One of them exclaimed, "'What a long nose she had! She must have been very difficult to kiss, Mr Spencer!" "Yes indeed," he brightly acquiesced, to our intense delight at the apparent admission. He laughingly protested that he was only speaking "theoretically" but would Herbert Spencer, the philosopher, have generalised from *a priori* reasoning?'[52] In those later years she had become a very rich woman and a much-respected sage, but she still lamented the fact that she had become 'a hideous hag'.[53]

Her life-partner, George Henry Lewes (1817–1878), was in no position to complain about this. He was described by a contemporary (Douglas Jerrold) as 'the ugliest man in London', and by a scholar of our own day as 'a Victorian Clive James'.[54] He was a good match for George Eliot, however, being a man of huge intellectual range, though not her rival in depth or weight. While Marian Evans was translating Strauss, Lewes had been engaged in writing his chatty *Biographical History of Philosophy* – perhaps the most readable book of its kind before Bertrand Russell and Father Copleston, SJ made their comparably encyclopaedic compilations in the mid twentieth century. He reviewed on every subject, from drama (in his youth he had written plays and aspired to be an actor) to Alexandre Dumas, Disraeli (as a novelist), Shakespeare, and German literature. One of the foremost English exponents of Positivism, he was in correspondence with Comte, whom he knew slightly. 'Votre ami Lewes', as Mill called him when writing to Comte.[55] When he took up with Marian Evans, and they travelled to Germany together, he was writing a biography of Goethe, the first in English.

He was a rogue, of course. The various stories he helped to put about, suggesting that his legal wife was mad or in an asylum, were all untrue. All through the years of George Eliot's fame Mrs Lewes lived in Kensington with a bachelor son – Edmund, a successful dentist – and her daughters Rose, Ethel and Mildred.[56] What money Lewes ever thought to send to them came, most certainly, not from his own commercially unsuccessful literary outpourings but from the royalties of

George Eliot's novels. Yet without him, it is generally agreed, she would probably not have been sufficiently encouraged to make her first essays in *Scenes from Clerical Life*.

It is hard not to feel Schopenhauerian levels of gloom descend as one follows the career of Lewes. Ever since he and George Eliot moved into The Priory, St John's Wood (November 1863), one feels, ugly female novelists have been setting up house in North London with pushy liberal-minded journalists. One has to concede, however, that while they might be viewed as archetypes of a thousand inferior imitators, 'the Leweses', as they came, not quite accurately, to be known, were an impressive pair. Their innumerable modern equivalents might produce a comparable sinking of the spirits in any who consider them, but they have not produced Lewes's *Life of Goethe*, still less *Adam Bede* or *Middlemarch*.

In 1878, when they had been together for nearly thirty years, Lewes died, a little over sixty years old. The funeral was in that unconsecrated haven of famous outcasts and unbelievers, Highgate Cemetery. The minister of the Rosslyn Unitarian Chapel in Hampstead conducted the service. According to one witness, there were only about a dozen 'out and out rationalists' present, and Dr Sadler, the minister, almost seemed to apologize 'for suggesting the possible immortality of some of our souls'.[57] George Eliot herself was too grief-striken to attend. She kept to her room, not in their London house but in The Heights, her hideous suburban mansion in Witley, Surrey, reading *In Memoriam* over and over again and copying passages into her journal. There is something extremely poignant about this, since if George Eliot was the sibyl of Victorian Rationalism, the great exponent of the inadmissibility of belief, then Tennyson was the poet of the Honest Doubters who nevertheless saw the validity of 'believing where we cannot prove'. *In Memoriam* is the great poem of bereavement, but it is also a work which explores the agonizing processes of religious doubt, from the position not of nihilistic atheism but of a faith which is strong enough to hold on

> When the blood creeps, and the nerves prick
> And tingle; and the heart is sick,
> And all the wheels of Being slow.

It is surely no accident that Comte, Strauss, Feuerbach, Herbert Spencer, Lewes, and indeed nearly all the intellectuals who bolstered

George Eliot's position of unbelief, should today be unread and unread-able, whereas her friend and contemporary Alfred Tennyson, in his con-frontation of raw doubt and the complicated agonies of a broken heart and a troubled mind, speaks as directly today as when his poem was first published.

> I wage not any feud with Death
>> For changes wrought on form and face;
>> No lower life that earth's embrace
> May breed with him, can fright my faith.
>
> Eternal process moving on,
>> From state to state the spirit walks;
>> And these are but the shattered stalks,
> Or ruin'd chrysalis of one.
>
> Nor blame I Death, because he bare
>> The use of virtue out of earth:
>> I know transplanted human worth
> Will bloom to profit, otherwise.
>
> For this alone on Death I wreak
>> The wrath that garners in my heart;
>> He put our lives so far apart
> We cannot hear each other speak ...[58]

There is more in Tennyson, too, of the theological implications of sci-entific discoveries and the fear that evolution reduces us all to the con-dition of 'rubbish', cast into the void, than in many a wordy article in the *Westminster Review*.

In the end, some of George Eliot's contemporaries found her insis-tence upon a position of unbelief somewhat arid. The most famous instance of this occurs in a mellifluous essay in *The Century Magazine* by F.W.H. Myers, who describes himself walking with the great lady in the Fellows' Garden of Trinity College, Cambridge, on a rainy evening:

She, stirred somewhat beyond her wont, and taking as her text the three words which have been used so often as the trumpet-calls of men – the words, *God, Immortality, Duty* – pronounced, with terrible earnestness, how inconceivable was the *first*, how unbelievable the *second*, and yet how peremptory and absolute the *third*. Never, perhaps, have sterner accents affirmed the sovereignty of impersonal and unrecompensing law. I lis-tened, and night fell; her grave, majestic countenance turned toward me like a sibyl's in the gloom; it was as though she withdrew from my grasp, one by one, the two scrolls of promise, and left me the third scroll only, awful with inevitable fates. And when we stood at length and parted, amid the columnar circuit of the forest-trees, beneath the last twilight of starless skies, I seemed to be gazing, like Titus at Jerusalem, on vacant seats and empty halls – on a sanctuary with no Presence to hallow it, and heaven left lonely of a God.[59]

8

A *Passion for Generalizing: Herbert Spencer and the Modern*

'There is no life of which I have a really intimate
knowledge which seems to me so inexpressibly sad
as the inarticulate life of Herbert Spencer.'
                    Beatrice Webb, 5 May 1883

FUNNY OLD HERBERT Spencer deserves a mention. He is in some ways symptomatic of the whole difficulty of writing about this subject, the demise of faith among the Victorians; for one begins it, as a reader or as a chronicler of events, under the impression that these issues might all remain in some senses the same for us as they were for them. Such huge and eternal questions – Is there a God? Are the Gospels true? Can we look forward to life beyond the grave? Are there Moral Absolutes? Did the Universe have a Creator, or did it all just happen by chance? If there are answers to these questions which are objectively or verifiably true – or, at the very least, palatable to the minds of one generation – then surely they are 'valid' for all time? And though the theologians and the metaphysicians would want to insist on the rationale of this line of thinking, the more dispassionate modern reader senses that things aren't quite like that. Questions of faith and doubt and religion, if not like humour actually ephemeral, seem very different from one generation to another. Nothing enforces this sense so poignantly as the complete evaporation of Herbert Spencer from human consciousness.

Like Mark Pattison, Herbert Spencer was a keen fly-fisherman who found in angling one of the few pursuits which calmed the hyperactivity of his fertile brain. He made his own flies, which on one occasion were regarded askance by the other fishermen at Inveroran in Scotland, where he was passing a vacation. Spencer took the view that salmon and sea-trout are far less discerning then most fishermen suppose, and will leap at anything they mistake for a fly. 'Consequently my aim was to make the best average representation of an insect buzzing on the surface of the water.' In recounting this to George Eliot, Spencer prompted the retort named in his expansive autobiography as an example of the novelist's wit: 'Yes,' she said, 'you have such a passion for generalizing you even fish with a generalization.'[1]

Even those readers who do not find George Eliot's joke as hilarious as Spencer evidently did might believe that the phrase sums him up pretty well: A PASSION FOR GENERALIZING might have been written on his gravestone. 'He was', we are told, 'one of the few British thinkers who have deliberately attempted the construction of a comprehensive philosophical system.'[2] From 1851, when he published his pioneering work of sociology, *Social Statics*, and for the next forty years, he expounded with a prolixity matched only by his breadth of range what he described as *A System of Synthetic Philosophy* (1860). *First Principles* appeared in 1862 (one volume) followed by *The Principles of Biology* (two volumes) in 1864–7, *The Principles of Psychology* (1870–2), *The Principles of Sociology* (1876–96), as well as *The Data of Ethics* (1879) and *The Principles of Ethics* (1892). The sheer volume is colossal. It is no surprise to learn that he barely had time to read up any of these subjects before writing about them, and that he lived on his nerves. He was particularly terrified of being over-stimulated late at night by conversation. If you managed to lure him to a dinner table (and this was quite an achievement, for he became increasingly eremitical with the passing years), you had to be careful not to say anything too witty or interesting lest it agitate his grey cells and keep him awake. If in the middle of a conversation he foresaw such a calamity, Spencer would hastily take a pair of ear-plugs from his top pocket and block out the threatened stimulus. No wonder that some (even disregarding other brusqueries of his manner) found him rude.

For every one who has actually read Freud, there must be a million who have a general idea that he unearthed our subconscious or, somehow or another, the notion that many facets of human behaviour are to be explained by recovering forgotten childhood traumas. Equally, for every one who has read a line of Marx, there must be ten million, a hundred million, who know that the guiding factors in the affairs of men are the fluctuations of economics, the control of wealth supply and the class struggle which these factors underlie.

When we speak of Marx or Freud as 'influential' thinkers, we mean that popularized versions of their ideas have for a number of reasons got about, and become a received wisdom for a generation or two. Certainly for those born between, say, 1870 and the First World War, Spencer's was a name on this level of popularity and significance.

The ideas he popularized were that science had somehow 'disproved' religion; that God was an obsolete term for something which could be termed, impersonally, a force or an energy. He also believed that race-memory or inherited characteristics – inherited by whole races rather than by individuals – could explain conundrums which had puzzled the minds of Hume and Kant – for example, the puzzle of how we *appear* to have certain types of knowledge intuitively, or to accept certain truths *a priori* rather than as a result of personal experiment. With his materialist view of acquired characteristics, Spencer tried to attribute his own rebellious or nonconformist streak to his supposed descent from Huguenots, even from refugees from the Hussite wars in Bohemia in the fifteenth century.[3] If he wished to glamorize the ancestry of Harriet Holmes, his mother, who was the daughter of a plumber in Derby, is it necessary to blame him?

It would be hard now to find any intelligent person in the Western world, other than those who have studied the History of Ideas at university or read the biographies of his two most famous female friends, George Eliot and Beatrice Webb, who possesses even a hazy idea of what Spencer stood for. No real philosopher today has the smallest interest in him, since his use of language is so inexact that it is usually difficult to know precisely what he means. Even his great phrases, like 'the Inconceivable and the Unknowable' (designed in a nebulous way to suggest the Mystery of Things), remain undefined. He makes no effort to inform his readers what he means by 'know' or what he means by 'conceive'. 'How can an adult man spend his time in trying to torture an accurate meaning into Spencer's incoherent accidentalities?' asked an exasperated William James in August 1886.[4] And yet when William's brother, the novelist Henry James, wrote from London, 'I often take a nap beside Herbert Spencer at the Athenaeum and feel as if I were robbing you of the privilege',[5] it was without irony. Herbert Spencer's was a name to drop, and the brother who had chosen to reside in England had absorbed the contemporary English notion that Spencer was something of a great man and a great thinker.

While for professional philosophers there will always be something unsatisfactory about Spencer, this might actually go some way to explain his vogue as a popular thinker. He leaves unanswered and unexplored the basic epistemological problem on which metaphysics rests: How can we know anything at all – and what would we mean by know if we knew? It could be said that, since no one has ever been able to give satisfactory answers to these questions, it is asking a lot of an untrained journalist like Herbert Spencer to succeed where Plato, Aristotle, Aquinas, Descartes, Hume and Kant have failed.

The trouble with Spencer as a thinker is that he appears to adopt the sceptical/empiricist view of knowledge, best expounded by Hume, without seeing that this view makes it impossible to entertain what is sometimes called a 'scientific' outlook, since science, from an empirical viewpoint, can never be anything more than a disconnected number of observations of phenomena. Some inductive principle must be introduced in order to make sense of data. (This is the first principle of Kant's *Critique of Pure Reason*.) Spencer, while seeming to reject Kantianism, adopts Kant's phrases of *phenomena* and *noumena*, to distinguish between things we observe, and concepts which we have of things-in-themselves. So it is all quite a muddle. Yet, just as Coleridge was influential in the 1820s and 1830s precisely because it was difficult to understand what he was saying, so Spencer, for the generation of mid to late Victorians, bolstered up two of their key superstitions: the idea of life as perpetual progress – the life of the universe itself as well as the life of societies and individuals; and, secondly, the idea that Science would provide the key instrument of progress.

Many, many muddled thoughts here, which you have only to follow Spencer's sad life to see. Evolution is hardly a cheering paradigm for the political development of human society. The 'dragons in their prime That tear each other in their slime', as Tennyson called prehistoric monsters, were hardly role models for those – Spencer and all his friends among them – who aspired to universal suffrage and a peaceful extension of civilized values through the ballot box.

Like many self-made men, Spencer was a fascinating mixture of political contradictions. With part of himself he was an individualist, a Manchester Liberal who became increasingly obsessed by the belief that the State was introducing what he called Slavery by Tax, and interference in private liberty. On the other hand, the unchecked aggression of individuals and nations – the political equivalent of the Survival of the Fittest – filled this gentle humanist with abhorrence. He was brave enough to denounce British aggression in Africa at the time of the Boer War, and so furiously opposed was he to war that at the end of his life he was unpopular in England. Yet, when he died, the Italian Parliament observed a minute's silence. The United States did not have an official mourning, but it was agreed in America that one of the most popular thinkers and sages had been lost.

Not by William James, though, who saw that Spencer had been not so much an influential philosopher as a man who embodied and gave voice to a whole bundle of ill-thought-out Victorian prejudices. In his first lecture on Pragmatism, in 1907, James bemoaned Spencer's 'dry schoolmaster temperament, the hurdy-gurdy monotony of him, his preference for cheap makeshifts in argument, his lack of education even in mechanical principles, and in general the vagueness of all his fundamental ideas, his whole system wooden, as if knocked together out of cracked hemlock boards – and yet half of England wants to bury him in Westminster Abbey.'[6]

Like Carlyle, like Marx, Spencer was primarily a journalist. He had come to London (appropriately, perhaps, since he was destined to be so archetypically a mouthpiece of the age) in 1837, the year of the Queen's accession, to work as a railway engineer at the new-built Chalk Farm station in the Hampstead Road. The London and Birmingham Railway Company had not, at that stage in its history, decided to penetrate the capital as far as Euston Square, so this was the furthest south reached by that particular line.

Spencer, then seventeen, had found employment with the company as a result of string-pulling by an uncle. He came of Methodistical stock in Derby. His father belonged to that tough, Nonconformist tradition which refuses to be impressed, or to kow-tow. It was Spencer *père*'s proud boast that when writing their names on envelopes he had never in his life addressed anyone as The Reverend or as Esquire, but had called everyone Mister. He also refused ever to doff his hat to anyone. Herbert Spencer's own political stances, when boiled down and considered, do not advance much beyond this provincial cussedness. Perhaps one sees, in this delight in awkwardness for its own sake, how Spencer can both welcome the political reforms brought about as a result of agitation by Mill and the Utilitarians, while at the same time resenting even such obvious benefits as the new drainage systems in cities, which prevented the regular outbreaks of cholera that had hitherto dogged English life, as mere 'state interference'.

They worked Herbert Spencer very hard on the railway, first in London and then further up the line, as far as and beyond Worcester, where he was based for a number of years. He was a clever young man, with an amateur's interest in all branches of science and a good engineer's delight in applying scientific know-how to practical problems.

The railroad company was anxious to expand as fast, while employing as few people, as possible. They therefore commissioned cast-iron girders to be pre-fabricated in Birmingham – before measuring the spans involved in the bridges they required. It was left to the twenty-year-old Spencer to go down to Bromsgrove and construct a bridge which would neither require new girders to be made, nor collapse under pressure from the new-built machines. Trains were now running at thirty miles an hour.[7] Somehow, even when the company was working him from 8 a.m. to 3 a.m. (*sic*), Spencer found time for reading. Lyell's *Geology* was one of his proudest purchases at this period.

Lyell's *Principles of Geology*** was one of the seminal scientific works of the nineteenth century. When Tennyson read it in 1836 he was troubled, like many readers, by Lyell's declaration, based on fossil evidence, that 'the inhabitants of the globe, like all other parts of it, are subject to change. It is not only the individual that perishes, but whole species.' It inspired his lines

> From scarped cliff and quarried stone
> She cries, 'A thousand types are gone:
> I care for nothing, all shall go ...'

Against this relentless and heartless Nature, man is seen as a fantasist,

> Who trusted God was love indeed
> And love Creation's final law –
> Though Nature, red in tooth and claw
> With ravine, shrieked against his creed – [8]

In the light of the Darwinian controversies of the 1860s and afterwards, it is interesting that Lyell's earlier conclusions from geological evidence were disturbing to faith because they suggested that every species, including the human, was ephemeral. Already in the 1820s he had attacked those who would measure the facts of nature not by observation but by an appeal to the literal text of holy scripture.[9] He read Lamarck, the first great evolutionary theorist, and concluded: 'How impossible it will be to distinguish and lay down a line, beyond which

---

* Published by John Murray, volume 1 in January 1830, volumes 2 and 3 in 1832 and 1833 respectively, the whole work printed in four volumes in 1834. It underwent constant revision as the state of knowledge changed, and it was always widely popular.

some of the so-called extinct species have never passed into recent ones.' From the late 1820s onwards Lyell was maintaining that geological evidence suggested, for example, that birds and mammals coexisted in the earliest times. This was a view which he came to revise only after his friend Charles Darwin's construction of a theory of the Origin of Species which was different from Lamarck's. Lyell (Sir Charles, 1797–1875) was largely instrumental in getting Darwin's theory published: it is typical of this modest and self-effacing scholar that he should have so saluted and welcomed Darwin, even when his ideas suggested that much of Lyell's own earlier work needed to be reviewed. If this had disturbed its readers by suggesting that everything was hurtling towards a meaningless destruction, Darwin's undermined the notion of human distinctiveness by suggesting that species, far from being wholly destroyed with each phase of eco-history, pass into one another, evolve into one another.

But these are matters which await our attention in a later chapter. One can't help being impressed by young Spencer, though, starting work at eight and often clambering into bed at three in the morning, yet being so hungry for knowledge that he invested in a set of Lyell.

As soon as the railroad was complete, the company sacked their staff. 'Got the sack – very glad' Spencer wrote in his diary. His parents, now slightly less impoverished than during his boyhood, were able to support him when he went back to Derby and entered a period of wide general reading and hack schoolmastering. He regarded himself primarily as an inventor, and devised and patented a velocimeter for gauging the speed of engines during trials.

Since this was by now the 1840s, and railway mania was sweeping the country, such an invention was potentially important. But Spencer was nothing if not a generalist, and in his twenties he threw his prodigious energies in all manner of different directions. Politically he supported the Chartist agitation, and became local secretary of the Derby branch of the 'complete suffrage movement'. He became obsessed, as so many did during this period, by phrenology, the belief that by feeling and measuring the lumps on a human skull, character can be reliably assessed. The theory bears no more scrutiny than the medieval idea that human character was determined by a balance of the Four Humours. Spencer can hardly be said to have had a novelistic interest in the mysteries of human motivation and character, but it must have been a comfort to him to feel that character itself, like every other manifestation of life on the planet, had now been classified, labelled, and scientifically explained. He studied astronomy. He eagerly devoured Lamarck's evolutionary theories (and, interestingly enough, he never really wavered from them, remaining unconvinced by Darwin). Whatever their truth, Spencer must have delighted in the notion, easily extractable from Lamarck, that Nature, like society itself, and like Victorian England, was on an exciting, buoyant, optimistic course, bouncing onwards and upwards.

Spencer's inventions became increasingly ambitious. That for a flying machine failed to find a buyer with sufficient foresight to develop it on his behalf. Perhaps it is emblematic of the direction to be taken by Spencer's later life that the only invention to make much money for him when patented was the binding pin, a stapling device for use with large numbers of printed periodicals. He certainly covered many a printed page with his own reflections, and it was as a journalist that this self-taught polymath from the provinces was to transform himself into a national sage. After a spell working as sub-editor on a radical paper in Birmingham (*The Pilot*), Spencer got his lucky break. In 1848, the year of revolutions, he was appointed a 'sub' on *The Economist* at a salary of 100 guineas a year.

Everyone took Mark Pattison to be the model for Mr Casaubon, but in the all-consuming egotism of that character there is surely a dash of Spencer? After she had got over her crush on the young Herbert, George Eliot was always able to see what was funny about him.[10] In 1854, when she had known him a few years, she wrote:

> He will stand in the Biographical Dictionaries of 1954 as, 'Spencer, Herbert, an original and profound philosophical writer, especially known by his great work xxx which gave a new impulse to psychology, and has mainly contributed to the present advanced position of that science, compared with that which it had attained in the middle of the last century. The life of this philosopher, like that of the great Kant, offers little material for the narrator ...[11]

This did not stop Spencer, in old age, writing an enormous *Autobiography* and therein jealously moulding the image of himself which he wished to survive for posterity. He called in all his letters when he was working on this book, extracted those passages which confirmed his own view of himself, and destroyed the manuscripts. A week after her death, he wrote to the newspapers denying the statement in an obituary that he had had anything to do with George Eliot's education. And he badgered Johnnie Cross (the man who married George Eliot when

Lewes died) to scotch the widely-held belief that he and the great novelist had ever been lovers. He asked Cross 'to contradict these statements in some general way, and indicate the fact that, big as was my admiration for her, and great as my feeling of friendship, yet my feeling did not grow into a warm one – or something to that effect'.[12] Nevertheless, he made no secret of the fact that George Eliot was 'the most admirable woman, mentally, I ever met'.[13]

Perhaps the second most remarkable woman was one in whose education he did indeed play a great role – Beatrice Potter (1858–1943), best known to the world as the sociologist and political reformer Beatrice Webb, whose marvellous diaries record many unforgettable vignettes of poor Spencer in old age. Her father was a self-made railway millionaire, and Spencer was a frequent visitor to his house. The *Diaries* recount her solemnly loyal reading of all Spencer's principal works, and there can be no doubt that, with her taste for monsters (she was in love with Joseph Chamberlain for years), she had a genuine sympathy for one whom she described as 'the old philosopher'.

Reading Spencer was for Beatrice Potter in many respects a disillusioning experience. She was profoundly religious by temperament, and her early commitment to Christ was more than a little shaken by her discovery of Spencer's scientific agnosticism. 'One had always feared that when orthodox religion vanished, no beauty, no mystery, would be left, nothing but what could and would be explained and become commonplace, but instead of that each new discovery of science will increase our wonder at the Great Unknown and our appreciation of the Great Truth'. That was what she thought on her initial reading of Mr Spencer's *First Principles*. But it did not take her long – about three months – to realize that 'the religion of science has its dark side. It is bleak and dreary.'[14] The point was reinforced in July 1878 when she and Spencer looked round Cologne Cathedral. 'Even the philosopher does not criticize the interior', she noted, though he objected to the 'excessively monotonous' service which was in progress when they entered. Beatrice told him she rather liked the rhythmical chant of Vespers:

> 'I confess to a certain amount of superstitious awe,' say I defiantly. 'I should be sorry that these cathedrals should pass out of the hands of the Catholic Church with its beautiful ritual.' The philosopher simply cleared his throat of any disposition to dispute this last contemptible suggestion and continued, 'Awe is quite legitimate. It arises in our minds from a perception of power, but we must bear in mind when we

give way to this feeling that these cathedrals were erected by the Princes of the Church, who were military chieftains, and as bloodthirsty as their secular neighbours ...' This little tirade over, we passed out of the church.[15]

The image of the sparrow flying from the darkness of a Northumbrian winter into the light and warmth of the mead-hall and then out once more into the unforgiving dark appeared to the Saxon thane as an image of the human pilgrimage. 'Of what follows, we are ignorant.'[16] Such being the condition of men and women, it seemed wise to seventh-century man to be prepared to test Christianity in the spirit of faith, precisely because we do not know. 'If the new faith has with it anything more certain, it seems a good thing to follow it.' That was how it seemed when the English people adopted the Christian faith. By the 1870s it had begun to seem, even to believers, that the English people were about to abandon that faith; that the story which began in the pages of the Venerable Bede was to end in the highbrow periodicals. 'One may almost say,' lamented W.H. Mallock in *The Nineteenth Century* (1878) 'with us one can hear faith decaying ... This decay has been maturing for three hundred years, and their effects prophesied for fifty; indeed, not prophesied only but in some degree accomplished.'[17]

To the generation which looked to Spencer as to a great philosopher, the selfsame flight from darkness to darkness, from unknown to unknown, which in earlier generations had been the foundation of religious beginnings, prompted talk and feelings of religious endings; compelled not a trust in religious certainties but a dogged assertion of metaphysical uncertainties.

> An entire history of anything must include its appearance out of the imperceptible and its disappearance into the imperceptible. Any account of an object which begins with it in a concrete form, is incomplete; since there remains an era of its existence undescribed and unexplained. While admitting that we have by implication asserted that the sphere of knowledge is coextensive with the phenomenal – coextensive with all modes of the Unknowable which can effect consciousness.[18]

If we late twentieth-century readers wonder whether sense can be made of that – or indeed of *any* of Spencer – it is perhaps a good idea to remind ourselves of how high his position once was. My own pocket edition of *First Principles*, from that now vanished list of Agnostic Golden

Oldies 'The Thinker's Library', is a reprint of 1946. As late as this, the introduction could describe the book as 'one of the most important contributions to modern philosophy'. Who, nowadays, reads Herbert Spencer at all? In *A Hundred Years of Philosophy* John Passmore probably says as much as can be said in writing that 'it was left to Herbert Spencer to develop an agnostic-evolutionary philosophy which swept the world'.[19] He does not develop the point. Frederick Copleston, SJ gives a kindly summary of Spencer's views in his *A History of Philosophy*. When the Jesuit historian of ideas is obliged, in the interests of truth, to record that 'Spencer's thought is so closely wedded to the Victorian era that it can scarcely be described as a living influence today', the understatement is almost gleeful.[20] Copleston's view is broadly reinforced by *The Oxford Companion to Philosophy*, which declares Spencer's reputation to have 'sunk to hitherto unfathomed depths'.[21]

Yet perhaps we retain more Victorian prejudices than these clever men would suggest? Some of Spencer's racial and social theories might, perhaps, raise a few eyebrows today. But do we not still generally believe that societies, like organisms, move *on*, and by implication do we not think that *on* means *up*? Do we not share with Spencer a generalized belief that the scientific outlook, however that may be defined, compels the religious outlook to be modified, if not actually abandoned? And if we do have such beliefs, then the existence on this planet of two generations of Europeans who believed Herbert Spencer to be the greatest thinker of their time might have something to do with our own outlook. Even the *Oxford Companion* finds more Spencerian influence in the sphere of political thought than moderns would perhaps wish to recognize – which is something we must revert to at a later stage.

Does the human mind acquire knowledge merely by receiving the multiplicity of sense-impressions cast upon it by phenomena, as a magic lantern casts slide-pictures on a screen? Or does it do so by an innate capacity to make judgements and to form categories, without which the sense-impressions would be inchoate, meaningless? Into this complex epistemological territory the autodidact railway-engineer from Derby boldly marched. Matters which had challenged the ingenuity of Berkeley, Hume and Kant were confronted with the self-assurance of the Victorian self-made man.* His *First Principles,* a kind of *Summa,*

---

* When George Eliot complimented Spencer on the lack of wrinkles in his forehead, he replied that nothing had ever really puzzled him.

seems in itself like a paradigm of the Kantian dilemma. Is it merely a picture of what was going on inside Herbert Spencer's cranium, or is it a picture of the nineteenth-century *Weltanschauung*? Or is Herbert Spencer's importance to be found in this: that it makes no odds how you answer the question? Was he a man so characteristic of his time that *First Principles* conveys a picture of how the Victorians in general, and not just he, saw themselves and the world? If so, would it not explain his enormous popularity, and his high reputation?

As with a large Victorian interior, or one of the great Victorian museums, one is arrested by the impressive fullness of *First Principles*. Everything is here – metaphysics and physics; theology, geology; psychiatry, sociology; physics and chemistry; art history, linguistics, town-planning.

Philosophers will cavil at the imprecision of Spencer's language. For example, in a famous passage he posits that there are three possible views to be taken about the origin of the Universe: 'self-existence, self-creation and an external agency'. Spencer plods through the implications of these views. None of them seems satisfactory to him, and he dismisses them as 'literally unthinkable'. As with many Spencer statements, the reader wants some qualification. To any late Darwinian – in our own times, for example, Dr Richard Dawkins, but there are hundreds of others – the notion of the 'self-existence' of things, of the universe, existence without a beginning, is perfectly conceivable; or, to put it differently but not significantly so, it is perfectly possible to banish teleology from the mind when considering the origin of species, or astronomy. Likewise, the existence of Spinoza and his followers shows that it is perfectly possible to conceive of a universe which is, in the sense which Spencer seems to hint, 'self-creating'; and a majority of the human race have been happy to subscribe to a 'creationist' theory. Yet 'by no mental effort', Spencer believes, can we truthfully subscribe to any of these three views. It all remains an unutterable mystery, sometimes becoming in his prose a Mystery.

Whether Spencer's epistemological criteria are satisfactory, we may leave to the judgement of metaphysicians. It is well known that he decided to abandon reading Kant's *Critique of Pure Reason* when he reached the section, quite early in the book, about our conceptions of space and time.

We do not presume to ask whether Herbert Spencer was right or wrong; merely to see how the world looked to him. And *First Principles* is a magnificent showing-forth of this.

With the common sense of an Englishman, Spencer casts aside the unanswerable conundrums posed by the dwarfish genius of Königsberg. But, with the quasi-mysticism of the Englishman, he also regards the Mystery as Unknowable. It is worthy of our reverence. If we are unable to know anything about how we know things, and if we cannot say, or even think, whether this universal frame began as a divine decree, we can at least go up and down and round about, collecting specimens. There had never been an age when scientists noticed more, saw more, in this sense understood more. There had never been more data. Therefore, the second half of Spencer's book – entitled 'The Knowable' – is about four times longer than the first, 'The Unknowable'. As a record of what Herbert Spencer had come to know before he was forty years old, it is undeniably impressive: as I have already said, there seems to be scarcely any area of human knowledge in which Spencer had not taken an interest. Unable to fix his mind (and who should complain?) on any metaphysical catch-all theory of knowledge, he none the less felt compelled to look about for some universal truth which would unify, synthesize and explain the multiplicity of phenomena collected in the museum-like cranium of Herbert Spencer. He established to his own satisfaction that the indestructibility of matter, the continuity of motion and the persistence of force are the three observable facts about the universe. But how do matter and motion redistribute themselves? Spencer answered this by asserting as a general 'law' or 'principle' or 'formula' – the words are never very nicely defined – the grand nine-teenth-century idea: evolution. Moreover, this universal law, this process of evolution, is to be seen at work in every area of life, following the same pattern, from the simple to the complex, from the small to the crowded, from the homogeneous, as he calls it, to the heteroge-neous. 'The chemical composition which is almost uniform throughout the substance of a germ, vegetable or animal, gradually ceases to be uniform ...'[22]

Here we are in territory which we should expect to be covered by the term 'evolution': 'In plants the albuminous and amylaceous matters which form the substance of the embryo, give origin here to a prepon-derance of chlorophyll and there to a preponderance of cellulose ...' Most of Spencer's thesis, incidentally, had been formed before the appearance of *The Origin of Species*; but, of course, when he had read Darwin's masterpiece, he was able to add far more detail to his picture.[23] And it is detail that Spencer so hungrily mops up. Frustrated by his hundred pages contemplating the Unknowable, he gobbles up the Knowable with a relentless appetite – plants, bees, mammals, vertebrates and invertebrates, stars, clouds, men, women and their habits and customs are all noted obsessively. It is rather like an overcrowded canvas by Frith. And everything, from the smallest molecule to the greatest industrial city, is a manifestation of the grand evolutionary principle.

No one could ever accuse Herbert Spencer of writing a poem, but strangely enough the effect of reading *First Principles*, and in particular chapters xiv–xvii on the Law of Evolution, is a little like that of having taken in *a vision*. At one moment we are attentively contemplating the head and thorax of a lobster; a few pages later, we find that 'in the social organism integrative changes are abundantly exemplified. Uncivilized societies display them when wandering families, such as those of Bushmen, join into tribes of considerable size ...'[24]

There is something both innocent and shocking, to the modern sensibility, in the ease with which Spencer applies the knowledge acquired from biology to the anthropological field. Clearly, to Spencer, the speed of evolution had not maintained an equal pace on every inch of the earth's turbulent surface. It had been much faster in Europe, for example, than in more 'primitive' parts of the world.

> In proof of the first of these statements may be cited the fact that, in the relative development of the limbs, civilized men depart more widely from the general type of the placental mammalia than do the lowest men. Though often possessing well-developed body and arms, the Papuan has very small legs; thus reminding us of the man-apes, in which there is no great contrast in size between the hind and fore limbs. But in the European, the greater length and massiveness of the legs has become marked – the fore and hind limbs are relatively more heterogeneous.

Likewise when we consider the components of the skull, 'the higher forms being distinguished by the relatively larger size of the bones which cover the brain, and the relatively smaller size of those which form the jaws, etc. Now this trait, which is stronger in Man than in any other creature, is stronger in the European than in the savage.'[25]

It was Spencer and not Darwin, we recollect, who coined the phrase 'survival of the fittest'. When one tries to imagine the effect of reading aloud such passages from *First Principles* to a university audience today, one appreciates the gulf which separates our own generation from that of the Victorians.

After the colonial experiment, and the various examples of social engineering in the twentieth century based on the idea of one race being more advanced than another, many human beings have returned with some relief to the myth that we are all alike the creatures of one Maker. Herbert Spencer and his innocent contemporaries were not proto-Nazis. Having scrambled and fought to make their own way in the world, it seemed natural to them to think that the whole universe was made in the image and likeness of self-made, scrambling provincial men, who had to fight to *get on*. Spencer sees the expanding suburbs of English cities as manifestations of the evolutionary principle:

> We have integrations consequent on the growths of adjacent parts per-forming like functions; as for instance, the junction of Manchester with its calico-weaving suburbs. We have other integrations which arise when, out of several places producing a similar commodity, one gaining more and more of the business, draws to it masters and workers, and leaves the other places to dwindle; as witness the growth of the Yorkshire cloth-districts at the expense of those in the west of England; or the absorption by Staffordshire of the pottery-manufacture, and the conse-quent decay of establishments at Derby and elsewhere ...[26]

Presumably, if such a 'decay' had not happened in Derby there would have been more prosperity in the town, and more chance for Mr Spencer senior to earn his living as a teacher, rather than being forced to go, ignominiously, to Nottingham and seek work as a lace-maker. Doggedly, however, Spencer sees this as part of the thrusting, cruel process of Nature itself – his own driving ambition to make himself not merely a successful writer but *the* supreme intellect of the age being part of the same relentless 'force', as he would call it. The acquisition of knowledge was his own method of rising from the evolutionary slime, but it also is a principle of things which is manifest to anyone prepared to see the world through Spencer's eyes, or hear it (perhaps a strange metaphor to employ of an adept of the ear-plug) through his ears. Language itself has been 'progressing'. 'Among uncivilized races, the many-syllabled names of not uncommon objects ... show that the words used for the less-familiar things are formed by uniting the words used for more familiar things.'[27] We discover that among the languages of North American tribes there are fifty polysyllabic names for 'common objects'. The Ricaree and Pawnee languages are regarded as 'uncivilised' and 'lower' than English for their persistence in saying *ashakish* when they could be saving time with the English word *dog*. Even Hebrew is further back in the evolutionary scale than English: 'If we compare, for instance, the Hebrew scriptures with writings of modern times, a marked difference of aggregation among the groups of words is visible ...'[28] There is very little 'complexity', according to Spencer, in Hebrew. 'Compare a number of verses from the Bible with some paragraphs from a modern writer, and the increase in heterogeneity of structure is very conspicuous.'[29] Incidentally, it perhaps goes without saying that a Victorian three-decker novel is more 'heterogeneous' and therefore more advanced in the evolutionary scale than simple narratives, such as those of Homer (Spencer had a low view of Homer).

He makes the improving suggestion that we should visit Sydenham to see the 'restored Assyrian architecture'; it is possible (in the Crystal Palace) to watch the gradual evolution of culture – from scratches on the walls, men evolved the idea of the bas-relief. 'While a walk through the British Museum will afford an opportunity of observing transitions, it will bring into view much evidence that the independent statues were derived from bas-reliefs ...'[30] The history of art itself, and of calligraphy, and of design, all tell a tale of evolution from the friezes on a Greek temple to an interior which is perhaps the one which Spencer himself looks up from his writing-desk to observe:

Strange as it seems, then, all forms of written language, of painting, of sculpture, have a common root in those rude drawings on skins and cavern-walls by which savages commemorated notable deeds of their chiefs, and which, during social progress, developed into the politico-religious decorations of ancient temples and palaces. Little resemblance as they now have, the bust that stands on the console, the landscape that hangs against the wall, and the copy of *The Times* lying upon the table, are remotely akin. The brazen face of the knocker which the postman has just lifted, is related not only to the woodcuts of the *Illustrated London News* which he is delivering, but to the characters of the *billet-doux* which accompanies it. Between the painted window, the prayer-book on which its light falls, and the adjacent monument, there is consanguinity. The effigies on our coins, the signs over shops, the figures that fill every leader, the coats of arms outside the carriage panel, and the placards inside the omnibus, are, in common with the dolls, blue-books and paper hangings, lineally descended from the sculpture-paintings and picture-writings in which the Egyptians represented and recorded the triumphs and worship of their god-kings ...[31]

There is something so impressionistic about paragraphs such as these that they almost become surreal; yet there can be few passages of prose which convey in more energetic detail what it felt like to be an intellectually curious, agnostically baffled Victorian of 1860.

It is sad to record that Spencer's 'religion of science', as Beatrice Webb called it, did not make him very happy. In July 1883 she found him looking 'absolutely wretched. No better. "I have no patience with what is disagreeable. I don't know what to do with myself. Even if I go fishing what can I do with my evenings without pleasant society? I am terribly bored." '[32] Three years later, when he gave her some leaves of his *Autobiography* to read, Beatrice was stabbed with a yet more tender pity for him.

'I was never in love,' he announced when I put the question straight. 'Were you never conscious of the wholesale sacrifice you were making, did you never long for those other forms of thought, feeling, action you were shut out from?' Strange, a nature with so perfect an intellect and little else, save friendliness and the uprightness of a truth-loving mind ... I pressed him to continue his autobiography rather than his other work, those long-drawn deductions, wearisome to all except his blind disciples.[33]

Wise advice from one so young (twenty-eight) to one so old; but of course the mind was only truth-loving up to a point. Poor old Spencer wanted reassurances like everyone else, not least the reassurance that posterity would think well of him: the result is an autobiography so prolix and so full of self-vaunting and self-justification as to be all but unreadable. In 1887 she went down to see him in Brighton. He had moved to the coast, and now lived in a small house 'with sunny aspect and glimpse of the sea'. He lay there on a day bed 'in a living death'. The doctors could find nothing wrong with him, but he suffered an agonising succession of imagined or hypochondriac symptoms, constantly sounding his pulse, and a martyr to sleeplessness and indigestion.[34]

The hopes and fears which tormented him were of the very kind which, as a scientific agnostic, he might have expected would be banished by the rational mind. Towards the end of his life, in 1902, he published a series of fragmentary thoughts about the possibility of the consciousness surviving bodily death. 'After contemplating the inscrutable relation between brain and consciousness, and finding that we can get no evidence of the existence of the last without the activity of the first' – a typical Spencerism! Do get on with it, man – 'we seem obliged to relinquish the thought that consciousness continues after physical organisation has become inactive.'

So that's that, then? We do not survive our bodily death? And we should not have expected the apostle of scientific agnosticism to imagine anything else. It is with some surprise that we find there is a 'but' in the case ... 'But it seems a strange and repugnant conclusion that with the cessation of consciousness at death, there ceases to be any knowledge of having existed. With his last breath it becomes to each the same thing as though he had never lived.'

Spencer is unable to face this fact with stoicism. Rather, he speculates that there might come a time when there could be found some form of scientific proof that the human consciousness does survive bodily death. His capacity for generalizing stands him in good stead. Evolution (or Creation) explains a good deal about how the mysteries of *objects* are presented to our senses. But no such theory has yet explained or plumbed *space*. 'Theist and Agnostic must agree in recognising the properties of Space as inherent, eternal, created – as anteceding either creation or evolution. It is impossible to imagine how the marvellous space-relations discovered by the Geometry of Position came into existence. The consciousness that without origin or cause infinite Space has ever existed and must ever exist, produces in me a feeling from which I shrink.'[35]

Spencer's friend and follower John, by that time Lord, Morley read these sentiments with some dismay. 'It made some of the narrower or the firmer among us quake,' he records in his *Recollections*.[36] He went down to Brighton to quiz the old man about what was meant by Geometry of Position, and to discover whether he really was wavering in his unbelief. When he thought he understood Spencer's position, Morley interjected that Space was, after all, only a subjective impression. 'With flashing eye and astounded gesture, as if hearing the incredible, he exclaimed, "Then you have turned Kantian, have you?" I saw that things could be carried no further, so with remorse in my heart, I quitted him.'[37]

It is hard to know Spencer's state of mind at the last. He died in December 1903. He asked for no religious ceremony, but for a speech at his funeral, to be delivered by Morley. 'I do not like the thought of entire silence, and should be glad were there given a brief address by a friend. On looking round among my friends, you stand out above others as one from whom words would come most fitly; partly because of our long friendship, partly because of the kinship of sentiment existing between us, and partly because of the general likeness of ideas which distinguishes us from the world at large.'[38] In the event, Spencer died while Morley was abroad. We have already alluded to the tributes which were paid him in death. His mortal remains were cremated at Golders Green crematorium (in Morley's absence Mr Leonard Courtney gave the address). Few of us are in a position to guess, still less to know, whether his consciousness survives, somewhere in Infinite Space; or, if it does, whether Spencer considers that the hours, weeks, months, years of dyspepsia, solitude, depression and loneliness – the price he paid for writing millions of words which no one now reads – were, in the end, worth the effort.

9

Science

'Are God and Nature then at strife?'
Tennyson

THE ENORMOUS COMMERCIAL success in our day of 'popular science' books might be attributable to the profound interest and enjoyment which we all derived from the study of science in our childhood. Unable to kick the habit of the chemistry set, the hour in the physics lab testing basic electric circuits or in the biology lab dissecting frogs, we the reading public continue our voracious scientific interests by reading works of astronomy, cosmology, genetic biology and biochemistry.

Maybe. Or maybe we buy, in the greatest numbers, not those books which humbly seek to explain the unfolding fascination of what Thomas Kuhn (with, one assumes, deliberate dismissiveness) calls 'normal science'[1] but those which would induce the belief that science offers universal explanations for angst-ridden metaphysical inquiries. Stephen Hawking, for example, modestly suggests that his book *A Brief History of Time* might help his readers to 'know the mind of God'.[2] Darwin's most ardent representative on earth (since the death of Thomas Huxley), Richard Dawkins, begins his superbly readable account of the Darwinian theory of cumulative selection with a sentence which deserves a prize: 'This book is written in the conviction that our own existence once presented the greatest of all mysteries, but that it is a mystery no longer because it is solved.'[3]

Do those of us who enjoy these books – and they are certainly addictive – feel that we have our money's worth? After all, you would think that once we had seen into the mind of God or solved the greatest of all mysteries, that would be that. We should not need to read another book on the subject. But then ... so readable are these popular scientists, and so interesting the substance of what they have to say, that when the next of them appears on a TV chat-show, often cunningly put up against some dyed-in-the-wool creationist or religious believer, we rush out to the book stores next morning to buy the book.

The old Victorian Big Fight, first popularized by Thomas Huxley, with God in the Blue Corner and Science waiting in the Red Corner to punch His teeth out, still has the capacity to draw the crowds. Indeed, it possibly has more pull now than it ever did then, since in our 'post-modern' world there have been plenty of arts graduates and would-be clever thinkers prepared to borrow Kuhn's words and say that science is, after all, only a paradigm, a way of talking about the universe: which we, with our ear cocked for literary ironies and the uses to which texts can be put, can see is only *one* way. Science, they tell us, is only 'true' in its own way. Theology could just as readily be 'true' in another ... Plenty of room for confusion of thought, here.

In all likelihood, our post-modern habit of viewing science as only a paradigm would evaporate if we developed appendicitis. We should look for a medically trained surgeon who knew what an appendix was, where it was, and how to cut it out without killing us. Likewise, we should be happy to debate the essentially fictive nature of, let us say, Newton's Laws of Gravity unless and until someone threatened to throw us out of a top-storey window. Then the law of gravity would seem very real indeed. What shocks us about science, compared with the other areas of discourse with which we entertain the vacant hours, is that science seems like an accurate language for talking about real things, actual phenomena. So if a scientist starts telling us that all the 'mysteries' have been solved, we take that literally, too, and flock to him with the credulity of the crowds who might once have climbed through the steep olive-groves of Delphi to consult the oracle. Indeed, there are many of us who believe, at least most of the time, that there were scientific discoveries in the nineteenth century which were the primary and definitive contributory factors in the so-called Death of God.

Before considering the Victorian obsession with science, however, it is worth analysing the singular quality of historico-theologico-metaphysical-scientific muddle involved in the question of a First Cause. When we rush out to buy the books, we very likely do so in the quasi-superstitious spirit of the careless pre-Darwinian thinker ascribing the origin of everything to God.

The advantage of doing this – of talking about a First Cause – is that it stops us worrying our heads with an unanswerable and ultimately pointless question. 'Deists' such as Voltaire, Gibbon or (in some of his phases of thought) Kant were not making the crude mistake which modern Darwinians sometimes attribute to them. They weren't baby-

Thomas Hardy, whose poem 'God's Funeral' epitomizes the atheism of his generation

Some Enlightenment precursors: *(clockwise from top left)* David Hume, Immanuel Kant, Edward Gibbon and Georg Wilhelm Hegel. Did their work destroy the God of Faith, o merely the Deism of philosophers?

The resemblance of Karl Marx to the Zeus of Oticoli was noted by an admirer, who presented him with a cast. As the 'consciousness of the nineteenth century', Marx had small influence. It is in the twentieth century that we have witnessed the growth of atheist Marxist states in Russia and China

Thomas Carlyle voiced the
anxiety felt in Britain in the
1840s that Christianity might be
untrue. But what could take its
place?

John Henry Newman was one
of the most mellifluous defender
of orthodoxy, but many
contemporaries found Carlyle
more persuasive

remy Bentham's Philosophic
adicalism had a critical
nfluence on the development of
ne nineteenth-century secular
ate. His skeleton, still wearing
is old clothes, continues to sit
n University College, London

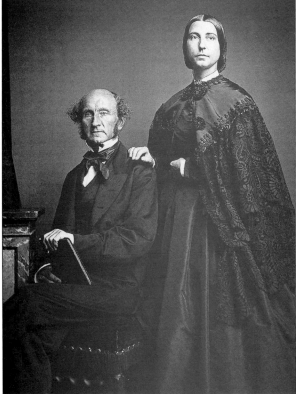

ohn Stuart Mill, 'the saint of
ationalism', pictured here with
is step-daughter, pioneered
arliamentary reform, feminism
nd state socialism

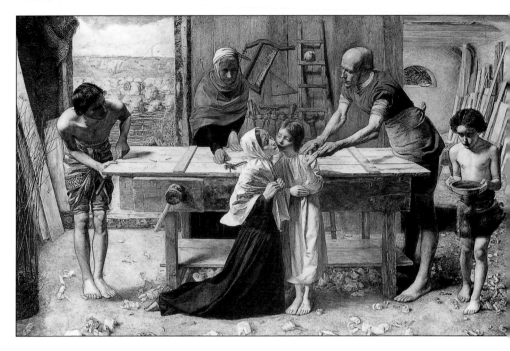

Millais's painting *Christ in the house of his parents* caused a storm of protest when exhibited in 1850

Secular Lives of Jesus, of which the most popular was Ernest Renan's, did even more to disturb the belief of Christians

Herbert Spencer, now largely unread, was seen as a great philosopher in his day. As a young man he befriended George Eliot *(below left)*; in old age he knew the socialist Beatrice Webb *(below right)*, who told her diary: 'There is no life … so inexpressibly sad as the inarticulate life of Herbert Spencer …'

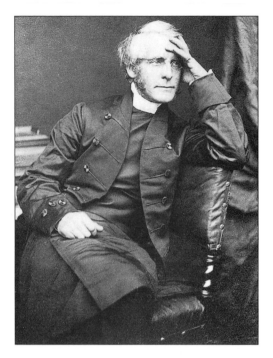

Bishop Colenso dared to question the historicity of Noah's Ark. He was deposed for heresy

Sir Charles Lyell was not himself an atheist, but through his pioneering work in geology he did more than any other scientist to disturb the religious faith of the 1830s and the century that followed

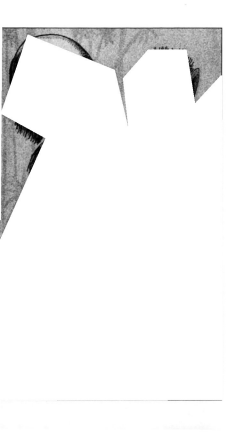

T. H. Huxley *(above)* was the Apostle of
Unbelief. He coined the word 'Agnostic'
and was a great popularizer of the work of
Darwin, whose inexorable exposure of the
process of natural selection removed the
need to posit a First Cause as the origin of
Life on Earth

The endearing if slightly absurd Master of Balliol Benjamin Jowett *(above left)* was definite in his belief in God, albeit vague about the Divine Nature. His most celebrated pupil Algernon Swinburne *(above right)* became the great poet of Atheism, whereas Jowett's old friend Alfred Tennyson *(below)* was the poet of the honest doubters, 'believing where we cannot prove'

Did God go to Balliol? To read Matthew Arnold is to suppose that He would have done so, had He existed. Arnold's niece Mrs Humphry Ward wrote bestselling novels about Doubt. John Ruskin *(below)* rediscovered the Catholic aesthetic but could not believe its theology

The case of Charles Bradlaugh *(left)*, the MP who refused to take the Oath in the House of Commons, highlighted the extent to which, by 1883, unbelief had become commonplace. The Anglo-Catholic Gladstone *(below left)* defended Bradlaugh's position – 'I have no fear of Atheism in this House'. Lord Queensberry *(below)*, Oscar Wilde's Scarlet Marquess, refused to take the Oath in the Lords, dismissing it as 'Christian tomfoolery'

When Annie Besant ran away from her clergyman husband, she seemed destined for a life of atheistic socialism; but she missed religion, and became seduced by the Wisdom of the East

Her friend Eleanor Marx died too young to waver. She 'refused to recognize the beauty of the Christian religion'

God is dead … or did they really mean that God is Dad? Sigmund Freud in his lectures on psychoanalysis paraded as scientific truths the prejudices which animated such figures as the novelist Samuel Butler, pictured with his friend Henry Festing Jones: 'MY MOST IMPLACABLE ENEMY from childhood has certainly been my father', Butler wrote

Might it not be possible to hang on to religion even when its mythologies were exposed?
Attempts to do so by the Catholic modernists, among them *(clockwise from top left)*
Alfred Loisy, George Tyrrell and the Baron von Hügel, were ruthlessly suppressed by
the Vatican

The genial philosopher/psychologist William James defended the reality of religious experience. He had no truck with the Absolute Idealism of his great contemporary Josiah Royce. These photographs were taken by James's daughter near Chocorua, New Hampshire. In the first frame he is saying, 'Royce you are being photographed.' In the second he cried 'Look out! I say, Damn the Absolute!'

ishly saying that someone came along and pressed a button which would enable the whole show to proceed – though it is precisely this anthropomorphic myth with which the Book of Genesis begins. Critics of the First Cause theory have no difficulty in pointing out its inadequacies by asking what or who caused the First Cause. As an explanation it is hopeless. As a way of stopping head-spin, it has much to recommend it. After all, as Richard Dawkins disarmingly admits in that very book which began so confidently, 'we still don't know exactly how natural selection began on Earth'.[4]

Biology and biochemistry have indeed more or less cleared up any mystery about the manner in which characteristics within species are genetically transmitted. It would be a person of considerable boneheadedness who did not believe in, and see the stupendous significance of, Watson and Crick's discovery of DNA in Cambridge in 1953. By discovering the molecular structure of DNA, Watson and Crick really wrote the final paragraph of the story begun by Wallace and Darwin a hundred years earlier. We could now see, beyond reasonable argument, how it worked; how Darwin's intuition was right, and that all life is related, and could – or, more than could: does – derive from a common source.

One suspects that the question of *origins* – with which this whole matter has been concerned since Darwin published his most famous book in 1859, with that word in its title – betrays a mistaken picture of the *kind* of information science could pass on to us. It has been noticeable that once they stop their fascinating analyses of *how* and begin to attempt to formulate answers to *why*, the scientists seem every bit as clumsy as the most amateurish theologians, either falling back on the imagery of science-fiction, with J.B.S. Haldane's vision of life climbing out of 'the primordial soup', or succumbing to Francis Crick's own touching but lame view (he is a non-believer in God, one should hasten to say) that 'the origin of life appears to be almost a miracle, so many are the conditions which would have to be satisfied to get it going'.[5] These days even the most hard-nosed materialists, if they get themselves into conflict with the religious, find themselves wanting to say how awe-struck they are by the complexity and wonders of nature, and end up sounding like Louis Armstrong with his 'wonderful world'.

This is the one area of life where, more than in any other, we seem the children of the Victorians. So far in this book, we have hinted at various reasons why the men and women of the nineteenth century might have abandoned their religion. There is the relentless time-bomb of 'enlightenment' thought – above all, David Hume's scepticism about the very notion of Causation, and the distrust of a metaphor which considered it probable that there was a Mind behind the Universe. We remembered Kant's demolition of the Arguments by Design, or the Cosmic arguments. We thought of Gibbon, exposing in chapter after chapter the fact that the early and medieval Christians were a shabby and badly-behaved collection of individuals, considerably less impressive in many respects than the admirable Stoics and Epicureans who lived in the age of Cicero.

For the generation who read Strauss, there was the deadly twin assault of Hegelianism and empiricism: the one suggesting that the march of history had put away childish things, and Christianity with them; the other reminding the sceptical mind of the sheer unlikelihood, the basic, common-sense improbability, of angelic apparitions, a virginal conception, loaves and fishes which could be multiplied, a human body which could rise from the tomb.

Out of the many doubts which nagged at the minds of men and women in the 1840s and 1850s there came a word to describe the prevailing mid nineteenth-century metaphysic: agnostic.*

> Behold, we know not anything;
> I can but trust that good shall fall
> At last – far off – at last, to all,
> And every winter change to spring.[6]

Interestingly, indeed, the figure who inspired the agnostics to coin the word for their set of opinions was a clergyman of the Church of England. Nor was he the type of clergyman whose views were wishy-washy, by the standards of the ecclesiastical spectrum. Indeed, Henry Longueville Mansel was in many respects an old-fashioned High Churchman – certainly closer to Pusey than to Dr Arnold in theological flavour and in the more nebulous but unmistakable area known by the semi-definable Anglican term 'churchmanship'. He was a much merrier man than Pusey, to be sure. 'His humour was irrepressible,' remembered a friend, 'and the coming joke was to be seen spreading

---

* It was in 1869 that Huxley coined the term agnostic, at a meeting of the Metaphysical Society; *vide infra*, p. 199.

gradually over his face.' Mansel had the High Victorian taste for awful puns, worthy of the most excruciating *Punch* jokes. As an examiner at Oxford, he came across someone whose name was Field-Flowers. 'That man', he exclaimed, 'was born to be either *ploughed* or *plucked*.' Someone who upset the gravy at dinner began to dab it with a cloth, and said, 'What a filthy mess!' 'Not exactly,' rejoined the wit, 'but it is lamb-on-table [lamentable], certainly.' When he (briefly, before his premature death, of heart failure) became Dean of St Paul's, Mansel was showing a visitor around. The puritanical tourist pointed to a statue of Neptune and his trident, and asked crossly, 'What has that to do with Christianity?' 'Tridentine Christianity, perhaps?' asked Mansel.[7]

He was born in 1820, and educated at Merchant Taylors' and St John's College, Oxford.[8] Of his prodigious memory for verse a school friend (the Reverend Leopold Bernays) remarked that 'if all the English poets were lost, Mansel would be able to reproduce them'. As an undergraduate he worked so hard that he injured his health, conquering his natural languor by the invention of a Heath Robinson-ish alarum clock, the weight of which, when it descended, pulled off his bedclothes and compelled him to rise – sometimes as early as 4 a.m. He was rewarded by a Double First.

The important thing about Mansel, destined to become by his mid thirties a Reader in Metaphysical Philosophy (eventually the first Waynflete Professor of Moral Philosophy), is that he was one of the few Englishmen of the date to have read and absorbed Kant.

Bertrand Russell, the godson (if such a thing does not seem a contradiction in terms, in such an impeccably free-thinking tradition) of John Stuart Mill, remembered the anecdote of someone once mentioning Kant to James Mill and receiving the answer, 'I see well enough what poor Kant would be at.'[9] This general English ignorance of the greatest metaphysician of modern times was only matched by the general English ignorance even, or especially, in intellectual circles up to and including our own day, of science.* Hence, perhaps, the particularly surreal quality of the Victorian Religion versus Science controversies.

In 1858 Mansel delivered the Bampton Lectures (always given from the pulpit of the University Church in Oxford on a Sunday morning). It was thirteen years since Newman, the most electrifying preacher in

---

* Consider the remark of Mrs Sumner, wife of the Warden of All Souls, to Lindemann (The Prof): 'My husband always says that with a first in Greats, a man can "get up" science in a fortnight.'

memory, had joined the Church of Rome; fifteen years since he had spoken from that pulpit and filled that church, of which he was the vicar, with appreciative congregations. Since then a great change had come upon Oxford, as upon England. The cynicism of Mark Pattison, the honest doubts of Froude and Clough and Arnold, had changed the intellectual climate. *The Times* reported that 'Sunday after Sunday, during the whole series, in spite of the natural craving for variety, and some almost tropical weather, there flocked to St Mary's a large and continually increasing crowd of hearers, to listen to the discourses on the Absolute and the Infinite, which they confessedly could not comprehend'.[10]

Mansel was unashamedly steeped in German philosophy. Unlike most of those who spoke so freely about 'the Germans', he was able, authoritatively, to state that 'it would probably astonish some of the critics who talk so comprehensively of German metaphysics and German Theology, as if all Germans held the same opinions, to be told that the purport of the philosophy of Kant is to teach a lesson in humility, to inculcate the very limited nature of human faculties and human knowledge'.[11]

He was not an uncritical Kantian. There were many passages in Kant which he believed were needlessly obscure, or vague. He distrusted Kant's idea of appearances and his stress on the active nature of the human mind, for he believed that transcendental idealism led inevitably to the waffly pantheism of Fichte, and the windier passages of Hegel. Mansel had a good-humoured trust in English/Scottish 'common sense' solutions to philosophical problems. But the first and fundamental lesson which he derived from Kant was one which he believed had been forgotten: 'the true lesson of philosophy is a knowledge of the limits of human reason'.[12]

Mansel's Bampton Lectures attempted to separate out what can and can't be usefully said, what can and can't be legitimately known. To encapsulate the central message of the Bamptons – published as *The Limits of Religious Thought* – it would be enough to say that merely because an adequate conception of God is unattainable, this does not mean that belief in God is impossible. Indeed, the ineffability of God, His invisibility, incomprehensibility, and unknowability, are central to the Biblical as to the Christian Mystical Conception of God.

The Deist God who could be inferred from Design or Cosmology is not the God of Scripture, who is known through Revelation. Mansel did not believe that it was possible, given the nature of the human mind, for people to intuit God either through the sensibility or through the understanding:

> If our whole thinking is subject to certain laws, it follows that we cannot think of any object, not even of Omnipotence itself, except as those laws compel us ...[13] It is no matter from what point of view we commence our examination, whether with the Theist, we admit the coexistence of the Infinite and the Finite, as distinct realities; or, with the Pantheist, deny the real existence of the Infinite; on each of these suppositions alike, our reason appears divided against itself, compelled to admit the truth of one hypothesis, and yet unable to overcome the apparent impossibilities of each.[14]

By a series of mental gymnastics, Mansel managed to argue that unless one conceded the possibility of the Infinite, and of Revelation, it was not truly possible to criticize the Bible. For the Bible presented humanity with regulative, not speculative, principles that 'do not serve to satisfy the reason, but to guide the conduct; they do not tell us what things are in themselves, but how we must conduct ourselves in relation to them'.[15] And:

> If Revelation is a communication from an infinite to a finite intelligence, the conditions of a criticism of Revelation on philosophical grounds must be identical with those which are required for constructing a Philosophy of the Infinite ... Whatever impediments, therefore, exist to prevent the formulation of such a philosophy, the same impediments must likewise prevent the accomplishment of a complete criticism of Revelation.[16]

No wonder there were those, as the 1850s drew to a close, who were so excited by Dean Mansel that they supposed him to be, 'single-handed, confounding a host of unbelievers – some with unpronounceable names and unintelligible theories; and sending them flying before him like dust before the wind'.[17]

While the gentlemen of Oxford, without fully understanding what they were about, absorbed Professor Mansel's defence of revealed religion, Charles Darwin was on the verge of publishing *The Origin of Species*. It is doubtful whether he would have gone into print so soon – perhaps at all – had it not been for the fact that another biologist, Alfred Russel Wallace, was on the verge of publishing a paper suggesting a theory of natural selection to explain the evolution of species. Wallace's paper on the subject reached Darwin at about the time that Dean Mansel was expounding Kant from the pulpit of St Mary's; and he was persuaded by his friend Charles Lyell, the great geologist, that he must put something on paper '... if only a fragment – pigeons if you please'.[18] This is a reference, as any reader of *The Origin* will know, to Darwin's having devoted time to the study of racehorse breeders and pigeon-fanciers, noting that these men appeared to be doing, in a speeded-up fashion, what Nature did as a matter of course: producing a species which was stronger and more likely to win in its chosen field than its forebears. It was not achieved by some spurious Lamarckian passing-on of learned or acquired characteristics – this was not possible. It was done genetically. Forty years before Mendel's genetic revelations were published, and a century before the discovery of the exact structure of DNA, Wallace had begun to have an inkling that the key to evolution in species was genetic. Species evolve by a process of selection – natural selection, since the 'survival of the fittest' could alone account for survival at all.

Darwin had been slowly, and in some ways reluctantly, accumulating evidence during the preceding quarter-century. His modesty and diffidence partly explained his silence – at least, his silence in print. He was a private gentleman, comfortably circumstanced thanks to his Wedgwood inheritance, and with no wish for notoriety. Moreover, as he was not slow to recognize, the metaphysical implications of his work were inimical to faith; and he felt tenderly towards his beloved wife Emma – also a Wedgwood – who held orthodox religious opinions. His own change had been slow, imperceptible; 'I gave up religious belief almost independently from my own reflections,' he told Francis Galton;[19] and he had come to believe, with many of his age, that 'The Old Testament was no more to be trusted than the sacred books of the Hindoos', not only because of 'its manifestly false history of the world' but because of its 'attributing to God the feelings of a revengeful tyrant ... Beautiful as is the morality of the New Testament, it can hardly be denied that its perfection depends in part on the interpretation we now put on metaphors and allegories ...'[20] Nothing very original about these ideas. Since the beginning of Queen Victoria's reign, however (1837), Darwin had been confiding to his notebooks some radically new ideas about the origin of species. 'If we choose to let conjecture run wild,' he had written even so early, 'then animals, our fellow brethren in rain, disease, death, suffering and famine – our slaves in the most laborious works, our companions in our amusements – they may partake of our origin in one common ancestor – we may all be melted together.'[21]

The Wedgwoods were high-minded Unitarians, and the Darwins were 'church' by reason of squirearchical position only, not by conviction. Even on the *Beagle* all those years before, when as a young naturalist he began to notice the speed – a matter of generations – with which the beaks of finches in the Galapagos islands adapt themselves for survival, Darwin, though still a church-goer, had not retained any belief in miracles: 'The more we know of the fixed laws of nature the more incredible do miracles become.'

Darwin's theory of natural selection was decidedly his own – though it is interesting that Wallace should have reached almost identical conclusions at an almost identical moment in history. This in itself is certainly a fact which should make us ask how much it was a scientific discovery – falsifiable, in Popper's terms – and how much the expression of a metaphysical idea having much in common with *laissez-faire* economics, competition, progress, and the other ideas of the time.

> All the plants of a given country ... are at war with one another. The first which establish themselves by chance in a particular spot, tend, by the mere occupancy of space, to exclude other species – the greater choke the smaller, the longest livers replace those who last for a shorter period, the more prolific gradually make themselves master of the ground, which species multiplying more slowly would otherwise fill.

This could be Marx, talking of the class struggle; or Bismarck, a little later in the century, talking of the struggle of nation states for supremacy in militaristic power; but it was in fact a Swiss botanist quoted by Lyell in his *Principles of Geology*.[22]

Lyell was, like most early nineteenth-century scientists, a gentleman of independent means. (There were hardly any 'jobs' for scientists in nineteenth-century England and the universities, unlike those of the Germany of the post-Kantian years, were slow to accept the need to teach science as an academic discipline.) He was the least likely revolutionary in the world, and the evidences he gradually discovered, *as a geologist*, of new data strongly inimical to the traditional Christian world-picture, were painstakingly collected over a long period. As the foremost palaeontologist of the century, he was able to demonstrate the sheer impossibility of believing that the world had been created all in one go, some thousands of years BC. The progressions, volcanic and otherwise, by which the surface of the earth came to its present shape were, Lyell demonstrated, much slower and much more gradual than the traditional picture as given in the Bible.

The eighteenth-century philosopher Bishop Berkeley defended the traditional view that the world was little more than six thousand years old on the grounds that there would surely be palaeontological evidence of earlier life-forms, had these existed. If Berkeley (born 1685) had lived to read Lyell his rhetorical question 'How comes it that no remains are found?'[23] would have been answered. No doubt Berkeley would have shared our astonishment that the human race, with all its ingenuity, had waited until the nineteenth century before guessing the age of the planet.

In the course of Lyell's encyclopaedic investigations of geological remains – in the Auvergne, in Italy, in his native Scotland, in North America, and in the Canaries – he discovered the existence of fossils of extinct mammalian species in Jurassic and Triassic strata; Tennyson was not the only one to work out some of the implications. Nature was wasteful. Species could, in the words of *In Memoriam*, be cast as rubbish to the void. And, moreover, the more the evidence accumulated, the more it looked, not as if one species became extinct to be replaced by another, but as though one evolved into the other. Lyell was always cautious about making his findings public. But it was he who arranged to publish Darwin's *Origin of Species* – the first time the theory of natural selection was made public was through a paper of Lyell's given to the Linnean Society. Without the palaeontological evidence, Darwin's views could (until the discovery of DNA) have been regarded as speculative: though the evidence Darwin himself had accumulated began to look overwhelming.

Similarly, Robert Chambers's (1802–1871) *Vestiges of Creation* had caused disturbing waves among the doubting classes when it was anonymously published in 1844 (some people thought it was written by Prince Albert!).[24]

> It is clear from the whole scope of the natural laws that the individual as far as the present sphere of being is concerned, is to the Author of Nature a consideration of inferior moment. Everywhere we see the arrangements for the species perfect; the individual is left, as it were, to take his chance amidst the *mêlée* of the various laws affecting him. If he be found inferiorly endowed, or ill befalls him, there was at least no partiality against

him. The system has the fairness of a lottery, in which every one has the chance of drawing the prize.[25]

Darwin's view was in a sense the opposite: there are no *chances* in his system. He was anxious, for a number of reasons, to play down the metaphysical implications of his theory of natural selection. He concluded *The Origin* with the suggestion that the process of natural selection was a series of 'laws impressed on matter by the Creator ...'

> These laws, taken in the largest sense, being Growth with Reproduction; Inheritance, which is almost implied by reproduction; Variability, from the indirect and direct action of the external conditions of life, and from use and disuse; a Ratio of Increase so high as to lead to a Struggle for Life, and as a consequence to Natural Selection, entailing Divergence of Character and the Extinction of less-improved forms.

There is very little here to suggest inheritance of the earth by the meek of any species. The best-endowed, by inheritance; the most competitive; the most ruthless; the most thrusting: they, it would seem, had inherited the earth. Was this Darwin the naturalist speaking? Or Darwin the grandson of one of the most famous and successful of capitalists, Josiah Wedgwood – inventor, social climber, aesthete, potter, businessman of genius, who did not allow the loss of a leg in early life to prevent his magnificent, exuberant, energetic rise through society. (How Balzac would have loved to contemplate old Jos – Owd Wooden-Leg, as his workers called him!) One can imagine Adam Smith cheering the Darwinian idea, but not St Francis of Assisi. 'There is a grandeur in this view of life,' Darwin concluded that bombshell of a book, 'with its several powers, having been originally breathed by the Creator into a few forms or into one; and that, whilst this planet has gone cycling on according to the fixed law of gravity, so from so simple a beginning endless forms most beautiful and most wonderful have been, and are being, evolved.'[26]

Thus, the author himself. But his readers were surely right to conclude, as has Richard Dawkins, that 'although atheism might have been logically tenable before Darwin, Darwin made it possible to be an intellectually fulfilled atheist'.[27] This is not, as we can see by rereading the final paragraph of *The Origin of Species*, what Darwin actually says; but it is indeed the unavoidable conclusion. Hitherto, in order to explain how the universe came to be as it was, and in particular how life on earth came to be as it is, there had been the itching temptation among scientists and among metaphysicians – even the ones who had read David Hume and knew it was not logically necessary – to supply some paradigm of *design* when speaking of nature; and having drawn the paradigm of design, to conclude not only that Nature had a designer, but that it had been designed, or created, for a purpose.

Many people to this day believe that it is necessary, in order to be an honest theist, to subscribe to some such collection of views. Perhaps the Marxists were right who linked their views with those of Darwin, since Darwin's truly distinctive contribution to the nineteenth-century world-view was not to promote materialism, nor to propose a theory of evolution – plenty of scientists and philosophers had already done that; it was to expound a theory of natural selection which removed any necessity for a metaphor of purpose when discussing natural history. Evolution proceeded, in the Darwinian view, by a series of ineluctable progressions, the stronger form always eliminating the weaker. Once the process had been recognized for what it was, there was no need to personalize it at all. There was no need to pretend that Natural Selection had a view of things, or loved the world, or the people in it, any more than it had once loved amoebas or brontosauruses. The bleak impersonal chain of being rolled on with the inevitability of the other 'laws of nature': there was absolutely no need, if this was an accurate picture of what happened in nature, to posit the existence of a 'Creator'.

When Lyell first approached a London publisher to propagate his friend's ideas, he turned to John Murray (1808–1892), the son of Byron's publisher. Murray (an ardent amateur geologist) was unimpressed; in fact, when Lyell tried to explain it to him, he thought the thesis completely absurd – 'as absurd as contemplating the fruitful union of a poker and a rabbit'. When told that Darwin had tested his theory in relation to racing pigeons, the bookman brightened a little, and implored that this should be brought into the earlier part of the thesis: 'Everybody is interested in pigeons.'[28] In fact, of course, the idea of The Struggle for Life seems to us fundamental to the Nineteenth Century and its idea of itself. 'There exists but one animal. The Creator used only one pattern for all organized beings. An animal is an entity taking its shape, or rather its different shapes, from the environment in which it develops. Zoological species are the result ...' Darwin? No: Balzac, in his preface to *La Comédie Humaine* of 1842. Mr Murray need not have been apprehensive. The shy naturalist had written the ultimate three-volume shocker. Perhaps Mr Murray guessed it was going to do well, since he increased the print run on the first edition from 500 to 1,250. A pirated American edition of 3,000 sold out almost at once. Thereafter, it became The Book, selling in quantities to rival the novels of Dickens. Balzac's Comedy displays a perpetual warfare and struggle of selfish genes preying upon one another, yet there remains in his over-energetic creations, such as Vautrin and Rastignac, a perpetual sense that they are free to escape their fore-ordained destinies by acts of will (literally, in Vautrin's case, since he escapes the scaffold at the last minute and becomes a chief of police). Darwin's picture of the universe does not really allow for such liberties. Shortly before he died, Dean Mansel said to an Oxford friend: 'Prepare to defend the Existence of God and the Free Will of Man. Those are the points of controversy upon which the world is turning at present.'[29]

Even Darwin, of course, irreligious as he had privately become by 1859, did not *set out* to make it possible to be an intellectually fulfilled atheist. And it is perhaps worth remembering that the publication of Chambers's *Vestiges*, Lyell's *Geology*, and Darwin's *Origin of Species*, troubling as they were on many levels to faith, did not lead, in the world of science, to widespread unbelief. On the contrary. Most of the leading scientists of Great Britain retained a Christian commitment. In 1874 Darwin's step-cousin, Francis Galton, sent detailed questionnaires to 189 leading Fellows of the Royal Society, and to three others distinguished in scientific fields. When asked their religious affiliation, seventy per cent described themselves as members of the established churches (Scotland and England), where that was relevant, or as adherents of the recently disestablished Church of Ireland. The others were divided between those who when asked their religious affiliation replied 'None whatever', and those who said they were 'established Church with qualification', Unitarian, other Nonconformist, Wesleyan, Catholic, or Bible Christian. Asked whether the religion taught them in their youth had had a 'deterrent effect on the freedom of your researches', almost ninety per cent replied 'None at all'.

It would be true to say that among Victorian men of science, Christian commitment was not the exception but the rule. James Challis, Michael Faraday, John Herschel, James Prescott Joule, James Clerk-Maxwell, Charles Pritchard, G.G. Stokes and William Thomson (Lord Kelvin) were all devout, though not necessarily orthodox, representatives of the physical sciences. The leading geologists of the day were

Sedgwick, T.G. Bonney, James Dwight Dana, J.W. Dawson, Joseph Le Conte, Sir Charles Lyell, Roderick Murchison, William North Rice, Alexander Winchell, and George Frederick Wright. They were all firm believers in a Deity. Among the better-known naturalists in holy orders were the Reverends J.C. Atkinson, M.J. Berkeley, C.A. Johns, R.T. Lowe, W.W. Newbould, J.G. Wood and H.B. Tristram.[30] In 1868 an Austrian monk, Gregor Mendel, totally unknown to Darwin, was conducting experiments which would vindicate the Darwinian position and destroy the plausibility of Lamarck. Father Mendel's experiments in breeding pea-plants established the existence of what he called hereditary particles and are now called *genes*, and he was the first scientist who demonstrated that natural forms can be subdivided into discrete traits which are transmitted genetically from one generation to the next. This was the discovery which prepared for Watson and Crick's discovery of DNA in 1953, and it was in many ways more important than anything discovered by Darwin – though of course it was entirely compatible with Darwin's brilliant deductions and propositions. Father Mendel showed no unwillingness, day after day, to rise before the dawn and sing a psalm which proclaimed that it is God 'who hath made us and not we ourselves'; he died in his monastery.

So, although with hindsight it may seem that Darwin made it possible to be an intellectually fulfilled atheist, it was by no means considered by his scientific colleagues that he had made such a position intellectually inescapable.

It is also worth adding that Darwin, such a brilliant naturalist, was not a trained theologian; and he was mistaken in supposing that the immutability of species – that is, the idea that God created all the species ready-made and that they can never evolve or change or become extinct or evolve into one another – is, or ever was, a part of Christian doctrine.

Of course, in *Paradise Lost* this is how the Creation is depicted. Having populated the seas and the sky at one and the same evolutionary moment with fish and birds, Milton's God tells the Earth to bring forth beasts:

> The Earth obey'd, and strait
> Op'ning her fertil Woomb teem'd at a Birth
> Innumerous living Creatures, perfet formes,
> Limb'd and full grown: out of the ground up rose
> As from his Laire the wilde Beast where he wonns

In Forrest wilde, in Thicket, Brake or Den;
Among the Trees in Pairs they rose, they walk'd:
The Cattel in the Fields and Meddowes green; ...

and so on, down to the charming moment where

scarse from his mould
Behemoth biggest born of Earth upheav'd
His vastness: Fleec't the Flocks and bleating rose,
As Plants; ambiguous between Sea and Land
The River Horse and scalie Crocodile ...[31]

It has been said, and it seems strongly plausible, that Darwin spent twenty years trying to blot this picture 'out of his *imagination*' (my italics).[32]

It is hard for us to remember how popular *Paradise Lost* once was. Lord Macaulay, the most widely read historian in Victorian England, was said to know the whole of the great epic, all twelve books, by heart. It was very easy for English gentlemen, particularly those of Darwin's level of education, to believe that Milton's poem had the status of official Christian doctrine, but as a matter of fact it did not and does not. Indeed, in terms of Christian orthodoxy, Milton was wrong. At the time of the Darwinian 'crisis' in the Church of England Dr Pusey, of all people, hardly in the vanguard of modernism, preached a sermon before the University in which he reminded his congregation of St Augustine's doctrine that the earth produced grass and trees and species *causaliter* – that is to say, it received from God the power to produce them *of itself*, as it were impersonally.[33]*

It was Aubrey Lackington Moore, curator of the Botanical Gardens in Oxford in 1887, who perhaps argued more forcefully than anyone else that what Darwinism destroyed was not Christianity but eighteenth-century Deism, with its picture of a World Architect rather than a Creator. To him, the Darwinian theory was 'infinitely more Christian than the theory of special creation' because 'it implies the immanence of God in nature, and the omnipresence of his creative power ... Deism, even when it struggled to be orthodox, constantly spoke of God as we might speak of an absentee landlord, who cares nothing for his property

---

* And Lord Shaftesbury, he who thought the harmless *Ecce Homo* the 'most pestilential book ever vomited from the jaws of hell' (*vide supra*, p. 139), was untroubled by Darwin's theories: Finlayson, *Shaftesbury*, p. 387.

so long as he gets his rent ... Yet', he concluded, 'anything more opposed to the language of the Bible and the Fathers can hardly be imagined.'[34] Moore, who was a High Church clergyman, felt it necessary to contradict any idea that Darwinism invested the world with the power of self-unfolding. That would, he conceded, contradict belief in God. Many Darwinists today, particularly if they have read Richard Dawkins and agreed with him, would say that this begs the entire question; after all, that surely is what the theory of natural selection does – it invests life on earth with the power to be self-generating, self-regulating and impersonal. One only mentions Moore – who was one of the contributors to the famous volume *Lux Mundi*, a book designed to reconcile Christianity with developments in modern thought and scholarship – to show that, as a matter of empirical fact, the publication of Darwin's *Origin of Species* did not cause everyone with any scientific knowledge to abandon his faith. Widely read in theology and philosophy, Moore was more than an amateur botanist; he was what we should describe as a proper scientist. 'I am bound to say that I never met any man who combined such large stores of knowledge in all these several departments,' said George Romanes after his death.[35]

If, in the opinion of a man as learned as Aubrey Lackington Moore, and of many other Christians of the time, Darwinism only challenged the heresy of Deism and not the Christian idea of an immanent Creator perpetually and lovingly involved with what He has made; and if the majority of scientific opinion in Britain (and, we may conclude, in Europe and America) was not instantly converted to atheism by Darwin's discoveries – how do we derive the impression that the Victorian Age was a battleground between Science and Religion? The answer must partly lie in the brilliance of the anti-religious propaganda put out by the materialists; and partly, it must be said, in the boneheaded response to scientific development on the part of the louder Christian apologists. When we think of Oxford and the Darwinian crisis we do not think of the Reverend Aubrey Lackington Moore tending his rare species in the hothouses of the botanical gardens in the 1880s. Instead, we think of the famous rowdy contest, in the summer of 1860, between the Bishop of Oxford – 'Soapy Sam' Wilberforce – and the Apostle of Unbelief, Thomas Huxley.

The British Association for the Advancement of Science met for a week each year in a different town. Its meetings – 'duller each year' according to T.H. Huxley,[36] one of its leading lights – were usually well-attended, with large public gatherings in town halls, lecture theatres and Winter Gardens. It was obvious that the BAAS meetings in the summer of 1860 were likely to attract considerable attention, as it was the first such assembly since the publication of *The Origin of Species*. Sales of this had outstripped all expectations: clearly it had touched something in the public. Was that something an obsession with theology, as its enemies supposed? Or was it in fact a new vision of man, which only tangentially had to do with God – driving God out of the picture, not so much because His existence had been disproved as because it had been – to use a twentieth-century term – marginalized?

Long before the famous BAAS meeting in Oxford in the hot summer of 1860, the different forces had been mustering their troops and their weapons on each side. Huxley, who was Darwin's St Paul or the Devil's Disciple, depending on your point of view, had been wearing himself out with lecture tours and public demonstrations. ('I am drilling for the Rifles and will "pot" with my first shot the man who should dare to find fault ... with any tittle of the book,' he said.) What drove him on was the stupidity of his opponents: 'there is a wonderful tenacity of life about this sort of opposition to physical science. Always crushed it seems never to be killed, and after a thousand defeats it is as rampant now as in the days of Galileo.' This was certainly true, and it is no surprise that Huxley saw his mission as one of 'Science versus Parsonism'. Bishop Wilberforce had already sneered at Darwin's book, telling Sir Charles Lyell that he thought it 'the most unphilosophical he had ever read'.

The analogy with the plight of Galileo was seriously meant. Huxley believed the refusal of the Church Establishment to accept the truth was politically and intellectually sinister. At a lecture at the Royal Institution on 10 February 1860 he had given voice to an almost evangelical belief in Science's power to transform British society. Britain, he said, 'may prove to the world that for one race at any rate Despotism & Demagogy are not the necessary alternatives of polity – that freedom & order are not incompatible – that Reverence is the Handmaid of Knowledge – that truth is strength & that free discussion is the very life of truth'. Science was something which could change human life for the better.

Cherish her, venerate her, follow her methods faithfully ... and the future of this people will be greater than the past. If you do otherwise I fear the day will come when our children see the glory of England vanishing like Arthur in the mist and cry too late the woeful cry of Guinever:

> It was my duty to have loved the highest
> It surely was my profit had I known
> It would have been my pleasure had I seen ...

When the meeting of the BAAS came to pass in the summer, Darwin was too ill to attend – just as he had been ill on the even more important occasion of making his discoveries public at the Linnean Society, when his place was taken by Joseph Hooker and Charles Lyell. The absence of the author of *The Origin of Species* probably added to the drama of the occasion in Oxford.

On Thursday morning, 28 June, the Zoology section of the conference held its meeting. The Bishop of Oxford, a keen amateur ornithologist and a Vice-President of the BAAS, was in the audience to hear Sir Richard Owen, one of the most eminent anatomists of the time, deliver a speech attacking Darwin, and Huxley. *Pace* Huxley, Owen maintained that the brain of a gorilla bore no close resemblance to that of a human being – it was much more like that of a lemur.

There was 'a background' to all this. Owen had given a blistering (anonymous) review to the *Origin* in the *Westminster Review*, claiming that the book was a flash in the pan which would be 'forgotten in ten years'. ('I wish', Darwin wrote, 'for auld lang's sake he had been a little less bitter ... Some of my relations say it cannot possibly be Owen's article, because the Reviewer speaks so very highly of Prof. Owen. Poor dear simple folk!')

Huxley had not been slow to defend Darwin against Owen's charges on earlier occasions, in London; nor was he now, in Oxford, slow to rise to his feet and point out that the Glasgow anatomist had just dissected a chimpanzee's cerebrum and written to Huxley confirming 'its extraordinary resemblance to the human brain'.

On Friday, the next day, Huxley felt exhausted, 'as tired as a dog', having been giving papers at the conference all week (on the subject of sea-squirt eggs). He decided to leave the conference early and take the 4 p.m. Saturday train to Reading. The weather had broken and it was raining heavily as he made a hasty tour of the colleges 'to look at some of the chapels which are very beautiful'. It was then that he ran into Robert Chambers, he of *Vestiges*, who implored him not to go. When the BAAS had last held their meeting in Oxford, in 1847, Bishop

Wilberforce had lashed out at the mild-mannered Chambers for his 'foul speculations' about the age and origin of the earth. Science needed the energy and rumbustious love of a fight which Huxley could put up against Parsonism, and to leave now would be desertion.

So Huxley stayed. The Saturday meeting attracted a huge crowd to the new-built University Museum to hear a visiting American, Doctor Draper, talk on the subject which was on everybody's mind: 'The Intellectual Development of Europe considered with reference to the views of Mr Darwin'. Alongside Dr Draper on the platform were Bishop Wilberforce, Huxley, Hooker, Lubbock, and the president of the section, Huxley's old teacher, Henslow.

The American spoke for an hour: 'Are we a fortuitous concourse of atoms?' he asked in accents which to the English ears of an audience of between seven hundred and a thousand seemed almost painfully slow. His hearers became restless. There were interjections. A man who got up and tried to debate the probability of Darwinism on mathematical grounds was shouted down. The clergy, who were there in force, shouted for their bishop to speak.

Soapy Sam was a clever man (a First in mathematics) who had been raised to the sacred purple at the age of forty. At the time of his consecration, Prince Albert had written to remind him that he must never allow himself to take the part of a 'mere *Churchman*, but always that of a *Christian*'. He must be 'meek and liberal, and tolerant to other confessions; but let him never forget that he was the representative of the Church of the Land, the maintenance of which is as important to the country as that of its Constitution or its Throne'.[37] Wilberforce took these charges seriously, and it is perhaps a little unfair to describe him as 'at fifty-four a bluff, shallow, good-humoured opportunist'.[38] He was a good orator, and this was perhaps his downfall since, like many good orators, he loved the sound of his own voice, and of an audience reacting to it. They laughed at his jokes. It is rather a fascinating example of the way oral tradition sometimes *doesn't* work, that no one can exactly remember what Soapy Sam said at the peroration of his talk. Everyone agrees that it was a throwaway line – a gag which pleased some of his audience. And it was something to this effect: he turned with mock politeness to Huxley and begged to know 'was it through his grandfather or his grandmother that he claimed his descent from a monkey?'

Huxley slapped his knee and said to the scientist at his side, 'The

Lord hath delivered him into mine hands.' As the clergy clapped and roared, as the Bishop sat down, there were calls for Huxley to reply.

Huxley rose – a tall, slightly-built, high-shouldered man in a long black coat and an enormous high collar. His hair and eyes were very dark. His handsome face was, according to some witnesses, white with anger. He said that he

> had listened with great attention to the Lord Bishop's Speech but had been unable to discern either a new fact or a new argument in it – except indeed the question raised as to my personal predilection in the matter of ancestry – That it would not have occurred to me to bring forward such a topic as that for discussion myself, but that I was quite ready to meet the Right Reverend Prelate even on that ground. If, then, the question is put to me, would I rather have a miserable ape for a grandfather or a man highly endowed by nature and possessed of great means of influence and yet who employs these faculties and that influence for the mere purpose of introducing ridicule into a grave scientific discussion, I unhesitatingly affirm my preference for the ape.[39]

This produced laughter too, and the audience thereafter listened respectfully to what Huxley had to say. He said that he was only there in the interests of science. He said that Mr Darwin's theory was very much more than an hypothesis: it was the best explanation of species yet advanced. When he had finished speaking he had the crowd on his side, and the applause was tumultuous. Walking away from the meeting, Huxley told Joseph Hooker that he now saw the practical value of public speaking, and that he would try to conquer his hatred of it. For the next thirty-five years, Darwin's bulldog was to be the most eloquent public defender of the notion that Science and Christianity – anyway, orthodox Christianity, as popularly understood and officially defended by the Establishment – were incompatible.

There can be no doubt that, in some circles, men of science felt it was their duty not merely to express doubt about religion, but actively to promote atheism. Such a man was William Kingdon Clifford (1845–1879). Admitted to Trinity in 1863, he was an Apostle, and quickly recognized as a mathematical genius. At this stage he was an ascetic and devout Anglo-Catholic, and enjoyed the attempt to support Catholic doctrines with scientific analogies. He quoted Thomas Aquinas. In 1868 he was elected to a fellowship, and it was at about this time that he began to read Darwin and Herbert Spencer. In 1870 he suffered a shipwreck, as part of the English expeditionary team to witness the eclipse. His ship the *Psyche* (how apt) sank off the east coast of Sicily, near Catania. By the time he came back to Cambridge he was a confirmed atheist, and in 1871, at the age of twenty-six, he was appointed Professor of Applied Mathematics at University College, London. Everyone testifies to his charm, eloquence and wit. And as the 1870s advanced and his beard grew longer, Clifford developed an almost Nietzschean obsession with the death of God being the necessary preliminary to the coming of the 'kingdom of Man'.[40] Destined to die of consumption at thirty-four, Clifford was also consumed with hatred of the very trappings of the religion he had once loved. He saw Christianity as idolatrous, barely distinguishable from the pagan abominations condemned in the Bible. The enthronement of a bishop in 1869 provoked him to observe: 'the entire town is in an uproar for the ecclesiastical fuss that is to take two hours in the streets and the cathedral tomorrow: enthronization of the new bishop, parade through the public ways of him and minor fetishes as the mace, cocked hat and Sword of the Civic Functionary, and subsequent grand banquet to the priests of Baal'.[41]

Clifford's professional work was largely taken up with applied mathematics, but he had always enjoyed metaphysics, and felt the two were naturally related. In *On Theories of Physical Forces* (a book which in important respects anticipated Einstein's Theory of Relativity) he tried to establish that 'the word "cause" has no legitimate place either in science or philosophy'. The scientist asks 'What precisely does happen?', not 'Why do things happen?' Clifford's posthumous work on *Commonsense of the Exact Sciences* asserts the importance of distinguishing between pure and applied geometry. It is as improper to describe one sort of geometry as 'correct' as it would be to describe ludo or dominoes as 'correct'. Geometry as a whole can only be 'correct' when applied and empirically tested.[42]

W.K. Clifford is perhaps now most famous for making Lockean caution about the nature of propositions into a strait-jacket. Locke had asserted that there is 'one unerring mark by which a man may know whether he is a lover of truth for its own sake, namely, the not entertaining any proposition with greater assurance than the proofs it is built upon will warrant'. Clifford in 'The Ethics of Belief' took this one stage further. 'It is wrong every where and for anyone', he asserted, 'to believe anything upon insufficient evidence.'[43]

It was Professor William James who immortalized this sentence of Clifford's for us, and indeed rescued Clifford from dwindling to no more than a footnote in intellectual history. How James tackled the assertion will be the subject of a later chapter of this book.

Clifford's violent reaction against Christianity, and his sense that it was not merely mistaken but wicked, evil, must have had some of its roots in those years of early manhood when he had been not merely 'pious' ('so devout that men commented')[44] but in love with God with an intellectual passion.

A similar rage possessed Tyndall, Professor of Surgery at the University College Hospital, when the nation prayed as the Prince of Wales recovered from a bout of typhoid fever. The High Church periodical *The Guardian* called for more of this 'moral regenerating power' – prayer – in place of impious science. But if the killer plague of typhoid was on the decrease in Victorian England it was not because of prayer, but because of the spread of proper sanitation and advances in medical techniques. When the Prince recovered there was a service of thanksgiving in St Paul's Cathedral, from which the medical profession was virtually excluded. That was when the doctors responded with the idea of a Prayer Gauge, to be put up in London hospitals to test the efficacy of intercession. In fact no such test took place, nor did Tyndall (though he was asked to do so by Huxley's friend Dr Clark) give a lecture at his own London hospital on 'The Pointlessness of Prayer'. Francis Galton noted, however, that insurance brokers offered no discounts to 'the praying classes'.[45]

And yet, agnosticism mysteriously found itself unable to leave religion alone. It is hard to imagine such a body as The Metaphysical Society meeting in London today, but nine times a year, from 1869 to 1880, the great Prime Minister W.E. Gladstone, Cardinal Manning, R.H. Hutton, the Editor of *The Spectator*, Dean Stanley and F.D. Maurice, with other luminaries of the believing persuasion, met to discuss and debate theology with the unbelievers – men such as Huxley, Clifford, J.A. Froude, John Morley and Herbert Spencer. (Newman would not join – typical.)

It was at the meetings of the Metaphysical that Huxley became embarrassed by the fact that he did not have a word to describe his position. He did not wish to describe himself as an out-and-out atheist, nor as a materialist. Influenced by Spencer, who had been in too much of a hurry to read Kant but had nevertheless skimmed through bits of Dean

Mansel, Huxley and friends decided that Mansel's Kantian distinction between the Knowable and the Unknowable exactly expressed their scientific outlook. The Christian and the atheist 'were quite sure they had attained a certain "gnosis" – had, more or less successfully, solved the problem of existence; while I was quite sure I had not, and had a pretty strong conviction that the problem was insoluble.'[46] Since most of the great men of the age appeared to be 'ists' of one sort or another, Huxley felt 'forced to invent what I felt to be the appropriate title of "agnostic", and I took the earliest opportunity of parading it at our society'.

Hutton, who chronicled proceedings of the Metaphysical Society for the wider audience of *Spectator* readers, hinted that the Agnostic was one who worshipped the Unknown God – as in St Paul's famous sermon on the Areopagus. But Huxley was adamant in his denial of this:

> The term 'agnostic' was not suggested by the paragraph in the Acts of the Apostles in which Paul speaks of an inscription to the Unknown God (*agnosto theo*). It is obvious that the author of this inscription was a theist – I may say an anxious theist – who desired not to offend any God not known to him by ignoring the existence of such a deity. The person who erected the altar was therefore in the same position as those philosophers who in modern times have brought about the apotheosis of ignorance under the name of the 'Absolute' or its equivalent. 'Agnostic' came into my mind as a fit antithesis to gnostic – the gnostics being those ancient heretics who professed to know most about those very things of which I am quite sure I know nothing – Agnostic therefore in the sense of a Philosophical System is senseless: its import lies in being a confession of ignorance – a warning set up against philosophical and theological phantasms which was never more needed than at the present time when the ghost of the 'Absolute' slain by my masters Hume and Hamilton is making its appearance in broad daylight.[47]

Agnosticism is a peculiarly Victorian word, coined to express a particular state of mind. Unable to believe any of the old formularies, the agnostics of Huxley and Spencer's breed continued to be overwhelmed by the moral seriousness of life, and indeed by its mystery. They cast down religion from its pedestal because, as they thought, it was pretending to certainties which it was only proper for a scientist to possess.

But what if you were in the sad position of certainty in both domains? In most case-studies of the nineteenth-century Science and Religion debate, certainty in one field drove it out from the next. Pious 'creationists', particularly in the United States, to this day do not trouble their heads with assessing the probability of the data of Darwinism. They are sure that there is a God who made the world, and who loves them, and who redeemed them. Why should they waste their time looking at the 'evidence' of some blasphemer whose ideas sound just as wildly improbable? A fish turning into a bird over a number of years? What was it supposed to do about breathing in the transition phase? How do you fly with a pair of transitional wings?

Similarly, there must be many like W.K. Clifford – and, one suspects (though he denies it), Richard Dawkins – whose discovery of what Darwin had to say filled their mind with such honest conviction that they could not any longer hold on to 'the junk and treasure of an ancient creed'. But what if your mind stubbornly refused to lose faith in either? What if you remained the most dogged and fundamentalist believer that God made the world in one mighty act; *and* believed in the evidence of geology that the rocks, and the very shape of the planet, and the species in it – plant, fish, fowl, mammal – all bear an evolving and interconnected relationship?

This was the dilemma of Philip Henry Gosse – perhaps not the greatest zoologist of the age but, what Huxley once called him, 'an honest hodman of science'.[48]

The nineteenth century is the great era of museums, collections, classifications, categorizations, lists. To this essential hodman's task Gosse brought a keen eye (he was the son of a miniature painter and himself no mean draughtsman) and an inquiring intelligence. Like nearly all nineteenth-century British scientists Gosse began and ended as an amateur; but, unlike the big names, he was never rich. It was when he was sent as clerk to a whaling office in Newfoundland that he bought his first microscope; *The Entomology of Newfoundland* was his first work. A spell as a farmer in Canada led him to make innumerable studies of the local flora and fauna. After a tour of the United States (and a spell as a village schoolmaster in the remote township of Dallas) he returned to London where, once again, schoolteaching supported a life which he wished to devote to science. So impressive was his second book, *Introduction to Zoology,* that the British Museum paid him to go to Jamaica to undertake a collection of undescribed birds: *Birds of Jamaica*, a folio volume with splendid plates, was the result.

It would be quite wrong, then, at least on one level, to imagine that Philip Gosse was a narrow man. He was widely travelled and, as an observer of the natural scene, passionately devoted to scientific truth.

But there was another side to his nature. He was also a fervent Bible Christian – and so was his wife, whom he married in 1848. The only child of their union, Edmund Gosse – destined to grow up into a late Victorian/Edwardian man of letters, snob, man-about-(literary)-town, friend of Hardy, James, Conrad, and so on – has left an unforgettable account of what it was like being raised by these fervent devotees of evangelicalism.

Gosse *fils* tells us that 'every instinct in his [father's] intelligence went out at first to greet the new light' when the discoveries of Lyell and Darwin and Wallace made it seem that the planet and the universe had come into being much longer ago, and much more gradually, than the opening chapters of Genesis would appear to suggest. Clearly, a compromise could not be reached. Either the world was 6,000 years old, or it was much, much older; either the species had come into being immutably, and all at once, or they had evolved. You could not believe *both*. The lower-middle-class Philip Gosse had developed a personal antipathy to the 'famous "Lord Chancellor manner"' of Sir Charles Lyell.[49] He therefore decided to put pen to paper and, more rashly, to go into print, offering a scientific solution to the religious difficulties of evangelicals such as himself. Adam, after all, had appeared on the scene possessing hair and bones and teeth which in any other human being would have taken years to develop and grow. Why should the same not be true of the earth itself? Suppose the Almighty had made the earth and the universe in one great catastrophic act of creation, but had given it the appearance of aging?

> This 'Omphalos' of his, he thought, was to bring all the turmoil of scientific speculation to a close, fling geology into the arms of Scripture, and make the lion eat grass with the lamb. It was not surprising, he admitted, that there had been experienced an ever-increasing discord between the facts which geology brings to light and the direct statements of the early chapters of 'Genesis'. Nobody was to blame for that. My Father, and my Father alone, possessed the secret of the enigma; he alone held the key which could smoothly open the lock of the geological mystery. He offered it, with a glowing gesture, to atheists and Christians alike. This was to be the universal panacea; this the system of intellectual therapeutics which could not but heal all the maladies of the age. But alas! atheists and Christians alike looked at it and laughed, and threw it away.[50]

To the ears of any reasonably sensitive twentieth-century observer the laughter sounds hollow – but also depressingly familiar. What seems astonishing is that 140 years after Darwin published *The Origin of Species*, we in our generation should still be allowing ourselves arguments between 'scientists' and 'creationists'. Science was the Victorian fundamentalism. Of course it found out things which were 'really true'. But not enough scientists and not enough religious believers would seem to have absorbed the message of Kant — namely, that the human mind is not a camera. It does not take snapshots of some external thing called 'reality'. The mind is a doer, not just a contemplator. This does not mean that there is no reality-in-itself to contemplate. It does not mean that there is no universe for science to explore, or no God for the soul to worship. But it does mean that the Science versus Religion match is usually conducted most loudly by people who would benefit from a few months spent reading a third discipline — philosophy. Indeed, it was in the United States, not previously a noted hotbed of philosophy, that these truths began to dawn, towards the close of the century.

Meanwhile, the Europeans and the Americans were left with the essentially silly questions with which Soapy Sam Wilberforce and Thomas Huxley had bothered their heads — such as whether it was their grandfather or their grandmother who was descended from a monkey. In England, of course, it had always mattered who your father was. Perhaps, as *Father and Son* shows, it mattered even more how you got on with him.

10

Swinburne and the Gods

'The forties was the time of doubts, in the plural
and with a small d; turmoils of Arthur Hugh
Clough or John Sterling or young James Anthony
Froude. In the sixties Britain and France and
Germany entered the age of Doubt, in the singular
and with a capital D.'

Owen Chadwick, *The Secularization*
of the European Mind

If the 1860s was the Age of Doubt with a capital D, then the laureate of mid nineteenth-century unbelief was Algernon Charles Swinburne (1837–1909). If figures like Herbert Spencer or Morley gave Unbelief an articulate voice, it was Swinburne who set it to the most intoxicating music. 'The supreme evil, God' was a line which Christina Rossetti crossed out in her copy of *Atalanta in Calydon*. Swinburne as it were returned the compliment when, in his own old age, he read an edition of her poems, and wrote to her brother, one of his oldest friends, W.M. Rossetti: 'Good Satan! what a fearful warning against the criminal lunacy of theolatry! It is horrible to think of such a woman – and so many otherwise noble and beautiful natures – spiritually infected.'[1] For a whole generation, however, Swinburne had been the poet who celebrated their liberation from the sexual constraints and intellectual absurdities (as they saw things) of Christianity. Hardy's Jude and Susan, in the famous condemned novel, naturally quote Swinburne's 'Thou hast conquered, O pale Galilean; the world has grown grey from thy breath'. For Hardy and his coevals, whole clusters of Swinburne's unforgettable phrases and images bolstered their atheistic adventure.

> We thank with brief thanksgiving
>> Whatever gods may be
> That no life lives forever;
> That dead men rise up never;
> That even the weariest river
>> Winds somewhere safe to sea.
>> ('The Garden of Proserpine')

or

> The ghosts of words and dusty dreams,
>> Old memories, faiths infirm and dead.

> Ye fools; for which among you deems
> His prayer can alter green to red
> Or stones to bread?
>
> ('Félise')

or

> Is his life but as other gods' lives? is not this
> Lord God of your trust?
> Is not this the great God of your sires, that
> with souls and with bodies was fed,
> And the world was on flame with his fires? O fools,
> he was God and is dead.
>
> ('Hymn of Man')

Atheism is not incidental to Swinburne's art: it is something which feeds it at its deepest centre. And having cast off boyhood piety, Swinburne was remarkably constant about his lack of religion, what he habitually called his antitheism. Whether as the promising young student-friend of the Pre-Raphaelites, or as a Bohemian roué in London, or as the timid, stone-deaf suburban hermit of Putney, his atheism was constant. Politics were different. He veered from being a supporter of Irish Fenianism to being an enthusiastic Unionist, an admirer of Joseph Chamberlain. By turns an ardent Republican and a Jacobite, and sometimes (for why should poets be as consistent as logicians?) both, he found himself in old age saluting Queen Victoria as a new Gloriana:

> No braver soul drew bright and queenly breath
> Since England wept upon Elizabeth ...

Only in his implacable hostility to religion did he remain steadfast; and to those readers today who allow themselves to be intoxicated by his melodies, and to retrace the footsteps of this unjustly neglected great poet, it is the atheism which perhaps has the most dated, the most 'period' quality. Whatever song we choose to sing after the century of Lenin, Stalin, Hitler, Mussolini, Mao Tse-tung, Pol Pot, Franco, Atatürk, and politicians and scientists who pioneered nuclear bombs, it is not very likely to be Swinburne's

> Glory to man in the highest! for Man is the
> master of things.

206

Like Shelley and Byron, and unlike most English poets since the time of the Renaissance, Swinburne was an aristocrat. His mother, Lady Jane Henrietta, was the fifth daughter of the third Earl of Ashburnham; his father (Lady Jane's second cousin) was Rear-Admiral Charles Henry Swinburne, connected on his mother's side with the Dukes of Northumberland. Swinburne's particular brand of exhibitionism and rebelliousness against accepted bourgeois codes of behaviour – his early republicanism, for example, his apparent inability to handle money, his cheerful espousal of 'extreme' political views, his idolization of political revolutionaries on the Continent – had a recognizably aristocratic flavour, instantly familiar to students of this English type. The Swinburne who hero-worshipped the 'decadent' Baudelaire or the revolutionary Mazzini was at one with his grandfather, the sixth baronet, who, having discarded the Jacobitism of *his* forebears, as MP for Launceston found another way of being against the Government by becoming an extreme radical and a friend of Mirabeau and Wilkes. One sees the genes at work in the career of Swinburne's cousin Bertram Mitford, first Baron Redesdale, idolizing mad King Ludwig and giving money for the foundation of the Bayreuth Opera House; or again in the bizarre careers of some of Lord Redesdale's celebrated grandchildren, with their enthusiasms for European politics. Certainly the breathless tone of Swinburne's youthful letters could easily be seen as having a family likeness to, say, those of his cousin the Hon. Nancy Mitford. On being introduced to the works of the marquis de Sade he wrote to his friend Richard Monckton Milnes (Lord Houghton):

> At first I quite expected to add another to the gifted author's list of victims; I really thought I must have died or split open or choked with laughing. I never laughed so much in my life ... One scene between M. de Verneuil and Mme d'Ersteval I never thought to survive. I read it out and the auditors rolled and roared. Then Rossetti read out the dissection of the interesting Rosalie and her infant, and the rest of that refreshing episode; and I wonder to this minute that we did not raise the whole house by our screams of laughter.[2]

This is pure 'Mitfordese'.

The origins of Swinburne's obsession with flagellation have been traced by some to relations with his supposedly stern father, the Admiral. Others have read into his obviously autobiographical novel

Lesbia Brandon the suggestion that it was a family tutor whose excessive interest in punishment pushed Swinburne into that direction. '"Twelve next month is he? Ever been flogged, yet, my boy?" "I can answer that if he won't," said his sister. "Herbert has that pleasure still to come."'[3]

By the time he was twelve Swinburne had been sent to Eton where, according to that novel and to the repeated and overwhelming testimony of nineteenth-century Etonians, flogging was exceptionally severe even by the standards of the times. Eton birches were grotesque instruments consisting of three feet of handle and two of a thick bunch of birch twigs. Birchings in both the Upper and the Lower schools were public. 'It was, in my time, so far from being a punishment administered on special occasions only, or with any degree of solemnity, that some half dozen boys were flogged every day. It was entirely public; any one who chose might drop in. I have sometimes been one of three spectators and sometimes one of a hundred,' recalled one Etonian of the years 1841 to 1844.[4] In his thorough and fascinating study of Victorian flagellation, Ian Gibson makes a direct link between Swinburne's sadomasochism and his religious hatred of Christianity. Drawing particular attention to the antitheistic choruses in *Atalanta in Calydon,* Gibson points out that Swinburne's God ('The lord of love and loathing and of strife') is a sadist who

> Smites without sword, and scourges without rod;
> The supreme evil, God.

He adds, 'whether God is responsible or not, one of the functions of shame is certainly to slay desire – or to turn it into unnatural channels',[5] believing that it was Christianity's denial of the body which inspired Swinburne's particular loathing.

The trouble with any simple identification of cause and effect in the shadowy areas of psychosexuality is that such assertions can be countered with examples which precisely contradict them. W.G. Gladstone, an Etonian of an earlier generation, used to whip himself with a 'discipline' (the gift of the learned Doctor Pusey*) when he felt himself threatened with lust. In all likelihood he got prostitutes to do this for

---

* Pusey, also an Old Etonian, gave two whips to one of his Anglican convents, urging the nuns to use the five-tailed whip daily 'in memory of the scourging of Our Lord' (quoted in Jan Marsh, *Christina Rossetti*, p. 196).

him while trying to persuade them to desist from their life of vice; but in the whole of the nineteenth century it would be hard to find a more pious Christian. So, the link between masochism and unbelief is not compelling. True, what we would call 'S and M' was highly popular among the Victorians. In grown-up life Swinburne and a fellow-addict, Monckton Milnes, enjoyed the discovery of this advertisement in the High Church weekly *The Guardian*:

> WANTED, by a Widow lady, a PERSON who is experienced, in the art of whipping, and well-qualified to administer a severe flogging with a new birch rod to two young children of the ages of nine and ten. Wages 30 l. per annum. The children are very wilful and troublesome. Address to S.N.N., Brooks's Club, Suffolk Street, London.

In his inebriated twenties, notoriously, Swinburne liked to patronize 7 Circus Road, 'in Regent's Park, a lovely little villa presided over by a well-educated lady, well-versed in the birchen mysteries'.[6] Such was the extent of thrashing, walloping, beating, thwacking and birching in Victorian childhoods that we might wonder why such establishments were so comparatively thin on the ground. Swinburne continued, all his life, to delight in such contemplations:

> Oh, hold his shirt up, Algernon,
> Hold the boy's shirt up high;
> Let us all have a view of his bottom, Hugh,
> Oh, doesn't the pain make him cry, by Jove!
> Oh, doesn't the pain make him cry.[7]

The surviving Swinburne pornography is extensive, with many a loving description of boys begging for mercy as blood spurts from the weals on their buttocks and cruel tutors or insatiable dominatrixes continue to thwack away.

> A pretty boy with fair upturned face,
> Dark eyebrows and dark eyes, and yellow hair,
> With breeches down for flogging, in disgrace;
> With the birch hanging over him in air,
> With scar on scar and bloody trace on trace
> Of flogging all across the parts laid bare,
> All his fair limbs and features drawn with pain,
> As the birch showered its strokes on him like rain.[8]

But for every ten thousand flagellants who have passed through Eton, there have been only a handful of memorable poets; and, of that handful, perhaps only two of genius – Shelley (1792–1822) and Swinburne. Both aristocrats, both atheists, both sent down from Oxford, both left-wing, both destined, in their different generations, to give voice to the spirit of rebellion felt by the young of their day; both notably inventive and varied metrists. In our day, which is so comparitively uninterested in poetry, they are largely unread. A letter preserved by his cousin Mrs Disney Leith records how, even as a boy at Eton, Swinburne was experimenting with Galliambics:

> I should feel at every line as if I were writing down my own name in the bill: besides I might make false quantities – and *then*! … And *then* I showed my verses indignantly (after the catastrophe) to another master, and he said they were very good, and there was but one small slip in them, *hard* as the metre was; and I told my tutor with impudent triumph (knowing he had done his very worst!) and he was shut up I can tell you … but that did not heal the cuts or close the scars which had imprinted on [my] mind and body …[9]

Incidentally, his tutor was the much-loved William Johnson [Cory], perhaps one of the most inspired and inspiring of all Victorian schoolmasters. 'He was by nature a lover of youth,' as the historian David Newsome reminds us.[10] 'In 1872 Cory was compelled by Dr Hornby to leave Eton; not for any very good reason save that it was dangerous for a schoolmaster to allow his emotions to carry him so far that they were capable of being misunderstood.'[11] Cory is best known to us for one lyric – his haunting translation 'They told me, Heraclitus, they told me you were dead'. Generations of boys remembered him fondly. It was he who fired them with a love of Greek literature – 'Item, my favourite bit of Plato, where Theodorus introduces to Socrates the teachable, quick, even minded Theaetates, the ideal listener, telling Socrates that the boy is like him in having a snub nose and ugly eyes, but speaking with motherly joy of his sweet nature.'[12] All the boys seemed quite equal to Cory's emotional attentions, nor do the favourites seem to have been scarred for life by his affectionate habit of rubbing his whiskery cheeks against their smooth pink faces; though no doubt a schoolmaster who behaved like that in the England of the late 1990s would be sent to prison.

Classical learning had been the ideal of scholars and gentlemen since the eighteenth century, and was the compulsory task of middle-class boys educated at the public schools (old and new) which rose to such importance in the post-Thomas Arnold (1795–1842) era. At most of the public schools, and well into this century, the cleverer boys became fluent in Latin and Greek prose and verse, learning to compose it themselves; and they had read a good smattering of Greek and Latin literature before they were eighteen. English literature – let alone French, German or Italian literature – of the Christian eras would seldom have appeared in an English classroom of the date. The English love affair with the ancient world is a fascinating object of study.[13] For the purposes of our consideration of the loss of religious faith in the nineteenth century it is remarkable that a man like Dr Arnold, who believed it was his mission to make boys Christian, should have seen nothing odd about them spending the four or five most formative years of their lives being filled with knowledge of pre-Christian culture, made to learn odes by Horace in which it was asserted that, contrary to what St Paul believed, we are but dust and shadows, with no future life to look forward to. While English law, following St Paul, told them that homosexuality was the most heinous of sins, Plato and Sappho told them otherwise. While their Bibles told them to mortify the flesh, their Catullus told them to celebrate its joys while they could. A confusing diet. No wonder Gladstone, a conscientious but unimaginative man, spent so much of his early manhood writing an impressively absurd three-volume disquisition devoted to proving that Homer and the Old Testament patriarchs worshipped the same God.

Studying Classics opened Victorian minds to the possibility that not every generation has meant quite the same by the word *God*; that the sterner dictates of monotheism were, even in the Scriptures, quite a late development in Hebrew literature and consciousness. In the polytheistic pluralistic world which gave birth to all the great literature of Greece and Rome, there was a multiplicity of Gods. Lucretius, the most influential religious thinker of the first century BC, popularized Epicurus's atomistic view of the universe. The basic idea of this is remarkably similar to Big Bang physics – namely, that the universe consists of a fixed number of atoms whose movement and changes constituted 'creation'. The universe coheres. It does not require, for its explanation, some external agency to have 'made' it. The permanence of matter does not make Lucretius a determinist (as Democritus was); nor does it make him an atheist – he begins his great poem *De Rerum Natura* with an invocation to Venus. But it makes it unnecessary, and impossible, to accept the Leibnitzian or Deistic theory of God as an individual intelligence outside what is. What is there, is there. There is nothing beyond there. And this view permeates nearly all post-Lucretian Latin literature. No need, then, to prove that Swinburne had or had not read Lucretius to show that he had registered the world-view contained in the *De Rerum Natura*, and was to make powerful poetic use of it himself when he had in turn rejected Christianity and absorbed the Darwinian *Weltanschauung*.

But at first Swinburne's taste in Classical literature consisted in a mastery of the Greek Anthology – this was the most-often used text at Eton at the time – and the fascination with metre which the letter quoted reveals. He was in his teens a devout Anglo-Catholic, as were his mother and sisters. 'Kneel, Algernon, kneel!' his sister Alice said furiously to the (by then unbelieving) poet at their mother's funeral in 1896. No such injunction was required in his teens, as he told his friend William Rossetti when describing the 'very strong religious Christian feelings he used to have from the age of 15 to 18 or so'. Swinburne himself believed that this partly accounted for 'the continual use he makes of a Christian or biblical framework in his poems'.[14]

Lady Jane Swinburne was distinctly *dévote*. Swinburne's view that he was brought up 'quasi-Catholic' is confirmed by the later liturgical practices of his High-Church sisters. Rather like characters in the novels of Charlotte Mary Yonge, Lady Jane and her children raised money for a new church, to be built at Bonchurch in the Isle of Wight in 1848; the young Algernon, echoing the 'soft ... rather sing-song intonation' of his mother's 'Ashburnham voice', would lisp his belief, Sunday by Sunday, that Christ had 'suffered under Bonchurch Pilate'. Lady Jane gave him Newman's sermons to read; and there was a family connection in that his aunt, Elizabeth Swinburne, had married Newman's close friend John William Bowden. The first letter in the magnificent six-volume Yale edition of Swinburne's correspondence is to his father, dated April 2, 1854 (when the poet was almost 17), wishing 'darling Pino', as he called his father, 'many very happy returns of your birthday ... I suppose you had Holy Communion today as well as we here. I thought this morning of that, and how nice it was to be all communicating together on your birthday.'[15]

Swinburne lost his faith at Oxford, where he also acquired his taste for alcohol and for the poetry of Charles Baudelaire. His college was

Balliol, and his tutor the Regius Professor of Greek, Benjamin Jowett.*

Jowett's scholarly work during the 1850s was on the subject of St Paul. His edition of the Epistles to the Thessalonians, Galatians and Romans had earned him the reputation of a heretic. Far from regarding St Paul as an infallible oracle, he frankly asserted that the apostle's thoughts often outran his powers of expression. Some of the most sacred of Christian doctrines, such as the Atonement, were examined by Jowett with the same cool detachment which might be accorded to the thought-processes of a primitive tribe. And he made his principle quite clear in his essay on the 'Interpretation of Scripture': '*Interpret the Scripture like any other book*. There are many respects in which Scripture is unlike any other book; these will appear in the results of such an interpretation. The first step is to know the meaning, and this can only be done in the same careful and impartial way that we ascertain the meaning of Sophocles or of Plato.'[16]

How much did Jowett believe? And how much of his belief was specifically Christian, as opposed to a wishy-washy blend of Platonism, Hegelianism and liberal Protestantism? Rigorists might permit themselves the answer, *Not much*. For those of a religious disposition, but who wish to retain their intellectual integrity, there will always be something appealing about the 'modernist' or extreme liberal position in theology. 'A confusion of the heart and head may lead sensitive minds into a desertion of the principles of Christian life, which are their own witness, because they are in doubt about facts which are really external to them. Great evil to character may sometimes ensue from such causes ...'[17]

Some such 'injury to character' perhaps allowed Swinburne to soar so exotically from the straight and narrow path. In the first part of the new syllabus Jowett had invented – the examination in Latin and Greek literature which is called Honour Moderations – Swinburne achieved a decent second. But that was the last exam he was to pass in Oxford.

Like many Balliol men (of both sexes) since, Swinburne was left-wing. He and a small group of pals founded a club called The Old Mortality at which they met to extol the virtues of republicanism and the superiority of J.S. Mill over the Bible. Their hero was the Italian republican leader Mazzini – who was to inspire so much of Swinburne's

---

* *Vide supra*, Chapter 5.

political verse. 'An Ode to Mazzini' was finished and declaimed at an Old Mortality meeting in 1857.

The worthier side of Balliol life, however, what one could call the Rugbeian strain, never appealed to Swinburne. He found Matthew Arnold's Lectures on Poetry boring (which they are), and he was not uplifted by T.H. Green, 'who preached Hegel with the accent of a puritan'. Something much more exciting was about to happen in Swinburne's life. One of his Old Mortality friends knew two undergraduates from Exeter College, Edward Burne-Jones and William Morris. And in the autumn of 1857 he became involved with them in the task of decorating the Debating Hall of the Oxford Union. They were working under the supervision of an exciting painter-poet from London (though of Italian ancestry) named Dante Gabriel Rossetti.

Unfortunately, Rossetti did not know enough about fresco techniques, and the ceiling painting in what is now the library of the Union at Oxford has faded to inky black. But Rossetti and his friends met Swinburne – Little Carrots, as they dubbed this diminutive, red-headed and hilarious young man. By the time the pictures were finished – scenes from the *Morte d'Arthur*, naturally – Swinburne had become the darling of the set. The limited world of college, tutorials, and undergraduate friendships no longer held any charm for him. By 1860, having omitted to do any work, Swinburne had left. Jowett managed to cover things up, but he was in effect sacked. In his distinguished old age Swinburne turned down the offer of an honorary degree from Oxford, and this has been seen as pique.[18] Yet he remained on good terms with Jowett – they had a happy Cornish holiday together in 1874* – and he returned to his old college from time to time without awkwardness. It was at a Balliol dinner in the 1870s, by which time he was the most famous poet of his generation, that he spoke of *Poems and Ballads* – the volume which made his reputation.

There were three poems, he said, which beyond all the rest were biographical – 'The Triumph of Time', 'Dolores' and 'The Garden of Proserpine'. 'The Triumph of Time' was a monument to the sole real love of his life – a love which had been the tragic destruction of all his faith in woman. 'Dolores' expressed the passion with which he had sought relief, in the madnesses of the fleshly Venus, from his ruined dreams of

---

* The subject of one of Max Beerbohm's more amusing caricatures.

the heavenly. 'The Garden of Proserpine' expressed his revolt against the flesh and its fevers, and his longing to find a refuge from them in a haven of undisturbed rest.[19]

Perhaps there is something too neat about this self-mythologizing, reported as it is by the prig Mallock. But there is also undoubtedly some element of biographical truth here. The disappointment chronicled in 'The Triumph of Time' is the failure to marry his cousin Mary Gordon. They were very close, but what is abundantly clear from her recollections of Swinburne is that he felt able to present to her only one side of his nature. It was clear she was not lying when she made the amazing claim, after his death, that she knew him to have been 'in communion with the Church of England all his life', and that he was 'never intoxicated in all his life'.[20] The truth is that Swinburne was devotedly fond of his family, and the polite, well-behaved and sober character he presented to them for most of his life was quite at variance with the side seen and brought out by the Rossettis and their rakish, druggy 'set'. Mary Gordon and Swinburne wrote a novella together – *The Children of the Chapel*.[21] The hero, Arthur Savile, is painfully bullied at Eton and, needless to say, is beaten. But for the most part this tale is as innocent as the productions of Charlotte M. Yonge it imitates.

No doubt his autobiographical novel *A Year's Letters*, written in the 1860s, gives us a glimpse of Swinburne's real feelings for his cousin. He makes her into someone from a sensual Pre-Raphaelite canvas, her hair as loose and as lustrous as Rossetti's Lady Lilith or Aurelia: 'I never saw her look so magnificent, her hair was blown down and fell in heavy uncurling heaps to her waist; her face looked out of the frame of it, hot and bright, with the eyes lighted, expanding under the lift of those royal, wide eyelids of hers.' But the feelings of lust it was so easy to express to the public in his verses, or to the prostitutes of St John's Wood, would not come when he tried to speak to his beloved Mary. 'I could hardly speak to her for pleasure, I confess: don't show my avowals. I rode between her and the sea, a thought behind, a gust of wind blowing off land drove a mass of her hair across my face, upon my lips; she felt it somehow, I suppose, for she turned and laughed.'

While writing highly-charged descriptions of this serious love, Swinburne was also amusing himself and his friends with a fantasy about a clerical family, the High Church Bishop Buggeridge, his Broad Church relation Dean Buggeridge, and The Hon. and Rev. Onan

Buggeridge whose friend is the Reverend Simplicius Pricksmall of Little Pissing, together with the living of St Onan's. What would Mary have made of it if she had ever read it?

For his part, Swinburne's was like many dissipated natures. The loves and friendships in his life which had nothing to do with the darker side of his nature were especially pure, innocent and unclouded by alcohol or sadistic lust. If not 'in love' with Mary – but perhaps he was? – he was at any rate in love with the calm and the emotional stability which family life and cousinship provided. When he turned away from it, it was to the wild and self-consciously wicked world of Dolores. When we read this, our minds supply images of the hectic, lusty heroines of Rossetti's canvases. One thinks of the 'singular housemaid of advanced ideas' who inspired Rossetti's Ligeia Siren, firm naked breasts unashamedly aroused, massive swimmer's shoulders, skeins of red hair falling down her back.[22]

> I have passed from the outermost portal
> To the shrine where a sin is a prayer;
> What care though the service be mortal?
> O our Lady of Torture, what care?
> All thine the last wine that I pour is
> The last in the chalice we drain,
> O fierce and luxurious Dolores,
> Our Lady of Pain.

For a generation brought up on Tennyson's *Lady of Shalott*, the publication of Swinburne's *Poems and Ballads* (1866) must have been electrifying, intoxicating. Apart from the exciting contents, the sheer technical variety and brilliance of the new young poet brought a new music into English literature. 'Instead of the old, dull iambic measures, the tedium (let us be honest about this) of Wordsworthian blank verse, their ears were ringingly assailed by dactyls, anapests, cretics, in a multitude of complex measures; by all sorts of stress variants, which, though they had been used sparingly by earlier poets from Dryden onwards, now appeared moulded with astonishing deftness as the basic metres.'[23]

Rather like the Sixties of our own century, the 1860s was a decade in which the younger generation felt inclined to overthrow *in toto* the values and mores of their parents. D.G. Rossetti, Swinburne and their friends, long-haired, famously dissipated, promiscuous, abandoned to narcotics and alcohol, occupied something of the same position in the nineteenth-century public mind that pop idols were to fill in the 1960s. There were moments of high merriment, such as the legendary evening at the Arts Club when, unable to find his hat in the cloakroom, Swinburne tried on all the members' top hats, and stamped them flat with his feet if they did not fit.* Other stories had him bending his fork double at the dinner-table, making 'a scandalous noise', or 'wildly kicking out' at a book in the Club library which had annoyed him. Ezra Pound used to tell the story, handed on by oral tradition, that Swinburne's friend the American painter Whistler interceded on Swinburne's behalf with the Club committee: 'You ought to be proud that there is in London a club where the greatest poet of your time *can* get drunk if he wants to, otherwise he might lie in the gutter.'[24]

Whether or not this anecdote is authentic, the sentiment behind it was not unique to Whistler. We read of the painter Hungerford Pollen and his wife finding D.G. Rossetti quite exhausted, having been woken the previous night at 3 a.m. by a tremendous knocking to discover Swinburne being held up in the arms of a policeman, surrounded by excited urchins. Mrs Pollen had banned Swinburne from her house some time before, when he became blasphemous and abusive after partaking of her sherry. 'Oh, my dear!' Pollen had responded, 'we must never be unkind to him; he is just a child.' Evidently Swinburne's size, as well as his recklessness, contributed to his friends' feeling that he was not really responsible for his own actions.

But like some pop stars of the 1960s, Swinburne and his raffish friends knew sad and sinister moments as well. Most famous of all, perhaps, at least in the annals of painting, was the terrible evening of 10 February 1862 when Swinburne dined with Dante Gabriel Rossetti and his wife Lizzie at the Hotel Sablonière in Leicester Square. It was some twelve years since a friend of Rossetti's had first spotted Lizzie Siddal over the blind of a glass door at the back of a bonnet shop in Cranborne Alley (only a stone's throw, as it happens, from the Sablonière). During the time she spent with Rossetti, Lizzie was one of the most stunning of the 'stunners' admired by his circle. Her face is forever familiar to us. She it was who nearly died of pneumonia when John Everett Millais made her pose in the bath for hours and hours – the result being his *Ophelia*. She was Holman Hunt's *Sylvia*, and she

---

* A variant of the story has Swinburne and another inebriated club member making two lines of hats and pancaking them in a three-legged race: *see* Rooksby, *Swinburne*, p. 129.

appears in innumerable poses for Rossetti, whom she eventually married. There was even a cult of her own drawings: Ruskin, who had a chaste crush on Guggum, as the circle nicknamed her, was wild about them and claimed, absurdly, that they were better than Rossetti's own. Her marriage put her under enormous strain. Rossetti, a much bigger man than Swinburne, could take even more alcohol and narcotics. Though frequently ill, he began to balloon in size. In later photographs of DGR his physical resemblance to Luciano Pavarotti is uncanny. Lizzie, by contrast, who was suffering from phthisis, was wasting away, and trying to kill the pains of her illness and the unhappiness of her relations with an unfaithful husband by means of a devotion to laudanum which became an addiction. 'He grew fatter, she thinner.'[25]

Having dined at the hotel the Rossettis parted from Swinburne at about eight, and went home. A hour later, however, Rossetti went out 'for a walk'. When he returned at half-past eleven he found that Lizzie had consumed a two-ounce bottle of laudanum, and was unconscious; she died the next morning at 7.20. Afterwards Rossetti had no more stomach for living in the house where it happened, and there followed the ill-starred attempt to share a house in Chelsea with Swinburne, ending with Swinburne's frequent collapses into *delirium tremens*.

Like Swinburne, Rossetti produced his best work when abusing his body with dangerous substances. His grief for Lizzie did not diminish his alcohol intake. The celebrated progress of his bereavement – the burial of his verses with Lizzie's body in Highgate Cemetery, and their exhumation seven years later, his obsession with seances and life after death (how very 'Victorian'), have attracted sneering as well as sympathetic judgements from posterity. It would be a foolish person, however, who did not see that *Beata Beatrix*, his translation of the dead, pale Lizzie into the saving heroine of Dante's *Paradiso*, was one of the greatest works of art of the entire nineteenth century, not merely in England but in Europe – perhaps the greatest. It reflects depths of grief, despondency (Rossetti 'spoke daily of suicide' during the long period he was at work on the picture),[26] and religious hope – none of them, one suspects, areas of experience which Swinburne ever made his own. His masterpieces, it must be said, sprang from a much more limited nature and experience than those of Rossetti. Even before his virtual imprisonment at Number 2 The Pines, Putney, he had not known much in the way of emotional adventure. He had hoped to marry his cousin, she had turned him down; he had been to brothels; he had taken more alcohol than his tiny frame could stand. He was aware of not being a 'deep' person, and after the *succès de scandale* caused by *Poems and Ballads* he deliberately set out to write on religious and political themes which would add *gravitas* to his wild reputation.

If 'The Triumph of Time' told the story of his loss not merely of his cousin Mary Gordon but of the very possibility of a 'normal', stable, heterosexual relationship in his life, and if 'Dolores' celebrated the side of his nature which delighted in self-conscious wickedness, there was, as he told the Balliol men during that dinner of the 1870s, a third poem which was deeply revealing of Swinburne's inner self: it is one of his most celebrated anthology-pieces, 'The Garden of Proserpine'.

> Here, where the world is quiet;
> Here, where all trouble seems
> Dead winds' and spent waves' riot
> In doubtful dreams of dreams;
> I watch the green field growing
> For reaping folk and sowing,
> For harvest-time and mowing,
> A sleepy world of streams.

Swinburne manifestly had a profound need for domestic peace and quiet, a need which advanced upon him during his forties when the accursed deafness began to imprison him in silence. Everyone who cared about him worried about his health. There were frequent collapses. He would pass out, as if epileptic. His drunkenness became a social embarrassment even to his closest and most tolerant friends. So it was a great relief to his mother and his respectable friends when Theodore Watts (known later in life as Theodore Watts-Dunton – like many Victorians he changed his name as the result of an inheritance) 'rescued' him.

Watts (-Dunton) was a lawyer who initially entered the circle of Swinburne's friends when he was recommended to William Morris to sort out the legal problems consequent upon the wholly unlooked-for commercial success of Morris and Co. The circle soon discovered that Watts was a man of literary discernment (D.G. Rossetti used to show him his poems, and ask for criticisms and corrections). In the surviving photographs Watts, with his bushy walrus moustache, looks a figure of great absurdity. And the bourgeois domestic life lasting nearly thirty years which he arranged for Swinburne at Number 2 The Pines has, understandably, been mocked.

Certainly the stultifying boredom of the regimen followed by Swinburne in Putney – the daily walk on the Heath, when he would stop and admire any babies in perambulators he could find (he had a passion for young babies), the one small bottle of Bass a day, the bellowed and often unheard observations of Watts or of visitors – was a kind of death; so perhaps it was appropriate that he should have foreseen it in 'The Garden of Proserpine'. Though he did not know it at the time, it was not of the underworld but of Putney that he wrote when he said:

> There go the loves that wither,
>   The old loves with wearier wings;
> And all dead years draw thither,
>   And all disastrous things;
> Dead dreams of days forsaken,
> Blind buds that snows have shaken,
> Wild leaves that winds have taken,
>   Red strays of ruined springs.

Some people like to defend Watts by claiming that he 'saved' Swinburne. True, in his perpetually sober and often lonely life at Number 2 The Pines Swinburne had the leisure to become one of the most prolix of all English poets. It is inconceivable that his collected poetic works, filling two enormous volumes, will ever be reprinted in their entirety; or, if they were, ever read. Of course, he lost none of his technical skill, and it must be said that many poets have written their best work in their twenties and thirties. One can't blame Watts-Dunton for the fact that Swinburne in his fifties and sixties did not rise to the passionate eloquence, the sonorous sensuality or the shockingness of his great early works.

That said, the later works of Swinburne are a poor argument for near-teetotalism and suburban virtue. In the years when he was being picked up from under tables at parties, trampling on hats and offering drunken insults to famous people, Swinburne wrote the four dazzling volumes which made his name – two volumes of *Poems and Ballads*, containing his finest lyrics; *Atalanta in Calydon*; and another drama, less good than *Atalanta* but formidably impressive, *Erechtheus* – and also wrote much of his finest prose work, particularly his study of William Blake. Like many writers since – Scott Fitzgerald, Dylan Thomas ... but why begin a list which could fill pages? – Swinburne demonstrated that whatever alcoholic excess might do to a writer's liver it does not diminish the quality of the work; in fact, quite the opposite.

The popularity of Swinburne must have derived very largely from the intoxicating music of his verses. But it is ridiculous to suggest that they are no more than 'music' or sensual sounds. By modern tastes, Swinburne is perhaps an excessively didactic writer, concerning himself in his poetry (particularly in the volume entitled *Songs Before Sunrise*) with political matters, issues arising from current affairs and contemporary events. And central to his poetry, central too, surely, to its popularity, is its repeated proclamation that Christianity is finished, done for, discredited.

In private, Swinburne was much more virulently atheistic than, let us say, the Rossetti brothers, or the agnostic Morris. To Dante Gabriel Rossetti in February 1870, he wrote his own version of the Death of God joke:

> I expect you will see shortly in the papers, 'Suicide of an elderly pauper lunatic, formerly an unlicensed pawnbroker and receiver of stolen goods. His linen was marked JAH. A young man of dissipated appearance and a Jewish cast of feature who announced himself as the son of the deceased, is more than suspected of being the same person who was sentenced to the gallows some time since for a nameless offence and taken down before the proper time, and restored to life after undergoing the extreme penalty of the law. Since then, has been known to the police under a variety of aliases, and among his companions of infamous notoriety, by the slang term of "the Lamb".'[27]

Of the many attempts by Christianity to reverse the tide of unbelief sweeping through Europe, none was bolder than Pius IX's summoning of the First Vatican Council in Rome in 1869. It was destined to be broken up by the onset of the Franco-Prussian war, when the French troops who had been protecting the Pope withdrew and the Italian republican forces of Garibaldi entered the Holy City.

As far as the republicans Mazzini and Garibaldi were concerned, the Papacy was the last bastion of the old royalist absolutism which had held back the progress of human rights and intellectual freedom for centuries. Swinburne, who hero-worshipped Mazzini, actively supported this view of the Vatican and its proceedings. Not only did the Pope and the Council Fathers set out to attack the 'pantheism, materialism and atheism of the time',[28] but the more extreme among them (none more extreme than the English representative, Cardinal Manning) proposed declaring the Pope to be infallible. This last idea was too much even for many of the Council Fathers themselves. The trains out of Rome were jammed with cardinals and bishops escaping from the Council before the matter came to a head. In the event, just before the Council broke up the Infallibility issue was put to the vote. In a thunderstorm of Biblical loudness and violence, the Holy Father proclaimed himself infallible. Of the seven hundred bishops who had assembled at the beginning of the Council in 1869, a mere 533 were present to vote for the notion that one of their fellow human beings could speak with total infallibility on matters of faith and morals. Some of the bishops, notably in Germany, Austria and Switzerland, broke away and joined the 'Old Catholics' of Utrecht, unable, in conscience, to accept the new doctrine. The majority of European Catholics were committed to the belief.

The Vatican did not merely now make the claim of papal infallibility. In the nineteenth century, in its assaults on every development in scientific knowledge, every glimmering of light shed in the field of biblical scholarship, every advancement of technical skill (it even issued condemnations of the electric light), the Vatican was the great powerhouse of reaction, posing very grave difficulties for those who wished to practise the Catholic faith without committing intellectual suicide. Such brave souls undoubtedly existed. Newman – a bigot in youth and a liberal in old age – wrote a highly cautious defence of theism entitled *A Grammar of Assent*; the Catholics who came to be known as modernists – brave men like Abbé Loisy in France and Baron von Hügel in England – tried to be loyal to the Church in their own way;* but they were destined to be driven out by the condemnatory decree of Pius X, *Lamentabili* – perhaps an appropriate title. After that, until the Second Vatican Council made life slightly more sane for Catholics of an intellectual bent, they were placed in a ridiculous position. For example, Catholic students were forbidden to read books on the Index (which included the works of Voltaire, and Charles Kingsley's *The Water Babies*). Students of theology, however devout, were forbidden to absorb *any* modern wisdom about the evolution of the biblical texts.

Is it any wonder that with bigotry on this scale at the very heart of European Christianity – a bigotry more than reflected in the Protestant world – the young men and women of the 1860s and 1870s should have

---

* Their story makes up our final chapter.

fallen so hungrily on the works of Swinburne? 'I for one cannot understand how a man can so believe in God personal and moral as to be convinced of him, unless he believes in some revelation Christian or other: i.e., unless his reason abdicates in favour of his passion.'[29] He tried to get William Rossetti, as a 'fellow atheist', to sign a letter protesting against the Vatican Council, but Rossetti replied that he did not consider himself an atheist; regretted, indeed, that Swinburne should use the word of himself. Swinburne conceded that

> I feel it my mission as an evangelist and apostle (whenever necessary) to atheize the republicans and republicanize the atheists of my acquaintance. I have in my head a sort of Hymn for this Congress – as it were a 'Te Hominem Laudamus', to sing the human triumph over 'things' – the opposing forces of life and nature – and over the God of his own creation, till he attain truth, self-sufficiency, and freedom.[30]

As we have seen, what Darwinism destroyed, irrevocably, was the Deist world-picture of matter, or the universe, or simply 'what is', as something distinct from the creative process which 'made' it or 'caused' it. Lyell's *Geology* had made it impossible *(pace* poor Philip Gosse) to think that the world and the stars and the planets came into being, in their present constituent state, during a seven-day programme. The existence of geological strata made it clear to Lyell's generation – as it was not to Paley's – that the Watchmaker, if He had 'made' the world, had done so, not all at once, but in a gradual process. The existence of fossils confirmed not just the *age* of the earth, but the fact that species are mutable. In order to survive, they have to mutate. Milton's picture (based on Genesis) of fixed species arriving on the surface of the planet by divine decree was not borne out by the evidence. And what Darwin was able to demonstrate beyond reasonable doubt was not merely that the species mutate, evolve, change, but that they do so within a system which requires for its 'explanation' no theory of volition by a creator – no Watchmaker, coming in from outside to 'make' what is. On the contrary, what is, is. And 'this' – this immense continuum of time and space – is what there is. All the pictures which humankind had crudely made for itself of the here and now – depending for their existence on some exterior agency – had to be discarded.

Darwinism succeeded, in brief, because it was true; or as true as any description of the evolution of species could be. However much the 'creationists' might scream about it, the truth could not be gainsaid; any more than it can now when, a little pathetically, they try to rehearse this positively flyblown old set of arguments.

But this is not to say – as we can now see, and Darwin's generation could not – that Darwin had all the answers to all the questions. He did not know about DNA. We do. He did not know what we know, post-Hubble, about the observable, demonstrable fact that our universe is ever-expanding. And it follows that the Victorians were not in a position to debate whether a coherent God, a God who breathes through His creation, lives within it, a God who is *here*, not *there*, might not be the true God. In the world of post-Big Bang Theory it is open to theologians, physicists, and indeed to all intelligent people who are interested in this question, to ask whether our Victorian forefathers did not get the whole question the wrong way about. Thinking of God as an 'explanation' for things, they could not come to terms with the sense – very commonly experienced in life, though perhaps never better expressed than in the nature-mysticism of Wordsworth – that God was actually *in* His universe. This was not the pantheism of Spinoza, who spoke quite openly of *Deus sive Natura* (God, that is to say, Nature). Rather, in Wordsworth you have 'something much more deeply interfused'.

Wordsworth himself, for a whole range of social and psychological reasons, turned aside from radicalism and 'mysticism' to follow his friend Samuel Taylor Coleridge's journey to rabid reactionary membership of the Established Church. It is a journey many have made since. Being so terrified of the implications of scientific materialism and Unbelief, they huddle for shelter beneath the arms of Orthodoxy. It is an attractive but a dishonourable position. Those who care for the truth have to recognize the implications of what Darwin and Huxley were saying. They have to recognize that the Watchmaker-God of Deism was destroyed in the last century. He was laid to rest.

Darwin and his friends became, many of them, atheists, people who believed that there was no God at all; that the Universe was empty and without soul. This is an honourable position because, unlike the huddlers-under-Orthodoxy's-umbrella, such stark atheists were guided by the truth. But were they guided by the *whole* truth? Does Big Bang alter our perception of their truth? Does it not supply an answer to the one question which Darwinism so dismally refuses to address: namely, how (let alone why!) *anything happens to exist at all*. It is existence itself which is surely the greatest of all mysteries. How we, with what we call our consciousness, come to be observing existence, our own and that of all that is, is not a mystery outside the mystery. We are not like the Old God, *outside* existence, peering into it through a microscope or a telescope. We are part of it; so, if it makes sense to speak of Him, is the coherent Deity. Students of the medieval Jewish mystical texts known as the Kabbalah have begun to remind us of a different way of looking at God. 'To the Kabbalist, the fundamental fact of creation takes place *in* God ... The creation of the world, that is to say, the creation of something out of nothing, is itself, but the external aspect of something which takes place in God Himself.'[31] For the Kabbalists, the process of creation happened *within* God. They use the metaphor of wine skins which, however often they are rinsed, retain the smell of wine: so the 'smell' of God remains in everything and everyone. There is 'a residue of divine manifestation in every being'. Very similar perceptions enable a modern scientist to be able to say 'The world is incredible – just the fact that you and I are here, that the atoms of our bodies were once part of the stars. They say I am on some sort of religious quest, looking for God, but God *is* the way it's put together.'[32]

It is a paradox of intellectual history that – given the state of knowledge in the nineteenth century, and given the addiction of religious people to the notion of God as a Being outside Existence, outside the Cosmos, outside the world 'which is the world of all of us' – only an 'atheist' such as Swinburne was likely to glimpse what for us, over a hundred years later, is the only possible means by which a religious view of the universe can be sustained. God had to die in order for such truly religious perceptions to grow. As Professor Friedman has written,

> When the deity asks Job, 'Where were you when I laid the foundations of the earth?' Job might answer, truly and reverently in a way, 'I was there'. To the extent that the universe still reverberates with the Big Bang, it reverberates in all beings; and those beings with the furthest developed state of consciousness – which on this planet includes humans – may be capable of being in touch with that part of our formation: through tools of the intellect if they are cosmologists (including observation, deduction), through tools of mysticism if they are Kabbalists (including meditation, introspection). And there are, no doubt, some tools that the two have in common as well (aesthetics, logic, instinct).[33]

If this line of approach makes sense to our generation, then we can turn back to Swinburne the atheist and find insights into the nature of things which are in fact very far from irreligious. If Swinburne had been an atheist of the purely cynical Baron Holbach variety, he would hardly have been such a devotee of William Blake, for example. Swinburne, the Rossettis and their circle kept the memory of Blake green when that great genius had sunk from public consciousness. When Gilchrist died leaving his Life of Blake unfinished, it was suggested that Swinburne might help to complete the book. Instead, he wrote a book of his own, expounding Blake's thought and genius.

> Blake could not conceive an impulse to mendacity, a tortuous habit of mind, a soul born crooked. This one quality of falsehood remains damnable in his sight, to be consumed with all that comes of it. In man or beast or any other part of God he found no native taint or birthmark of this. Upon all else the divine breath and the divine hand are sensible and visible.
>
> > The pride of the peacock is the glory of God;
> > The lust of the goat is the bounty of God;
> > The wrath of the lion is the wisdom of God;
> > The nakedness of woman is the work of God ...

At no point in his book did Swinburne ridicule Blake's religious view of the world; indeed, he obviously saw Blake's rejection of 'Nobodaddy' in the Prophetic Books as on a par with his own rejection of the Victorian God, the petulant personal 'Creator' with prudish suburban ideas about sex. From Blake's Prophecies Swinburne learnt the lesson that 'Churches have cast out apostles; creeds have rooted out faith. Henceforth anger and loneliness, the divine indignation of spiritual exile, the salt bread of scorn and the bitter wine of wrath, are the portion of the just man ...'[34]

It was undoubtedly from Blake that Swinburne derived his sense that virtue and abstinence, no less than 'sin', are in need of forgiveness:

> > What ailed us, O gods, to desert you
> > For creeds that refuse and restrain?
> > Come down and redeem us from virtue,
> > Our Lady of Pain.

If this is self-consciously 'naughty', there is also something more grown-up, more fundamentally serious, about Swinburne's concept of 'theanthropy', the Blakean idea that Man, or rather the Soul of Man, *is* God. The 'Jewish and Christian God is an active but prolific force at variance with the Eternals ... He it is who is the source of the religion which wars against "the large and liberal laws of right".'[35]

It is no wonder that McTaggart, the most austere of the British Idealist philosophers, should have been so devoted to the poetry of Swinburne, particularly to 'Hertha' and 'By the North Sea'. What is remarkable about these poems is the extent to which, by decades, Swinburne *anticipates* philosophical developments. And though 'Hertha' is a meditation upon a godless universe, or at the least a universe without a personal God, it is something rather more than 'Darwinian' in the narrowly-defined sense. McTaggart felt it was incumbent upon philosophy to find a metaphysic which would justify a 'religious attitude' – that is, 'a conviction of harmony between ourselves and the universe at large'.[36] Such a 'religious' attitude is what underlies and defines 'Hertha'. A case can surely be made for saying that it is the most important religious poem, in English, of the nineteenth century. Arnold's 'Dover Beach' does not after all *say* anything. It does not advance a metaphysic. Its thesis, inspiring to generations of quasi-humanists, makes its appeal through vagueness. The sea of faith, once 'at the full', is now ebbing out. The world

> Hath really neither joy, nor love, nor light,
> Nor certitude, nor peace, nor help for pain ...

So, we must 'be true to one another'. Fine as far as it goes; and no wonder Arnold's poetry gets into all the anthologies. But it hardly amounts to an account which you could set beside, or against, Wordsworth's as a *Weltanschauung*. Swinburne, in the two poems I have named, worries less about the portent of the Sea of Faith; but stares with Goethean awe at the sea itself:

> As the waves of the numberless waters
> That the wind cannot number who guides
> Are the sons of the shore and the daughters
> Here lulled by the chime of the tides:
> And here in the press of them standing
> We know not if these or if we
> Live truliest, or anchored to landing
> Or drifted to sea.

'Hertha' is, precisely, the awestruck but non-superstitious attitude to nature which we feel instinctively. She begins by speaking to us: 'I am that which began.' Swinburne is not whimsically making Nature into a Goddess, or even into a person.

> I bid you but be [she says];
>   I have need not of prayer;
>   I have need of you free
>   As your mouths of mine air;
> That my heart may be greater within me, beholding
>   the fruits of me fair.

It is not the humanly-invented deities which command our devotion,

> ... the Gods of your fashion
>   That take and that give,
> In their pity and passion
>   That scourge and forgive,
> They are worms that are bred in the bark that falls off;
>   they shall die and not live.

The 'naughty' Swinburne probably thought he was shocking Christian sensibility by filling 'Hertha' with so many Biblical references. They actually serve to remind us of how much the Jewish Scriptures are punctuated with accounts of the falsity of human attempts to make unto themselves idols and Gods. Of course, in the earliest parts of the Pentateuch Yahweh, their God, wants them to forsake these false Gods and to follow him. But little by little Yahweh himself withdraws. Whereas in the Books of Genesis or Exodus, God is doing everything Himself from weaving the clothes for Adam and Eve after the Fall to killing the Egyptian first-born, latterly – having revealed the moral law through the Torah – He withdraws. He 'hides his face'. By the end of the historical cycle you find a Scriptural book – Esther – in which God is not mentioned at all; and the Psalmists speak of a God who has withdrawn Himself completely from the human scene.

This is actually the scriptural picture, and it is one of the reasons, I suspect, that the Victorians, who were so well-versed in the Bible, found the religious developments in their century so alarming or exciting, depending on temperament. For they realized that they were living out the Bible: the book on which their faith rested and depended was the book in which God eventually disappeared. In Swinburne's 'Hymn of Man' he taunts the Catholics:

> Cry aloud; for your God is a God and a Saviour;
>   cry, make yourselves lean;
> Is he drunk or asleep, that the rod of his wrath is
>   unfelt or unseen?
> Is the fire of his old loving-kindness gone out, that
>   his pyres are acold?
> Hath he gazed on himself unto blindness, who made
>   men blind to behold?

All this is a direct allusion to the story in the First Book of Kings, Chapter XVIII, when Elijah the prophet challenges the prophets of Baal to a contest. They are to sacrifice a bull, place it on the altar and call upon Baal to set it alight for them. The four hundred prophets of Baal do as he suggests. They make their prayer to Baal. They cry out his name. They cut themselves with swords and lances. They bleed. They shriek. And all the while, their god, who is but an idol, is silent, and the prophet of Yahweh taunts them: 'Cry aloud, for he is a god; either he is talking, or he is pursuing, or he is in a journey, or peradventure he sleepeth and must be awaked' (I Kings xviii.27). However, like so many robust stories in the Hebrew theology, this is not a simple tale of the triumph of one god over another god. Sure enough, when the prophets of Baal have finished slashing themselves with knives and shouting themselves hoarse, Elijah shows them what a real God can do – and just for good measure, he douses the altar with water before he asks Yahweh to set it ablaze. Of course Yahweh obliges; and then, to oblige Yahweh, Elijah kills all four hundred of his rivals. But there is, written into this story, the human experience that Yahweh, more often than not, behaves like Baal. He doesn't come when he is called. Peradventure he sleepeth. Or – and in the 'Hymn of Man', Swinburne spells it out for his audience –

> Cry, cut yourselves, gash you with knives and with
>   scourges, heap on to you dust;
> Is his life but as other gods' lives? is not this the
>   Lord God of your trust?
> Is not this the great God of your sires, that with
>   souls and with bodies was fed,
> And the world was on flame with his fires? O fools,
>   he was God, and is dead.

You can't get more specific than that. The attitude of Christian obscurantists, as of any other kind of religious fundamentalists, provokes an exasperation which can at times be childish. You just want to shout 'Yah boo sucks!' But that isn't the only attitude. The 'Hymn to Man' is what Swinburne felt when he contemplated the figure of an Italian minor aristocrat, in the eighth decade of the nineteenth century, carried on a litter like one of the Roman emperors and wafted with ostrich feathers before being told, by those assembled bishops too cowardly to deny the nonsense, that he was infallible. But the universe did not become less awesome because the childish fantasies of Christianity had been discarded. As Darwin himself had written in *The Origin of Species*, 'there is a grandeur' in his view of life, too, and 'whilst this planet has gone cycling on according to the fixed law of gravity, from so simple a beginning endless forms most beautiful and most wonderful have been and are being evolved'.[37]

11

In the Name of the Father

'The people which first succeeded in . . .
concentrating the divine attributes was not a little
proud of the advance. It had laid open to view the
father who had all along been hidden behind every
divine figure as its nucleus. Fundamentally this
was a return to the historical beginnings of the
idea of God. Now that God was a single person,
man's relations to him could recover the
intimacy and intensity of the child's relation to
his father . . .'

        Sigmund Freud, *The Future of an Illusion*, iii

'My parents were – in a sort – visible powers of
nature to me, no more loved than the sun and the
moon: only I should have been annoyed and
puzzled if either of them had gone out; (how
much, now, when both are darkened!) – still less
did I love God; not that I had any quarrel with
Him, or fear of Him; but simply found what
people told me was His service, disagreeable; and
what people told me was His book, not
entertaining.'

        Ruskin, *Praeterita*, I.50

E DMUND GOSSE'S *Father and Son* (published 1907) is one of the great texts of Victorian unbelief. Gently subtitled 'A Study of Two Temperaments', it leaves the reader in no doubt which of the two is the more charming. The paradox is, of course, that Edmund Gosse was a bore; whereas the parental religious maniac whom he depicts is, however awful, touchingly awful. Once the boy Gosse has discovered the beauty of poetry, and of art, the reader knows that he can not survive long in the Plymouth Brethren, among fanatics like the girl who believed, not merely that the Crystal Palace was the 'Temple of Belial', but that this entitled her to smash all the plaster casts of heathen deities in the sculpture gallery there; or the preacher who referred to Shakespeare as 'a lost soul now suffering for his sins in hell'.[1] The son gives his father his due: Gosse *père* remarks,

Brother So-and-so was not, in my judgement, justified in saying what he did. The uncovenanted mercies of God are not revealed to us. Before so rashly speaking of Shakespeare as 'a lost soul in hell', he should have remembered how little we know of the poet's history. The light of salvation was widely disseminated in the land during the reign of Queen Elizabeth, and we cannot know that Shakespeare did not accept the atonement of Christ in simple faith before he came to die.[2]

By then, of course, Gosse *fils* has already felt himself (aged sixteen) to be 'a bird fluttering in the network of my Father's will'.[3] Edmund Gosse grew up; went to London. What astonishes him as he looks back is that his father, still in Devonshire, did not worry himself about the young man's moral welfare in the sinful capital city. What the elder man's obsessive letters demand is a chronicle of Edmund's adherence to the faith – to an evangelical faith which he had come to hate. The postal inquisition leads eventually to young Gosse admitting to his father that

233

he no longer believes, and this spells the end of their relationship – not because the son cannot tolerate the father, but because the father demands 'Everything or Nothing'. 'If the written Word is not absolutely authoritative, what do we know of God?' asks the father. 'What more than we can infer, that is, guess – as the thoughtful heathens guessed – Plato, Socrates, Cicero – from dim and mute surrounding phenomena.'

It is the childhood scenes in *Father and Son* that we all remember. One recalls, for example, the incident which occurred while his mother was still alive and they were living in Hackney, East London.

> My parents said: 'Whatever you need, tell Him and He will grant it, if it is His will.' Very well; I had need of a large painted humming-top which I had seen in a shop-window in the Caledonian Road. Accordingly, I introduced a supplication for this object into my evening prayer, carefully adding the words, 'if it is Thy will'. This, I recollect, placed my Mother in a dilemma, and she consulted my Father. Taken, I suppose, at a disadvantage, my Father told me I must not pray for 'things like that'. To which I answered with another query, 'Why?' And I added that he said we ought to pray for things we needed, and that I needed the humming-top a great deal more than I did the conversion of the heathen or the restitution of Jerusalem to the Jews, two objects of my nightly supplication, which left me very cold.[4]

It is perhaps not surprising, since both were addressed by the same name, that Gosse confused his Father 'in some sense with God'. The discovery that his father was not omnipotent, omniscient and infallible was perhaps, like the beginning of doubt over the humming-top, a double-disillusion. When belief in the Earthly Father evaporated, the belief in the Heavenly could not survive.

The Christmas pudding incident is one of the most ridiculous as well as one of the most poignant in the book. To précis it would not do it justice. It deserves to be quoted in its entirety:

> On the subject of all feasts of the Church he held views of an almost grotesque peculiarity. He looked upon them as nugatory and worthless, but the keeping of Christmas appeared to him by far the most hateful, and nothing less than an act of idolatry. 'The very word is Popish,' he used to exclaim, 'Christ's Mass!' pursing his lips with the gesture of one who tastes asafoetida by accident. Then he would adduce the antiquity of the so-called feast, adapted from horrible heathen rites, and itself a soiled

relic of the abominable Yule-Tide. He would denounce the horror of Christmas until it almost made me blush to look at a holly berry.

On Christmas Day 1857* our villa saw a very unusual sight. My father had given strictest charge that no difference whatever was to be made in our meals on that day: the dinner was to be neither more copious than usual nor less so. He was obeyed, but the servants, secretly rebellious, made a small plum pudding for themselves ... Early in the afternoon, the maids – of whom we were now advanced to keeping two – kindly remarked that 'the poor dear child ought to have a bit, anyhow', and wheedled me into the kitchen, where I ate a slice of plum-pudding. Shortly I began to feel that pain inside which in my frail state was inevitable, and my conscience smote me violently. At length I could bear my spiritual anguish no longer, and bursting into the study, I called out, 'Oh! Papa, Papa, I have eaten of flesh offered to idols!' It took some time, between my sobs, to explain what had happened. Then my Father sternly said: 'Where is the accursed thing?' I explained that as much as was left of it was still on the kitchen-table. He took me by the hand, and ran with me into the midst of the startled servants, seized what remained of the pudding, and with the plate in one hand and me still tight in the other, ran till we reached the dust-heap, when he flung the idolatrous confectionery on to the middle of the ashes and raked it deep down into the mass. The suddenness, the violence, the velocity of this extraordinary act made an impression on my memory which nothing will ever efface.[5]

The barely-suppressed violence of the scene and its completely grotesque comedy could almost have made it a subject for a novel by I. Compton-Burnett.

These subversive novels (written between 1925 and 1961) have almost passed out of knowledge in the English-speaking world, except among a handful of lucky addicts; but there will surely come a time when Compton-Burnett is recognized as one of the great twentieth-century English writers. Her mannered, arch, camp stories (Sophocles meets Mrs Henry Wood, or The English Eugene O'Neill) burrow into the ways in which human beings exercise power in families. Most of her characters (often grown-ups condemned through penury and membership of the upper-middle class to remain at home) are living in a fascist state – but that state is their family home, and the tyrant is not a Hitler or a Mussolini – it is their grandmother or their father, the only person in the household actually to have any money. Treading that borderline

---

* Edmund Gosse would have been eight years and two months old.

between farce and tragedy which is her special territory, Compton-Burnett has many unsettling things to say about sex, money, the crushing of human individuality by stultifying 'family values'. That is why so many of the free spirits in her books, and nearly all the funniest, are the unmarried – particularly those young men with Wildean epigrams on their lips; or the scowled-upon governesses or ladies' 'companions' who recognize that by being mere appendages to the family-structure they are in some measure free of it.

If I. Compton-Burnett's novels have a manifesto it is to be found in the amoral confession of Alfred who in *Daughters and Sons* alienates the affections – though not, as is rumoured, the fortune – of one of the most memorable tyrants in the *oeuvre*, old Sabine, who at eighty-four is still causing governesses to wither and grown-up offspring to shrink beneath her lacerating tongue: *'I hold no brief for any family.'*[6]

Compton-Burnett was by birth a late Victorian; she died in 1969, full of years, something of a mystery-woman, whose 'life' would appear to have been poured into her books. All the novels are set in the late years of the nineteenth or the very earliest years of the twentieth century, and on one issue they are unanimous: that religion has had its day, that belief is an impossibility for the generation to which she herself belonged. In *A Family and a Fortune* (1939), the old grandfather, Oliver, following a funeral, asserts a belief in life after death:

> 'I have those who belong to me on both sides. It gets to make less differ-
> ence to me on which side I am.'
>
> His grandsons looked at him with incredulous eyes, startled by the
> faith of a man who was in other respects a normal being.[7]

In *Daughters and Sons* the point is made even more forcefully of Sabine (who belongs to the same generation as Oliver). This novel (written in 1937) is set in 1894; Sabine keeps to the old custom of beginning each day with family prayers:

> She came to a pause for her audience to kneel, and led them in prayer,
> remaining in her seat. The Almighty would allow for her rheumatism,
> as his conception of her had in some way required its infliction, and
> would hardly be struck by any unsuitability in her abasing herself less
> than her household. She saw the matter as he would see it, as she assumed
> that she saw most matters. Her feeling for him was of such a nature that
> she only needed to have been born fifty years later than her date of eight-
> een hundred and ten, to fail to recognize him at all ...[8]

Something which has been a natural belief for one generation becomes unthinkable (literally) for the next. One generation allows public hanging or slavery; pass a hundred years, and no serious person (in Europe, at any rate) can tolerate such things. Animal rights and sexual morality have changed in comparable ways. In this constantly evolving human pattern, in which one generation's virtue becomes another's vice, one's truth the next's falsehood, the idea of God is pinpointed quite specifically by Compton-Burnett as the property of the Newman/Manning/Gladstone generation. Thereafter was born her own breed. One of her friends recalled a luncheon party with her in old age at which allusion was made to a contemporary, Rose Macaulay, reverting to the practice of Christianity.

> She carved up Muriel Spark and Iris Murdoch at the same time as the bacon. Marriage and religion were discussed and deplored. I felt guilty to be married and to have stayed married so long, and almost thankful not to be religious. Rose Macaulay has never been forgiven. To have such a thing happen – when for a lifetime she had been a perfectly sound agnostic like everybody else.[9]

The relentless, unforgiving agnosticism of Ivy Compton-Burnett is surely an essential part of what Anthony Powell called her 'unreconstructed pre-1914 personality'. The origins of her hatred of the family, and of religion, are to be found in her hero, Samuel Butler, whose *Notebooks* she obsessively re-read and underscored.

Samuel Butler (1835–1902), like Karl Marx, had a far greater influence after his death than during his lifetime. Perhaps 'influence' is the wrong word for Butler, though. When Shaw saluted him (in the preface to *Major Barbara*) as 'in his own department the greatest English writer of the latter half of the XIX century'; and when Lytton Strachey and the Bloomsberries took him up as their prophet; and when Ivy Compton-Burnett not only read and re-read his *Notebooks* but, as it were, dramatized them in nineteen novels – none of this was the result of his *influence*. Their bosoms all returned an echo to Butler's iconoclasm. In regard to his two great themes – dismissal of Christianity, and hatred of family life – they all felt they had been there before. He merely put their experiences into words.

Even so, the posthumous book (published 1903) which made such an impression upon them, *The Way of All Flesh*, deserves to be studied as a record of late Victorian family life and the peculiar psychological kinship between religious belief and the child–parent relationship. It was a book on which Butler had been working intermittently for twenty-nine years. He began it the year Sigmund Freud entered Vienna University as a medical student. Butler had just completed the semi-Swiftian satire *Erewhon* (1873), whose sarcastic and overtly anti-Christian tone had, according to his father, hastened his mother's death;* he was still tinkering with *The Way of All Flesh* in the last weeks of his life. By general consent, the novel is an autobiography, and the insufferable, bullying figure of Mr Pontifex is a cruel portrait of Butler's own father, a clergyman. 'MY MOST IMPLACABLE ENEMY from childhood onward has certainly been my father. I doubt not whether I could make a friend of my brother more easily than I could turn my father into a cordial well-wisher,' Butler wrote in his *Notebooks*.[10] And he added: 'He never liked me, nor I him: from my earliest recollections I can call to mind no time when I did not fear and dislike him; over and over again I have relented towards him, and said to myself that he was a good fellow after all; but I had hardly done so when he would go for me in some way or other which soured me again.'[11] In the light of Freud's theories, which were coming to fruition precisely during the gestation-period of *The Way of All Flesh*, it is interesting that the enmity between father and son in Butler's novel exists from the very beginning. Theobald Pontifex was sad when he believed his wife to be barren, but he did not truly wish his son to be born, and he certainly 'had had no idea how great a nuisance a baby was'.[12] The birth of the child and the subsequent illness of its mother 'was another nuisance and an expensive one ... Theobald had never liked children. He had always got away from them as soon as he could, and so had they from him; oh why, he was inclined to ask himself, could not children be born into the world grown up?' Therefore the poor little brute, Ernest, was punished for existing:

> Before Ernest could well crawl he was taught to kneel; before he could well speak he was taught to lisp the Lord's prayer, and the general confession. How was it possible that these things could be taught too early? If his attention flagged or his memory failed him, here was an ill weed which would grow apace, unless it were plucked out immediately, and the only way to pluck it out was to whip him, or shut him up in a cupboard, or dock him of some of the small pleasures of childhood.

---

* Butler himself commented that doctors had given cancer as the cause of his mother's death.

But as in Larkin's poem in which 'man hands on misery to man', poor old Theobald Pontifex had received similar treatment from his own father. 'Mr Pontifex may have been a little sterner with his children than some of his neighbours, but not much. He thrashed his boys two or three times a week and some weeks a good deal oftener, but in those days fathers were always thrashing their boys.'[13]

Butler realized that the enmity which lay at the heart of the father–son relationship was not something over which either party could exercise control. He pitied his grandfather, in *The Way of All Flesh*, as 'not the man to trouble himself about his motives'; and observed (he died two years after the publication of Freud's *Die Traumdeutung*: had he read it, heard inklings of what was going on in Austrian medicine? Or was it merely that this was the true *Zeitgeist?*):

> Man forsooth prides himself on his consciousness! We boast that we differ from the winds and waves and falling stones and plants, which grow they know not why, and from the wandering creatures which go up and down and after their prey as we are pleased to say without the help of reason. We know so well what we are doing ourselves and why we do it, do we not? I fancy that there is some truth in the view which is being put forward nowadays, that it is our less conscious thoughts and our less conscious actions which mainly mould our lives and the lives of those who spring from us.[14]

The Way of All Flesh suggests that the enmity between fathers and sons is a peculiarly nineteenth-century phenomenon. Butler points out that in Shakespeare, fathers and sons tend to be friends, as they do in the literature of antiquity. It is in the novels of Jane Austen that we first begin to suspect that fathers are *capable de tout*. Several ideas are sounded out, though not fully developed, in *The Way of All Flesh*. One is the suggestion that those of the *rentier* class, and beneficed clergymen in particular, have a relation with their children which is unlike that of fathers in the past. To begin with, these men, living on either their investments or their clerical stipends, are at home. All the time. Whereas fathers in the past left the house, to hunt, to fight, to study, to till or to farm, the Victorian father, either in his parsonage or simply in the house paid for by the interest on *capital*, hovers about all the time as a figure in the child's development. Not only do the children exasperate him with their noises and smells, but they pose a threat of a purely practical and economic kind: they cost money, with their entourage of nannies and governesses, their school fees, their allowances. And there can hardly be anything more Oedipal than the knowledge that they cannot live as their fathers are living until they in turn inherit the family fortune – that is, until *the father is dead*.

The fathers of the *rentier* and clergy class needed powerful allies against their natural enemies, their sons. And they did not hesitate to enlist the most powerful ally of all: Jehovah. Puritan sullenness came to the aid of the Mammon-worshipping Victorian *bourgeoisie*, the evangelical reading of the Old Testament serving perfectly, as Butler saw it, the purposes of the dour Victorian Father figures who had made his generation so unhappy:

> I dare not say that we owe no benefits to the Jewish nation, I do not feel sure whether we do or do not, but I can see no good thing that I can point to as a notoriously Hebrew contribution to our moral and intellectual well-being as I can point to law and say that it is Roman, or to our fine arts and say that they are based on what the Greeks and Italians taught us. On the contrary, if asked what feature of post-Christian life we had derived most distinctly from Hebrew sources I should say at once 'intolerance' – the desire to dogmatize about matters whereon the Greek and Roman held certainty to be at once unimportant and unattainable.[15]

As we read Butler's works and follow his life, we feel that the earthly father is attacked with the same fervour with which he set out to dethrone or disprove the Heavenly Father; and then again, as the wheel comes full circle, we sense that his ineradicable theological obsession, his inability to leave God the Father alone, has something to do with unconscious dramas buried in childhood, from which he was unable wholly to escape. The very fact that Samuel Butler did not 'grow up' (to use a loose populism which contains several layers of truth) presumably explains his appeal to the generation which flourished between 1900 and 1930, so many of whose writers – Shaw, Strachey, Woolf – built their literary *personae* on essentially adolescent foundations: the desire to shock or to upset their parents. For most of them, God had already flown out of the window; but the God in whom they did not believe is very recognizably Butler's God, the Hebraic, intolerant deity of their fathers and grandfathers.

Butler was a child of the parsonage. His grandfather had been Charles Darwin's headmaster when the naturalist was a boy at Shrewsbury; Dr Butler had then gone on to become the Bishop of Lichfield. His son –

the novelist's father, and the model for Theobold Pontifex – was the Rector of Langar, and it was in the parsonage house in that remote Nottinghamshire village that the psychodramas took place which were to be written up as *The Way of All Flesh*.

His grandfather the Bishop had been a man of substance, and his death during Samuel's boyhood guaranteed that whatever the emotional deprivations of rectory life, it was not without its material compensations. The boy was allowed to sit at table and sip wine when there were guests for dinner. He never tasted claret again for years, writing about it, indeed, as if it were barely worth tasting, as if anything associated with his father was to be deplored, hated. Years later, when he was dining with his college friend Jason Smith, the taste of the wine set before him recalled, in Proustian fashion, memories of time past in Langar. 'There was no mistake about it. I asked Jason what the wine was. He said it was Château Lafite and very fine. I have no doubt that my father when I was a boy was finishing up my grandfather's cellar.'[16]

We must not expect the man who could dismiss the wondrous Château Lafitte as 'like weak port wine' to be dispassionate. Indeed, the whole reason for directing our attention towards him in the context of Victorian unbelief is that he was so passionate, so extreme, and by many standards so odd. And yet this freak 'spoke' for a generation.

At Shrewsbury and at St John's College, Cambridge there were no manifestations of profound unbelief. He prepared to take holy orders as his father and grandfather had before him. Then followed, in the crucial year of 1859, a six-month period spent living in London and testing his vocation. He was apprenticed, as it were, to a curate at St James's, Piccadilly – the Reverend Philip Perring. A little to his surprise he found, as he assisted this good man in his parish work, that the great mass of people were supremely indifferent to religion. Doubts began to set in, especially when he heard the absurdity of Christian claims on his own lips. Conducting an evening class, Butler was asked why God permitted evil in the world. 'My good man,' he replied, 'don't you see? If Adam had not eaten the apple you would now be in the Garden of Eden; whereas, things being as they are, you have a chance of Heaven, which is a much better place.'[17]

It was not long before he began to wonder whether he was altogether cut out for the Church. He wrote to his father and asked if there was any chance of his being allowed to pursue the career of an artist. 'I have no objection to your taking up drawing as an amusement,' replied his father, 'I said that long ago. But as to the wild scheme of making it a profession with no knowledge whatever how far it may answer, and to the neglect and ruin of every other prospect, to this I will give no countenance at all ...'[18] Nor was the Rector impressed by the lad's puzzlement over doctrines such as the bodily Resurrection, or the means of grace through baptism.

The great question of money then arose to guarantee that Butler father and Butler son would hate one another forever. By the terms of Bishop Butler's will, Samuel was the eventual heir to a considerable estate which included some property in Shrewsbury. Alas, in his final year as an undergraduate Samuel was persuaded by his father to sell this house and some of the land which went with it, to a cousin. The matter was still irritating him nearly fifty years later. 'Re the sale of the Whitehall Shrewsbury to my cousin. How they bamboozled me!' he exclaimed in 1901.[19] The result of his quarrel with his father was that Samuel Butler decided to emigrate, to seek his fortune as a farmer in New Zealand. It was a decision full of omen. On a cold, wet autumn day he went on board his ship in East India Docks and began to unpack his belongings – books for the voyage – Darwin, Gibbon ...

> Prayers are to men as dolls are to children. They are not without use and comfort, but it is not easy to take them very seriously. I dropped saying mine suddenly, once for all without *malice propense* on the night of the 29th of September, 1859, when I went on board the *Roman Emperor* to sail for New Zealand. I had said them the night before and doubted not I was always going to say them as I always had done hitherto. That night, I suppose, the sense of change was so great that it shook them quietly off. I was not then a sceptic; I had got as far as disbelief in infant baptism but no farther. I felt no compunction of conscience, however, about leaving off my morning and evening prayers – simply I could no longer say them.[20]

He may have left off the morning and evening prayers, but the obsession with Christianity would appear never to have left him for the remaining forty-three years of his life. Five years of pioneering and farming life in various parts of New Zealand still left him time to paint (his lifelong passion), and to compose articles for the Christchurch *Press*: 'Darwin on the Origin of Species: A Dialogue', et cetera. Darwinism, maintained one of the voices in the Dialogue, 'is utterly subversive of Christianity; for if this theory is true the fall of man is entirely fabulous;

and if the fall, then the redemption, these two being inseparably bound together ...'[21] He was also able to write long theological letters to his Cambridge contemporaries ('For the present I renounce Christianity altogether'), in which he began to air some hobby-horses he was to ride for the rest of his career – for example, that Jesus Christ did not die on the Cross, but was taken down and resuscitated.

It was in his latter days in New Zealand that Butler formed one of those strange close male friendships, which was to dog him all his days. Charles Paine Pauli (educated at Winchester and Oxford) was the son of a German businessman. 'Very handsome well-dressed men are seldom very good man,' Butler observed, looking back on it all more than thirty years later. But a particular evening they spent in one another's company changed their lives. 'His visit was unexpected; I had not called on him and had no intention of doing so: I was surprised at his calling on me, but he was doing his best to please, and when he left I was aware that I had become suddenly intimate with a personality quite different to that of anyone whom I had ever known.'

Pauli had come to hate New Zealand. He had tried working up-country, and had then moved into Christchurch where he worked on *The Press* as an accountant. His swashbuckling handsomeness and his sportiness ('a fearsome fast bowler')[22] did not prevent him from being a hypochondriac; he said he needed to go back to England to consult medical specialists, but that he had no money. After that he would like to read for the Bar, if only there was money. Butler, like a character in a New Testament parable, had been a good husbandman of his grandfather's inheritance. He had expanded a small sheep station, bought quite a bit of land, and turned a capital of around £4,800 into something over £8,000. He decided to leave the capital in New Zealand, where he could get ten per cent for it, and return to London with Pauli. He paid him a hundred pounds for his passage home, and advanced him two hundred a year for his legal studies. Pauli was to sponge off him for the next thirty years.

The young men found neighbouring sets of rooms in Clifford's Inn, off High Holborn. This was to be Butler's home for the rest of his life. In the intervals of nursing Pauli through illnesses (typhoid in February 1866) Butler studied at two art schools (Cary's, Streatham Street and Heatherley's, Newman Street, where a fellow student was John Butler Yeats, father of the poet W.B. Yeats). He became a goodish painter, but even his paintings – *Family Prayers* (1864), a *faux-naïf* picture of misery in Langar Rectory, or the much more accomplished *The Christening at Fobello* (1871) – reflect the theological preoccupation.

Erewhon (an anagram of Nowhere) had been turned down by George Meredith, publisher's reader for Chapman and Hall, so it was published by Trubner, in 1872. It was the only one of Butler's books which made him any money (£62 10*s*. 10*d*. – rather less profitable than sheep farming). It's a Swiftian journey-novel in which he uses his travel experiences and matches them to his intellectual hobby-horses. Having crossed a previously unexplored chain of mountains (obviously in New Zealand, though it is described merely as 'the colony'), the unnamed narrator finds another country. It is, needless to say, Victorian England with its values upended and inverted – so poor Mr Nosnibor is treated as a great invalid because he has embezzled a large sum of money, and those who suffer physical ailments are punished; for in Erewhon, moral and physical failings have been inverted as objects of censure. The Goddess of their religion is Ydgrun (Mrs Grundy), an embodiment of decency and common sense. Those who follow her are not religious in the true sense of the word.

> Being inured from youth to exercises and athletics of all sorts, and living fearlessly under the eye of their peers, among whom there exists a high standard of courage, generosity, honour, and every good and manly quality – what wonder that they should have become, so to speak, a law unto themselves; and while taking an elevated view of the goddess Ydgrun, they should gradually have lost faith in the recognized deities of the country?

The 'satire' of *Erewhon* feels a bit leaden today; *Erewhon Revisited*, which he wrote years later, is much funnier, particularly from the theological point of view. In the first book the narrator (we learn in *ER* that his name was Higgs) escaped Erewhon in a hot-air balloon. When he returns twenty years later, he discovers a religious cult in progress: his ascension in the balloon has come to be regarded as miraculous, and he himself is worshipped as the Sunchild. The 'Musical Banks' (that is, the churches) encountered in the first book are now divided between the theories of Professor Hanky and Professor Panky, fundamentalism and modernism. When at the end of the story Higgs settles down with the leading Erewhonian theologues, one of them asks, 'What would those who in your country come nearest to us Musical Bank managers do if they found they had made such a mistake as we have, and dared not own it?'

This is the central question for nineteenth-century Christianity. Those in Erewhon who sell relics of the heavenly chariot in which Higgs rose to Heaven, and who insist upon the reality of his Resurrection and Ascension, naturally feel discountenanced when he turns up twenty years later as a very ordinary man. But he answers them: 'Our religion sets before us an ideal which we all cordially accept, but it also tells us of marvels like your chariot and horses, which we most of us reject. Our best teachers insist on the idea, and keep the marvels in the background. If they could say outright that our age has outgrown them, they would say so, but this they may not do ...' In the revised (1901) edition of *Erewhon*, Butler conceded that the 'Musical Banks, and perhaps the religious systems of all countries, are now more or less an attempt to uphold the unfathomable and unconscious instinctive wisdom of millions of the past generations, against the comparatively shallow, consciously reasoning, and ephemeral conclusions drawn from that of the last thirty or forty.' That is a sentence which shows how deeply Butler belonged to that category singled out by W.H. Mallock, those 'whose hearts are aching for the God they no longer believe in'.[23]

Christianity was not the only belief-system in which Butler lost faith. It did not take him long to discover that he no longer subscribed to Darwinism. As an art student he had confided in J.B. Yeats that reading *The Origin of Species* had completely destroyed his faith in a personal God.[24] But the sheer irreligion of the Darwinian position, its absence of purposive metaphysics, its destruction of teleology, were more than Butler's formerly-Christian soul could bear. Having subjected Christianity to a literalist demolition-job in books such as *The Evidence for the Resurrection of Jesus Christ as Contained in the Four Evangelists Critically Examined* (1865), he turned his attention to what he had come to feel were the inadequacies in Darwin's claims. In 1871 he read *The Genesis of Species* by the Roman Catholic biologist St George Mivart. It argued that while evolution was true, Natural Selection could not account for the whole of it. 'Butler's whole nature', wrote his friend Festing Jones, 'revolted against the idea that the universe was without intelligence ... But where was the architect of the universe? He could not return to the Jewish and Christian idea of God designing his creatures from outside; he saw, however, no reason why the intelligence should not be inside.'[25] So he incorporated God within the creatures, as the Life Force. Butler believed that Darwin claimed a unique status for his work, when in reality the idea of evolution had already been expounded in the work of his grandfather Erasmus Darwin, in Buffon and in Lamarck. *Evolution Old and New* (1879) was Butler's attempt to set the record straight, and to expound the contribution to evolutionary science of these founding fathers.* He further came to believe that Charles Darwin, unlike his sainted ancestor, was a humbug, an imposter, a man of straw whose ideas were only correct when stolen from other people.[26] 'It is not bishops and archbishops I am afraid of,' he wrote to his sister. 'Men like Huxley and Tyndall are my natural enemies, and I am always glad when I find church people recognising the differences between them and me are, as I believe myself, more of words than of things.'[27] Darwin fully acknowledged that he had no explanation for the origin of the variations upon which natural selection has to work. It is the great gap in the Darwinian theory; but it is perhaps questionable whether Lamarck's theory of 'will' accounts for it as fully as Butler would have wished.

His father, long since become Canon Butler, died at Christmas 1886. He was, and always had been, the 'implacable enemy' of the son; but in latter years their quarrels about money and religion had diminished, and Butler was present with his father at the last. So was their cousin Archdeacon Lloyd, who began to utter prayers for the dying over the Canon's bed. With the removal of his clergyman father from the scene, Butler's hostility to religion grew markedly less. The year after his father's death he was able to write to one friend, 'it is against superstition and more especially against the Christian superstition that I have fought to the best of my ability', while to another he wrote:

> Do you – does any man of science – believe that the present orthodox faith can descend many generations without modification? Do I – does any free thinker who has the ordinary feelings of an Englishman – doubt that the main idea underlying and running through the orthodox faith is substantially sound? ... Tell me that Jesus Christ died upon the cross, and I find not one tittle of evidence worthy of the name to support the assertion. Tell me that therefore we are to pull down the Church and turn everyone to his own way, and I reject this as fully as I reject the other. I want the Church as much as I want free-thought; but I want the Church to pull her letter more up to date or else to avow more frankly that her letter is a letter only. If she would do this, I for one would not quarrel with her ...[28]

---

* Butler's book on evolution was less popular than Darwin's, however, selling only 541 copies (Muggeridge, *The Earnest Atheist*, p. 173).

This seems a very long way from the open satire of the early writings. It is almost as if Butler's God, with whom he was battling so fiercely in his teens and early manhood, was psychologically indistinguishable, for him, from the Rector of Langar. Perhaps, if his somewhat eccentric personal life had not by then fixed itself into a routine, he would have become what is known as a Modern Churchman or modernist; but at that date of the Church's history, such a flagrant breaking of the code would probably not have been approved.

An inability to commit himself, a horror of family life and an obsession with money perhaps, when combined, made it inevitable that Butler would find a sexual outlet of only one sort. He met Lucie Dumas somewhere near the Angel, in Islington. She had had predecessors in his life, but for twenty years she had no rivals. For the first thirteen of these he paid her a pound a week but did not reveal to her so much as his name.[29] Lucie was a strict Catholic who kept the Church's fasts, even imposing them on her cat, Marquis. Butler would visit her on a weekly basis, not always with great enthusiasm. 'Oh, bother, Alfred,' he would say to his manservant, 'it's Wednesday today and I've got to go to Handel Street.' He would leave at about half-past two and return about five. Meanwhile, Pauli remained much the greater emotional and financial drain on Butler's resources – though Butler was not his only victim. He had also battened on to Algernon Charles Swinburne.

Pauli was eventually replaced in Butler's affections by a lawyer called Henry Festing Jones, his inseparable companion for the last twenty years of his life, and his biographer. The friendship encouraged both men in hatred of their respective families. 'Your people are beasts' is a typical exchange between the two men. They make a strange pair; bearded, bespectacled, they shared more and more: trips to the music-hall, holidays, crushes on the same boys – an obsession with a Swiss, Hans Rudolph Faesch, kept them both very excited while Butler was writing his slightly crazy book on Homer – and, of course, until she died of consumption, Lucie Dumas. The only day they were apart was Sundays, when Butler stayed in his flat in Clifford's Inn and did the chores. He continued with his Wednesdays in Handel Street, and Jones visited Lucie on another day. When she died, it was 'a very heavy blow, to Jones as to myself'.[30]

We remember Samuel Butler today as the author of two or three semi-amusing books, rather than as a pioneer of metaphysical thought. But did any Englishman of the period articulate more fully or sharply the idea of God and the hateful father-figure as inextricably linked?

It is not wise to generalize. We do not know whether the 'Victorian' Father, so heavy-handed and so odious, was any more prevalent in the nineteenth century than in previous ages; but it is one of the perceptions which literary Victorians had of themselves – from Mr Barrett of Wimpole Street to the Marquess of Queensberry, it seems like a century peopled with fathers making impossible emotional demands on their sons and daughters, Lear-like demands for affection which cannot possibly be forthcoming and which in any event belongs elsewhere. Auden saw Matthew Arnold as an archetypical figure in this respect:

> But all his homeless reverence, revolted, cried:
> 'I am my father's forum and he shall be heard,
> Nothing shall contradict his Holy Final word,
> Nothing'. And thrust his gift in prison till it died.

> And left him nothing but a jailor's voice and face,
> And all rang hollow but the clear denunciation
> Of a gregarious optimistic generation
> That saw itself already in a father's place.[31]

Arnold is a ripe example to choose, since his grandest effort at a sub-Homeric epic, *Sohrab and Rustum*, is a Persian tale in which, by a series of accidents, a father and son end up on opposite sides in a war and, by the misty banks of the Oxus, engage in single combat, in which the son is slain by the father.

The same point is made in F. Anstey's comic novel *Vice Versa* (1882), possibly the best and certainly the most 'Freudian' (*sans le savoir*) school story ever written: a pompous, overbearing father, Mr Bultitude, remonstrating with his young son Dick (who does not want to go back to his boarding-school), expresses the wish that they could swap places and that he could be young again. What Mr Bultitude does not know is that he is holding in his hand a magical Indian charm which brings the bearer's wishes to pass; and the High Victorian adult stuff-pot is immediately transported into the body of a child, and forced to undergo the torments of boarding-school life while his son's spirit, now inhabiting an adult's body, stays at home and enjoys an endless surfeit of jellies, sweets and childish parties. Anyone – well, any English male – who has undergone the experience of being sent away to board at an uncongenial school will respond to this brilliant tale. Only when you read it again in grown-up years do you notice the relentlessly parricidal theme, the sheer sadism of it – for the torments of the grown-up at school are even worse then they could ever be for a child, since Mr Bultitude's stiff, over-bearing manner is interpreted by teachers as cheek and by the other boys as an unfunny prank. This certainly deeply adds to the enjoyableness of the book when read in childhood.

But all this stuff – this sense that we men are naturally at war with our Dads – is no more than a hunch, surely? One sees, from the point of view of metaphysical projection, how it could be made to fit into the theological debate. In this period, for whatever reason, boys did come to hate their fathers. Family life, which in earlier generations perhaps simply *went on* in the background of things, like the weather, started to loom too large. They were all together too much in their large houses? The men did not have enough to do? The unwontedly long peace made the latent aggression of English males turn internecine upon its own kind? (From Waterloo to the outbreak of the First World War, there was no European battle on land or sea involving the British; the Crimean was for nearly everyone in Britain a spectator's war, read about in news-papers; the skirmishes and troubles of the Empire, in India and Africa, only involved a handful of chaps. For the most part, it was a 'weak piping time of peace'.) Whatever the reasons we can find for the half-true generalization, the Victorian Age produced the Victorian Father and the tension, peculiar to its time, that we discern in texts as differ-ent as *Sohrab and Rustum*, *Father and Son*, and *Vice Versa*.

So, we might argue, it is in this age that we should expect men to discard a belief in the Heavenly Father; or, at the very least, an attempt by English males to persuade themselves that 'Christianity is a woman's religion, invented by women and womanish men for themselves'.[32]

Of course, if we accepted any of these broad-brush impressions and dignified them with the name of argument, we could see that they work both ways. On the one hand you could say that God the Father was the ultimate projection of a phantasmagoric psycho-figure from our pre-pubescent nightmares. But, equally, you could argue that the desire to *discard* God is not a rational thing: it is part of one's Oedipal need to assert oneself. We tell ourselves that God is dead, when what we mean is God is Dad, and we *wish* him dead.

Dr Freud (1856–1931) would think differently. As well as living through the age in which these parricidal fantasies were 'in the air', waiting to be formalized, he also lived in the great age of scientific lit-eralism, the time when science could be expected to solve all the questions which religion (except for the stupider of its adherents) had always been content to leave in the air.

In 1875 Freud visited Britain for the first time, and was enraptured, in spite of the 'fog and rain, drunkenness and conservatism'. (Like Engels', his first experience of an English city was Manchester, where his half-brothers lived.) He had decided that he loved 'reading English poems, writing English letters, declaiming English verse, listening to English descriptions, and thirsting after English views'.[33] After that summer, as he told his school-friend Silberstein, his heroes were British natural scientists: John Tyndall, Thomas Huxley, Sir Charles Lyell, Charles Darwin.[34] The first Marxists idolized Darwin because they felt that he had proved, scientifically, what the Young Hegelians had merely felt in their bones: that progress, relentless and pitiless progress, materialistically determined, was the only law of nature. It was how things were. Any doctrine which suggested purposiveness, or freedom of the will, any sentimentality which clung to the idea of a 'mind behind the universe', could now be discarded. What Darwin had done for the scientists, Marx appeared to have done in the sphere of politics, economics, history itself: laid bare its relentless march, its functioning process.

Freud did not graduate as a Doctor of Medicine until 1881. Only during his passionate friendship with Wilhelm Fliess between 1887 and 1902 did the distinctive doctrines of Freudianism begin to emerge: the importance, indeed predominance, of the Unconscious as an explanation for human behaviour; dreams as wish-fulfilments which can be interpreted through psychoanalysis; the Oedipus Complex as the great psychological fact about male human beings and their personal myths and histories. It is not for a book of this length and on this subject to trace the reasons why these doctrines came to be so widely believed; or why they are now so largely challenged in psychological fields. What we can notice, however, is that in the period between the mid 1870s, when the medical student visited England, and the late 1930s, when the venerable old Dr Freud took refuge in London from Nazi persecution, his doctrines were accepted widely, one is tempted to say almost universally, among the Western intelligentsia.

During that troubled but not altogether unhappy exile in London (where Freud was destined to die, in 1939), a young Oxford philosopher called on him at the house in Maresfield Gardens which is now the Freud Museum. They talked of psychoanalysis, and of Freud's escape from the Nazis after the recent *Anschluss*. The clock ticked round to about five o'clock on that Friday afternoon. Old Martha Freud, Sigmund's wife of half a century, came into the room and said to the visitor, 'You must know that on Friday evenings good Jewish women light candles for the approach of the Sabbath. But this monster – *Unmensch* – will not allow this, because he says that religion is a superstition.'[35]

To our generation – although we recognize that this was a marital joke which had been gaining momentum for forty years – there is something heavy about Freud banishing the candles. If it reminds us of anyone, it is not of the free-thinkers but of Philip Gosse, busily burying a Christmas pudding lest it encourage idolatrous thoughts. Freud saw it as his function, his mission, to banish superstition and illusion. Atheism was, for him, an essential premiss of the psychoanalytical movement. Ernest Jones, Freud's first and most fervent English disciple and his biographer, who mixed in the Viennese psychoanalytical circle from the beginning, asserted that 'it has never been my fortune to know a Jew possessing any religious belief' – and this in spite, rather than because, of the fact that he had spent his life among Jewish analysts. Freud's cranky book on *Moses and Monotheism* (arguing that Moses was Egyptian, not Jewish at all) was interpreted as an attack on his ancestral religion; but he rebutted this charge. 'It is an attack on religion only in so far as, after all, every scientific investigation of a religious belief has unbelief as its presupposition.'[36] Famously, he asked: 'Why did none of the devout create psychoanalysis? Why did one have to wait for a completely godless Jew?'[37]

His contemporaries, particularly those of a religious disposition, tried to reassure themselves that there was in fact something old-fashioned about Freud's religious stance: 'Your substitute religion is in essence the Enlightenment thought of the eighteenth century in proud fresh modern guise,' complained Pfister;[38] and his modern biographer Peter Gay calls Freud the 'last of the *philosophes*'.

In 'The Future of an Illusion' (*Die Zukunft einer Illusion*, published in 1927), Freud's most sustained attack on religion, he singles out his own people, the Jews, for particular mockery. They have been egoistical enough to want to make themselves not just believers, but God's Own Special Child, his Chosen People. 'Very much later, pious America laid claim to being "God's own Country"; and, as regards one of the shapes in which men worship the deity, the claim is undoubtedly valid.'[39]

Once the figure has been created, personalized and made like Daddy, he can be hated, like Daddy, and dethroned, killed. As Freud had argued in *Totem and Taboo*, all mankind must forever labour under the primal crime, the killing and eating of the father, which constituted 'the founding act of civilization'.[40] The Jews bore, throughout history, the burden of having killed Moses, and of the 'harsh, self-punishing religion' they developed after that killing.

It could easily be argued that the ideas of Freud have been more socially disruptive than those of Marx. Marx believed in disruption only as a temporary measure in history, while the Proletariat awaited its Destiny; until that day dawned, it was legitimate for the Faithful to support any act of terrorism, sedition, or social disruption which might hasten the fall of the old order. But when Socialism became the dominant party of Government, in preparation for the coming of pure Communism, then a rigid order would follow.

Freud, with a comparable optimism, believed that when humanity could throw off its illusions, it would also destroy neurosis, the thing which made it unhappy. But his diagnosis of what made it unhappy was family life. He taught us that in order to become sane, we must undermine and question what for most of us is the bedrock of our social and emotional security – our trust in, and love for, our parents. By teaching that neurosis can only be eliminated by overt hatred of our parents, he re-drew the inner map of millions of European and American human beings, making what had been a safe place into a battleground. This was a monumental achievement; not necessarily one for which he should be given all the credit – as we have seen, it was very much the fad among nineteenth-century families to Blame Dad – but an achievement none the less. Gosse, Butler and the rest achieved their effects because everyone still believed, *au fond*, that they were very naughty to dislike their fathers. Freud prepared us for a generation who would think it virtuous to sue their parents in a court of law, or blame them for all the miseries of existence. Nadezhda Mandelstam told us (in *Hope against Hope*) that it was Stalin's achievement to make everyone in the Soviet Union distrust one another. Freudianism was a cultural revolution on this scale of success. He created a generation who not only believed that the virtues of his ancestral religion – to honour father and mother – were vices; but who also subscribed to the view that our inner selves are inescapable: the story which we believe might be alterable by effort or luck has already been written in the forgotten or half-forgotten years of infancy. Like Marx, and like Darwin, he provided an imaginative framework in which Determinism could continue without Illusion. We struggle through our unfolding destinies with the Calvinistic certainty that they cannot be escaped, but without the Calvinistic God. The brooding presence gazing at us in our guilty nakedness is not the Deity in the Garden of Eden but our parents in the Garden of Childhood.

'I don't feel I'm going to meet my Maker,' says the formidable old grandmother in one of I. Compton-Burnett's novels. 'And if I were, I should not fear him. He has not earned the feeling.'[41] And the most sympathetic character in the book remarks of the tyrannical father of the woman he loves: 'I have never believed in God. I believe in him now. We have known he is a father. And I see that he is yours. Here are the anger, jealousy, vaingloriousness, vengefulness, love, compassion, infinite power. The matter is in no doubt.'

12

Two Prophets: Arnold and Ruskin

'There is henceforward for man, neither alpha nor omega – neither beginning nor end, neither nativity nor judgement; no Christmas Day except for pudding; no Michaelmas except for goose . . .'

Ruskin, *Fors Clavigera*

I F, LIKE SO many distinguished English statesman of the last century – Gladstone, Salisbury, Balfour – God had beguiled His leisure hours with a little anonymous reviewing, what sort of notice would He have given to Matthew Arnold's *Literature and Dogma* – subtitled 'An Essay Towards A Better Apprehension of the Bible'? The date of the piece was 1873; the author was nearly fifty years old.[1]

Assuming that He, in common with other well-informed Victorians, had followed Matthew Arnold's career, God might well have been prepared to view the Essay with sympathetic interest. The author was the son of the great Doctor Thomas Arnold of Rugby. In his youth, he had been a dandified poet, friend of the languid Clough. But his poetic gift, a minor one at the best of times, had fizzled out. He entirely lacked Swinburne's ear, and his garish Baudelairean imagination; he was not in the same league as the great Tennyson or Browning; he was technically less accomplished than Coventry Patmore; and certainly, unlike the later generation of poets, Meredith for example, he would have been incapable of dramatizing the contemporary experience.

It is not unusual for someone with only semi-poetic gifts to find their talent for versifying has deserted them by the time they reach middle age. But in Arnold's case, it is rather fascinating that the gulf between his art and what he called 'this strange disease of modern life' should be so great. Arnold saw more modern life than did Tennyson, Browning, Patmore or Clough. He was a pioneer of education, in some ways more influential and more important than his father. Whereas Dr Arnold's headmastership of Rugby had led to the cleaning-up of the public schools and the spawning of dozens, probably hundreds, of imitation Rugbys for the middle and would-be middle classes, not only in the British Isles but throughout the Empire, Matthew Arnold interested himself in the class below that. He was a pioneer of State education. The 'grammar schools' which gradually came into being in the closing decades of the nineteenth century, the schools for those who were clever enough to benefit from but not rich enough to afford the sort of education purveyed by Dr Arnold, had a transforming effect on England. For some fifty or sixty years in England it really did become possible for anyone of good brains, regardless of their income, to achieve a sufficient mastery of academic subjects to get into university. To this extent, the reforms of Matthew Arnold and his friends were revolutionary, empowering a whole class who hitherto had only been able to throw up the occasional autodidact of brilliance, such as Thomas Hardy or Herbert Spencer.

Matthew Arnold's actual profession was that of Inspector of Schools. He did this from 1851 until Gladstone procured for him a Civil List Pension in 1883. His particular responsibility for many years was Nonconformist schools, which inevitably took him into the industrial towns – far away from the Oxford about which he wrote so sentimentally ('city of dreaming spires', et cetera) and from the somewhat rarefied atmosphere of his own family homes. On the one hand, you could say that this more than explained – since he could see Dickens's Coketown for himself every week of a busy working life – why he called modern life 'a strange disease'. But it is somewhat odd that a man who devoted all his professional energy to educating the lower ranks of society should have viewed his own time and culture in a purely elegiac mood.

His famous essay on *Culture and Anarchy* envisaged perpetual warfare between, on the one hand, cultivated fellows such as himself, who read Homer and Dante and who, if they wished to have a breath of modern culture, rushed off to France and Germany; and contemporary England, which was largely populated by the Philistines (that is to say, the governing aristocratic class) and the rising class – the class Arnold himself was trying to educate – whom he flatteringly called the Barbarians.

You can tell what he thinks of the lower orders themselves from his fastidious essay on 'The Function of Criticism'. Arnold, having opined that the culture of Victorian England is in every way inferior to that of fourth-century Athens or the London of Shakespeare or that of any era in France or Germany, falls to musing on how hideously vulgar English journalism is by contrast with such estimable journals as *Revue Des Deux Mondes*. He has recently 'stumbled on' a paragraph in an English newspaper which causes his nose to wrinkle.

A shocking child murder has just been committed at Nottingham. A girl named Wragg left the workhouse there on Saturday morning with her young illegitimate child. The child was soon afterwards found dead on Mapperley Hills having been strangled. Wragg is in custody.[2]

This is the sort of sad story which the sympathy of George Eliot (as in *Adam Bede*) or Hardy (as in *Tess*) might have seen as a personal tragedy. Dickens would have perhaps seen some comedy in the name Wragg, but this would not have stopped him appreciating Wragg's dignity, the pathos of her situation. Arnold, however, was so intellectually snobbish and so pathologically anti-British that he could only use the incident to deride those simpleton-journalists who, in their dull-witted patriotism, believed that the Anglo-Saxon breed was the best in the world.

If we are to talk of ideal perfection, of 'the best in the whole world' [he muses], has any one reflected what a touch of grossness in our race, what an original shortcoming in the more delicate spiritual perceptions, is shown by the natural growth amongst us of such hideous names – Higginbottom, Stiggins, Bugg! In Ionia and Attica they were luckier in this respect than the 'best race in the world'; by the Ilissus there was no Wragg, poor thing! ... Wragg is in custody. The sex lost in the confusion of our unrivalled happiness; or shall I say, the superfluous Christian name lopped off by the straightforward vigour of our old Anglo-Saxon breed? ...[3]

The high-minded attempts to bring Homer to the masses, which seems to be the general idea both behind his criticism in *Culture and Anarchy* and his professional career as an Inspector of Schools, falls away; and beneath its carapace we see the grinning spectre of that other by-product of the good old Anglo-Saxon breed, the crashing snob. It turns out that all those years spent on trains, going to see that the people of Birmingham, Bradford or Bridlington were fed with spoon-sized doses of Sweetness and Light, had only served to remind the Oxford Professor of Poetry and son of the Headmaster of Rugby what irredeemably coarse fellows they all were, compared with those delicate, beautiful Greeks.

Arnold's brand of intellectual snobbery, which places Greek-reading Oxford graduates not merely above poor waifs like Wragg but also above the 'philistines' of industry, the popular press, et cetera, is one of the most durable strands of 'high thinking' to survive in England. Almost every generation has spawned some son or daughter of Arnold's peculiar way of looking at the world. You would never guess from his writings that while he was alive England was enjoying a cultural and socio-political heyday with (apart from the disaster of the Crimean War) very little bloodshed or conflict. Arnold's lifetime saw all the novels of Dickens and Thackeray published, not to mention the poetical works of Tennyson (which Arnold heartily despised); it overlapped with the marvellous architectural achievements of Pugin and Barry (does their Palace of Westminster have a rival among the buildings of London?), while Sir George Gilbert Scott built St Mary Abbott's, Kensington, the Catholic Apostolic Church in Gordon Square (1853), and Pearson built the superb St Augustine's, Kilburn (1870). Until Arnold was nearly thirty years old, Turner was still painting; Rossetti was producing some of the most stupendous canvases in the history of English art. Nor was the prodigious prosperity of the commercial classes entirely failing to 'percolate' to the poor. Yes, the condition of the working classes in England was terrible in, say the 1870s; but in many perceptible ways it was less terrible than when Engels observed it in 1848. The Factories Acts meant that they worked shorter hours. Chadwick's drainage systems reduced, eventually eliminated, water-borne diseases such as cholera and typhoid. The middle classes – upper, middle and lower echelons thereof – became immeasurably more prosperous in this man's lifetime. And what is more, their *popular* culture was of a high order – witness the ingenuity of their music-hall songs, or the light operas of Gilbert and Sullivan.

But for Arnold, almost everything he saw in his own country caused him to draw in his breath. The sheer vulgarity of modern England appalled him.

Like his bossy headmaster father, he would have liked to knock a bit of Latin, Greek and Christian morality into the populace, but he was far too lofty to wish to dirty his hands with them; and he was too intelligent not to see that such an undertaking would be a hopeless task. He was not really like his father at all in temperament. But he did inherit from the headmaster the sense that while old-style Christianity was unbelievable, it should be possible to devise some way of so watering the mixture as to make it palatable even to the high-minded agnostics whom Matthew Arnold would deign to regard as his intellectual peers.

Hence *Literature and Dogma* in 1873. And hence my perhaps profane speculation that God Himself, like one of the heavily-bearded statesman of the age, might try to encapsulate in a few thousand words, for the editor of the *Fortnightly* or the *Quarterly*, what He thought of Matthew Arnold's view of religion.

God might very well have shared Matthew Arnold's worry that, having rejected the possibility of miracles, so many philosophers and scientists should have regarded Christianity as a mere 'cheat' or 'imposture'.[4] Arnold begins his survey of *Literature and Dogma* with a frank acknowledgement that to 'reinthrone the Bible as explained by our current theology, whether learned or popular, is absolutely and for ever impossible! – as impossible as to restore the feudal system, or the belief in witches'.[5] God would surely have been grateful to Arnold, however, for thinking that it was still vitally important that religion, in some form or another, should survive. All that is required is to lay aside the older and more superstitious ways of reading the Bible – those propagated, for example, by the Roman Catholics and the Protestants – and to read the Bible in the 'right manner',[6] as a work of 'literature'.

'Hebraism', as God will remember if He has read Arnold's book *Culture and Anarchy*, is a habit of mind which we may contrast with the much more attractive 'Hellenism'. The Hellenes, like Matthew Arnold, have an intuitive, intellectual and imaginative approach to life (and of course they would never name a person *Wragg*, or *Stiggins*); sweetness and light mean more to them than balance-sheets and literal-minded legalism. The 'Hebrews' by this definition include all the Nonconformists with whom Arnold had professionally to work, the chapel-going mill- and factory-workers and managers, the Northern mayors, the Bradley Headstones. But although he used the term emblematically, he was quite happy to use it literally, as well. He dismisses Disraeli, for example, for 'treating Hellenic things with the scornful negligence natural to a Hebrew':[7] an obvious reference to the fact that Disraeli was actually a Jew.

For Arnold's purposes it is rather a pity that so much of the Bible, an admirable book to be sure, seems to have been written by these Hebrew fellows. Luckily many of them, when you boil down what they have to say and ignore their superstitious miracle-stories and their barbaric laws and customs, do share Lofty Matt's view that religion can be defined as 'morality touched by emotion'.[8] Even more fortunate, though, is the fact that Jesus had no sympathy at all either with Judaism or (an even happier chance) with the 'common multitude', who were 'dull of feeling and gross of life'.[9] The message of Jesus is that if you follow His teachings (which are almost identical to those of Arnold himself in *Culture and Anarchy*), you will 'conquer and annul' your 'sensuality'.[10] It is of course unfortunate that so many of Jesus's followers were 'men liable to err, full of the turbid Jewish fancies ... which were then current',[11] who wanted to put their own rather crude ideas into the mouth of Jesus. Hence the passages of the Gospels – the miracle stories, many of the parables, the prophecies of a Messianic consummation, the Virgin Birth, Passion, Crucifixion, Death and Resurrection – which seem so woefully unArnoldian in colouring. Luckily the true spirit of Jesus survives in some of His choicer sayings, though even these have to be altered to capture their true flavour. 'Blessed are the *meek/poor*' will lead us disastrously into the company of the hapless Wragg unless we, with Arnold, rephrase it *Blessed are the mild*.[12] The essence of the religion of Jesus is His *sweet reasonableness*.[13]

So far we can envisage God sitting anonymously at His table in the Athenaeum Club with His eyes moving over the pages of *Literature and Dogma*, feeling intense gratitude to Mr Arnold. After all, He would surely have shared with Arnold a fear that Mr Herbert Spencer[14] had somehow persuaded the masses that there was no point in maintaining any pretence that religion was true. And we are all agreed, surely, with Arnold, that 'religion is the solidest of realities, and Christianity the greatest and happiest stroke ever yet made for human perfection'.[15]

Arnold was in the habit, rather a good one perhaps, of keeping what he called 'touchstones'. He used to write down quotations from the great books, uplifting thoughts, into a small pocket notebook, and consult them throughout the day, rather like a priest dipping into the Breviary. When he was sitting, hungrily, in station waiting-rooms in Blackburn or Bootle, having just inspected some Methodist board-school or other, it must have been comforting to remember the words of Homer, Dante and Shakespeare. And it is on this level of sweet reasonableness and uplift that he would appear to have understood the religious emotion.

God, however, might have felt tempted, as He began His review, to point out that Arnold showed not the smallest glimmering of understanding of religious emotion detached from morality or 'uplift'. The awestruck Aeneas who sacrifices at the Temple of Apollo at Cumae and then confronts the shrieking sibyl before descending to the underworld is not sweetly reasonable. Nor is the J.S. Bach of the St Matthew Passion or the Mozart of the Requiem. Nor are the thousands of anonymous icon painters in the tradition of Eastern Christian Orthodoxy ... One does not need to elaborate the list to make the point. The sense of the holy, the sense of the numinous, the feeling that humankind is not alone but, rather, watched over by a Presence – sometimes loving, sometimes threatening: these are surely essential ingredients in the religious emotion? Arnold does not really have this sense at all. He lovingly quotes Goethe – *der Aberglaube ist die Poesie des Lebens* (extra belief is the poetry of life)[16] – but he does not believe that God is a person.

'Our very word *God* is, perhaps, a reminiscence of those [actually these] times when men invoked "The Brilliant on high" ... as the power representing to them that which transcended their narrow selves and by which they lived and moved and had their being.' But the object of religion, says the son of Rugby School, is '*Conduct*'.[17]

It is hard not to feel the pathos of our imagined Reviewer, sitting at a library table in His Anonymity. Other members of the Athenaeum if they watched Him might blink and wonder if they had been drinking too much port after their dinner. For little by little, as Arnold's pages unfold, it will have become clear to the Anonymous Reviewer that God, as a Personal or independently existent entity, has faded away into a number of vague terms. He is Brightness. He is Sweet Reasonableness. He is Sweetness and Light. He is Eternal. But He does not do anything quite so coarse, quite so Philistine, quite so Wragg-like as to Exist.

As they sit there in the Athenaeum library, the bearded ones in their frock coats – Darwin, Spencer, Trollope – they watch the equally bearded Ancient of Days close Arnold's book and, with a misty decorum, fade from their sight.

Arnold's most celebrated anthology-piece, 'Dover Beach', contains some confusing imagery. The noise of the waves raking the shingle outside his hotel bedroom on his honeymoon night at Dover were, in his mind, bringing 'The eternal note of sadness in'.

> Sophocles long ago
> Heard it on the Aegean, and it brought
> Into his mind the turbid ebb and flow
> Of human misery; we
> Find also in the sound a thought,
> Hearing it by this distant northern sea.
>
> The sea of faith
> Was once, too, at the full, and round earth's shore

Lay like the folds of a bright girdle furl'd;
But now I only hear
Its melancholy long withdrawing roar,
Retreating to the breath
Of the night-wind down the vast edges drear
And naked shingles of the world ...[18]

There is much to ponder here. Unlike the English Channel, the Aegean is not a tidal ocean, so it would be extremely surprising had Sophocles heard, on his own native shore, anything like the sound outside Arnold's bedroom window at Dover. But even if he had done so, why should this be considered a good image for the decline of religious faith? If Arnold had written a poem about his wife's bath-water running out while he awaited her arrival in the bedroom, this might better have provided the imagery he was after: the image of water which was running out, never to return. It is clear from the poem, as from his prose works on the subject, that he sees no more hope of a religious revival among the cultivated classes than he does for a revival of the feudal system. So he is not really thinking of Faith as a Sea. Had he been doing so, he would have seen the scientific revolutions of such as Spencer and Darwin as no more than a temporary aberration. Tides turn. The sea comes back in. Arnold appears not to have noticed this rather simple bidiurnal fact.

We might wish to ask the Victorian sages the central, the fundamental, question: Why does loss of faith matter? For Arnold there was no doubting the answer to, and the significance of, this question. 'This is what everyone sees to constitute the special moral feature of our times: the *masses* are losing the Bible and its religion. At the Renascence, many cultivated wits lost it; but the great solid mass of the common people kept it, and brought the world back to it after a start had seemed to be made in quite another direction. But now it is the *people* which is getting detached from the Bible.'[19]

Arnold here seems to be enunciating a view which came to be repeated so often in the nineteenth century that it turned into a cliché: that religion was a sort of glue which held society together. Take but religion away, untune that string, and hark what discord follows. Whether you think religion is true or false, it is socially useful. So we find the reactionary Dostoevsky fearing that if God does not exist, anything will be permitted; Arnold dreading the 'anarchy' which would befall society if, in losing faith in a personal God, it also lost the habits of decorum and piety; or Marx believing that religion was the opium which numbed the people's sense of their oppressed condition.

To read the defenders of the religious *status quo* in the nineteenth century is to be persuaded that Marx had a point, particularly when these defenders make it quite clear that they do not believe in religion themselves; they merely regard it as a useful vehicle for preserving what is beautiful from our European past (Gothic cathedrals, for example) while giving the simpletons a little romance in their lives. Some *Aberglaube*.

'What a delight', exclaimed the sceptical Renan in *Études d'histoire religieuse*, 'for the man who is borne down by six days of toil to come on the seventh to rest his knees, to contemplate the tall columns, a vault, arches, an altar; to listen to the chanting, to hear moral and consoling words!' ... True, 'criticism' can see the errors of religious dogma; but for the poor people 'it is the privilege of pure sentiment to be invulnerable, and to play with poison without being hurt by it'. No wonder honest Lord Morley[20] was so shocked by these words. He remembered sadly that in 1779 the Academy of Prussia had announced the title of an annual prize essay, 'S'il est utile au peuple d'être trompé'. Two prizes were awarded that year, one showing that error was useful, the other that it was not.[21]

It is hard not to remember this sort of thing when we read the vows taken by the Companions of the Guild of St George, founded by John Ruskin (1819–1900) in 1871.

> I trust in the Living God, Father Almighty, Maker of heaven and earth, and of all things and creatures visible and invisible. I trust in the kindness of His law, and the goodness of His work. And I will strive to love Him, and to keep His law, and see His work, while I live.[22]

That was the statement that any worker was obliged to make when he or she embraced membership of Ruskin's Quixotic neo-medieval guild, whose purpose was to undo the evils of capitalism, industrial pollution and squalor. The strongly religious tone of all Ruskin's economic and political utterances interestingly disguises the extent of his scepticism.

His early passion for mineralogy meant that he was forced to confront the disturbing theological implications of Lyell's *Geology*. 'You speak of the flimsiness of your own faith,' he confided in his undergraduate contemporary and lifelong friend, the medic Henry Acland in 1851 – when they were just past thirty. 'Mine, which was never strong, is being beaten into mere gold leaf, and flutters in weak rags from the letter of its old forms; but the only letters it can hold by at all are the old Evangelical formulae. If only the Geologists would let me alone, I could do very well, but those dreadful Hammers! I hear the clink of them at the end of every cadence of the Bible verses.'[23]

It is rather fascinating that Ruskin, like Matthew Arnold, was an undergraduate at the height of the Oxford Movement, yet remained entirely unaffected by it. Though a gentleman-commoner of Pusey's own college, Christ Church, his childhood evangelicalism guaranteed that he was not to be tempted by the High Church palaver of Pusey, Newman and friends. Indeed, Ruskin's strong attraction to Catholicism came much later, when he recognized, in one of those defining epiphanies with which his life was punctuated, that Catholicism had shaped European consciousness in a way that Protestantism never could and had never attempted. He came to see that Protestantism was, a good phrase, the mere 'débris of Catholicism'.[24]

Not that Ruskin ever concerned himself with the Catholic–Protestant debate as it might occur to the mind of an ecclesiastical obsessive. No more did he find prosaic, either/or solutions to the problems posed by science to religious faith. His was one of the truly original minds of the nineteenth century – 'philosophically the best-equipped mind of his generation'.[25] His doubts were productive doubts. Unlike Arnold, who merely threw up his hands in dismay at the philistinism and Hebraic thought-processes of the capitalist, and hoped merely to instil into the lower orders such sweetness and light as his father had offered to the middle-class boys of Rugby, Ruskin saw nothing wrong with being working-class, nothing wrong with being ignorant – but a great deal wrong with being idle, being exploited, being polluted by smoke and industrialization, and a great deal wrong with being alienated from one's roots. As well as one of the proto-socialists, he was right to call himself a 'violent Tory of the old school.'[26] As well as having doubts about religion, he was the first Victorian to have serious and intelligent doubts about science.

Long before the 'green' movement of our generation, Ruskin perceived that life on this planet could only become sane when human beings recognized their rightful place within it; when they stopped trying to exploit Nature for gain or to 'explain' it away in the name of physics and biology, and came instead to a submissive humility in relation to it, a true understanding. Perhaps nowhere is this attitude of Ruskin's better expressed than in *The Ethics of the Dust*, a series of lectures given to the girls of Winnington School in 1865, principally on the subject of crystals and mineralogy. He asks them to imagine walking on an over-trodden path on the outskirts of a manufacturing town, and picking up an ounce or two of the blackest slime, containing soot, sand, brick-dust, water and clay. Then he asks them to imagine the mud being allowed to rest a long age.

> Let the clay begin. Ridding itself of all foreign substance, it gradually becomes a white earth, already very beautiful, and fit, with help of congealing fire, to be made into the finest porcelain, and painted on, and be kept in kings' palaces. But such artificial consistence is not its best. Leave it still quiet, to follow its own instinct of unity, and it becomes, not only white, but clear; not only clear but hard; not only clear and hard, but so set that it can deal with light in a wonderful way, and gather out of it the loveliest blue rays only, refusing the rest. We call it a sapphire ...[27]

Ruskin continues in this vein, imagining the sand turning to opal, the soot to diamond, and finally the water, perhaps most beautifully of all, turning into a snowflake. 'And for the ounce of slime which we had by political economy of competition, we have, by political economy of co-operation, a sapphire, an opal, and a diamond set in a star of snow ...' It was, he says, human cruelty and iniquity which turned the precious stones of this earth into an ugly slime, and it must be by human mercy and justice that the earth be put right. Hence his idea of founding the Guild of St George, to which wealthy people such as himself would donate a tenth of their income in order to allow working people, who were so willing, to do useful tasks in what we would call an unpolluted environment. A high priority was to be given to reclaiming land wrecked by industrial pollution. The ideas which led Ruskin's disciple Octavia Hill and his admirers Sir Robert Hunter and Canon Rawnsley to found the National Trust, protecting British coastlines, mountains, and areas of natural beauty from building and wreckage, began with his Guild of St George.

As a system of organizing labour Ruskin's reinvented medieval guild was not to prove so successful, and was overtaken by the Trades Union Movement. Nevertheless, the influence of Ruskin on the British Labour

Movement in general was wide and deep. 'I have met in my lifetime some extremely revolutionary characters,' said George Bernard Shaw in one of his *Fabian Essays*; 'and quite a large number of them, when I have asked, "Who put you on this revolutionary line? Was it Karl Marx?" have answered, "No, it was John Ruskin."'[28]

Why, since he was so plainly an agnostic for much of his life (and with much of himself, for *all* his life), did Ruskin insist upon a religious dedication for members of his Guild? Partly, no doubt, he shared the fear expressed by Darwin, Arnold and so many others, that without a belief in God, society would break up. And no doubt there were psychological reasons why this closely protected rich only child of evangelical parents found it impossible to make a public acknowledgement of doubt, still less of unbelief. But whatever his faults, Ruskin was neither a sophist nor a coward.

I think he held on to the outward expression of religious belief because, both in the art criticism with which his life's work began, and later in his political thoughts, he had a dread of shutting his eyes to life's imaginative possibilities; and he knew that one of the easiest ways of doing this was to think that one's own way of viewing the world (whether as an individual, or as a member of a class, or as a representative of any particular age or generation) was the only way. He knew how difficult it was to maintain a clear vision of reality. 'The fact is, we are all, and always, asleep, through our lives; and it is only by pinching ourselves very hard that we ever come to see, or understand anything.'[29]

Rather than simply stating, with Arnold, that the Sea of Faith had gone out, was it not possible to study the religious faith of our forefathers (whether medieval Catholics or 'pagan' Greeks), and to learn from them?

In *Ethics*, Ruskin made the point that it ill became nineteenth-century Christians to assume that their way of looking at life was superior to that of the 'pagans'.

> The vice existing among certain classes both the rich and the poor, in London, Paris, and Vienna, could have been conceived by a Spartan or a Roman of the heroic ages only as possible in a Tartarus, where fiends were employed to teach, but not to punish, crime. It little becomes us to speak contemptuously of the religion of races to whom we stand in such relations; nor do I think any man of modesty or thoughtfulness will ever do so of any religion, in which God has allowed one good man to die, trusting.[30]

In *The Queen of the Air*, the lectures Ruskin gave to the University of London in 1869, he explored the way in which religious myth *works*. Not at all lofty about the simple believers, Ruskin acknowledged that 'to deal with Greek religion honestly, you must at once understand that this literal belief was, in the mind of the general people, as deeply rooted as ours in the legends of our own sacred book; and that a basis of unmiraculous event was as little suspected, and an explanatory symbolism as rarely traced, by them as by us.'[31] He spoke of the myths of Demeter and Poseidon, but there can be no doubt of the applicability of his words. As with all Ruskin's work, particularly that of his maturity, *The Queen of the Air* lectures, notionally on one subject (Greek mythology), have by the concluding lectures encompassed a variety of subjects – Turner, the economy, the evil of railways, the ugliness of suburbs, the purity of quartz – all the Ruskinian obsessions.

Although he became a great friend of Carlyle, and although he may be seen, after Carlyle, as the second great sage of Victorian England, Ruskin is totally different. Carlyle remained to the end of his unhappy days a disgruntled and disillusioned radical of the 1830s, a man with a perpetual sense of loss, which included a sense of the loss of God. He looked backwards through the ruins to a world irrecoverably despoiled. And, preacher *manqué* that he was, he loved to generalize, he loved to tell the benighted middle classes where they had gone wrong. He was the greatest of the pulpit journalists.

Ruskin seems a little like this at first. Like Carlyle, like Matthew Arnold, like so many nineteenth-century intellectuals, he appears to be in despair about the nature of capitalist society; and happy enough to mount the podium, if not the pulpit, to suggest remedies. As in the case of Carlyle, much of what he has to say relates to the Godlessness of the age. He deplores, while sharing, the doubts of nineteenth-century humankind.

But as we read on in the works of Ruskin, and particularly as we read *Fors Clavigera*, those extraordinary encyclicals which he wrote to the guild-members of St George, or his final great work of autobiography, *Praeterita* (much of it drawn from *Fors*), we realize that we are in the presence of a quite different order of being. Carlyle and Arnold wanted to generalize. Ruskin, whether he was looking at a capital in the Doge's Palace in Venice, or botanizing, or collecting minerals, had a fascination with the particular. He recollects that, having been thoroughly trained as a water-colourist and a draughtsman, and taught by the likes of

Copley Fielding to make competent production-line washes and sketches, he made an individual discovery on the road to Norwood – then a country village south of London. He was in his twenty-fourth year.

> One day on the road to Norwood, I noticed a bit of ivy round a thorn stem, which seemed, even to my critical judgment, not 'ill-composed'; and proceeded to make a light-and-shade pencil study of it in my grey paper pocket-book, carefully, as if it had been a bit of sculpture, liking it more and more as I drew. When it was done, I saw that I had virtually lost all my time since I was twelve years old, because no one had ever told me to draw what was really there! All my time, I mean, given to drawing as an art; of course I had the records of places, but had never seen the beauty of anything, not even of a stone – how much less of a leaf![32]

Thereafter, Ruskin's genius was released. As a visual artist, staggeringly competent though he was, he would never rise, nor aspire to rise, to keep company with his great master, Turner. But he had seen that the distinctive vision of one person, one individual, was a useful enough prism, by which to discover at least partial truths. He proceeded on this basis for the rest of his days, never fearing his own prejudices. Ruskin's intemperate judgements – Byron a great poet, Wordsworth no more than 'a Westmoreland peasant'; the church of the Salute, and indeed all the Renaissance architecture of Venice, a disaster; and so on, and so on – contribute to his charm. You never know, quite, where he will jump. He could not escape his own fairly extraordinary upbringing, nor the distinctiveness of his own personality. Very well. These were the eyes, and the particular genius, which were his inheritance; and these were what he would use to look at the world, at the nineteenth century, at art, at nature, at God. You can see why Ruskin was Proust's master.

To paint mist rightly, space rightly, and light rightly, it may often be necessary to paint nothing else rightly, but the rule is simple for all: that if the artist is painting something that he knows and loves, as he knows it, because he loves it, whether it be the fair strawberry of Cima, or the clear sky of Francia, or the blazing incomprehensible mist of Turner, he is all right; but the moment he does anything as he thinks it ought to be, because he does not care about it, he is all wrong.[33]

Ruskin's hero Turner had died on 19 December 1851. A low winter sunbeam caught the artist's face as he murmured 'The Sun is God', and expired. Such 'heathenism', as he was to call it, saved Ruskin from open unbelief, but the greatest Victorian aesthete did not arrive at this position easily. His intensely over-protective parents were a perpetual, brooding presence in his life, and in particular his rigidly evangelical mother. She only died when he was fifty-two. From his boyhood she had read the Bible aloud with him – he and she reading alternate verses. When they had read all the way through from Genesis to Revelation, they went back to Genesis and started all over. It was very much her Protestant prejudice which determined, for example, that when the Ruskins travelled to Switzerland, they gingerly selected the Protestant cantons in which to stay. Ruskin must have been the best-travelled English boy of his generation; and yet in another way it is hard to think of any upbringing, even Mill's, which was narrower.

His father was an immensely wealthy, art-loving sherry-merchant. There was hardly a county in the British Isles where Mr and Mrs Ruskin and their preternaturally gifted only son John had not travelled, with the aim partly of selling sherry to the grandees, and partly of appreciating the picturesque scenery and the great art to be seen in stately homes and country houses. France, Belgium, Italy, Switzerland had likewise been traversed, all in high style, in the Ruskin family travelling-carriage.

When they sent their son to Oxford, it was to the grandest college, Christ Church, and as a gentleman-commoner: that is, he enjoyed a status (spacious rooms, a golden tassel on his cap) normally only accorded aristocrats. The real aristocrats at first mocked and then came to love the eccentric millionaire suburban boy. Even as an undergraduate he had his mother in tow. She went with him everywhere, except to his wedding to Euphemia Gray ('Effie'), which she regarded, rightly, as a disastrous mistake. Certainly Margaret Ruskin did her best to increase poor Effie's misery, and played her part in the inevitable dissolution of that wretched match.

It was Ruskin's cursed fate, when he met the true love of his life – Rose La Touche – to find that she, too, was of the rigidly evangelical persuasion. Rose was thirty years younger than Ruskin – and just nine years old when they met and Ruskin fell in love. She called him, as readers of *Praeterita* will know, Saint Crumpet. He called her Rosie, Rosie Pet, or Rosie Puss. It was one of the great love-stories of the nineteenth century.

In the late twentieth century it is regarded as sinister for grown men to love girls very much younger than themselves. Other cultures differ – witness Islam, where the age at which girls are permitted to marry is twelve. Mrs La Touche, an Anglo-Irish lady who had been attracted to Ruskin by his lectures on art and introduced to him by his pupil, the gifted amateur artist Lady Waterford, was sometimes alarmed by the intensity of his devotion to Rose, but it was not the age difference *per se* which made her come to fear and dislike the notion of having Ruskin as a son-in-law: it was in part the fact that he had been married before. Divorce was all but unknown in Victorian England, and Ruskin had allowed his unconsummated marriage to Effie to be annulled on the grounds (strictly-speaking, untrue) of his impotence.[34] His pathetic attempts to reassure Mrs La Touche on this matter could only achieve the opposite. Much the greatest objection to the match, however, when Ruskin (aged forty-seven, to Rose's seventeen) made formal matrimonial proposals, was on the grounds that he was not a true believer. The La Touches considered him a heathen, and their minds were not set to rest by bossy letters in which he told them: 'If she is to be a Christian, she can only read her Bible with complete understanding in the Septuagint and Greek Testament; if she is to be a heathen, Greek is the greatest language of mankind, the chief utterance of the nations ... To have learned *one* Greek verb accurately will make a difference in her habits of thought for ever after.'[35] Poor Rosie had the first of her severe nervous breakdowns shortly after her mother received that letter.

'It is to me so fearful a discovery,' Ruskin confided in his American friend Charles Eliot Norton, 'to find how God has allowed all who have variously sought him in the most earnest way to be blinded – how Puritan – monk – Brahmin – Churchman – Turk – are all merely names for different madnesses and ignorances; how nothing prevails finally but a steady, worldly-wise labour – comfortable – resolute – fearless – full of animal life – affectionate – compassionate ...'[36]

Of course he did not allow the purely evangelical Mrs La Touche to know exactly what he thought about her faith, but she (as did his mother Margaret) pretty easily sniffed out the truth. In 1862 he wrote to his father, having tried to explain to the La Touches why he admired Bishop Colenso:

Rosie's mightily vexed about my heathenism [she was perhaps thirteen at the time] and sends me a long little lock of hair to steady me somewhat if it may be; of sending which – nevertheless – she won't take the grace – or responsibility – herself, but said, 'Mama cut it off for you'. 'But for the sake of all truth, and Love, you must not give the one true God – containing all others – God – up.' I can set her little wits at rest on that matter at any rate, and tell her that being a heathen is not so bad as all that.[37]

Ruskin had a long agonizing journey to follow before Rosie died of consumption in 1875. For much of this time he was forbidden to see her, and 'by a last refinement of cruelty' (Evans's phrase)[38] she told him at the end that he could only come into the sick-room for a visit if he would say that he loved God more than he loved her. How proud any Ruskinian feels of their honest hero to read that he would not submit to this blackmail. He did in fact see her one last time – in February 1875, when she was delirious and incapable of recognizing him. He heard the news of her death in May, when he was in the midst of delivering his Slade lectures at Oxford.

The Proust who chronicled an obsessive love for Albertine would have understood Ruskin's Rosie-worship. 'All art is praise ... There is no wealth but life' – these are Ruskin's creeds. Rosie came to be a saint in his inner life. He identified her with the *St Ursula* of Carpaccio, a painting which he painstakingly copied in water-colour. He attended seances, and she communicated with him from Beyond. And he became, in his latter years, more conventionally Christian. But the whole drift of his religious development was towards individualism. It was primarily as an aesthete that he discovered Catholicism. Since in old age he told Kathleen Olander that he would become a Catholic at once 'if he fully believed',[39] the fact that he did not do so is eloquent.

It was in the Campo Santo at Pisa in 1845 that Ruskin had his epiphany of the Catholic vision of things – so to say, the *mythology* – as a whole thing, a complete thing, a tradition which, for better or worse, was the tradition into which Western men and women had been born. It was the mythology which they inhabited. It was their home. The frescos at Pisa display the whole story – the triumph of Death; the coming of the Patriarchs, and the sufferings of Job; the localized and idealized lives of the saints (in this case, of St Ranier of Pisa and the Desert Fathers); and, finally, the return of Christ in Glory, and the Last Judgement. 'Now this code of teaching is absolutely general for the whole Christian world.

There is no papal doctrine, nor antipapal; nor any question of sect or schism because the painters saw them, and painted them, naturally, as we paint the nineteenth century product of common councilmen and engineers.'[40] He recognized that the paintings did not resolve modern scientific doubts of the kind raised by Huxley – 'as for instance that if Christ came to judgment in St James's Street, the people couldn't see him from Piccadilly' – but he had seen something which he recognized as larger and bigger than the doubts which threatened to engulf it. He had seen something bigger than nineteenth-century industrial life, or than the post-Romantic 'me-culture' (as we should call it). 'Whatever charge', he was to write in another context, 'may justly attach to the saying, "There is no God", the folly is prouder, deeper, and less pardonable in saying, "There is no God but me".'[41]

The epiphany at Pisa when he was twenty-six was followed by another in Turin when he was considerably more mature – nearly forty. He attended the Protestant (the Waldenstein) chapel there one Sunday morning and heard 'a little squawking idiot ... preaching to an audience of seventeen old women and three louts that they were the only children of God in Turin; and that all the people in Turin outside the chapel, and all the people in the world out of sight of Monte Veso would be damned.'[42] In one of those instantaneous moments of mental illumination which occurred to Ruskin, he realized that this insular and self-complacent preacher was symptomatic of the whole Protestant mindset – that of Ruskin's own parents, above all that of his mother. It was a moment of liberation akin to that experienced by John Stuart Mill when he escaped the crushing materialism of his father's world-view by reading Wordsworth. Ruskin ceased to be an Evangelical Christian, ceased trying to be one and feeling guilty about not being one. It was an experience, this 'unconversion' as he called it, which was to colour the whole of his life – his aesthetic life as well as his ideas of political economy. It was to change him from fastidious hermit, living in luxury, to a social prophet who eventually unloaded almost all his personal fortune in a series of prophetic, quixotic attempts to undo the evil effects of capitalism. It explains that electrifyingly embarrassing but somehow cheering moment in Oxford in 1884 when he was lecturing on 'The Pleasures of Truth'. As a pure type of Catholic witness, Ruskin produced a copy of Carpaccio's *St Ursula*, that beautiful dreaming form who had been the object of his meditations for decades and who had become conflated in his imagination with Rosie-Puss. To summarize the spirit of Protestantism, he displayed an enlargement of an engraving of a pig by Bewick.

It was really meant to be a joke, of sorts. Of course, it was a crazy kind of joke. We are told that the Oxford scientists began 'to slink out of his way as if he were a mad dog'.[43] What was the Pig versus St Ursula contrast but a vivid illustration of what he had been saying, and seeing, for years? (As when, in Rouen some fifty years before, he 'saw that art (of its local kind), religion, and present human life, were yet in perfect harmony. There were no dead six days and dismal seventh in those sculptured churches ...')[44]

In Victorian England you could attack God or, as Arnold did, loftily vaporize Him out of existence. But it really did not *do* to attack Protestantism. The London press deplored 'this academic farce'. The University which had been only too happy to accept benefactions from Ruskin – the endowment of the Drawing School, the gift of his Turners, and so forth – asked Jowett, Acland and others to have a word with the Slade Professor. When he announced that his next lecture would be a denunciation of vivisection and the disgusting experiments on animals then beginning in the laboratories in the South Parks Road, they realized that he *was* out of his mind.

Those of us who love Ruskin find something splendid in these 'mad' utterances. He retired to his lakeside retreat, Brantwood in Cumberland. He resigned the Slade Professorship. For the next fifteen years, until in 1900 he died, Ruskin inhabited a twilight of semi-sanity, interrupted by periods of total lunacy. His beard grew to luxuriant proportions beside which the facial embellishments of Marx and Darwin look like mere goatees. In his periods of mental stability he wrote his most charming and approachable work, the autobiographical *Praeterita*.

One could not have a book about the Victorians and the death of God which did not include Ruskin. Yet in some senses he does not belong here at all. Even in his bleakest moments of doubt he remained what Joan Evans has pertinently called an agnostic Deist.[45] Like Tolstoy in Russia (who admired Ruskin this side idolatry) he came from a background of privilege, and he had an extraordinary psychological personal history, yet he managed to speak directly on many levels to 'ordinary people'. He had a very instinctive sense of what religion was, and why it mattered, both to individuals and to societies. And he saw very clearly the ways in which God was being killed in the nineteenth century – by the sophistries of the Matthew Arnolds at the top of society, and by the grinding misery of the Wraggs at its bottom. Yet the mystery of things – the composition of crystals, the skill and vision which could produce a landscape by Turner or a face by Carpaccio – were part of the same unnameable Something which also made the over-privileged and solitary Ruskin aware, as few social observers had been, of what did or did not allow societies to cohere. Catholic art was an expression of a unity, a social unity, in the Middle Ages which was impossible for people living in an industrial society. How to live in such a society, how to live with pollution – industrial, moral, personal, collective – is the underlying problem which he faces, now earnestly, now whimsically, in the 'Letters' of *Fors Clavigera*, 'at once the portrait of a great man and the portrait of his age'.[46] Impossible to summarize either what the letters are like or what they are about; nevertheless, I would say that if I were allowed to keep only one English book from Victoria's reign, compelled to witness a bonfire in which were destroyed every copy of *David Copperfield*, *In Memoriam*, *The Origin of Species*, Browning's *Men and Women*, *Vanity Fair*, Wilde's plays – yes, even the first series of Swinburne's *Poems and Ballads* – I should feel tempted to keep *Fors Clavigera* – Fortune or Fate, carrying the Key (or a club). The title, mysterious and odd, is open to many interpretations.

No more paradoxical sentence about Ruskin was ever penned than R.G. Collingwood's 'Ruskin was a modernist'.[47] But it is true in the sense that Ruskin found himself opposed in almost every way to the Spirit of the Age, but strangely and intimately aware of what was going on, of the particular ways in which the decline of religion affected the 'feel' as well as the composition of society. He saw that what was going to be destroyed by modern industrialization was not simply God, but the whole Western tradition – what Professor Harold Bloom calls the Canon – and with it our memory of the past. Orwell's vision of 1984, in which 'Oranges and lemons/Say the bells of St Clements' is an inexplicable fragment of the past surviving in a new and wholly alien world, is profoundly Ruskinian. 'A day will come when we shall have men resolute to do good work, and capable of reading and thinking while they rest; who will not expect to build like Athenians without knowing anything about the first king of Athens, nor like Christians without knowing anything about Christ.'[48] In the previous letter he has a playful (and prophetic) meditation on the habit of eating a goose pie at Michaelmas.

> I don't suppose a more savoury, preservable, or nourishing dish could be made, with Michael's help, to drive the devil of hunger out of poor men's stomachs, on the occasions when Christians make a feast, and call to it the poor, the maimed, the halt and the blind. But putting the point of economy aside for the moment, I must now take leave to reply to my said correspondents, that the importance and reality of goose-pie, in the English imagination, as compared with the unimportance and unreality of the archangel Michael, his name, and his hierarchy, are quite as serious subjects of regret to me as to them; and that I believe them to be mainly traceable to the loss of the ideas, both of any 'arche', beginning or princedom of things, and of any holy or hieratic end of things; so that except in eggs of vermin, embryos of apes and other idols of genesis enthroned in Mr Darwin's and Mr Huxley's shrines, or in such extinction as may be proper for lice, or double-ends as may be discoverable in amphisbaenas, there is henceforward for man, neither alpha nor omega – neither beginning nor end, neither nativity nor judgement; no Christmas Day except for pudding; no Michaelmas except for goose; no Dies Irae, or day of final capital punishment, for anything ...'[49]

In England, in the United States and, in some diffuse manner, throughout Western civilization, Ruskin's influence continued to be felt, in rather the same way as Tolstoy's. While some commentators feared the political consequences of unbelief, dreaded (as Arnold did) the collapse of society into anarchy without religion's glue, Ruskin and Tolstoy looked at the problem from the other way about. They were not particularly concerned with defending orthodoxies. They dreaded, however, what would happen when it could no longer be said that human beings were spiritual, moral entities, fashioned in God's image and likeness. They feared the effect on individuals of trying to live in a society which had no Christmas Day except for pudding. As we have seen, Tolstoy did not worry when he read that some clever German professor had disproved the very existence of Christ; but, like Ruskin, retained a sense of God's reality, the only reality which enables men and women to preserve the notion of themselves as individuals. This was why Lenin attacked Tolstoy with more virulence than he did any of his other intellectual or political enemies.[50] Similarly, Lenin and Trotsky found England, the England which had lapped up *Fors Clavigera* and *Unto This Last*, a sadly inconsistent place. In the days when Lenin visited London – in 1902 he lodged there for a whole year – he did not feel, as Engels had half a century before, that the populace was ripe for revolution. Trotsky once took Lenin down to the East End of London on a Sunday evening. They attended a meeting, quasi-political and quasi-religious, in which speeches and songs about socialist brotherhood alternated with hymns. 'Lord Almighty, let there be no more kings or rich men.'

Many of us are old enough to remember the British Labour movement when it still had much of this semi-religious, semi-chapel quality. Lenin was puzzled. 'There are many revolutionary elements among the English proletariat, but they are all mixed up with conservatism, religion and prejudice, and somehow the socialist and revolutionary elements never break through the surface and unite.'[51] Trotsky agreed. 'British Marxism is not interesting,' he wrote. Both revolutionaries in every way preferred the thorough-going Germans.[52]

They were not alone, of course. Many English intellectuals, and some non-intellectuals, as the nineteenth century wore on, had glimpsed a secular future and longed to bring it swiftly to pass.

13

The Most Inexpressible Calamity

O weariness of men who turn from GOD . . .
To schemes of human greatness thoroughly
  discredited . . .

T.S. Eliot, 'The Rock'

WHEN ANNA KARENINA and Vronsky run away to Italy, in Tolstoy's great novel (published in parts between 1875 and 1877), they encounter a painter, Mikhaylov, who is described by another Russian in these terms:

> You know, he is one of those wild, modern folk one so often meets nowadays; you know! One of those freethinkers who have been brought up from the beginning in disbelief, negation and materialism ... Formerly a freethinker was a man brought up with ideas of religion, law, morality, who himself, through struggle and pain, had attained freedom of thought; but now a new type of born freethinkers has appeared. These grow up without so much as hearing that there used to be laws of morality and religion, and that there was once authority in these things; they grow up simply with the idea of negation – that is, as heathens.[1]

Such sentiments could have been expressed about the rising generation in any country of Europe. Tolstoy himself (born 9 September 1828), baptized and brought up in the Orthodox faith, describes the fascination with which, at the age of eleven, he heard a school-friend divulge the discovery that 'there is no God and that all we are taught about Him is a mere invention'.[2]

In England George Eliot, John Morley, Matthew Arnold, Mark Pattison, Darwin himself and countless others 'attained freedom of thought', but came from positions of firm religious belief. The closing decades of the nineteenth century were the true era of 'the death of God'. Almost more disturbing than the philosophy of Nietzsche with which the phrase is associated was the fact that 'the background of all the world was not merely atheism, but atheist orthodoxy, and even atheist respectability. That was quite as common in Belgravia as in Bohemia. That was above all normal in Suburbia.'[3] This was the new state of things. This was the new world in which the ideas which had existed only in coteries in the 1840s, '50s and '60s were now commonplaces. It was a world preparing itself to absorb the Darwinian theory of Survival of the Fittest – a world in which the great powers, guided not by morality, nor by a sense of a common European past, fought out a struggle for supremacy as if they were amoebas beginning the processes of life on Earth all over again; or dinosaurs preparing to extinguish one another. The studied godlessness of the Marxist creed was to give birth to convulsions all over Europe which excited reactions of Nietzschean and Wagnerian tragedy.

It would be a bold historian who claimed that Lenin, Stalin, Hitler came about because of the nihilistic atheism of the decades in which they were born. But their contemporaries certainly lived with a *Weltanschauung* so different from that of their grandparents that it would have been surprising if the world had not changed radically in the period. Whether we attribute this to the weakness of Christian institutions at the time or to the vigour of the ideas, to something as nebulous as *Zeitgeist* or as measurable as industrial progress or economic growth, the change is palpable.

'It was because no one doubted, and because everyone was too idle to examine and to probe, that Christianity became so corrupted in the Middle Ages. I must make a faith for myself, and I must work, until I have,' Beatrice Potter told her diary on 4 April 1874.[4] And again, 'since I cannot accept the belief of my Church without inward questioning, let me try and find a firm belief of my own and let me act up to it.'[5] Throughout the period of her life which she described as her 'apprenticeship', Beatrice Potter had a quasi-secret religious life, on the one hand doing social work in the East End of London among the poor Jewish immigrants, or collecting social data from the working-class communities of Bacup in Lancashire (some of them her own relations!), on the other secretly praying, nipping into churches and receiving the Sacrament. She pined for a great religious organization which would possess her body and soul and command her absolute allegiance. At times she considered herself an adherent of that already somewhat outdated creed, Auguste Comte's Religion of Humanity. At other times she showed a wistful respect for the Roman Catholic Church. Having long since admitted that 'I very much doubt' the very existence of God,[6] she could still contemplate, on a visit to Rome, the thrill of belonging to the Church of the Ages:

The Protestant ... declares virtually the supremacy of his own reason ... But the Catholic Church deals differently with the question ... The Church declares herself to be the supreme reason. She does not ask you to interpret her, she provides her own interpreter in the priest and suits her doctrine to the individual and the time ... Could not the agnostic, if he felt that his nature was not sufficiently developed to live without an emotional religion, could he not renounce his freedom to reason on that one subject, and submit to the authority of the great religious body on the subject of religion, as he would accept that of the great scientific body on the subject of science, even if in the latter case his own reason should lead him to different conclusions, on any phenomena of nature, to those arrived at by scientific man?[7]

Hindsight enables us to see that it was to the pursuit of such a church, an authoritarian church of humanity, that Beatrice Potter, after her marriage to 'the socialist Sidney Webb', was to devote her life until, when half a century had passed after that diary entry had been penned, there was indeed in existence a world religion which made just such demands and promises. 'Sidney and I', she proudly told a nephew by marriage in her old age, 'have become icons in the Soviet Union.'[8]

On 24 May 1883 Beatrice Potter 'went in afternoon to British Museum and met Miss Marx in refreshment rooms'. It is highly characteristic of both women that they should have fallen to discussing religion. Eleanor Marx, now twenty-eight, had travelled a long way since as a young child she so shocked her father by saying she had felt the 'call of religion' in the Roman Catholic church near their house in Maitland Park.

In the highly-charged atmosphere of the 1880s, the question of religion and the question of the socialist struggle marched hand in hand. George William Foote (1850–1915), one of the friends of the atheist MP Charles Bradlaugh, had been imprisoned for blasphemy in 1883 for printing his magazine the *Freethinker*. While he was in prison Eleanor was carrying on his work, editing the monthly *Progress* and sowing unbelief and sedition as best she and her colleagues could. Beatrice Potter found the anti-religious jokes in *Progress* feeble, but Eleanor explained that

Ridicule is quite a legitimate weapon. It is the weapon Voltaire used and did more good with it than any amount of serious argument. We think the Christian religion an *immoral illusion* and we wish to use any argument to persuade the people that it is false ... The striking difference of this century and the last is that free thought was the *privilege* of the upper classes then and it is becoming the *privilege* of the working classes now.[9]

'It was useless to disagree with her,' Beatrice told her diary; '– she refused to recognize the beauty of the Christian religion.'[10]

A modern reader is haunted by the meeting between the two women – the intense, gypsy-like beauty Beatrice, twenty-five, whose political education had hardly begun, whose mentor was still Herbert Spencer (by now very right-wing, a Manchester Liberal in economics, an evolutionist in world-view, with a horror of State assistance for the poor or State interference in the lives of the better-off); still in the future was her infatuation with the Radical Imperialist Joseph Chamberlain, and the marriage to Sidney Webb that set her off on the journey which was to make her the godmother of the British socialist state who drafted the constitution of the Labour Party; and Eleanor Marx, 'dressed in a slovenly picturesque way with curly black hair flying about in all directions', heavy in countenance – no one could have found her beautiful – chain-smoking, her intensity given up to politics and the love of a scoundrel.

It was but two months since Eleanor had buried her father Karl Marx in Highgate Cemetery (17 March 1883). Only eleven people, Eleanor included, had attended the interment and heard Engels deliver his famous eulogy at the graveside:

> Soon enough men will come to feel the void which the death of this powerful spirit has torn into the fabric of things.
>
> Just as Darwin discovered the law of the development of organic nature, so Marx discovered the law of the development of human history: the simple fact, hitherto obscured by an overgrowth of ideology, that man must first of all eat, drink, have a roof over his head and clothe himself before he can pursue politics, science, art, religion, etc., and therefore the production of the immediate material means of subsistence and consequently the degree of economic development of a people or of a period of time form the base on which state institutions, legal conceptions, art, and even the religious ideas of the people concerned have been evolved, and in the light of which they must therefore be elucidated – not, as previously, the other way round.[11]

Engels moved forward to his peroration, making claims which have been the subject of dispute and ridicule on the part of historians ever since. Marx was, he claimed, 'the most hated and most calumniated man of his time', and yet, 'although he had many adversaries, he had scarcely a single personal enemy'.[12] This was a strange tribute to a man who had lost every single friend he possessed (except Engels) through feuding. 'He is dead, revered, beloved and mourned by millions of fellow-workers from the mines of Siberia and the whole length and breadth of Europe and America as far as California ...' Marx's world-wide admirers, who certainly existed, could probably have been numbered in thousands rather than millions. But the movement of events and of world history would change all that. Plenty of people in Siberia would know the name of Marx fifty years after he died. If at the time of the funeral he was not yet a household name, it must often subsequently have been pointed out that Christianity started with a handful as small as that which gathered to bury Marx in Highgate. Various others stepped forward when Engels had finished speaking, including the German revolutionary Liebknecht who said, in his and Marx's own tongue, that Marx was immortal, and God was dead. 'Dead and living friend, we shall follow to the very end the way you have pointed out to us.'[13]

The household in Maitland Road had been dispersed. Engels took over Marx's library, distributed his small estate (£250) among his heirs, took in to live with him in his own house on Primrose Hill the mysterious boozy housekeeper, Helene Demuth (who had, as investigations proved, given birth to Marx's son).*

The great work *Das Kapital* could hardly have made him famous in England at the time of his death. Volume One had been completed, but the remaining two volumes were no more than a profusion of incoherent notes, waiting to be put into shape by Engels. The work of translating the masterpiece of Communism into English was left to Eleanor Marx and her rather sinister friend Dr Edward Aveling, a Lecturer in Comparative Anatomy at the London Hospital. Part medic, part actor, with several pseudonyms and 'stage names', Aveling 'was short, with the face and eyes of a lizard and no physical charm except a voice like a

---

* Frederick Demuth, the only one of Marx's children to live long enough to see the coming of the Russian Revolution and the Communist Age. He worked for many years at Bryant and May's match factory, keeping himself to himself (fellow-workers were not even sure whether he was married). When he died, he had a housekeeper and a reasonably middle-class establishment in Stoke Newington. He was a moderate Labour Party supporter, with no interest in Communism. He died on 28 January 1929. Eleanor visited and befriended him after their father died, but it is not known whether Freddie (he pronounced his surname *Dee-moth*) ever knew, in Karl's lifetime, who his father was – though they did meet.

euphonium'.[14] The judgement is George Bernard Shaw's, who was to befriend both Aveling and Eleanor Marx in those secular 1880s.

Aveling (son of a clergyman) and his friend Annie Besant (runaway wife of a clergyman, who had been separated from her husband, allegedly on the grounds of her atheism) were for a time intimates, and thought alike on all the issues of the day: Irish republicanism, birth control, free love – all of which they favoured – and religion and God – which they deplored. The incident which brought them and so many unbelievers of the period together was the case of Charles Bradlaugh, a matter which seemed to throw into focus how the world had changed even in the short decades since Darwin published *The Origin of Species*. After Bradlaugh, secularism was recognized as a fact, and as a result many of the notions of England for which Coleridge, Newman, Pusey, Gladstone had struggled in the 1830s and 1840s were pronounced irrevocably dead.

On 3 February 1845 Gladstone had resigned from Robert Peel's Cabinet on the question of the Maynooth Grant. As a pious young Tractarian, Gladstone believed that the Established Church was a divine institution, not a mere Department of State; its sacraments and formularies were, he believed, as close to the Catholicism of the Primitive Church as was humanly possible. To tolerate other forms of Christianity within the British Isles was to imply that Anglicanism was but one sect among many, rather than the True Church which John Keble and his followers knew it to be. When, therefore, Peel's Cabinet voted to give a grant of £30,000 to the Roman Catholic seminary of Maynooth near Dublin (the only place of 'higher education' available to Irish Catholics, and one of the most distinguished seminaries in Europe), Gladstone felt moved to resign, thus imperilling his glittering political future. There are many strange ironies about the story – not least the fact that Gladstone in his old age became so convinced the Irish should have Home Rule that he was prepared to split the Liberal Party (of which he had by then become the Icon) over the matter.

But if the contrast between young Gladstone and old Gladstone provides a rich field for analysis of his fascinating character, and of nineteenth-century political life, it also gives us the chance to measure what had happened to English religious sensibilities in the thirty-five years between Gladstone's resignation as Peel's President of the Board of Trade and his extraordinary triumph in 1880 when, as 'an old man in a hurry', he was swept back into power as Prime Minister. It was his second term. From 1868 to 1874 he had presided over great political reforms. The sweeping victory in 1880 of the Liberal Party, under the leadership of Lord Hartington, brought Gladstone back (Hartington, to the Queen's disgust, refused to form an administration, insisting that Gladstone be Prime Minister)* to preside over one of the strangest Parliaments in British history, in which the questions of Ireland, South Africa and Egypt caused immense problems; in which very little of a reforming character was actually achieved; and in which old Liberalism in its various forms (Whiggery, Peelism, et cetera) and New Radicalism, Fenianism, and crypto-socialism formed an uneasy Commons coalition.

Perhaps there was no stranger moment in Gladstone's parliamentary career than the night of 26 April 1883, when the man who had once resigned over the Maynooth Grant rose, as Prime Minister, to defend the right of an atheist, Charles Bradlaugh, to affirm his intention, as a newly-elected Member of Parliament, to be a loyal servant of Her Majesty, rather than swearing it by Almighty God. Gladstone the man of prayer had not changed. He still attended Matins and Evensong on a daily basis whenever possible; he still went to Holy Communion; he still believed that the Almighty had inspired every word of Scripture (and, come to that, most of the words of Homer).

Charles Bradlaugh, a working-class radical from Hoxton, East London, had in 1880 been elected by the people of Northampton on a radical ticket. Since then hours and hours of parliamentary time had been wasted discussing his case. As a professional atheist and paid-up member of the National Secular Society, Bradlaugh (friend of Annie Besant, the ubiquitous Dr Aveling and others of the same seditious and unbelieving kidney) had averred his right to forgo the oath-taking. The House had rejected him; the people of Northampton had re-elected him; fisticuffs at the Bar of the House; imprisonment in the Clock Tower at the Speaker's behest; popular protests from the nonentity Tory leader Sir Stafford Northcote and the opportunist Lord Randolph Churchill: it had all been a wonderful time for the atheists. The Christian conscience of England was shocked. Gladstone's old friend Cardinal Manning posed the question in the *Contemporary Review* ('Without God, no Commonwealth'):

What should restrain such a Legislature from abolishing the legal obser-vance of Christmas, of Good Friday and of Sunday; of rescinding all

---

* 'Abandoning a woman in her hour of need,' said Disraeli.

restraints on the employment of women and children in mines, factories and poisonous trades; thereby destroying what remains of home-life among the poor? What shall hinder the multiplication of causes justifying divorce by the adoption of foreign and Oriental codes?[15]

Manning went further and pointed out that the propagation of atheism was an indictable offence under English law.

No doubt, no doubt. But things had mysteriously moved on; and Gladstone the practical politician recognized this, even though Gladstone the man must have agreed with every word Manning wrote. Certainly on a personal level the Etonian, scholarly Gladstone found the Hoxton-born radical repellent. But there was that third facet to Gladstone's strange character, the side of his nature where the Humbug and the Genuine Liberal seem so inextricably woven together that it is impossible to form a judgement of their genuineness. In the debate in the House of Commons on that night of 26 April 1883 it was this Gladstone who spoke; and he argued passionately for the liberty of a freeborn Englishman, elected by his fellow-countrymen, to take his seat in Parliament without having to make mock of religion by going through a form of words which everyone knew to be, for him, bogus. The Conservative Opposition tried to make the debate into one of God versus Bradlaugh; the question for them was whether or not 'to dethrone the Supreme Being in this House, and to wipe out the name of God from the records of Parliament'. Henry Chaplin, a keen racegoer and dyed-in-the-wool Tory, said the proposed measure 'shocks, horrifies, and outrages every sentiment and every feeling nearest and dearest to the hearts of the people, in every family, in every home, by every fireside, from the palace of the noble and the rich, to the dwellings of the poor and the lowliest cottage in the land – aye, and to millions upon millions of our race besides – wherever the English tongue is spoken on the face of the civilised globe.'[16]

But to the Grand Old Man such talk was not only ridiculous, it was almost blasphemous. 'I have no fear of Atheism in this house,' thundered that voice which had held in thrall crowds of thousands, for hours on end, during the Midlothian campaign; which had been echoing round the Chamber of the House of Commons, on and off, for forty years; and which so bored and irritated his sovereign. 'Truth', he declaimed, 'is the expression of the Divine mind; and however little our feeble vision may be able to discern the means by which God will provide for its preservation, we may leave the matter in His hands.' By insisting upon an oath which Bradlaugh had said was meaningless and offensive to him, and by refusing to accept the verdict of the electors of Northampton, the House had managed to identify religion with injustice. What was the upshot: 'the impairment of that religious faith, the loss of which I believe to be the most inexpressible calamity which can fall either upon a man or upon a nation.'

Many of Gladstone's family and friends believed that this speech was the finest of his whole life. 'It was the voice and manner, above all the voice, with its marvellous modulations, that made the speech majestic,' said Lord Bryce. How sad that today, if we heard it, many of us should think it hammy, theatrical, unreal. (Or so that voice seems in the fragmentary recording of it on cylinder which has survived.)

It did not, on that occasion, win the day. The Conservatives won the Division by three votes. Randolph Churchill had asked the House

> whether they could contemplate without alarm the revulsion that such an Act might occasion among those masses of the people who, with some hope of a happier state hereafter, were toiling their weary way through the world, content to tolerate, for a time, their less fortunate lot – the revulsion that would occur should they infer from the action of the Legislature that it was even possible that their faith was false? Surely the horrors of the French Revolution should give some idea of the effect on the masses of the State recognition of Atheism.[17]

There was humbug on both sides, then; but we shall have to enlist the help of Professor James, in a later chapter, to discover the extent to which Lord Randolph's arguments may be found to be defensible. Versions of the argument are still heard today in the United States, almost every month; and they surface in the more secular UK and Europe, too. Surely, the Conservative-minded person wants to know, it makes a *difference* whether we believe in a Divine Lawgiver, and a Future Life, or whether we don't? Surely it makes a difference to our children if we can tell them that our ideas of right and wrong are based on Divine Commands, ten of them, delivered to Moses and written in the Sacred pages of Scripture. And on the other side of the argument are those who would argue with Gladstone that God can look after Himself and does not need the State legislature to protect Him. But, would reply the angry Lord Randolphs, that's not the *point*. Of course God is not affected, whether we believe in Him or not. It is *we* who are affected. Ah, says Professor James. How can we be so sure of that ...?

If Charles Bradlaugh had been merely one eccentric individual, appearing in an atmosphere of religious orthodoxy to affirm his unbelief, then his case would not have occupied eight long years of Parliamentary time before finally being resolved in 1888. Thereafter, English men and women could, if they so chose, affirm rather than swear oaths 'in all places and for all purposes where any oath is or shall be required by law . . .' After a decade or more of campaigning on the matter, Bradlaugh had become almost moderate in his tone. He left it to the other Liberal MP for Northampton, Henry Labouchere, to draw Ohs and Ahs from the Opposition benches when he said: 'I confess that for my part, I do regard these words of the oath as an utterly unmeaning form – utterly and absolutely an unmeaning form. To me they are just the same superstitious incantation as the trash of any Mumbo-Jumbo among African savages.'[18]

The fact is that many English men and women in the 1880s would have agreed with Labouchere, even if they would not have chosen to express themselves so intemperately. Joseph Chamberlain, the most brilliant of Gladstone's Cabinet ministers, left the Liberal Party in 1886 because of his opposition to Irish Home Rule. Beatrice Potter was painfully in love with him during this year. 'My great love for him is acknowledged before God,' she told her diary when she realized that the affair was hopeless and that she could not be his wife (he married an American two years later). 'This morning I take the sacrament – the great symbol of sacrifice, of the sacrifice of the individual life and happiness.'

Chamberlain himself, as he had told Beatrice in the course of their many intimate talks, was an unbeliever. In 1884 she had been to hear him address one of his great rallies in his native Birmingham – thousands in the crowd thrilled to the oratory of 'Our Joe', '. . . for has he not raised Birmingham to the proud position of one of the great political centres of the universe'.[19] Beatrice felt in this assembly that the world was secularizing itself. The working class of Bacup still read their Bibles and attended their Methodistical chapels. Was the same true of the Birmingham radicals? She thought not. She recollected that Heine in the 1830s had written, 'Talk to an Englishman on religion and he is a fanatic; talk to him on politics, and he is a man of the world.'

It would seem to me, from my slight experience at Bacup and Birmingham that that part of the Englishman's nature which has found gratification in religion is now drifting into political life and when I suggested this to Mr Chamberlain he answered: 'I quite agree with you, and

I rejoice in it. I have always had a grudge against religion for absorbing the passion in man's nature.'[20]

These views would no doubt have been echoed by the eighth Marquess of Queensberry, who at the height of his obsession with his son Lord Alfred's most celebrated friendship asserted, 'These Christian English cowards and men, as they call themselves, want waking up.'[21] To his role as President of the British Secular Union the Scarlet Marquess brought the same manly vigour he displayed on the hunting field and in the boxing ring. It is interesting that his name, in sporting circles, should be forever associated with rules to limit the amount of damage which pugilists might inflict upon one another (the so-called Queensberry Rules); since it has been well observed that 'when it came to fighting, Queensberry was happier with a free-for-all'.

He had a Scottish peerage, but not an English one which would automatically entitle him to sit in the House of Lords. The Scottish peers periodically elect sixteen of their number to sit in the Upper House in London; in 1872 Queensberry thereby entered the Lords. He was seldom called upon to speak, but he managed to irritate their lordships by scattering secularist pamphlets 'over the seats of the Peers spiritual and temporal'. 'Everything', he thundered, 'is fair in war; and this is war. We Secularists and other bodies of Freethinkers are fighting now tooth and nail to be recognised as a body of people who have a religion and have a faith ... Our great difficulty at the moment is to get a hearing from our orthodox opponents ... I shall never scruple to use any artifice I can to get at them and bring them to bay.'[22]

He publicly announced his intention of refusing to swear an oath of allegiance to Her Majesty. He wanted to be the Bradlaugh of the Lords and, if his son Lord Alfred Douglas is to be believed (a perhaps breathtaking conditional), Queensberry dismissed the oath as 'Christian tomfoolery'. As it happens the matter was never put to the test, since his fellow Scottish peers, once he had become President of the British Secular Union, convened at Holyroodhouse in Edinburgh and decided unanimously to vote him out of the House. He never did get the English peerage he so much craved.

So angry was he with his fellow peers in Scotland that he never set foot in the country again but uprooted his bewildered family from their ancestral seat, Kinmount in Dumfries, and established them at a less romantic address: 67 Cromwell Road, a not particularly salubrious part of Kensington. Here he could furiously observe his children growing up into caricatures of all that he most abominated. Drumlanrig, the eldest boy, became private secretary to Lord Rosebery. Recognizing the unquestionably homosexual flavour of his son's relationship with the Foreign Secretary and future Prime Minister, Queensberry threatened to expose the 'affair'. Some of his anger was no doubt caused by Rosebery's decision to make Drumlanrig a lord-in-waiting to the Queen, with the right to sit in the House of Lords as an English peer. Furious, mad letters from the Marquess to Gladstone, to the Queen, to all and sundry, were dispatched. When Rosebery was ordered by his doctor to take a rest cure at Homburg, Queensberry followed him with a dog-whip. Faced with pressure of this sort, Drumlanrig got himself engaged to be married to an amiable upper-class girl, Alix Ellis; but before he was called upon to solemnize the union he turned a gun on himself during a shooting party in the Quantocks, in Somersetshire.

When Drumlanrig's brother, the robustly heterosexual Percy Douglas (now destined to inherit the marquessate), announced his engagement to marry, Queensberry violently objected to his choice of wife, and the two were for long estranged. Threats of disinheritance and lawyers' letters were exchanged.

So when Lord Alfred Douglas, the next brother, who had inherited much of his father's belligerence and sheer nastiness, formed his fatal attachment to Oscar Wilde, it was no surprise to anyone that the Scarlet Marquess reacted as he did.

The story is too well-known to repeat, but it demonstrates one thing at least: that being an atheist, as Queensberry was, in no way diminished prejudice in sexual and moral matters. Bosie, of course, compounded the crime of being homosexual by becoming (as did Wilde on his death-bed) a Roman Catholic. Queensberry had already watched with embarrassment as his own brother, Lord Archie, became a Roman Catholic priest with special care for St Vincent's home for boys; he must have been equally exasperated when his sister Lady Gertrude entered a convent, not once, but twice, and then, after a spell helping Father Lord Archie with his boys' home, became a keen advocate of women's suffrage.

Eleanor Marx was to devote her life, short as it was doomed to be, to the propagation of atheist–socialist ideals and to the love of Edward Aveling, with whom she had established a ménage in rooms near the

British Museum not long after her father's funeral. It was a period (well-captured in Henry James's *The Princess Casamassima*) of little groups of conspirators meeting in locked rooms, of socialist societies breaking into splinters and then into splinters of splinters.

The year after her father died, she and Aveling organized a demonstration. The Highgate Cemetery Company would not allow the crowd (said to be as large as 5,000) into the grounds singing the 'Marseillaise' and waving red flags, so they passed the graveyard gates and climbed up into Dartmouth Park where, according to Eleanor, Aveling delivered 'a splendid speech which touched the hearts of all his hearers'.

Others in their Social Democratic Federation were less impressed. Aveling was in every sense of the word an actor, and one by one those who sympathized with the socialist ideals of the federation – William Morris, Hyndman, Joynes (a former Eton master), Bradlaugh – found themselves suspicious of him, as well they might.

Friends like the Hyndmans urged Eleanor to break with Aveling, since he often betrayed her with other women; but she was addicted to him. Throughout the winter of 1897–8 she nursed him through a painful and disgusting illness, which involved the continual dressing of wounds which exuded a foul-smelling pus, changing bandages, washing him, and wheeling him in a bath chair up and down the sea-front at Margate, where she had taken him to recover. When he was somewhat better, they went to live in Sydenham, and it was while she was there that Eleanor received a letter and a newspaper cutting which revealed that on 8 June 1897 a certain Alec Nelson and a twenty-two-year-old actress named Eva Frye had been married at the Chelsea Register Office. Alec Nelson was one of Aveling's stage names.

The effect upon Eleanor (now forty-two) was shattering. Aveling had guessed she would eventually discover the extent of his deceitfulness (he had, for example, sold most of her possessions, behind her back),[23] and he had his plan ready. He suggested that the situation had become impossible. He was disgustingly ill, dying of a horrible disease, he said. He and Eleanor should enter into a suicide pact. He sent the maid, Gertrude Mary Gentry, to the chemist with a note: 'Please give the bearer chloroform and a small quantity of prussic acid for the dog – E.A.' When the maid returned with the poison, Aveling changed the note to read 'E.M.A.' (Eleanor Marx Aveling).

In imitation of Madame Bovary, Eleanor dressed herself in white and took the poison. (The maid had been sent back to the chemist with the poison book, and only Aveling was in the house.) Aveling, who for some weeks had been exaggerating his illness and was, for example, perfectly capable of walking, with no need of a bath chair, left the house and caught the first train to London. He made a point of establishing an alibi for himself by visiting the office of the Social Democratic Federation, and remembered to call the secretary's attention to the time – eleven o'clock. At a quarter to eleven Gertrude Gentry had returned from the chemist. She found Eleanor still breathing faintly, a bottle of prussic acid on the table beside her with a note: 'Dear, it will soon be over. My last word to you is the same that I have said during all those long sad years – love.'

Aveling lied to the coroner at the subsequent inquest. He told the court Eleanor had often made suicide threats, but that he had considered them to be idle. The chemist who had supplied the poison was made to believe it was Eleanor who got the prussic acid from him. Aveling – by establishing that he was in the office of SDF while Eleanor was still alive – was *just* able to convince the coroner that he had been out of the house when the poison was administered. No mention was made of the pact. He was, in effect, Eleanor's murderer.

One does not exactly blame Shaw for being taken in by Aveling; after all, many others were, too; but it is somehow rather typical of GBS to have found Aveling sufficiently enchanting to make him into Louis Dubedat in *The Doctor's Dilemma*. According to Shaw, if you asked What sort of man was Aveling?, the answer from anyone who knew him was a shriek of laughter and the question 'How much have you lent him?' Shaw half admired Aveling's 'hopeless and incorrigible deficiency in ordinary moral fibre', seeing in him, again approvingly, 'one who would have gone to the stake bravely rather than admit that Marx was not infallible or that God existed'. 'He seduced every woman he met and borrowed from every man,' recorded Shaw indulgently.[24]

Annie Besant saw through Aveling at an early stage of the game. When still under the powerful Liberal–radical influence of Bradlaugh she hated the ideas of Marx; and she resented Aveling's claim that he had become a Marxist as a consequence of five years' careful study. 'It is less than five years since Dr Aveling joined the Freethought party,' she told the readers of *Justice*, the journal of the Democratic Federation. 'As his friends closed their doors on him, I opened mine, and save for the time when he was with his pupils, and night time, he made my house his home. All his work was carried on with me ...' And, as she made clear, Aveling was happy to give the the impression that, far from being a Marxist, he was a free-thinking libertarian.

Annie Besant was mocked by many of her confrères at this time, though her early career, viewed with the kindliness of a later age, seems more tragic than absurd while her later life, so surprisingly different in tone and purpose, provides its own interesting commentary on the Death of God theme.

As a young woman she was devoutly High Church, enjoying nothing better than the perusal of Early Church Fathers (in an English translation) and the composition of pamphlets on the value of fasting. Such views did not really recommend themselves to her husband, a Low Church clergyman nearly twenty years her senior who was a mathematics master. The marriage was extremely unhappy. The honeymoon had nauseated her – she had had no preparation from her mother for what would be expected of her – and the Reverend Frank Besant was hot-tempered and violent. He took her to live in Cheltenham, where he was a master at the boys' College, and she found it stultifyingly boring. Two children – Digby and Mabel – were eventually born to the Besants but nearly lost in the spring of 1871, when Mabel at eight months and Digby aged two contracted whooping cough. Annie herself was very ill, and at only twenty-four suffered something amounting to a nervous collapse once the worst crisis of the children's illness was past: she discovered that she had lost her faith.

Two very different clergymen, whom she did not personally know, represented for her at this early stage the polarities between which she felt torn. On the one hand there was the Reverend Charles Voysey, whose name had appeared in every newspaper in the land.[25] As vicar of Healaugh in the diocese of York, Voysey had been deprived of his living for questioning the divinity of Christ and the existence of hell, while asserting the comprehensive nature of the love of God. Bravely but foolishly Voysey appealed, conducting his own defence before the Judicial Committee of the Privy Council itself. It was a case which caused uneasy feelings in many a parsonage-house or college common room. As Jowett the Master of Balliol remarked, Voysey had 'looked too far over the hedge'.[26] Many parsons and their wives, many schoolmasters, university dons, and intelligent laypeople must have read Voysey's words and found that they agreed with them. The Reverend Frank Besant himself had a brother, Walter, who had been sacked as a schoolmaster because he was 'unsound on the Atonement', and who spent years of exile in

Mauritius in consequence. The pressure in the Besant household not to think like Voysey was intense. Frank, a poor man as well as a bully, was determined to stamp out his wife's doubts. But the more she thought about it, the more she doubted.

On a visit to London to see her mother, Annie took the opportunity to write to a clergyman who represented the very opposite viewpoint to Voysey's liberalism: she consulted the great Dr Pusey himself, and he, disturbed by the thought of a clergyman's wife suffering from doubts, urged her to come up to Oxford on the train for an interview. She found a short, stout man dressed in a cassock and looking like 'a comfortable monk'. Pusey and she had nothing in common. He assumed that she was coming to him as a penitent, for spiritual direction. She wanted a learned scholar to resolve her genuine intellectual difficulties. How could a good God have allowed such suffering as she had seen in little Mabel when she had the whooping cough? How do we know that Jesus was all-perfect? But merely to ask this question made the Doctor raise his hand to silence her blasphemy. Were there no books he could recommend her, she asked. 'No, no,' Pusey replied, 'you have read too much already; you must pray, you must pray.'

It was not advice which she felt able to follow. As the 1870s progressed she started to write pamphlets, not this time on fasting, but *On the Deity of Jesus of Nazareth*. Having read Renan, she was no longer a Christian. Soon, other pamphlets came from her pen, published anonymously but acknowledged to be 'By the wife of a Beneficed Clergyman'. She pointed out the inconsistencies between the various gospels, and questioned the doctrine of the Atonement. In the light of the Voysey judgement, we can imagine that Frank Besant was frightened lest he himself might lose his position (after the children were born, he had become vicar of the remote Lincolnshire parish of Sibsey). He insisted that she recant from her heresy by attending all the services in his church, and by receiving Holy Communion. It was, as far as she could see, an ultimatum: 'Hypocrisy or expulsion, I chose the latter.'

With the help of her brother Annie drew up a deed of separation, by which it was agreed that Digby should live with his father at the Sibsey vicarage while Mabel stayed with her mother in London. As Annie became more and more outspoken in her criticisms of Christianity, Frank used the children as pawns in the matrimonial game. Mabel, who from the age of three onwards became used to travelling alone on trains with a luggage label tied round her neck for the purposes of identification, would be fiercely catechized by her father on her arrival at Sibsey, to make sure that she was not absorbing her mother's infidelity. When she was seven Mabel was finally taken, 'shrieking and struggling ... near frantic with fear and passionate resistance', to live with her father on a permanent basis. The judge decreed that since Annie had been involved with the publication of a pamphlet recommending artificial contraception, and since the pamphlet, Charles Knowlton's *Fruits of Philosophy*, was obscene, one could not in consequence 'expect modest women to associate with' Mrs Besant.

Annie told her readers in the *National Reformer* that the judge, the notoriously choleric Sir George Jessel, was 'skeptical to all sincerity, and contemptuous of all devotion to an unpopular cause ... The old brutal Jewish spirit regarding women as the mere slaves of men breaks out in the coarse language that disgraces him rather than the woman at which it is aimed.'[27]

Annie spent her thirties being intensely political. She stood on platforms with Bradlaugh, and became his inseparable helpmate and companion. Together with the great feminist Millicent Garrett Fawcett she campaigned for birth control because, as Fawcett said, 'pauperism would never be cured until the rapid and continuous growth of population could be checked'. Besant's concern for the poor, and especially for poor children, increased when her own children were taken from her, and in 1889 she stood for election as a member of the London School Board for the poverty-stricken Tower Hamlets district. At that date this was the closest a woman could hope to come to exercising any executive political power.

She spoke with great eloquence and passion. '*No more hungry children.* Children sent to school without breakfast and given but little dinner cannot profit from the education you parents and ratepayers pay for ...' This language spoke to the voters, even to those who might have been expected to hate her atheism: the Irish dockers and navvies, or the poor Jewish immigrants from Russia and Eastern Europe. (Her friend Lewis Lyons, an East End tailor, campaigned in Yiddish on her behalf.) She was elected by a staggering 15,296 votes – four times the number of votes polled by her male predecessor on the school board. Her campaign to feed the poor school dinners was opposed on all sides – even by such impeccably radical figures as Mrs Dilke. But although she never managed to get it accepted as a principle that children should be fed as well as taught at school, the London Schools Dinner Association was soon managing, by voluntary subscription, to give one free meal a day to 36,000 children.

By now, 1889, Annie Besant was a familiar figure on all leftist platforms. But the religious unbelief which was part and parcel of Fabian Socialism was at war with her true nature. When she first left her husband she had associated with Moncure Daniel Conway (1832–1907), a Unitarian minister at the South Place Chapel, Finsbury. Conway was an upper-class Virginian who had trained for the Methodist ministry. When he was twenty he had gone north to Massachusetts, and been inspired by the writings and example of Emerson. He studied at the Harvard Divinity School from 1854 to 1856 and became convinced of the wrongness of slavery. When he returned to *ante bellum* Virginia, his vague theology and his radical political views guaranteed him social ostracism. He was sent to England by the Northern Government in 1863 to put their case in an effort to counteract the overwhelming sympathy for the Confederacy which was felt in British political circles.

Conway was a religious libertarian who became increasingly secularist. He keenly supported Voysey in his troubles, and was enthusiastic for the Theistic Church which Voysey tried to found after he had been booted out of the Church of England. By the time Annie met Conway, though, South Place was well on the way to becoming an Ethical Society rather than a Unitarian chapel. Talks and lectures rather than religious services formed the diet of the congregation.

One incident which took place at this time demonstrated the painfulness of the 'vague' position which Annie had made her own: her mother came close to death. Troubled by Annie's unbelief, her mother said that she would rather be lost with Annie than saved without her; but that it would be her dearest wish to receive the Sacrament with her daughter. Annie could not lie. She went to several clergymen and explained the situation, confessing that she was herself an unbeliever but that she would be prepared to receive the Sacrament to gratify her mother's dying wish.

Having met with several refusals, she plucked up courage and went to see the Dean of Westminster, Arthur Penrhyn Stanley, next to Jowett perhaps the 'broadest' exemplar of the Broad Church. He consented to do what was asked, came to her mother's bedroom, celebrated Holy Communion and communicated both women. Annie spoke freely with the dean and asked him how, with his liberal views, he found it possible to stay within the Established Church; he said he felt he could do more good within the boundaries of the Church than if he left it. Though at this stage Besant declared herself to be an atheist, Stanley probably recognized that she was basically a very religious person; merely unable in all honesty to subscribe to the Christian creeds.

The atheism hardened when she became associated with Charles Bradlaugh. This was the stage of her life when she dismissed prayer as an absurdity. 'Who are we that we should take it upon ourselves to remind Nature of her work or God of his duty? ... Every day proves to me that the reading and thinking men and women are now doing for themselves in lightening the darkness that prevails in these subjects what I had hoped those in authority would have done long ago.' So keen was she on the secularist position that she often spoke on platforms for the Secularist Society, preaching the gospel of Bradlaugh. She broke with Bradlaugh for political reasons, since he disapproved of the violent Trafalgar Square demonstrations which she and her new socialist cronies enjoyed. The demos were for a variety of socialist causes, and the betterment of the working man; though the bloodiest of them was in support of seven anarchists, condemned to death by the State of Illinois as a result of a suspected bomb. Condemnation of the Chicago Anarchists' activities virtually destroyed the right of public meeting – or so their London sympathizers believed. Six thousand people or more demonstrated in Trafalgar Square on what came to be known as Bloody Sunday – 13 November 1887. Truncheons and bayonets were used by the police and the Scots Guards to break up the crowds. A hundred and fifty were taken to hospital; three hundred were arrested. It was Annie Besant who, three days after Bloody Sunday, at a meeting of the Metropolitan Radical Association, called for another demo. And it was she who organized the huge funeral for Alfred Linnell, killed in Northumberland Avenue on Bloody Sunday, whose cortège, led by fifty veterans of the Chartist agitations, was followed by a hundred thousand from Trafalgar Square, past St Paul's Cathedral, to Bow Cemetery. William Morris gave the address at the graveside.

Annie needed heroes, and the fact that Bradlaugh split from her during this period inevitably led her to another – this time to the campaigning journalist W.T. Stead, Editor of the *Pall Mall Gazette*. She fell in love with Stead, and it was not reciprocated. Stead wanted to found a 'church' which would bring about a regeneration of the Christian way of life without retaining too many of the old dogmas of the past. Annie felt it was time to admit that though Atheism had brought her temporary consolation from the torment of believing in an unjust God, she felt bereft 'without a father'. By coincidence, at the time she first met Stead they were both reading Carlyle's *Cromwell* and she came across this sentence of the Lord Protector: 'I find this only good; to love the Lord and his poor despised people; to do for them, and to be ready to suffer for them.'

Beatrice Webb when she first saw Annie was struck by her palpable unhappiness. 'I heard her speak, the only woman I have ever known who is a real orator, who has the gift of public persuasion. But to *see* her speak made me shudder. It is not womanly to thrust yourself before the world.'[28] By the end of the 1880s Annie had begun to feel that the message was not nourishing; that socialism was not enough; that her audiences, though appreciative enough when she campaigned for school dinners, were hungry for spiritual food. She began to dabble with psychical research, to investigate the paranormal, to attend seances. It was then that she discovered the Theosophical Society, Madame Blavatsky and the Wisdom of the East. The first half of her life was over. For the next forty years Annie Besant, destined to die an old lady in 1933, expounded such mysteries as reincarnation, spiritualism, avatars, and the lost secrets of Isis.

Bradlaugh was appalled by the direction in which his old partner in secularism was journeying. In the *National Reformer* he denounced the Theosophists:

> They appear to me to have sought to rehabilitate a kind of Spiritualism in Eastern phraseology. I think many of their allegations utterly erroneous and their reasoning wholly unsound. I very deeply regret indeed that my colleague and co-worker has with somewhat of suddenness, and without any interchange of ideas with myself, adopted as facts matters which seem to me to be as unreal as it is possible for any fiction to be.[29]

'We had been fearing this for some time,' noted Sidney Webb with sadness when Annie resigned her membership of the Fabian Society. Beatrice Webb was kinder, because with the powerfully religious strand to her personality she must have partly understood Annie's need to believe 'a wonderful fairy tale'.[30] Some of Annie's other friends, notably George Bernard Shaw, were less kind. Shaw, several years Annie's junior, has left some ungallant recollections of her in which he claims she proposed marriage to him. Whether his own ideas seem any stranger to our generation than those of Madame Blavatsky will depend very largely on one's taste.

You still sometimes meet very old people in England who take Shaw seriously as a religious, or rather anti-religious, thinker. They are invariably what used to be called 'genteel', walking embodiments of Chesterton's recollections that by the 1890s, atheism had become the religion of the suburbs. The Victorian father 'was the first man, for whom there were no household gods but only furniture'.[31] Shaw, with his rather ridiculous beard and his apparent air of speaking and writing in memorable aphorisms (but how many does anyone ever remember?) is the embodiment of late nineteenth- and early twentieth-century irreligion. The ephemerality of his literary reputation is one quite vivid example of the difficulty facing us when we consider the central theme of this book. It is not just that we have all moved on from the *religious* positions of a hundred years ago: our doubts and unbeliefs are different, too. Shaw seems as obsolete as Bishop Walsham How, never more so than in his pronouncements on the Life Force.

It is difficult to place Shaw altogether. For the first half of the twentieth century he seemed like one of the giants of British literature; but he becomes less impressive with distance. Naturally, in his lifetime he received the Nobel Prize and made himself very rich twice over, partly by writing perky, harmless plays, partly by marrying money. His outstanding virtue as a man was that he could be immensely kind: he was generous to spongers and – a big plus on anyone's mark-sheet because it was so rare – he was prepared to stick up for Oscar Wilde at the time of the disgraceful trials. As a youngish and middle-aged man Shaw devoted hours of his time to the largely unrewarding work of a councillor in the St Pancras Ward of London. Thanks to Shaw, the first ladies' lavatory in England was constructed at the top of Park Street, now Parkway, in Camden Town, London NW1. The campaign to build the loo was in its way an archetypical Shavian act of philanthropy, provoking gratifying howls from Tory shopkeepers and local residents, who believed that such a provision offended against public decency. Nowadays the increasingly elderly fans who clamber from their charabancs for matinée productions of *Major Barbara* or *The Doctor's Dilemma* have more cause to be grateful to GBS than they know. After all, thanks to the existence of public lavatories for women they can settle back for two or three hours of facile paradox and wholly unmemorable epigram, safe in the knowledge that they can be in all senses 'comfortable'.

It is no accident that Shaw continues to survive in England, if survive is the right word, at respectable theatres in Chichester, Malvern and Shaftesbury Avenue. This was always his audience – the comfortable bourgeoisie. The supposedly dangerous socialist with the red beard, carefully-maintained Irish accent and equally carefully-nurtured anti-bourgeois views was always the political equivalent of a flirt. His claim, made in the 1880s, that 'I was a coward until Marx made a communist of me' sounds stirring enough. On 13 November 1887 Shaw, then thirty-one, took part in the illegal demonstration for free speech on Bloody Sunday. He commended the bravery of the women on the march, and mocked the cowardice of the men. Annie Besant was the 'heroine' of the day, he told a meeting of sympathizers later that evening. He cynically and cheerfully admitted later that he had 'skedaddled and never drew rein' at the first hint of a mêlée. He quoted with appreciation R.B. Cunninghame Graham, who said that Shaw 'was the first man to run away from Trafalgar Square on Bloody Sunday' (Cunninghame Graham himself went to prison as a result of the riot). This is all of a piece with Shaw, once the youthful Fenian, having not the smallest desire to live either in the Irish Free State or the Irish Republic. Similarly, his gerontic adulation of Stalin and Hitler seems prefigured by his remark in 1908: 'if there is to be any shooting, the Fabian intends to be at the state end of the gun'.

Shaw's essential shallowness was perhaps the sort of intellectual position which the Conservatives in the Bradlaugh debate began to fear. Manning, Randolph Churchill and others dreaded a society which slithered into valuelessness. While Gladstone argued (with more fervour than conviction) that the Almighty could look after Himself, and radicals like Joseph Chamberlain fantasized that religious energy could be channelled into political ends (an idea which Lenin and Hitler were both able, in their interesting ways, to develop), Shaw's giggling brand of modishness showed how far the automobile could run on marsh gas rather than real fuel. And you see this in particular whenever he writes about religion, which he does with an invariably spurious fluency, a cheeriness which carries the reader along, guaranteed never to approach the heart of the matter.

For all the fervour with which Shaw was read by young socialists in the early years of this century, his political and religious stances seem now no more than absurd garments acquired, like the celebrated all-in-one Jaeger suit, as a way of playing to the gallery, delighting, in part by shocking, the bourgeoisie on whom his fortunes as a stylish middlebrow playwright depended.

Dr Gustav Jaeger, one of the many medical crackpots of his time, developed the Sanitary Woollen System in the mid 1880s. His famous recommendations included woollen sheets – more hygienic, naturally – and 'digital' socks, which resembled gloves for the feet. The use of wool was designed to encourage perspiration, which drew out 'poisons' from the skin: wool, according to Jaeger, absorbed and gave off 'natural vapours'. Shaw, who found it so difficult to believe in God, happily absorbed this claptrap – in that sense being a man typical of the age which took to its heart so many incredible fads. Passionately sceptical of conventional medical developments (he denounced Edward Jenner's discovery of vaccination as 'a mere stunt' which was 'nothing short of attempted murder') he was prepared to believe, or perhaps it would be more accurate to say, to adopt, the ludicrous whims of Dr Jaeger.

To celebrate the death of his unloved father – neglected and poverty-stricken, in Dublin, in 1885 – and to spend the insurance money which this event brought his way, Bernard Shaw went to Jaeger's shop in the West End of London and ordered the yellow knitted 'all-in-one' suit, 'the first new garment I have had for years.' (How much Samuel Butler would have approved of this father-hating gesture.) In this highly distinctive defiance of traditional mourning garb, purchased in the sultry month of August, Shaw might have been expected to perspire as freely as even Dr Jaeger could have hoped, particularly since he also kitted himself out with Dr Jaeger's Sanitary Woollen Braces, Woollen Shirt and Woollen Coat. Plenty to draw out the poisonous vapours there, it might be supposed, but the interesting thing is that none came, suggesting at the very least someone as devoid of animal substance as the paper-thin creations of his matinée-dramas.

He adopted the clothes in the belief, apparently borne out in practice, that they would make him odourless. Shaw was obsessed by personal cleanliness. When Beverley Nichols met him (appropriately enough in Malvern, home of Victorian quack medicines) in 1929 he exclaimed, 'The cleanliness of the man! He was like snow and new linen sheets and cotton wool and red apples with the rain on them. One felt that he must even smell delicious, like hay or pears.' Trying to persuade a friend to adopt vegetarianism, Shaw once assured him that his own evacuations were 'entirely odourless'. It was eating meat which would make them offensive, and if he were ever 'to pass such a motion, I should give myself up for dead'. In the Twenties, when Shaw was getting into the stride of that spindly senescence which seemed his natural or proper age, he was hoping that 'one day we shall live on air, and get rid of all the sanitary preoccupations which are so unpleasantly aggravated by meat-eating'.

It is not true that cleanliness is next to godliness, though it is probably a mere accident that so many of the godly, from the Desert Fathers to Samuel Johnson, have been human beings who exuded a stench. It is probably an accident too that Shaw, prophet of the sweatless armpit and the odourless motion, was the man who ushered in the century of the deodorant and the ethnic cleanser. But if evacuation without smell seems too predictable a trope for the general literary effect of Shaw, we can at least observe the paradox that to discard a belief in God led, for a whole generation of Shavians, to a humanity that was less earthy than its religious grandparents. GBS's hero and fellow-vegetarian Adolf Hitler would have loved to 'live on air' – and in a sense did, floating above the clouds in his Wagnerian fairy-palace of Berchtesgaden, and hoping to make the Fatherland clean and pure.

Dethroning God, that generation found it impossible to leave the sanctuary empty. They put man in His place, which had the paradoxical effect, not of elevating human nature but of demeaning it to depths of cruelty, depravity and stupidity unparalleled in human history.

14

—➤◆◄—

William James

'Mankind's most important function'
William James,
The Varieties of Religious Experience

A LICE JAMES (1850–1892), the sister of more famous siblings and a woman who took at best a quizzical view of religious questions,* noted in her journal that her psychologist-philosopher brother was endeavouring to give his children religious instruction. On 10 October 1890 she recorded:

> William has, for several years past, read the Bible to his boys, and expounded (!) as he went. The other day Billy exclaimed: 'But, Father, who is Jehovah anyhow?' This must have been a blow, after three years of complacently supposed lucidity. Some years ago, when Harry was five or thereabouts, William undertook to explain to him the nature of God, and hearing that He was everywhere, asked whether He was the chair or the table. 'Oh, no! God isn't a thing; He is everywhere about us; He pervades.' 'Oh, then, He is a skunk.' How could the word 'pervade' suggest anything else to an American child?[2]

Perhaps the most eloquent component of this gently satirical passage on the lovable Harvard professor is that exclamation mark in parenthesis. Anyone who has felt the sheer charm of William James, and yet been exasperated by the apparent non sequiturs in his philosophical arguments – whether expressed in letters, lectures or essays – will know what that exclamation mark means; it is punctuation's equivalent of eyes raised to the ceiling. James's fellow-philosopher, the one with whom his name is most frequently linked as co-exponent of the 'pragmatist' theory of truth, Charles Sanders Peirce (1839–1914), once read one of James's essays on popular religious philosophy and exclaimed,

---

* When she was cremated at Woking Crematorium, at the cost of six guineas, plus one guinea for the parson, the parson read a short service, 'the most Alice had agreed to put up with', according to the family biographer.[1]

I have lain awake several nights in succession in grief that you should be so careless of what you say ... The only thing I have ever striven to do in philosophy has been to analyse sundry concepts with exactitude; and to do this it is necessary to use terms with scientific precision ... But that being my own claim to consideration, and it being a deeper conviction with me that philosophy is either science or is balderdash, and that a man who seeks to further science can hardly commit a greater sin than to use terms of his science without anxious care to use them with strict accuracy, it is not very grateful to my feelings to be classed along with a Bergson who seems to be doing his prettiest to muddle all distinctions ... Very faithfully, lovingly, and gratefully, C.S. Peirce.[3]

There will always be those, on both sides of the religious question, who take a comparably rigorous view of the gentle Professor James. Or who, while admitting his personal charm, would echo G.K. Chesterton's joke: 'It was his glory that he popularized philosophy. It was his destruction that he popularized his own philosophy.'[4] All very funny; but, much as one reveres Chesterton, it is hard to place him in quite the same league as James when it comes to the great questions of religious thought.

An acquaintance of mine, lunching at the Reform Club in London in the 1930s, calculated that a very old waiter might conceivably, if he had worked at the club as a young man, have remembered the Master. Summoning the old man, he asked if he remembered a Mr James. 'Mr James? Now, let me see. Would that be the American gentleman who liked to express himself ... well, sir, shall we say, in a very *roundabout* sort of a way?'

Any of us who love the Master must have been aware of his family history, and of his brother William, an eminent psychologist at Harvard University who, in the closing decades of his life, became devoted to religious philosophy, and who, in 1901 and 1902, delivered the Gifford Lectures at Edinburgh, published under the title *The Varieties of Religious Experience*. For my part, I read this book when I was too young – in my late teens, when I was what James himself would have called 'a sick soul'; certainly when what he called 'the religion of healthy-mindedness' would have been so far from my ken as not to seem to be 'religious' at all.

Although I turned William James's pages during my morbid youth, only in sunny middle age did his words come as much refreshment; not merely his words, but his whole personality. No one could accuse him of speaking in 'a roundabout sort of way'. Indeed, much as he admired his brother Henry, he found the fogginess of his style a sometimes impenetrable irritant, always striving in his own works (hence the sleepless and miserable nights of colleague Pierce) for an intelligible, even a chatty style, laced with amusing asides and jokes.

Any of us who has surveyed the nineteenth century's struggles with religious scepticism must have wondered if it was possible to draw some objective line under the whole subject, to write FINIS. Surely we could say at least one of two things. The human race, which had worshipped God or the Gods time out of mind, from the era of the cave men until the French Revolution, went crazy and threw off God. It tried to justify what it had done, by prosaic Benthamism or verbose Hegelianism; by inventing new religions such as Marxism, or by telling itself that under the new Comtian materialist dispensation, it lived in an age of science which could disprove 'religion'. And, hey presto! at just the right moment in history, along came the scientists to show that the universe had no need of a creator, nor of a beginning, nor of an end ... So argument could run, but with one proviso: that this crazy loss of faith, this 'inexpressible calamity', to use the Gladstonian words, was only a strange phase in human development, comparable to an adolescent rebellion. For deep down, so this argument would run, men and women continued to know that they were souls with eternal destinies, who responded to the great moral imperatives which Immanuel Kant had recognized as the very foundation of a reasonable life. Perhaps – such an argument would wish to go on – some adaptation of the old theologies would be required. Perhaps it would be necessary to concede, for example, that the Biblical texts, far from being a single composition from one divinely inspired source, are a collection of writings only intelligible with reference to the times and places of their origin. And yet, and yet – this view would insist – humankind is essentially religious, and this alone should make us humble before the thought-patterns of earlier ages who found it legitimate to use the word 'God'. According to such a view, the 'death of God' announced by whomsoever first announced it is at worst a dreadful blasphemy, at best an adolescent folly; and above all, it is wrong. Definitely wrong. There *is* a God – or, in Clough's words, 'something very like him'.

Such, perhaps, one might have hoped would be one possible and reasonable conclusion to a survey such as the author and reader of this book have been conducting together.

Or we might have hoped to come to a different conclusion. Is it not strange, we could have concluded, that at the end of the nineteenth century, all over cities like New York and Chicago and London and Paris, human beings were still getting out their cheque-books and paying architects to build beautiful churches, in order to worship an entity whom we now recognize to have been a figment of the human imagination? Is it not *odd*, to say the least, that the era we have been discussing, the era in which God died, should have been one of the very greatest periods of church-building in human history?

Surely, these reasonable and intelligent readers of a non-religious bent would wish to say, the Nineteenth Century did indeed witness 'the death of God'. The decapitated chicken still ran around the barnyard a few times. But we cannot any longer write, or speak, or live, as if the revolutions in human sensibility which we have observed in these pages simply never took place, nor the developments in philosophy and science. The sceptical inferences so wittily sketched by David Hume in his *Dialogues Concerning Natural Religion* do not merely make us doubt the God of the eighteenth-century Deists; they kill Him stone dead. And if anyone should turn around and say, 'We do not believe in the God of the Deists, we believe in the revealed God of Scripture', then the German biblical critics destroyed *Him*. And in case anyone should turn from the God of the Bible and say that there is still some mileage in the Argument from Design, and in a nature-mysticism which claims a knowledge of God from the shape and pattern of Nature, Darwinism removes not merely the necessity of supposing a Designer, but its very plausibility. There is not much left here for the religious person to chew upon, surely? Why not see this as a simple story – as Thomas Hardy did in his great poem, in which,

> ... tricked by our own early dream
> And need of solace, we grew self-deceived,
> Our making soon our maker did we deem,
> And what we had imagined we believed.
>
> Till, in Time's stayless stealthy swing,
> Uncompromising rude reality
> Mangled the Monarch of our fashioning,
> Who quivered, sank; and now has ceased to be.

Theologues, metaphysicians and philosophers, in surveying the foregoing pages of our narrative, might by now be feeling the need to make just some such assertion. It is with some relief that I, who can make no pretence of belonging to such company, and can choose my own friends, turn now to spend some of the time we have left together considering the case, and some of the ideas, of William James.

It will give us the chance to revisit some old friends, and to tie up a few threads which were perhaps floating loose in our tapestry. When the great expounder of William James's life and philosophy of life sees it as 'the old gospel of Carlyle with which James had been impregnated in his childhood',[5] he takes us back from the raw-boned twentieth century in which he wrote to that much-frequented nineteenth-century drawing room, by now so familiar to us, a hundred yards north of the River Thames in Cheyne Row, Chelsea, where Mrs Carlyle, rising (or not) from 'the chair she sat in', that bobbin-spindle chair whose cushions she has so frugally upholstered while her husband, perhaps in his famous check dressing-gown and with a noxious tobacco-pipe alight, 'holds forth' – denouncing 'Parliament and its babble', or claiming that 'the Christian religion has lost all vitality'.[6]

Of Sir Edwin Chadwick, the great sanitary reformer and improver of drains – he who realized that diseases were water-borne and that epidemics such as cholera and typhoid could be avoided if only the English town-planners would insist on proper sanitation – Carlyle observed that the 'only religion left to us is ablution, and that Chadwick is the priest of these times'.[7] He made the observation to his friend Ralph Waldo Emerson, to whom he also observed abrasively in passing that he was vexed by American visitors. 'They dislike the coldness and exclusiveness of the English, & run away to France & herd with their countrymen, & are amused instead of manfully staying in London and confronting Englishmen, who really have much to teach them, & acquiring their culture.'[8]

Still, there were some exceptions; or, if not exceptions, Yankees who were prepared to acquire a *little* English culture before beating the well-worn path to Paris.

Carlyle was charmed, in the winter of 1843–4, by a young American, married, with two small sons, who came with letters of introduction from Emerson. This fellow's first visit to London, in the year of Queen Victoria's coronation, had been to acquire a cork leg instead of the wooden stump which had been in place since a childhood accident had burnt and cost him his own. Notwithstanding this injury, and a speech impediment which led him to stammer, Henry James had been intended for the Presbyterian ministry and had studied to that end at Princeton. But the orthodoxies of formal theological thought and the restraints of ecclesiastical institutionalism were not suited to his free spirit and, somewhat to his father's chagrin, he had pursued his own line.

James was not a poor man. His self-made father, who died eight years before the meeting with Carlyle, had been 'rich without parallel', according to one contemporary newspaper: second only to John Jacob Astor in New York State. The stern old Presbyterian, however, had not forgiven his son for leaving the seminary, and had tried to cut two of his children, this Henry, and William, out of his will. A fortune of some three million dollars was at stake. In the event, after a protracted legal battle Henry James ended with a substantial income from his father's estate, some $10,000 a year – easily enough to finance the London trip with his wife Mary and his two baby sons. He was engaged upon an impeccably liberal study of the Book of Genesis, endeavouring to demonstrate that the first of the Mosaic books was not intended as a literal account of the origins of the world, but as 'rather a mystical or symbolic record of the laws of God's spiritual creation and providence'.

He had set sail to England not merely with letters of introduction from Emerson in his pocket, but with the sunny optimism of Emerson in his heart. Carlyle wrote to the American sage: 'James is a very good fellow, better and better as we see him more ... Something shy and skittish in the man; but a brave heart intrinsically, with sound earnest sense, with plenty of insight and even humour. He confirms an observation of mine, which indeed I find is hundreds of years old, that a stammering man is never a worthless one.'[9]

The assembly of men and women whom the young American encountered in Carlyle's drawing-room – John Stuart Mill, George Henry Lewes, George Eliot, Tennyson – were by no means united in free-thinking, but James was able to sniff out what a modern reader senses in every paragraph of Carlyle's prose: that 'he names God frequently, and alludes to the highest things as if they were realities; but it almost looks as if he did it only for picturesque effect, so completely does he seem to regard them as habitually circumvented and set at naught by politicians.'[10]

Neither of Henry James senior's infant sons – also William and

Henry – was out of 'long clothes' when their father first introduced them to the Diogenes of Cheyne Row, but Carlyle became a family friend; when the babies grew to manhood and made their own journeys to Europe, there would be revisits and revisions.

The elder of these boys, William, was to grow up to be the most distinguished psychologist of his generation – perhaps ever; he was also destined to become a philosopher of rare penetration. In both capacities he was openly preoccupied with the God-question. His own inner journey of God-thoughts is the subject of this chapter; but clearly his journey would not have taken the shape and route it so memorably did had not an event occurred during that first trip to England, when he was two years old.

Henry senior and his wife had taken Frogmore Cottage, on the outskirts of Windsor Great Park, as the ideal place to settle with the babies. At a weekly rent of £4 10s. (and 8s. a week for the cook and chambermaid), it was highly affordable. As far as we can tell, Henry senior was happy at this time – his book on Genesis was going well, his marriage was harmonious, and he enormously enjoyed expanding his circle of acquaintance. They had extended their European stay with trips to Paris, and when May 1844 came round the young James family were still in Frogmore Cottage. His health was good; and there is no season of the year in which the lush meadows and magnificent trees of Windsor Great Park look more beautiful. Yet it was during this month that Henry James senior experienced something which would change all their lives, forever.

He had eaten a good dinner. The children had been taken to bed. He was left alone, a rich, clever young man, staring into the embers of the grate. Quite suddenly and without warning James suffered a panic attack, and became aware that there was a presence in the room, 'some damned shape squatting invisible to me within the precincts of the room and raying out from his fetid personality influences fatal to life'. He wanted to run away from this terrifying demon or devil, but he could not. He remained rooted to the spot, suffering from 'an ever-growing tempest of doubt, anxiety and despair, with absolutely no relief from any truth I had ever encountered save a most pale and distant glimmer of the divine existence ...'

This terrible experience was followed by two years of intermittent but profound depression. He consulted a wide variety of doctors, all of whom considered that he had been overtaxing his brain, and that the sense of the diabolic presence, and the subsequent panic attacks, were the simple consequences of overwork. But, of course, James had not been overworking by any normally accepted uses of the term. Leon Edel, the Freudian interpreter of the James family story, describes it as 'a nervous exhaustion after years of inner conflict. The inner terror of defying Fathers and escaping spectral eyes was finally too much for him. He chose that one escape possible: a relapse into the innocence and passivity of childhood.'

All of which might be true, or might be untrue. What William *fils* would perhaps have wanted to add (to the exasperation of the sceptical empiricists and the scholastic rationalists alike) is that the experience was a true one. William, of course, never publicly analysed his father's experience, but he was to arrive, after a long journey not without difficulties, at a position bold enough to accept two sets of data which, if not irreconcilable, sit uneasily beside one another. We can not doubt that it was the experience of Henry senior in Frogmore Cottage which was the primary factor in guiding William's thoughts about this subject in his philosophical maturity: on the one hand, there can be no rational ground for supposing that there is an ontologically necessary being 'outside' the tangible, the knowable and the known; on the other, experiences such as the manifestation of the devil at Frogmore do *happen*.

It was two years before Henry senior found peace; and this came about not because of any medical advice, but through the spiritual diagnosis of a Mrs Chichester, who opined that the young man was suffering from what Swedenborg calls a *vastation*. We do not know much about this sibylline figure who became so important a part of the James family legend. Henry senior, having encountered the lady at Windsor, immediately went to London to purchase some key texts: *Divine Love and Wisdom* and *Divine Providence*. He was also destined to form a friendship with the leading English Swedenborgian, J.J. Garth Wilkinson. It was no surprise that when in July 1845 his wife Mary gave birth to a third son, he was named Garth Wilkinson James.

The works of Swedenborg were to travel with the James family for ever afterwards, rather as Chaucer's Clerke of Oxenford carried around his twenty books of 'Aristotle bound in blak and rede'. Henry junior, recalling their ceaseless peregrinations from one European city to another, tells us that the red-bound Swedenborgian volumes were always in his father's luggage, forming the 'purplest rim of his library's horizon'. The family never considered themselves truly settled until these books had been taken out and placed on the shelf.

What happens in vastation is that the old ego, with all its clashing appetites and demands, is drained, emptied out, destroyed. Selfhood, which in Henry senior's Emersonian phase had been something to thank God for, had become, in this, 'a literal nest of hell within my own entrails'. The Secret of Swedenborg (the phrase was to give Henry James senior the title of one of his many books) was that God had an indiscriminate love for the human race; such were 'the calm, translucent depths of meaning that underlie the tormented surface of explication he puts upon the spiritual sense of Scripture'.

More than any other member of the family it was Henry James's first-born William* who, in the course of a distinguished life as a scientist and a psychologist, tried to make sense of his father's experiences. From the first he was aware that, from an intellectual point of view, his father's opinions were unsustainable; and therefore, or so it seemed to the young William, the comforts they provided were won too easily. It is a great tribute to both men, and to the fondness they bore one another, that William as a young man was able to explain to his father, in copious letters, why he could not share Henry senior's religious faith. When he called Henry his 'beloved old Dad'[11] or his 'dearest Daddy'[12] he was palpably sincere. What a contrast exists between the honest and open-hearted James family and the extraordinarily pinched coldness of John Henry Newman, who felt unable to remain on speaking terms with his agnostic brother!

'I find myself', William confessed to Henry senior in a letter from Berlin written when he was twenty-five, 'more and more drifting towards the sensationalism closed in by scepticism [that is, to the view of the universe advocated by Hume, that our perception of truth is determined by 'sensations']. I can understand no more than ever the world-wide gulf you put between "Head" and "Heart"; to me they are inextricably entangled together, and seem to grow from a common stem – and no theory of creation seems to me to make things clearer.'[13]

Yet it was impossible for the old cork-legged parent to exist, emotionally, without his vague Swedenborgian doctrines of universal love, however little they made sense to his son.

---

* There were five children: William (1842); Henry junior, the novelist (1843); Garth Wilkinson ('Wilkie', 1845); Robertson ('Bob', 1846); and Alice (1848).

Towards the end of the 1870s at Harvard, after William had become a university teacher, one of his pupils called at the house in Quincy Street hoping for instruction. The door was opened to him not by Professor James but by Henry senior, now forty years older than when Carlyle first met and liked him, 'a remarkable character, a kind of glorified Greek fury ... He was old, white haired, lame and wore a skull-cap.' An inquisition began. 'Who are you? ... What's your name? ... Are you one of William's pupils? ...' And then when the young man, whose name was George Angier Gordon, had finally been admitted to the house, and the pair were seated, awaiting the arrival of the professor, 'Are you a believer?' 'I said that I counted myself on that side. Then every sentence was kinder than the one that went before, and mellower and before the conversation ended he had taken me to his heart ...'[14] William James the psychologist puts his lecture-audiences perpetually on their guard against forming easy explanations for human behaviour; but if we are puzzled, sometimes, by the contrasts in William's writings on religious subjects, by the seeming paradox of a natural sceptic defending religious belief, it seems reasonable to recall the constant presence in his mind of this much-loved parent's question: 'Are you a believer?'

The answer, by the time he approached manhood, was quite definitely in the negative. This was a period, for William James, of great personal unhappiness. By the time he grew up, he had come to resent the peripatetic existence his father had made them all lead. (Yet, like other paternal habits, William found the nomadic drift hard to shake off; from the age of two and a half, when he first visited London and met Carlyle, to the day of his death, aged sixty-seven, he only once spent a period as long as six years continuously in America.) William had been sent to three different schools in New York before he was thirteen; he and his siblings were then taken to Europe, and put through a whole string of more or less unsatisfactory educational establishments in London, Geneva, Boulogne and Bonn. There was a brief spell back in Rhode Island, but in many serious ways the James brothers grew up as European polyglots.

William at first supposed that he wanted to be a painter – a false hope which surely forms the basis of his brother's tale *The Tragic Muse* – but having discovered that 'there is nothing on earth more deplorable than a bad artist', William enlisted, in 1861, in the Lawrence Scientific School in Harvard. Having studied chemistry for a couple of years, he

became attracted (largely through the influence of the legendary
Professor Louis Agassiz) to anatomy and physiology. By the time he was
twenty-one he was telling a cousin that he had four choices of career:
'Natural History, Medicine, Printing or Beggary'. He opted for medicine, and joined the Harvard Medical School in 1864. These studies
were interrupted by the decision of Professor Agassiz to lead a party of
field naturalists down the Amazon, an expedition William was anxious
to join. He became very ill – at the time it was said to be smallpox,
though it would seem in fact to have been varioloid; for a long period
the disease left him languid, and unable to read. Even when he resumed
his medical studies in March 1866 and started an internship at
Massachusetts General Hospital, he was prey to a variety of troubles:
'insomnia, digestive disorders, eye troubles, weakness of the back, and
sometimes depression of spirits, followed one another or afflicted him
simultaneously'.[15]

Much has been made of the fact that both the elder James boys,
William and Henry, suffered from psychosomatic symptoms in early
manhood at precisely the moment in their country's history when young
men from liberal-minded families such as theirs were flocking to join
the Federal armies. A trifling strain to Henry's back when putting out
a fire (faint echo of Henry senior's loss of a leg when stamping out a fire
in *his* early manhood ...) became, in the novelist's recollection, a major
'spinal injury'. 'Scarce at all to be stated ... the queer fusion or confusion established in my consciousness during the soft spring of '61 by the
firing on Fort Sumter, Mr Lincoln's instant first call for volunteers and
the physical mishap already having overtaken me at the same dark hour,'
wrote Henry in *Notes of a Son and a Brother*. Wilkie, who had a heroic
war and became an officer in a Negro regiment, hilariously ended one
of his letters home: 'Tell Harry [the future author of *The Golden Bowl*]
that I am waiting anxiously for his "next". I can find a large sale for any
blood-and-thunder tale among the darks.'

William's preoccupation with physical courage – and, by implication, his own self-reproach, not for his moral lack of it, but for his body
having taken care that he could not be a hero in the War – colours all
his later ethical writings. *Will*, and its lack – what it is, indeed – is one
of his constant psychological interests.

The psychosomatic symptoms became so bad that by the spring of
1867 William was obliged once again to interrupt his studies in
Massachusetts and make, once more, for Europe. It was during this

unhappy period, spent largely in Germany, that he unburdened himself, in letters to his father, of his religious scepticism. He found Germany depressing. 'The German character is without mountains or valleys; its favourite meat is roast veal; and in other lines it prefers whatever may be the analogue thereof – all which gives life here a certain flatness to the high-tuned American taste.'[16]

Nevertheless, the two years he spent among the veal-eaters of central Europe laid the foundations of all his future work, since it was while attending lectures on psychology at the University of Berlin that he began to realize the bent of his academic interests. 'It seems to me', he wrote to his friend Thomas Ward, 'that perhaps the time has come for psychology to begin to be a science – some measurements have already been made in the region lying between the physical changes in the nerves and the appearance of consciousness-at (in the shape of sense perceptions) and more may come of it. I am going on to study what is already known, and perhaps may be able to do some work at it ...'[17] It was to Ward, too, that he confessed his total religious scepticism, and his charming if wishy-washy conception of the brotherhood of man.

> And if we have to give up all hope of seeing into the purposes of God, or to give up theoretically the idea of final causes, and of God anyhow as vain and leading to nothing for us, we can, by our will, make the enjoyment of our brothers stand us in the stead of a final cause; and through a knowledge of the fact that that enjoyment on the whole depends on what individuals accomplish, lead a life so active, and so sustained by a clean conscience as not to need to fret much.[18]

This was his life-view when he eventually returned to the United States in November 1868 and, at the age of nearly twenty-seven, resumed his interrupted medical course. He eventually became William James, MD (the only academic degree he ever obtained by examination) in 1869. It was out of the question that he should practise as a doctor, however, since he was much too 'delicate', and he began to hope that he might work in laboratories, or 'pick up a precarious living by doing work for medical periodicals or something of that kind'. He lived at home for the next three years, suffering from severe depression. And it is to this sad period that most James biographers assign the devastating experience described in his chapter on 'the sick soul' in *The Varieties of Religious Experience*. He later admitted that it was his own experience, though in the lectures he claims that the account of panic fear came to him from a French correspondent: 'The original is in French, and though the subject was evidently in a bad nervous condition at the time of which he writes, his case has otherwise the merit of extreme simplicity.' I translate freely:

Whilst in this state of philosophic pessimism and general depression of spirits about my prospects, I went one evening into a dressing room in the twilight to procure some article that was there; when suddenly there fell upon me without any warning, just as if it came out of the darkness, a horrible fear of my own existence. Simultaneously there arose in my mind the image of an epileptic patient whom I had seen in the asylum, a black-haired youth with greenish skin, entirely idiotic, who used to sit all day on one of the benches, or rather shelves against the wall, with his knees drawn up against his chin, and the coarse gray undershirt, which was his only garment, drawn over them enclosing his entire figure. He sat there like a sort of sculptured Egyptian cat or Peruvian mummy, moving nothing but his black eyes and looking absolutely non-human. This image and my fear entered into a species of combination with each-other. *That shape am I*, I felt, potentially. Nothing that I possess can defend me against that fate, if the hour for it should strike for me as it struck for him. There was such a horror of him, and such a perception of my own merely momentary discrepancy from him, that it was as if something hitherto solid within my breast gave way entirely, and I became a mass of quivering fear. After this the universe was changed for me altogether. I awoke morning after morning with a horrible dread at the pit of my stomach, and with a sense of the insecurity of life that I never knew before, and that I have never felt since.* It was like a revelation; and although the immediate feelings passed away, the experience has made me sympathetic with the morbid feelings of others ever since. It gradually faded, but for months I was unable to go out into the dark alone.

In general I dreaded to be left alone. I remember wondering how other people could live, how I myself had ever lived, so unconscious of that pit of insecurity beneath the surface of life. My mother in particular, a very cheerful person, seemed to me a perfect paradox in her unconsciousness of danger, which you may well believe I was very careful not to disturb

---

* Compare Bunyan: 'There was I struck into a very great trembling, insomuch that at some times I could, for days together, feel my very body, as well as my mind, to shake and totter under the sense of the dreadful judgment of God, that should fall on those that have sinned that most fearful and unpardonable sin. I felt also such clogging and heat at my stomach, by reason of this my terror, that I was, especially at some times, as if my breast bones would have split asunder . . . Thus did I wind, and twine, and shrink, under the burden that was upon me; which burden also did so oppress me that I could neither stand, nor go, nor lie, either at rest or quiet.' James's own footnote.

by revelations of my own state of mind. I have always thought that this
experience of melancholia of mine had a religious bearing.

James asked his 'correspondent' to explain more fully what he meant by
these last words, he said, and the answer he wrote was this:

> I mean that the fear was so invasive and powerful that if I had not clung
> to scripture-texts like 'The eternal God is my refuge,' etc., 'Come unto
> me, all ye that labor and are heavy-laden,' etc., 'I am the resurrection and
> the life', etc., I think I should have grown really insane.

A footnote in *Varieties* points us to the similarity between the experience
of the anonymous young 'Frenchman' and that of 'vastation' in the life
of his father: 'For another case of fear equally sudden, see HENRY JAMES:
Society and the Redeemed Form of Man, Boston 1879 pp. 43 ff ...'

The difference between the two men is in fact heightened, however,
by the comparability of their experiences in early manhood of panic-fear
followed by some inner comfort being granted as a result of religious
hope; for whereas Henry senior was happy to believe that the comfort
he had received was itself *argument enough*, William's approach to the
whole question, both at the time and with the hindsight of more than
thirty years, was much more oblique. He was 'rescued', in any case, not
by reading Swedenborg but by the French philosopher Renouvier, who
converted him to a belief in mental causation. It was to have a profound
effect on his progress as an academic psychologist, since the belief in
causation led him to reject the notion that 'animals are automata', as
T.H. Huxley believed. Conscious states, according to James, though
they owe their existence to the physical brain-processes, can react in
such a way as 'to further or dampen the processes to which they are
due ... If we knew thoroughly the nervous system of Shakespeare, and
as thoroughly all his environing conditions, we should be able, according to the theory of automatism, to show why at a given period of his
life his hand came to trace on certain sheets of paper those crabbed little
black marks which we for shortness sake call the manuscript of Hamlet.'
Such 'scientific' absurdities were rejected by James, not for reasons of
sentiment but on empirical grounds.[19]

These were the directions in which William James's mind was
moving when he emerged from his vastation, panic attack, nervous
breakdown in his late twenties. In 1872 Charles W. Eliot, by now
President of Harvard University but formerly William's chemistry tutor

at the Lawrence Scientific School, offered him the post of Instructor of Physiology at Harvard. He accepted it, and for the rest of his life became a much-loved and distinguished senior member of the university. In 1876 he began to give his courses on physiological psychology and 'founded, almost without realizing it, the first laboratory for experimental psychology in the United States'.[20] This was also the year in which he met Alice Gibbens, his beloved life-companion whom he married in 1878. They had four children (including Henry James III).

It was only when he was far advanced in his study of psychology, and had begun to approach his fortieth birthday, that the university recognized the diversity of William James's interest and made him Assistant Professor of Philosophy. He became a full professor in this subject in 1885, retaining the post until his death.

In thirty-five years of teaching at Harvard, William James came to be so much loved, all but universally and intensely, by colleagues, family and pupils, that his good-humour, his jokey, sharp manner of expression, his very physique – that lithe, bearded five foot eight inches of a man with deep, piercing eyes – became almost a distraction from what he had to say; a distraction, too, from the divided and sometimes tormented sources of his inspiration. He wasn't bland – the reverse. But his capacity for sympathy, for getting inside temperaments and opinions other than his own, was matched by (or perhaps echoed?) a complimentary or different tendency in his public utterances: an ability to project sides of his own nature or opinions which were exaggerated versions of his own, and knock them down like Aunt Sallys. This is what makes his company so stimulating, I think, ninety years and more after he left the scene.

What we call science depends very largely on a correspondence theory of truth; that is, the theory that propositions are true if, and only if, they correspond with facts. It sounds ineluctable, but does such a theory indeed stand up? If we say that we accept it, are we saying any more than that we assent to the notion that there *are* facts, rather than positing a theory about how we may come to know them?

Many twentieth-century thinkers – Derrida, Wittgenstein, Quine, Dewey among them – have cast doubt on the pretensions of philosophy to determine what can or cannot be known. The old questions of epistemology, about which European metaphysicians have been quarrelling since the time of Descartes, have not truly come up with one single, cast-iron method by which you can test the truth of propositions while justifying the validity of that method. Any method you try will have you going round in circles. What do we mean by a fact? Is it not a tautologous way of stating that it is a true proposition? What do we mean by a true proposition? How do you explain the notion that our language systems, appearing to latch on to worlds of fact (or of value) outside themselves, can find no outside arbiter of meaning or value by which their claims to truth can be assessed?

It is into this knotty territory that William James, psychologist; William James, physiologist; William James, pragmatist philosopher, entered in the last decade of his life, with interesting if not finally authoritative things to say about the God of philosophers and the God of religion.

Let us say a word about the God of philosophers because, to a layman, His fate in the nineteenth century, and His ultimate demise, might seem rather surprising. Those who had not investigated the matter historically, but who were told of the empiricist versus idealist debate, would probably guess that the God of the Idealists had a better chance of survival than the God of the Empiricists. The empiricists cannot be relied upon to think alike on all matters. Many of them – especially the Benthamites and the Utilitarians – fail almost entirely to address the epistemological difficulty of how we make claims to know anything at all. But they must be said ultimately to stand for theories of truth and knowledge which can be tested by experience. That is why they feel so happy to live in a scientific age. It is why they embrace positivist doctrines of truth, suggesting that we can claim something to be true either when sense data tell us that it is true or when we accept its truth *a priori*. For the empiricist, this *a priori* knowledge – the truth of formal logic or of mathematics – is demonstrable in its own terms, and to this extent is completely unlike the formularies of theology, which might claim ontological sureness but are in no obvious sense demonstrable.

In all these ways we should expect the empirical cast of mind to lead towards religious scepticism, or at the least towards agnosticism. You can't test the truth of a religious proposition, and none of the conventional proofs for the existence of God have, in the philosophical world post-Kant, attracted many adherents. The only ones which might appeal to the empiricist are the Arguments from Design, and these seem to most readers of the evidence to have suffered a deadly blow at the hands of Lyell and Darwin.

The Idealist, however, seems to have, ready-made, a conception of knowledge which is in itself quite 'religious'. This is especially true if you follow Hegel in thinking that the universe itself, in so far as it has reality, is a spiritual reality. Human consciousness, itself a spiritual thing, responds to the spirit and truth of the universe. According to the Absolute Idealism of Fichte or Hegel, reality is a whole – that is, the Absolute. The great attraction of this seemingly mystical notion is that it jumps over the central stumbling-block of the empiricist position – namely, how there can be forms of understanding or perceptions of truth which transcend any verification-principle which we could devise.

These are the systems of thought which so attracted English and American academic philosophers such as T.H. Green, F.H. Bradley, Josiah Royce, and others; theirs was the way of 'doing philosophy' which was to dominate English and to a lesser extent American university faculties from the 1870s until the 1930s. But although in the first heady wave of British Hegelianism it seemed as if Idealism had saved God's bacon, such optimism as T.H. Green's turned out to be misplaced.

The true monist, the Absolute Idealist, is committed to the idea that everything is One. What we perceive as things or entities, what we entertain as notions, are all manifestations or phenomena of the One. Unless an entity is part of everything-that-is, it does not make sense, in Absolute Realist terms, to say that it exists. And this stricture must, logically, include God. If, like Spinoza, you feel able to use the word God as a synonym for Nature, or for What-is, then you can embrace a species of pantheism. 'If you identify the Absolute with God, that is not the God of religion,' wrote Bradley in his great work *Appearance and Reality*. This must be true, since it would not make sense to say that the Absolute had any of the qualities traditionally associated with the God of the Bible or the God of popular religion. The Absolute could not be said to love humankind, nor to answer prayers, nor to be a Person. Any such talk would be nonsense, and Bradley robustly rejected it as such. He even goes so far as to say that 'the God which could exist would most assuredly be no God'.[21] Thus, while many idealists had a 'reverent' attitude to life, it was hard to see, if they were subscribers to Absolute Idealism, how they could really believe in God.

Now, it is well known that William James and Charles Peirce are the two first American rebels against the Absolute Idealism of the neo-Hegelians. But James came to philosophy late in life, and by a circuitous route. Nor was his interest in philosophy entirely dominated by his religious concerns: though these undoubtedly coloured some of his more famous essays. It was while trying on idealist spectacles, and finding that they did not suit his eyesight, that James was also advancing theories of consciousness and psychology based on physiology; was becoming more and more deeply materialist, in fact. Hence his remark made towards the end of his life in a letter to Charles A. Strong, 'The "omniscient" and "omnipotent" God of theology I regard as a disease of the philosophy shop.'[22] This disease was diagnosed very early in his life, and he made absolutely no attempt to catch it, however attracted he might be to religion.

It is entirely characteristic of James, to whom the idealist system of philosophy was so uncongenial, that he should have been largely responsible for the appointment at Harvard of America's leading Idealist, Josiah Royce. The two men (Royce was ten years younger than James) met at a dinner party in Boston in 1875. Royce, a graduate of the University of California, had begun work on a doctoral thesis at Johns Hopkins. It would have been difficult to find two men more different, either in appearance, background or temperament. Whereas James had been brought up as a wealthy Swedenborgian nomad drifting between grand apartments and expensive hotels in London, Paris, Geneva, Royce came from the small mining town of Grass Valley, and his boyhood ambition had been to be a fur-trapper. Prodigious mathematical skill was what projected him to U. Cal., whose school president, Daniel Coit Gilman, sent him to Germany, where he absorbed his Idealist notions. Unlike James, who had been unable to decide upon a choice of career, Royce was made to be a philosopher. Unlike the dapper and well-bred James, Royce was socially maladroit, short and stocky, with an unusually big head, bright red hair and a harsh, unpleasing voice. When he obtained his doctorate from Johns Hopkins, Royce (the first of four doctors to emerge from that university) was devastated to be unable to find a philosophical post. The only job he could find (and, unlike the comparatively plutocratic James, he *needed* a job) was teaching English at Berkeley – hardly a fate worse than death, but very frustrating for an ambitious young man who felt that he had important things to do in philosophy. It was James who, sympathizing with his younger friend's plight, obtained him first a temporary and then a permanent post at Harvard, teaching philosophy.

A pair of photographs taken by James's daughter in 1903 captures the famous philosophical sparring partners, sitting on a dry-stone wall near William's New Hampshire home, Chocorua. In the first plate James looks straight ahead and Royce, his head cocked sideways, is obviously engaged in one of his monologues. But the click of the Kodak alerted the pragmatist, who in the second shot is pointing to a giggling Royce. 'Royce, you're being photographed!' he apparently cried. 'Look out! I say *Damn the Absolute!*'

It was the emotional, almost one might say the *atmospheric*, quality of Idealism which James found distasteful. He did not want to live in what he called 'a through and through universe' with

its infallible impeccable all-pervasiveness. Its necessity, with no possibilities; its relations, with no subjects, make me feel as if I had entered into a contract with no reserved rights[,] or rather[,] as if I had to live in a large seaside boarding house with no private bed-room in which I might take refuge from the society of the place. I am distinctly aware, moreover, that the old quarrel of sinner and Pharisee has something to do with the matter. Certainly to my personal knowledge, all Hegelians are not prigs, but I somehow feel as if all prigs ought to end, if developed, by becoming Hegelians. There is a story of two clergymen asked by mistake to conduct the same funeral. One came first and had got no further than 'I am the resurrection and the life' when the other entered. '*I am the Resurrection and the Life*' cried the latter. The 'through and through' philosophy as it actually exists, reminds many of us of that clergyman. It seems too buttoned-up and white-chokered and clean-shaven a thing to speak for the vast slow-breathing Kosmos with its dread abysses and its unknown tides.[23]

Nevertheless, though this is good knockabout stuff, James was sufficiently interested in philosophy, and sufficiently honest, to admit that he could not easily find an answer to the central Idealist problem of epistemology. *Damn the Absolute!* was a good enough creed for working purposes, but he found in 1887, when he read Royce's book *The Religious Aspect of Philosophy*, not merely that he could not refute it, but that its argument dumbfounded him.

The second half is a new argument for monistic idealism, an argument based on the possibility of truth and error in knowledge, subtle in itself, and rather lengthily expounded, but seeming to me to be one of the few big original suggestions of recent philosophical writing. I have vainly tried to escape from it. I still suspect it of inconclusiveness, but I frankly confess that I am *unable* to overthrow it.[24]

Royce's argument is a rather simple one, and it is a variation of an argument in which Idealism in any of its forms has been advancing as a critique of scepticism or sensationalism or materialism, certainly since David Hume woke Kant from his dogmatic slumbers.

In his critique of pragmatism, Royce goes to what he calls 'the very heart of scepticism itself'. Let us, he says, assume a totally sceptical viewpoint. Let us assume that nothing is objectively true – all is at best relative, so that a proposition can never establish the truth, it can only state 'what seems true to me'. Then, says Royce, at the very heart of such scepticism there is an inherent contradiction, a logical contradiction, which makes it an untenable and incoherent viewpoint. That is, the relativist presupposes the possibility of stating at least one non-relativist viewpoint: namely, the generalization that everything is relative.

James's eventual answer to this argument of Royce's was to say that an idea *and* its object are both part of human experience; that the dichotomy apparently posed by the rationalist as against the materialist viewpoint isn't a necessary one.

We have already rehearsed why Bradley and other Absolute Idealists dissented from any such view, and how their use of arguments similar to Royce's led them to believe in an Absolute which could not possibly be identified with the God of the Judeo-Christian experience. Nevertheless, Royce himself saw this series of reasonings as the fundamental justification for religious belief. The materialist claims that 'mind', 'consciousness', arguments of all kinds, are merely the product of the particular physiological constitution of the human brain; but this very statement, if it asks assent, must be calling upon some criterion other than itself if it is to avoid the charge either of tautology or of self-contradiction. If our senses and our immediate experiences are the only tools we have for helping us arrive at the truth, by what criterion do they command us to accept the first half of this sentence?

Such an argument lies at the heart of A.J. Balfour's popular work of philosophy-cum-apologetics, *The Foundations of Belief*. If naturalism, as Balfour called the materialist view of things, were demonstrable, then, however distasteful it might be to the theist, it must be accepted. But since it is not logically demonstrable, then we are at liberty to follow our feelings. More than this, since we don't accept 'naturalist' premises we are entitled to regard thought itself as a super- or supra-natural act which in itself argues for a world of 'spirit'. So the justification for a religious viewpoint can proceed. Balfour's work of 1895 must have bolstered many who already possessed religious faith; one wonders how many atheists it has ever converted to theism? C.S. Lewis claimed to have been much influenced by Balfour, and certainly reproduced his arguments, in a somewhat cruder and robuster form, in his own works of apologetics, the unsatisfying *Mere Christianity* and the much more trenchant *Miracles* (1947). But when Lewis himself was teaching philosophy at Oxford he was a Bradleyan Idealist–atheist, a fact which suggests that he found Balfour's *Foundations of Belief* a useful cudgel in the war against the infidel only *after* he had, on the basis of various spiritual *experiences*, decided that he believed in, first a God, then God, then Christianity. Proceed towards a belief in a Deity along the rationalist lines proposed by Balfour and Lewis, however, and you are then presumably caught in the trap of having to say that all religious statements have to be demonstrable by modal logic; and that no contradictory statement about the Deity is admissible. You will find yourself back in the schoolroom asking how a God of Absolute Love can allow suffering if He is also Omnipotent. For most philosophers, and indeed for most non-philosophical inquirers prepared to use their brains in inquiries which might conceivably reach a conclusion, such lines of interest quickly peter out. Very few philosophers since the days of James and Royce have considered this a fertile field for their professional endeavours.

The pragmatism, however, of Peirce and James was destined to have a legacy in our century – not least, perhaps, because the 'scientific' notion of truth is one which has recommended itself widely and consistently to Western, twentieth-century brains. Most serious attempts to determine what is true are in practice worked out *ambulando*, on the hoof, by processes of trial and error, and not by formal logic. Scientific experiments proceed, usually, on the basis of positing an hypothesis and then subjecting it to as many tests as will satisfy the inquirer that the hypothesis is true: that is what 'true' means in most usages. For the logical positivists who learnt many of their attitudes to language, truth and logic from the pragmatic approach, this was to rule out the use of true–false criteria when discussing such areas of life as aesthetics or even ethics. But where did it leave theology and, more important, where did it leave God?

If you were A.J. Ayer, who wrote an excellent book on the pragmatism of Peirce and James, it did not leave God anywhere. Clearly, Ayer was slightly baffled by the fact that his two heroes both professed belief in God. In his essay 'A Neglected Argument for the Reality of God' (*Hibbert Journal*, 1908), Peirce claimed that any normal man who pursues the right course of reflection will come to act as if God is real; and 'to be deliberately and thoroughly prepared to shape one's conduct into conformity with a proposition is neither more nor less than the state of mind called Believing that proposition, however long the conscious classification of it under that head be postponed'.[25] A version of this approach did the rounds in England in the early to mid twentieth century; R.B. Braithwaite, for example, defined religious belief as the preparedness to behave *as if* such and such a thing were true. Archbishop William Temple also embraced this notion and said that when he recited the Creed, he mentally prefaced it with the clause 'I am prepared to live my life as if ...' How one's behaviour could be altered by, for example, believing that the Holy Ghost did, or did not, proceed from the Father and the Son, or proceeded from the Father alone, these learned and pious men either did not know, or chose not to tell us.

But James's approach to all this a little different. In his article on 'Common sense' in *The Oxford Companion to Philosophy*, Professor Coady of Melbourne says: 'in spite of the excitement of esoteric theory, philosophers have always hoped that their thinking had important connections with ordinary life ...' This is unquestionably the case. But what Professor James did – hence colleague Peirce's sleepless nights, perhaps – was to reverse this process; to barge into the philosopher's lecture-hall, as it were, with the direct concerns of everyday life. Hence the devastating contrast, in his lecture 'The Present Dilemma in Philosophy' (*Pragmatism*), between the idealists' airy defence of the Absolute and the wretched misery of the poor clerk drinking carbolic acid, quoted on page 7 *supra*. Peirce wanted pragmatism to do useful work, hence its name, analysing truth and meaning. James wanted this too, but he was also concerned to use it as a tool by which mortal men and women, whether or not they are philosophers, decide or discover what is important for them in their lives. The rough and ready, slangy Jamesian criterion was, what is the cash value of such and such a belief?

It is perfectly possible that we shall disagree with William James in his conclusions about these questions; but, when we have surveyed the sixty or so years between the time he first met Thomas Carlyle and the time that he gave the Gifford Lectures at Carlyle's old university in

1900–1901, we might find ourselves falling upon what he had to say with some gratitude. For instead of using the tired, clapped-out old weapons of philosophy to 'justify' religious belief, he used the fresh lens of experimental psychology to observe actual religious experience. And instead of using the harsh new scientific method (in itself as intolerant as the old theology) to tell men and women what they could or could not believe, he used every fibre of his intellectual energy to defend and justify freedom of the will and, in his phrase, 'the right to believe'.

This is why his greatest book is the one which unites his skills as a psychologist, his agility as a philosopher, and above all his human warmth: *The Varieties of Religious Experience* is a great classic. It forcefully rebuts simple-minded 'medical materialism', or sexual neurosis, or any other attempt to 'explain away' religious experience. Religion, he recognized, 'like love, like wrath, like hope, ambition, jealousy, like every other instinctive eagerness and impulse ... adds to life an enchantment which is not rationally or logically deducible from anything else'. And there follows, in as leisurely, wide-ranging and generous-spirited a series of lectures as can ever have been heard in Edinburgh, a rehearsal of human religious experiences. The cheerful paganism of Walt Whitman, the American optimism of Emerson or Mrs Baker Eddy (who persuaded herself that evil did not exist); the torments of the 'sick soul' finding consolations in conversion, as witnessed by Augustine, Luther, Tolstoy; the fascination of the divided self, such as Bunyan's; the very distinct qualities of the saintly, which have no counterpart in the secular sphere; the flights of the mystics; from Plotinus to the Upanishads, from Saint Ignatius Loyola to unknown or unheard-of men and women in his own day: William James lays out dozens, hundreds of examples of the power and, in human lives, the reality of the religious experience.

James's biographer and disciple Ralph Barton Perry (1876–1957) wittily attributes motives to his hero. He says that pity was such a predominant motive in James's heart that he could not help himself taking sides with the 'under-dog – with the Boers and the Irish against England, with the Filipinos against the United States, with religion or psychical research against science, with privates or laymen against officers, with the disreputable against the respectable, with heresy against orthodoxy, with youth against age, or with the new against the old'.[26] It is true that tender-heartedness sometimes made William James behave with near absurdity in life. In Cambridge, Massachusetts there was an Italian banana man on the corner of Oxford and Kirkland whom

James would pass on his way to and from classes. The man's beseeching brown eyes made it impossible for James to pass him without buying bananas, even though another banana salesman used to call at his house. 'You must eat lots of bananas,' said Mrs James to a student when asking him to dinner, 'because we have more bananas than we can use.'[27]

Are we suggesting that James embraced his defence of religion in the same spirit as that in which he bought the bananas, because he felt sorry for the hopeless purveyors of the cause? There is, I think, an element of truth here, crazy as it may seem. 'I admit the canalization of pity to be a difficult engineering problem,' he said once.[28] At the same time, he patently believed that 'although all the special manifestations of religion may have been absurd (I mean its creeds and theories), yet the life of it as a whole is mankind's most important function'.[29]

There is in fact quite a strange mixture of belligerence and what you could call Emersonian moonshine in James's religious philosophy, particularly towards the end of the Gifford Lectures (*The Varieties*) and in the increasingly frequent references to religion in his last decade of life. 'We must, I think, bid a definitive good-bye to dogmatic theology,' he told the Edinburgh audience.[30] And he described the God of such theology as 'an absolutely worthless invention of the scholarly mind'. These are fighting words when, in the very same lecture, he has listed the Catholic Church in general, Cardinal Newman, Thomas Aquinas and Leo XI in particular, as those who, together with some modern Hegelian philosophers, still felt there was life left in 'the metaphysical monster'.[31]

To a correspondent he candidly admitted, 'I have no living sense of commerce with a God.' Nevertheless, he added,

> there is *something in me* which *makes response* when I hear utterances from that quarter made by others. I recognize the deeper voice. Something tells me: – *'thither lies truth'* – and I am sure it is not old theistic prejudices of infancy. Those in my case were Christian, but I have grown so out of Christianity that entanglement therewith on the part of a mystical utterance has to be abstracted from and overcome, before I can listen. Call this, if you like, my mystical *germ*. It is a very common germ. It creates the rank and file of believers.

Is James's God anyone else's God? Did he successfully justify the ways of this God to the sceptics of the nineteenth century? Would his empirical approach to these matters need to take into account – as *The Varieties of Religious Experience* very decidedly does not – the fact that the great majority of those who get cash value from their use of the word God in fact entertain beliefs to which James said they must bid a definitive goodbye? The great Professor Richard Rorty says that 'many readers of "The Will to Believe" feel let down when they discover that the only sort of religion James has been discussing is something as wimpy as the belief that "perfection is eternal".' And, he adds, 'they have a point'.[32] To put it another way, you cannot imagine many people being prepared to go into an arena full of lions for the sake of William James's God.

There is, moreover, something pretty odd about James's God if you attempt to defend Him in the 'realist' terms of James's own discourse. For in order to make a coherent claim for God's existence, James maintained, you must accept that He must be completely limited in His sphere of operations. He might pervade, but you can see why young Henry James III thought He was a skunk. All this, though (if a William James maniac may allow himself one final word of defence), is slightly to miss the point. When James had asserted as a matter of empirical fact that people had religious experiences which did not fit into any neat, scientific–materialist package of the universe, his work was done. If we make him stay behind after the lecture and say what God is like, that is our fault, not his. He never claimed to have had a religious experience of a definitive kind. All he did was to assert the legitimacy of religious belief, and the validity of religious experience.

When we remember the uses to which scientific atheism has been put in the twentieth century, we can see the point of James's generous insistence that we live in a pluralistic universe.

The form of monism against which James did battle – Absolute Idealism – has vanished, leaving almost no trace or memory. In order to break down the monism which at that date dominated the philosophical faculties, James proposed a strange truce.[33] The absolutists should concede that *a priori* proofs for the existence of God be abandoned in favour of his own pragmatist view that people have experience of God. The empiricist, on these grounds alone, would abandon his sceptical prejudice. Such a God must be finite:[34] 'I have been told by Hindoos that the great obstacle to the spread of Christianity in their country is the puerility of our dogma of creation.'[35] Viewed purely as an attempt to justify belief in God, it may be that James's finite deity will raise a few gentle smiles. His 'something more', 'coterminous and continuous' with one's own consciousness, a 'transmarginal consciousness' which seems to touch our own at times of religious awareness, glows like the very low pilot-light on a boiler. It is not true, as A.J. Ayer asserts in his critique of James's position, that 'he glosses over the negative consequences of his approach. He hardly makes it clear that he strips his religious hypothesis of all pretension to give any sort of explanation of the world; it is a license for optimism which is in fact devoid of anything that would ordinarily be counted as religious support.'[36]

James does not want to use God or the religious hypothesis to give 'an explanation of the world'. He is perfectly happy for science to do its job, and he does not want God brought in as a lazy short-hand for what we either cannot, or cannot be bothered to, explain about the material universe. The 'something more' is something more. If you have never felt the need of it, or have no experience of what James is talking about, or if there is nothing in you, as there was in James, which *makes response* when such questions are aired, then they are of no more than historical interest.

James was trying to rescue, and assert the legitimacy of, an all-but-universal though infinitely varied set of human experiences. It is, he contended, these experiences which led to the growth of organized religions and theologies; not the other way about. To this degree his pluralism, his glad embrace of heterodoxy, his individualism, is anti-European; certainly anti- the various monisms which he could either see flourishing in European universities or scent in the European air.

'I shan't get seriously better until I can get back onto some American vegetation with an American tree over my head and an American squirrel chattering at me,'[37] he wrote after a collapse in health during one of the later lecture tours in Europe. His last trip to England was made in May 1910, when desperate fears for the health of his novelist brother Henry made him overlook his own weak heart. He only just made it back to New Hampshire that August. When he finally got to Chocorua, he sank into a chair by his own fireside and sobbed, 'it's so good to be home'. He died a week later.

15

Conclusion: The Modernist Experiment

'One has to pass through atheism to faith; the old God must be quite pulverised and forgotten before the new can reveal himself to us.'

George Tyrrell

Ego sum primus, et novissimus, et vivus, et fui mortuus . . .
Apocalypse i. 17, 18

T HE GOD OF the philosophers lay dead. Thomas Hardy followed his coffin, imagining a twilit scene for the Deity's interment.

> Still, how to bear such loss I deemed
> The insistent question for each animate mind,
> And gazing, to my growing sight there seemed
> A pale yet positive gleam low down behind,
>
> Whereof, to lift the general night,
> A certain few who stood aloof had said,
> 'See you upon the horizon that small light –
> Swelling somewhat?' Each mourner shook his head.
>
> And they composed a crowd of whom
> Some were right good, and many nigh the best ...
> Thus dazed and puzzled 'twixt the gleam and gloom
> Mechanically I followed with the rest.[1]

The poem is utterly uncompromising. There is no consolation here, as there is in Hardy's best-known anthology-piece 'The Oxen', in which he rehearses the old legend that cattle fall on their knees on Christmas Eve and hopes 'it might be so'. In 'God's Funeral', he has accepted that it is not so. To this extent, he speaks for his generation.

It is certainly true that the old proofs for God's existence looked pretty threadbare, even before Lyell and Darwin came along to deliver their body-blows to the Creationist idea, or before the biblical critics dissected the traditional manner of reading the sacred texts. Was 'hoping it might be so' quite enough? What sort of a God were they left with?

It is unremarkable that in cases of extreme pain, or grief, or wonder, men and women should seek, and find, consolation. Perhaps it is more remarkable that the intelligent human mind, knowing all it knows about the arguments against God's existence, should continue to practise religious observances; to be led, on some instinctual level, to punctuate the day with *allah akhbar*, with *O God make speed to save us*, with *Glory be to the Father*.

Those who do such things would wish to say that the 'cash value' consisted not so much in immediate rewards or solace as in a generalized feeling that 'religion was the deepest kind of life'. The phrase is Baron von Hügel's. And I am bound to say that compiling this study of those who tried to live without religion, or who chose to live within the limitations of a purely materialistic explanation for the problems of metaphysics, has not made me wish to revise the baron's viewpoint.

Von Hügel himself (1852–1925), the Catholic mystic and scholar, struggled with only partial success to fight against Immanentism – that is, the metaphysical 'easy way out' of this difficulty. The easy way out, the easy way to explain the paradox of why intelligent people still practise their religion and still, presumably, believe in God, is to say that they and the unbelievers see the same world, but religious people discern 'God' where sceptics see merely 'Nature' or our sense of The Good. Presumably it has always been and will always be the theologians' greatest challenge to find some 'realist' way out of this conundrum. Mysticism perhaps hints at what such a way would look like.

Whatever conclusion the metaphysician draws, however, religion goes on. And by that one does not mean that some people, against all reason, continue to insist on the validity or otherwise of the Ontological Proof. One means that they live a life in God. In a sense which it would be extremely hard for a metaphysician to find meaningful, they feel they know God, or almost know Him. You can try to get to grips with this phenomenon by point-scoring. (Coleridge's high-scoring point when discussing Genesis: '"*And man became a living soul.*" Materialism will never explain those last words.')[2] Any attempt to explain the differences between falling in love and lusting or between Mozart and Salieri in terms of materialism looks lame. But the truth is that you reach a stage, whether you are a believer or an unbeliever, when you are no longer making up your mind on a purely rational basis. It becomes a matter of life, and how individuals wish to lead it, and whether temperament or experience makes this 'deep' kind of life something which appeals to them.

There was just as much hard Marxist dialectic in the early life of the loyal Leninist Alexander Solzhenitsyn as there has been Russian Orthodox theology in the life of Solzhenitsyn, novelist and sage. The definitive moments in Solzhenitsyn's journey were not, however, intellectual points scored. One thinks of him, after he had been taken prisoner, rumbling eastwards in the crowded prison-train.

> At a quiet station called Torbeyevo, ... Solzhenitsyn caught sight of a small peasant woman in the usual shabby clothing: her slanting eyes indicated a Mordovian or Chuvash. Suddenly the prisoners, who were lying on the top bunks, 'sat up to attention: large tears were streaming from the woman's eyes. Having made out our silhouettes ... she lifted a small, work-calloused hand and blessed us with the sign of the cross, again and again. Her diminutive face was wet with tears.' As the train started to move again, she still went on making the sign of the cross, until she was lost to view.[3]

Is the life represented by this woman 'deeper', more impressive, truer to the nature of what as human beings we actually are, than the impassive materialism of Stalin's regime? Such questions can readily create responses in the heart which appear to be completely anti-intellectual. Solzhenitsyn's own journey, his embracing of 'peasant' religion, is something we have witnessed before in Russian history. Tolstoy tried it, until a combination of honesty and cussedness made him rebel. Dostoevsky famously did it, seeming to suggest, in his journalism at least, that there was a straight choice – the anarchy, followed by tyranny, of the materialist/socialist/terrorists; the stability and righteousness of the life of the devout.

This choice appeared, as the nineteenth century wore to its close, to be a necessary one. It seemed as if there were no good arguments left for religion. If, either for emotional reasons or because you believed in religion as a socially conservative cement, you wished to preserve the forms, you could only do so at the expense of the intellect.

Unless – that is to say – a way could be found which would reconcile the advancements of modern thought with the religious instincts of human kind. Faced with the apparent clash between Religion and Science, Philip Gosse (of *Father and Son* fame) decided that, since God's Word of Truth, the Bible, could not lie, it must be that scientific evidence was somehow, if not at fault, then a trick, placed on earth by God Himself to tease us. The conclusion from his false premiss was in its way perfectly logical, though it provoked merriment from the cynics.

337

The alternative was somehow to modify the apparent contradictions between faith and the intellect by the discovery of what in a happier age would have been called a 'reasonable religion'. In other words, how could one be a Christian without committing intellectual suicide?

The liberal Protestant way had its charms. It involved minimalism in doctrinal observance, vagueness in theological definition, and cloudiness of expression when anything so dangerous as a definition was required. Its difficulty was one of historical plausibility. The Jesus in whom Jowett or Matthew Arnold might have believed – or, if not that, to whom they would have made a polite obeisance – does not bear very much resemblance either to the Christ of Faith or to any plausible first-century rabbi who might have lived in Palestine during the Procuratorship of Pontius Pilate. The liberal Protestants were obliged to discard not merely the miraculous elements of the New Testament but also much of its urgent eschatology. If Jowett contented himself with the knowledge that a bust of Hegel 'looks quite a gentleman',[4] one sometimes wonders what he felt when confronted with representations of the Saviour in Balliol College Chapel.

The uplifting thoughts he has about the Fourth Gospel, like the sermons of his friend Dean Stanley, make one suspect that, for Jowett, Jesus might very well have been to Rugby and won a scholarship to Balliol. Such conclusions, though never of course forced upon Jowett's reader, nor Stanley's, do seem as whimsically far removed from the intransigently difficult stuff of scripture and tradition as the soppier devotions of Catholicism.

And the other trouble with the liberal Protestant approach, whether we conduct it in English or in German, is that it leaves the religious believer on his or her own; whereas, if this book has established anything, it is that religious experience is not merely individual, but collective. Certainly, historically, the religious experience of men, women and children west and north of Jerusalem for the last 1900 years has been, overwhelmingly, an experience of communities, of groups, of churches or The Church. How could the institutional churches maintain their intellectual integrity while remaining true to that faith once delivered to the saints?

There are many ways in which this question could be answered. But one of the most fascinating would be to contemplate that phase in the history of the Roman Catholic Church known as the Modernist crisis. It stretched from about 1890 to 1910. It cast up stories of intense painfulness, of great intellectual ambiguity and difficulty, and of some heroism – if, like a non-Modernist Jesuit, you believe that the 'mind, mind has mountains'. And it is of interest, too, since its concerns are not purely esoteric, and certainly not fixed in the past. It could be said that the Modernist crisis, and the way in which it was handled by the Papacy, affected the entire course of twentieth-century religious history, shaping and leaving its scars on all subsequent religious debates in the West.

The funeral in Hardy's poem, God's Funeral, was a fiction – dated 1908–10 in the *Collected Poems*. It was just in this period, on 21 July 1909 to be precise, that forty or so people gathered in a cottage garden in Storrington, a village in Sussex. Inside the small house there was a coffin, containing the mortal remains of a Jesuit priest – more properly one should say, former Jesuit priest, for he had been expelled from his Order – named George Tyrrell, famous in his day, though now largely forgotten outside the circle of those who interest themselves in the byways of ecclesiastical history. The small congregation of Tyrrell's friends and family was addressed by an equally famous and, on an academic level, considerably more distinguished priest, also a former Jesuit, Henri Bremond. 'Before we bear our friend's body from the home where he spent some of the last years of his life,' said Bremond, 'and where he died, I will say one word. Catholic burial has been refused him by our ecclesiastical Authorities, and we will make no comment on this decision, accepting it in silence, as he would have told us to do.'[5] They then walked in procession to the parish cemetery in total silence, where the Abbé Bremond spoke a magnificent panegyric. He spoke of Tyrrell's love for the Church – for the old parish churches of England, and for the Anglican Church into which he had been born, but also for the Catholic Church which he had joined as a young man and of which he was the most devout and enthusiastic priest. 'We know that for him, the Roman Catholic Church, as a fact, stood for the oldest and the widest body of corporate Christian experience, for the closest approximation, so far attained, to the still far distant ideal of a Catholic Church ...'[6]

How could it be that a man who had given his entire grown-up life – a short life, for he died aged forty-eight – to preaching Catholicism, giving retreats, hearing confessions, could have died, if not quite excommunicate, then so far beyond the pale that he had been expelled from the Jesuits and (though he received absolution and extreme unction on his death-bed) denied Catholic burial? What offence had he committed? Any Protestant or unbeliever witnessing the scene might have guessed that he had led a scandalous life, but his sins were not those of the flesh. He was persecuted – the word is not too strong – by the Catholic hierarchy for being what was called a Modernist.

The term is a confusing one. In art and literature, it refers to a particular set of aesthetic convictions which led, for example, to the poetry of Ezra Pound, the Picasso of *Les Demoiselles d'Avignon*, the architecture of Le Corbusier, the music of Stravinsky. The Catholic Modernists, confusingly, were the contemporaries of these Modernists in art. But they were not men and women who wanted Cubist-style vestments, atonal liturgical music or concrete-built churches. Rather, they sought to bring to an end the warfare which had been fought throughout the nineteenth century between God and Science, God and progressive political thinking, God and the Higher Criticism of the Bible. A wholly satisfactory definition of Catholic Modernism is yet to be found. In Shane Leslie's amusing novel *The Anglo-Catholic*, an ecclesiastical *roman à clef*, Tyrrell appears, ill-disguised, under the name of Father Birrell, ugly as a gargoyle, twitchy, satirical, 'crabbed and cantankerous'.[7] 'He was a mixture of Celtic mysticism and modern scepticism.' One character asks another, 'What is Modernism?', to receive the reply from his Catholic friend, 'Nobody can really explain, not even the Modernists, but it is probably a very old heresy dressed up afresh. Father Birrell has probably hit on something needing reform, but he should have kept it to himself. Intellectual reform is always needed, but woe to those who bring it to the Church.'[8] One of the Modernists – and Tyrrell's closest friend – Maude Petre, adds to our confusion by saying, 'Modernism – yes; Modernist – no! Modernism was a movement, and a movement is not a sect.'[9]

The truth is that different Modernists approached the problem – how to maintain religion without sacrifice of intellectual integrity, or, to put it another way, how to reconcile Modern knowledge with the Old faith – in different ways. Some were troubled by the insistence of the Church that the only way to do philosophy was to study the medieval scholastics. Even this was undertaken in a very narrow way. A clever young seminarian could study 'philosophy' and never read one line of Descartes, Kant or Hegel. Others were worried that the Church had not addressed itself, as the Church of England had begun to do, to the new biblical criticism. Others were concerned that by ignoring the troubling discoveries of geologists and biologists the Church placed a burden on the faithful, to choose between accepting what appeared to be scientific facts and abandoning their faith. But different Modernist writers had different emphases; and some who were called Modernists by the Church were not really Modernist; and some who attacked Modernists seem pretty Modernist to the eyes of hindsight.

Most of the big names in the movement were French – Blondel, Hébert, Bremond. The most famous was the Abbé Loisy – of whom more later. There were English Modernists, of whom the most dogged as well as the most famous were Father Tyrrell and his friend Miss Petre. There was also their friend the Baron von Hügel, a baron of the Holy Roman Empire; he was born in Florence of a Scotch mother and Austrian father but, because resident in Hampstead most of his life, he counts as an English Modernist. Here we shall concentrate largely on Loisy and Tyrrell, but one should realize that they were not lone individuals. Indeed, as Catholics they all mistrusted 'private judgement' in religious matters and were genuinely trying to change the mind of the Church as a whole, rather than merely asserting private heresies.

What impresses us about them today is not necessarily their solutions to the conundrum, but their passionate conviction that, without some such solution, human life on this planet could never again be so rich. To deprive human beings of religion was, for them, to cut off a vital resource, and the rigidity of mind displayed by both the materialist–atheists and the Vatican die-hard reactionaries threatened to do precisely this, in making most ordinary people believe that religion and modern life were not compatible.

The favoured approach of Hébert, Loisy and Bremond was the absolute opposite of what could be termed liberal Protestant, even though, when the Pope came to condemn them in *Lamentabili* (3 July 1907) and *Pascendi gregis*[10] (8 September 1907), Liberal Protestants and Agnostics was what they were called. The Liberal Protestant wanted to adapt the old religion and make it more in tune with the sensible, moderate-minded men and women of nineteenth-century Europe and America. The Catholic Modernist, by contrast, was much more likely to accept the whole tradition, from Virgin Birth to Judgement Day, but to understand it in a modern way. It is true that Tyrrell, for example, got into trouble precisely because he questioned the doctrine of hell – a very Liberal Protestant thing to do. But then, Tyrrell was only a convert, and in other respects he would have shared with the French Modernists the idea of theology as *symbol*. It is difficult to pin down how much, exactly, Modernists actually believed. Tyrrell himself, in August 1908, wrote to a friend describing a visit from Baron von Hügel and the Abbé Bremond:

> The Baron has just gone. Wonderful man! Nothing is true; but the sum total of nothings is sublime! Christ was not merely ignorant but a téte brulé [*sic*]; Mary was not merely not a virgin, but an unbeliever and a rather unnatural mother; the Eucharist was a Pauline invention – yet he makes his daily visit to the Blessed Sacrament and for all I know tells his beads devoutly. Bremond's French logic finds it all very perplexing.[11]

Yet the Modernists, Tyrrell and von Hügel no exception, often had a high Christology and a great devotion to the Christ of Faith, especially in the Eucharist. For them it did not matter if, in historical fact, the Eucharist and the Catholic Church were not established by Jesus of Nazareth but arose as a cult after His death. The Christian altar was still a place where (to use the phrase of a poet who was a Modernist in both senses of the word, T.S. Eliot) 'prayer had been valid'.[12] The Modernists revered St Thomas Aquinas's eucharistic hymns. The Abbé Hébert wrote a dialogue, *Plato and Darwin* (1893), in which Plato is made to say: 'Darwin, do you not realize how small an influence is exercised, in the present stage of our evolution, by pure ideas? Myths and allegories are necessary, not only to slaves and to the people, but to philosophers and men of science ...' At the end of the dialogue, Hébert imagines himself hearing High Mass in the Duomo at Pisa:

> I listened, and I heard these words –
>
> > Sub diversis speciebus,
> > Signis tantum et non rebus,
> > Latent res eximiae!*

> I started. It was a complete expression of my own thoughts. Appearances, signs, symbols, which veil the mysterious reality, but which nevertheless adapt us to it, so that it penetrates us and makes us live – is not this one of the essential elements of all faith and of all philosophy?[13]

---

* Wondrous things lie hidden under the different species, which are only signs and not realities.

Such must have been the creed, too, of the Abbé Loisy, who even when he had been expelled from the Church and had drifted into a form of mystic agnosticism could speak feelingly to the young Alec Vidler of 'Le Grand Mystère'.[14]

The full title of Alfred Loisy's *Mémoires* – 'Memoirs to serve as a history of the religious history of our times' – might be seen as self-important. That they fill three volumes, some 1,800 pages in total, might suggest egomania. The paradox is that the pages of these memoirs, prolix and detailed though they are, passionate and even vituperative as they become, are not conceited. 'What touches me most', wrote Loisy's friend, the Abbé Bremond, 'is to see how the ego does not engross your autobiographies, as it does engross, deplorably, in my view, Newman's *Apologia*.'[15] The reader finishes the *Mémoires* (and for all their prolixity they are *compulsive* reading, so finish them one does) feeling that the title is fully justified. While many a reader must have finished Newman's *Apologia* and felt 'I have read an account of how an evangelical youth became a High Church parson who became a Roman Catholic priest, but I can draw no general conclusions of a religious character from this story', the reader of Loisy feels quite differently; more, 'Here is a flawed, disappointed but passionately truthful man. His story does tell us something about the religious history of his times. It encapsulates the dilemma of the nineteenth century which affected Carlyle, Ruskin, Darwin, Hegel, Marx, Huxley, Newman – indeed, all thinking and, ultimately, all unthinking men and women in Europe!'

That dilemma may be simply expressed. The advance of knowledge – not of opinions or atheistic views but of actual knowledge – made apparently destructive assaults on the old religious certainties. What were honest men and women to do? Were they supposed to discard as valueless all the moral, aesthetic, intellectual, architectural traditions of Christendom, merely because Lyell had demonstrated that the Book of Genesis would make a poor geological textbook? You might think not. But, on the other hand, as George Eliot and Renan in their differing ways had discovered, the new scholarly approaches to the Bible left the old Biblical certainties in tatters. Could they in honesty continue to say that they believed in the infallible truth of Scripture, insist that it was the inspired word of God? If so, in what sense? Certainly it was now impossible to believe that the Pentateuch was the work of one pen, that of Moses, dictated by the Almighty, or that the Gospels represented the *obiter dicta* of the historical Christ.

Alfred Loisy (1857–1940), by very virtue of the fact that he was not, like Newman, a genius, makes a representative case-study which does indeed show the mind of the nineteenth century torn this way and that.

He came from farming stock in the Marne district. His parents were not especially religious, and his father was disappointed when the young Alfred chose to become a priest. The religion of those country districts is well described in the *Mémoires*, more like the Church of England in Hardy's youth than the sugary, sentimental piety of late nineteenth-century Ultramontanism. Here the shepherds brought the lambs to be blessed at the Midnight Mass on Christmas Eve and the liturgical and agricultural years seemed to move together in a natural cycle. Loisy was a brilliant boy, and in spite of his enjoyment of the life of a country priest he was urged to take his studies further and to learn the Semitic languages as well as Greek in order to explore the new biblical criticism. He did so, and was for many years a lecturer, ultimately a professor, at the Institut Catholique in Paris, teaching students the historical evolution of the biblical texts. He was an admirer of Renan and used to attend Renan's lectures at the (secular) Collège de France.

Loisy was not alone in the French Church in realizing the implications of the new ideas. But these Frenchmen had the advantage – or so it seemed to them – of being Catholics. Whereas the Protestant faith was built solely on the notion of Almighty God having inspired the words of Sacred Scripture, the Catholic Church was based on tradition. If the new teachings undermined the authority of the Bible, they gnawed at the very heart of Protestantism. But this, Loisy and his friends believed, was not necessarily the case for the Catholic. Suppose Moses did not write the book of Deutronomy. Suppose Jesus was no more than a highly charismatic first-century rabbi, who had no intention of founding the Catholic Church. Suppose the Eucharist, the Sacraments and the doctrine of the Trinity, together with the stories of the Resurrection and the Ascension, were all the collective invention of the Church, the people of God? Would that really undermine the Catholic religion? There were others, like his and Baron von Hügel's friend the Bishop of Fréjus, Mgr Mignot, who disagreed with Loisy that the biblical stories were mythological, but took the delicate view (for Mignot *was* a Modernist, in all but name) that while the narratives of the Bible were not historical, there were historical truths which *related* to them: even the story of Adam and Eve had, in this reading, a psychological if not an historical truth. It was still possible, if this was what you believed, to continue going to Mass, and to confession; to advance, indeed, in sanctity, and to undermine nothing, by admitting the truth of the biblical criticism.

So Loisy came to believe. His enemies in later life accused him of having been a crypto-atheist who, from at least 1886 onwards, merely pretended to believe in Catholicism, while secretly trying to destroy the faith of theological students by his seditious lectures. But what the story of the Modernist movement reveals is something much more interesting: a touching belief by a group of intelligent individuals (mainly but not all French) that this set of views of theirs really might become acceptable to the Catholic hierarchy at large, even to the Papacy.

The reason that Loisy's story might justly be called a book which 'serves as a religious history of his times' is that he was one of the first to smoke out the Vatican die-hards and force the Western Church to make a declaration about its position. Where would it stand? Would it, like the Church of England, state its adherence to the ancient creeds but tacitly allow, by appointing them to professorships and indeed bishoprics, the existence of those who understood those creeds with modern minds?

During the pontificate of Leo XIII (born 1810, Pope from 1873 to 1903) hopes flickered that some such view would come from the Holy See. One of Loisy's friends, Mgr Hulst, a liberal more than a Modernist, left an audience with Leo XIII under the distinct impression that the Holy Father intended to adopt just such a *via media*: that is, that none who held a belief in the modern ways of reading the Bible would be specifically condemned by the Holy See.[16] This wholly false optimism was shared by others, such as the Baron von Hügel, another of Loisy's friends. But rumours reached them that in fact the Pope was being guided by die-hard conservatives who were not in the least sympathetic to the view that such ideas should be allowed to float about in the same atmosphere as that of the old dogmas.

Loisy was summoned to explain himself to the Cardinal Archbishop of Paris, an old Breton Royalist, Archbishop Richard. The *Mémoires* paint an almost affectionate portrait of this prelate, whose manners were 'oily rather than sweet'.[17] Loisy was completely candid with the Archbishop about his views, and his hopes that the Church would be able to accept them. Shaking his head, the Cardinal lamented the fact that Loisy had been reading the Germans. 'I confess that I failed to persuade him', Loisy remarks, 'that my doubts sprang from reading, not the Germans, but the Bible itself.'[18]

Hulst, who had been so optimistic when he met the Pope, now realized that the Modernists were about to suffer a purge. He warned Loisy that he was hurling himself under a moving steam-engine: the monstrous and destructive machine, mowing down everything in its path, was the Encyclical *Providentissimus Deus* of November 1893.

Leo XIII is seen by history, if not as a liberal Pope, then at least as one who appreciated that the world had changed in the previous three decades. Unlike his predecessor, or his successor, he was anxious that the Church should not become completely isolated in a position of intellectual and political obscurantism. When one recognizes this, one can read *Providentissimus Deus* as an attempt to introduce to the Universal Church the fact of the discoveries which now made it possible to view the Bible in a new way. It recognizes the importance of archaeology and literary criticism. This is the Pope who allowed the Dominican scholar Joseph-Marie Lagrange to start the École Biblique in Jerusalem. But in the Roman Curia there was no one who had much inkling of what modern biblical scholarship was. Nearly all the cardinals resident in Rome were either diplomats, bureaucrats or, if they concerned themselves with the religious side of life, liturgiologists. The tiny proportion of them who were interested in theology will have been unreconstructed Thomists. The Modernists' notion that such as these could be introduced in one sweep to complicated ideas about biblical origins which the University of Oxford (say) had refused to contemplate for half a century was unrealistic. Of course, Leo XIII had to assert in *Providentissimus Deus* that the whole of Scripture was written at the dictation of the Holy Spirit – *Spiritu Sancto dictante*. For Loisy, this was tantamount to closing hermetically a door which could have been opened to the currents of new thought and philosophy.[19] By insisting that God wrote the Bible, the Pope was in effect saying that nothing in history or Nature discovered by the human mind could contradict the Bible. And since common sense shows that science and history do, on occasion, contradict the Bible, the Pope was in effect committing the Western Church to the same absurd mental contortions which had made Philip Gosse such a figure of ridicule to his son and his friends.

'Le pape, il ne vivra pas toujours,' von Hügel wrote optimistically in May 1894. As so often happens in Roman Catholic history, the liberals predicted that when the Pope died, he would be replaced by someone more sympathetic to their point of view; and the exact opposite happened. The delicate, aristocratic Leo XIII died in 1903 and the Conclave elected as his successor the Patriarch of Venice, Giuseppe Melchior Sarto, the first non-aristocrat to occupy the See of Peter since the Middle Ages. His background was so different from that of the Catholic intellectuals whom he subsequently undertook to persecute that his pontificate makes a most tragic story of failed understanding, on both sides. He had grown up as a very pious peasant, scandalized at the near-destruction of the Christian faith by the Modern Age – by the democratization and unification of Italy, by the march of science and the insidious idea of progress. In his first year as Bishop of Mantua (1885) he had managed to ordain only one man to the priesthood in his entire diocese.[20] He saw Catholicism as in danger of extinction; and he had what has been called 'a pessimistic not to say masochistic conception of the Church in the world: a Church not inured to triumphs but, as in the Bible, rejected, misunderstood, isolated and humiliated'.[21] A man of exemplary humility and piety, he used the most brutal tactics possible to expunge the heresy of Modernism from the Church. One of his first acts was to excommunicate a popular novelist of Modernist views; Antonio Fogazzaro's feeble book *Il Santo*, having been favoured with papal anathema, became an instant international best-seller and alerted middle-brow lending-library subscribers all over Europe to the existence of a heresy of which they had not even heard. Within a few months Sarto, Pius X, also banned Loisy – who was doomed to be exiled from the Church altogether.

A witch-hunt now began in the Roman Catholic Church which could have given valuable ideas, if they read about it in their youth, to many twentieth-century political monsters from Stalin to Joe McCarthy. Utterly harmless old ecclesiastics such as Archbishop Mercier of Malines were watched as if they were crypto-atheists. Parishioners were encouraged to report any suspicion of Modernism in their parish priests; priests likewise were encouraged to sneak on their superiors. Cardinal Schuster of Milan recalled of those days that 'An atmosphere of suspicion and disapproval had developed, such that it was forbidden to read even respectable newspapers in the seminary in Rome.' Cardinal Gasparri, as a Devil's Advocate in the canonization process for Pius X, wrote that 'Pope Pius X approved, blessed, and encouraged a secret espionage association outside and above the hierarchy, which spied on the members of the hierarchy itself, even on their Eminences the Cardinals ...'[22] Giorgio La Piana, later a professor at Harvard, recalled as a young priest travelling from his native Sicily to Rome by train. In the carriage he fell into chat with a stranger who began to expound his own personal sympathy with the Modernist movement. La Piana naïvely and enthusiastically agreed with the stranger. They parted on Rome station. La Piana went to his seminary, but he only lasted a few days in the Holy City before being sent back to his diocese. The travelling companion had been a Curia official. How much Stalin would have understood and approved this story.[23]

As far as the Pope was concerned, no methods were too dirty to use in expunging the Modernist disease – the *mal francese*, as he called it, with his coarse wit.* 'Kindness is for fools,' he once retorted when someone begged him to show pity for a Modernist. 'They want them to be treated with oil, soap, and caresses. But they should be beaten with fists,' said Pius X, the only twentieth-century pope, so far, to be canonized.

Very few had the courage to resist. Many Catholics during the years of the Modernist crisis would learn the truth of Loisy's idea that fear is a 'contagious disease'.[24] Many harmless and unmodernist attempts to advance, for instance, Catholics' knowledge of the Bible, were suppressed. Père Lagrange was recalled from Jerusalem and his Biblical School there simply went into abeyance for the duration of Pius X's pontificate. 'Can one ever justify oneself against suspicion?' he asked, before submitting, with loyal humility, to whatever formulae the Church authorities required of him.[25]

Given the brutality of the papal authorities, it is not surprising that one of the most noted English Roman Catholic Modernists, George Tyrrell, the convert from Anglicanism, should have exclaimed, 'Church of my baptism! why did I ever leave you?'[26] He was a Jesuit priest when he wrote those words, forty-five years old, destined to live only another three years before, rejected by his Order and expelled by his Church, he was buried in the corner of the parish cemetery at Storrington in Sussex.

Anglicans of a certain colouring like to repeat Tyrrell's words as if they were a purely rhetorical question. But much as he had loved the genial and intellectually honest traditions of the church in which he was baptized, even in the worst of his troubles Tyrrell remembered his strong motive for joining the Roman Catholic Church. He was a seeker

---

* That is, the French disease: Italian slang for VD.

after truth. He was brought up Church of Ireland (the Anglican Church of Ireland) and as a youth he was an evangelical, like Newman. He was converted to quite conservative Roman Catholic beliefs, but even in those days a prime attraction of the Church was its universality. The Church of England might be, as he said in that famous letter, one which contained 'better-than saints', such as the biblical scholars Westcott, Hort and Lightfoot and the genius of Coleridge; but it would always remain a province in the Church at large and not, as the Universal Church of Rome had been, a household which had contained European humanity, later the humanity of the world, and attempted to nourish its religious aspirations.

The Abbé Loisy at the age of twenty-nine[27] came to feel that the Church was a 'necessary institution'. You could not start such an institution from scratch. For all the falsity of some of its accretions of legend and mythology, it remained a powerhouse – the 'principal remedy for the ills of humanity'.[28] It did not seem to him as a young man too much to hope that this Church, with all its wealth of experience and traditions, would one day be prepared to join 'with prudence and discretion in the endeavour of all seekers after truth who exist in this world'.[29]

This was very much the view to which Tyrrell himself inclined. A large-minded man, it was this breadth and wealth of experience which had attracted him in the first place to the Catholic Church. It was not just a church, like that of his baptism, of a few local heroes, of Hort and Coleridge. It was, rather, the Church of the Apostles and Martyrs; of the catacombs, of the early Platonist theologians, and of St Augustine. It was the Church of the mystics, and of the religious orders. It was the Church of heroic martyrs in modern times. It was a great educating Church which had founded the medieval universities of Padua, Paris, Oxford. It had built the cathedrals and abbeys.

After the Modernists had been formally condemned in the Papal Encyclical *Pascendi dominici gregis* (3 July 1907) Tyrrell believed that the 'present domination' of die-hard bigots in the church was 'but a passing episode in the Church's history ... Mortal, fallible men like ourselves!' In his 'much abused letter' Tyrrell compared the position of Catholicism in the early twentieth century with that of Judaism in the first century AD. 'May not Catholicism, like Judaism, have to die in order that it may live again in a greater and grander form? Has not every organism got its limits of development, after which it must decay and be content to survive in its progeny?'[30]

Tyrrell none the less remained in his own eyes a loyal Catholic. Like other Modernists, he took over Newman's idea of the Development of Doctrine (which Newman had coined as a way of explaining to Anglicans how modern Catholicism, so visibly different from the life, practice and doctrine of the early Church, could be said to be a continuation of it) and made it an idea that the Church itself could evolve into a kind of universal religion of humanity.

But though such ideas might be incompatible with St Thomas Aquinas, indeed on examination turn out to be untenable ideas on any level, they certainly did not spring from a wish to undermine the Church. Tyrrell was a dabbler, intellectually, not a thorough-going philosopher. Adopting William James's idea of the 'cash value' of an idea, he tested theology by its 'prayer value'; most of his books are devotional sermons. When they began to suspect him of heresy, the Jesuits moved him from the fashionable pulpit of Farm Street in London to the humbler parish of Richmond in Yorkshire. But no ordinary layperson, of whatever social class, would have suspected that Father Tyrrell, SJ was anything other than the most conscientious priest, assiduous in pastoral care, good at sick visits, often in the confessional, fervent in prayer and devoted to the Blessed Sacrament. Nor was he – a point made by his friend Abbé Bremond in the funeral oration – an advocate of private judgement in religion. Hence his clinging to the Church so pathetically when it tried to shake itself free of him. 'He wanted a church, both from the sense of necessity of a social organisation of the Christian idea, and still more, perhaps, from his profound belief in, and his intense love for, the sacramental side of religion. No dogma was dearer to his heart than the dogma of the communion of Saints, of which I confidently repeated to his dying ears the sweet, short and simple formula, *Credo in communionem sanctorum.*'[31]

It could be argued that it was as much Father Tyrrell's temperament as it was the intractability of Catholic dogma which led to his collision with the Jesuits and with the Church. He was aware that some Church atmospheres 'develop the Voltaire in me',[32] and he found that some of the devotional literature he was given to read as a novice was 'drivel'.[33] He had a highly-developed sense of humour: not always an asset for those following the path of Christian perfection. His great friend Miss Petre observed that 'the sense of humour is a close ally of the fundamental sense of truth, and it was an unsuppressible element of his temperament. It played over the most serious events of his life, as irresistibly as over the lighter ones; it was with him in joy and in sorrow, in rest and in work; it flashed over his most strenuous efforts and flickered over his death bed ...' Of such humour Maude Petre added, 'God and His perfectly holy ones are without it; faulty man is less faulty when he possesses it. It is associated with the pathos of wrong-doing and short-coming, with the sad clear vision of those who gauge the puny efforts of man with the vast universe in which he moves.'[34]

He really got into trouble when he wrote a piece entitled 'A Perverted Devotion'. He does not actually venture here to say that there is no hell, or even that he disbelieves in it – though it is fairly clear, reading between the lines, that he does not. What he attacks is the 'perverted devotion' to the idea of hell which is to be found in certain forms of Christianity. There is little in the essay with which a late twentieth-century Christian, Catholic or Protestant, would be likely to take issue. But from the publication of this essay may be dated the long and sad divorce between Tyrrell and his Order. These were cruel times for the Modernist, and Tyrrell was by nature a fighter, a controversialist. These two facts led to inevitable rupture, and when the General of the Society of Jesus wrote to him asking for a public repudiation of his heresies, he naturally refused.

Shane Leslie was right to see in Tyrrell ('Father Birrell') a combination of the mystic and the modern sceptic. In all his controversies there was the danger of a gradual wearing-away of his inner convictions, his life of prayer. In April 1906 he wrote to a friend: 'I quite understand your desire for a life of prayer – the nostalgia for the old days "when His lamp shone about my head". God knows I feel it. But I think they will return for us all in some better form. I find the Breviary lives for me again after a long transition period of death. One has to pass through atheism to faith; the old God must be pulverised and forgotten before the new can reveal himself to us.'[35]

Tyrrell wrote two articles for *The Times* in the autumn of 1907, in which he set out his understanding of the Pope's condemnation of Modernism and tried to explain them to the lay readership of that newspaper. He saw the Vatican intransigence as an act of 'juridical violence' and maintained that what was most to be regretted was 'the loss of one of the Church's greatest opportunities of proving herself the saviour of the nations'.[36] His reward for this was to be told by the Roman Catholic Bishop of Southwark, in whose jurisdiction he was then living, that he could no longer say Mass or receive the sacraments: that he was in effect excommunicate.

For some readers the life and death of Father Tyrrell will be more than enough to persuade them that Thomas Aquinas was wrong when he wrote that faith and reason cannot be in conflict.[37] These pessimists will assert that faith and reason are doomed to conflict and that the nineteenth century demonstrates the triumph of science and history against superstition and mumbo-jumbo. For such as these, God had been buried by the time Pius X ascended the Apostolic throne.

Others, and they would have included some of the Pope's victims, or enemies, within and without the Catholic Church, could point to the extraordinary resilience of the religious idea. Lyell could show that God, if existent, could not possibly have brought the world into being, in all its present geological formations, in six days. Darwin could make the even more disturbing discovery that Hume was right, and there was no need to posit a notion of purpose behind Nature at all. The Higher Criticism of the Bible made a nonsense of fundamentalism. But human beings continued to pray, and to need to pray.

Pius X thought that the only way human beings could preserve their religion was by turning a blind eye to all these intellectual developments, to pretend they were not happening. He died in the utmost gloom, three weeks after the outbreak of the First World War, convinced that atheism, mayhem and nihilism would engulf the world, and he was, of course, absolutely right. He would have been surprised, probably, by the marked revival of Catholicism after the First World War and by the mass of converts, many of them, such as G.K. Chesterton or Evelyn Waugh, minds of great delicacy and genius. A decade after Tyrrell died, his beloved friend Maude Petre wrote to Loisy of her belief that 'we are moving to a new religion but I think that nothing dies and that Christianity will be a great, if not the greatest element in it ...'[38]

The fact that she came of one of the oldest English Catholic families, and that she had a robust temperament, gave Miss Petre the confidence to continue attending Mass, even when the Prior of Storrington did his best to tell her she was excommunicated. Doughty champion for the truth, she lived on until the Second World War.

It has to be said that, as a movement, Modernism was, at least on the surface, a cataclysmic failure. Even when it came to reform itself in the late 1960s, with the Second Vatican Council, the Roman Catholic Church remained rigidly loyal to a 'realist' picture of such doctrines as Christ's Resurrection or His Real Presence in the Eucharist. The Pope who promulgated the Encyclical *Pascendi* became a saint. For many years afterwards the existence of this document delighted both the religious die-hards and the atheist cynics who were, perhaps, united in the cynical knowledge that the more preposterous the mumbo-jumbo, the more hungrily would human beings queue up to swallow it. In the first year of Sarto's papacy the theatre-goers of London were enraptured by Barrie's *Peter Pan*. Night after night they tried to save the life of Tinkerbell by asserting their belief in the existence of fairies.

There is, however, another way of viewing the pronouncements of Pope Sarto. When the Abbé Bremond was installed in the French Academy he began his speech, 'J'ai vécu sous quatres pontifes: Pie IX, Léon XIII, Bénoit XV et Pie XI.' Evidently the eleven years of Pius X's pontificate had not, for this intelligent Catholic, been a 'life' at all.[39] From this point of view, Sarto's desire to make Catholicism and Knowledge into enemies was a disaster in the religious history of the century.

Catholic conservatives lacked the mystic faithfulness of Simone Weil when she wrote, in the 1930s, 'Christ likes us to prefer truth to him, because, before being Christ, he is truth. If one turns aside from him to go to the truth, one will not go far before falling into his arms.'[40]

Pius X would undoubtedly have united with Marx, Huxley, Herbert Spencer and Darwin in considering these words to be nonsense. Certainly the life of Weil and her spiritual struggle and exile in the middle of the twentieth century, so passionate, so intense, so odd, is not something the contemporaries of George Eliot would have been able to foresee, or to fathom.

If some of the friends we have made in this book – Lord Morley, or George Eliot herself, for example – could return to earth today, they would perhaps be surprised by the extent to which religion survives. While Christian pessimists of the late twentieth century see church membership diminishing, the nineteenth-century agnostics, if they could see our contemporary religious scene, might have a very different vision.

They might think that the Catholic Modernists had in some ways been proved right: religion, after all, just about survives. Though many of its most popular forms would seem to be precisely those 'fundamentalist' or 'unenlightened' versions of the faith which crushed Loisy and his friends, it is not really the case that old-style realism persists. Go a little deeper. Among the intelligent church-going population, how many Catholics really believe, as a matter of historical fact, that Jesus instituted the Mass? Or would stop going to church if they thought He hadn't? How many really believe in hell? The new religion predicted by Maude Petre has haphazardly come to pass. With ideas about private morality and about doctrine which would probably have scandalized Pius X, most church-goers today are in some respects Modernists.

It would be a bold philosopher in the late twentieth century who thought he could prove the existence of God, as Pius X taught you could – and should. Yet many conscious unbelievers feel shaken by Loisy's 'Le Grand Mystère'. Those who share the Abbé Hébert's idea that God Himself is *La dernière idole*[41] would still acknowledge that the God-idea, so important a part of human consciousness, has not been discarded with anything like the readiness which the late Victorians would have predicted. One of the most extraordinary things about the twentieth century has been the palpable and visible strength of the Christian thing, the Christian idea. Just as Nietzsche's generation were declaring the death of God and Thomas Hardy was witnessing His burial, religious thinkers as varied as Simone Weil, Dietrich Bonhoeffer, Nicholas Berdayev and Teilhard de Chardin were waiting in the wings. During the pontificate of John Paul II (no Modernist, he – but what would Pius X have made of his hob-nobbing with Buddhists, Sikhs and others in Assisi?) the immense strength of the Catholic idea played a demonstrable role in the collapse of the Soviet Communist system in Eastern Europe. In other parts of the world, the roles played in the spiritual war against racism by the Southern Baptist minister Martin Luther King and by the Church of England monk Father Trevor Huddleston showed that there was immense potency, not just in the Christian ethical ideal, but in their biblical sense of God coming to earth with His winnowing fork in His hand, ready to clear His threshing-floor.[42] These world-changing men and women decided to ignore the death of God in the nineteenth century. They spoke in the name of a God who was First and Last. They put their trust in One who said, 'I was dead, and see, I am alive for evermore.'[43]

Notes

Chapter 1: God's Funeral

1. 'God's Funeral', Hardy, *Collected Poems*, 307.
2. Exodus xx.3.
3. Lubbock, 259.
4. Hardy, *The Early Life*, 132.
5. Ibid., 76.
6. *Tess of the d'Urbervilles*.
7. Quoted in William James, *Pragmatism*, 20–21.
8. Ibid., 22.
9. Annan, 70.
10. Ibid., 39.
11. Ibid., 43.
12. Ibid., 44.
13. Marcel Hébert, quoted in Vidler, *Variety*, 67.
14. Dostoevsky, *Diary*, 542.
15. Goethe, quoted in Vidler, op. cit., 52.
16. Ridler, 46.

Chapter 2: Hume's Time-bomb

1. Ker, *Newman*, 206.
2. Coleridge, *Table Talk*, 263.
3. In *A Vindication*.
4. *Decline and Fall*, ii, 876–9 (ch. XLV).
5. Gibbon, *Autobiography*, 124.
6. Ibid., 51.
7. Gibbon, *Decline and Fall*, ii, 425 (ch. XXXVII).
8. Op. cit., i, 580 (ch. XVI).
9. Norman Kemp Smith's introduction to his edition of Hume's *Dialogues concerning Natural Religion* (Edinburgh, 1935) provides some telling arguments that Hume deliberately weighted his dialogue to favour the sceptical viewpoint; and see A.J. Ayer, *Hume*.

10. Hume, *Dialogues*, ed. Kemp Smith; the whole of Boswell's last interview with Hume is reproduced in this edition, 76–9; dated 3 March 1777 in Boswell's Journal.

11. Ibid., 38.

12. Quoted in Gay, *Enlightenment*, 498: the letter to the Revd Hugh Blunt and others, 6 April 1765.

13. Ibid., 406, 409.

14. Hume, op. cit., 21.

15. Gay, *Enlightenment*, 413.

16. Hume, op. cit., 186.

17. Ibid.

18. Ibid., 168.

19. Ibid., 146.

20. Tennyson, *In Memoriam*, lv.

21. Hume, op. cit.

22. Ibid., 4.

23. Ibid., 40.

24. Knickerbocker; Morley, *Recollections*; *Dictionary of National Biography* (1922–30), 616–24.

25. Morley, *On Compromise*, 137.

26. DeLaura, 507.

27. Gross, 106.

28. Morley, *On Compromise*, 73.

29. Wilde, *Letters*, 238.

30. Hume, *Dialogues*, 169.

31. Hume, *Natural History of Religion*, Works, iv, 315.

32. See Strawson, *Bounds of Sense*.

33. *Kant Selections*, ed. Greene, 372.

34. Ibid., lxxi.

35. Allen W. Wood, 'Rational theology, moral faith and religion', in *The Cambridge Companion to Kant*, 414.

36. Russell, *History*, 678.

37. *Kant Selections*, 373.

38. *Critique of Judgement*, quoted in *Kant Selections*, 492.

39. Ibid., 490.

Chapter 3: The Religion of Humanity

1. Bentham, *Church of Englandism*, 176.

2. Ibid., 203.

3. Mill, *Autobiography*, 19.

4. Ibid., 22.

5. Speech 'On Secular Education', 4 Nov. 1850: ibid., 210.

6. Speech 'On the Church', 1828: ibid., 208.
7. Ibid., 81.
8. Ibid., 83.
9. Mill, *Three Essays*, 256.
10. Mill, *Essays on Theism*, in *Collected Works*, 259.
11. Hegel, *Lectures on the Philosophy of World History*, 40.
12. Ibid., 147.
13. Hegel, 'On the Consummate Religion', in *Lectures on the Philosophy of Religion*, 64.
14. Ibid.
15. See Gould, *Auguste Comte*.
16. Quoted by Cockshut in his Introduction to Mill's *Autobiography*, viii.
17. Mill, *Autobiography*, 60.

Chapter 4: Carlyle

1. Emerson, *Journals*, x (1847–8), 179.
2. Ibid., 335.
3. Ibid., 543.
4. Ibid., 542.
5. Ibid., 553.
6. Quoted in Heffer, 1.
7. Carlyle, *Reminiscences*, ii (*Collected Works*), 178.
8. Froude, *Carlyle ... his Life in London*, i, 29.
9. Mill, *Autobiography*, 130.
10. Froude, op. cit., i, 17.
11. Ibid., 93.
12. Carlyle, *Critical and Miscellaneous Essays*, iv (*Collected Works*), 130.
13. Ibid.
14. Froude, *Carlyle ... the First Forty Years*, i, 48.
15. Ibid., i, 232.
16. Heffer, 42.
17. Froude, *Carlyle ... the First Forty Years*, i, 48.
18. Carlyle, *Reminiscences*, i (*Collected Works*), 15.
19. Ibid.
20. Ibid., i, 102.
21. Ibid., i, 118.
22. Ibid.
23. Quoted in Heffer, 88.
24. Hazlitt, *Spirit of the Age*, 206.
25. Ibid., 208.
26. Carlyle, *Sartor Resartus*, Chapter iv (*Collected Works*), 21.
27. Heffer, 118.

28. Carlyle, *Sartor Resartus*, Chapter vii, 116.
29. *DNB*, X, 490.
30. Flegg, 360–8.
31. Ibid., 39.
32. Carlyle, *Past and Present*, Book III (*Collected Works*), i.
33. Marx–Engels, *Werke*, i, 525ff.
34. Carlyle, *Past and Present*, Book III, vi.
35. Op. cit., Book II, ii.
36. Ibid.
37. Ibid., vii.
38. Carlyle, *Reminiscences*, i, 319.
39. Ibid.
40. Ibid.
41. *DNB*, XVIII, 1082.
42. Carlyle, *Life of Sterling* (*Collected Works*).
43. Ibid., 57.
44. Ibid., 62.
45. Ibid.
46. Ibid.
47. Ibid.
48. Quoted in Heffer, 275.
49. Carlyle, *Life of Sterling*, 145.
50. 'The State of German Literature', in Carlyle, *Critical and Miscellaneous Essays*, i (*Collected Works*), 49.
51. Ibid.
52. Op. cit., 72: 'On the State of German Literature'.
53. Carlyle, *Heroes and Hero-Worship* (*Collected Works*), 263.
54. Ibid.
55. Ibid.
56. Ibid., 297.
57. Ibid., 310.

Chapter 5: Not Angles but Engels

1. Carlyle, *Chartism*, Ch. 10 (*Collected Works*).
2. Inglis, 135.
3. Engels, *Condition of the Working Class . . .*, 62.
4. Inglis, 22.
5. Liddon, III, 32.
6. Inglis, 71.
7. Mayhew, I, 21.
8. Ibid.
9. Emerson.

10. Engels, op. cit.
11. Carew-Hunt, 51.
12. Marx and Engels, *Communist Manifesto*.
13. Ibid., 24.
14. Barzun, 125.
15. Berlin, *Sense of Reality*, 129.
16. McKown, 50.
17. Ibid.
18. The biography of Marx from which most of the details in this chapter are drawn is Robert Payne's.
19. Payne, Marx, 252.
20. Ibid., 323.
21. Berlin, *Marx*, 7.
22. Ibid., 195.
23. Ibid., 218.
24. Payne, *Marx*, 399.
25. Nietzsche, *Zarathustra*, prologue, section 3. I have emended Thomas Common's translation of *Übermensch* to 'Over-man' (from 'Superman').
26. Friedman, 170.
27. Hegel, ... *Philosophy of World History*, 37.
28. Ibid., 147.
29. Berlin, *Sense of Reality*, 134.
30. McKown, 105.
31. Tumarkin, 67.
32. Ibid.
33. Ibid., 80.
34. Ibid.
35. Ibid.
36. Ibid., 166.
37. Ibid.
38. Ibid., 198.
39. Ibid., 225.
40. Ibid., 259.

Chapter 6: Living in a Lumber-room

1. Dunn, 47.
2. Froude, *Nemesis of Faith*, 157.
3. J.H. Newman, *Apologia*.
4. Quoted in Dunn, 10.
5. Froude, op. cit., 157.
6. Dunn, 145–6.
7. Quoted in Dunn, 145.

8. *DNB*, xxii, 679–87.

9. Quoted ibid.

10. John Mander, *Our German Cousins* (John Murray, 1974), 55

11. Muirhead, 127.

12. Things improved in certain limited spheres (see Mander, op. cit., pp. 60ff.), most notably in Scotland, and among Carlyle's and Coleridge's London disciples.

13. Francis Newman, 167.

14. Hegel, ... *Philosophy of Religion*, iii, 323.

15. Scruton, *Short History*, 175.

16. Eliot, *Middlemarch*, Book ii, ch. xxi.

17. *New Revised Standard Version of the Bible*, New York, 1989, xxxv.

18. *DNB*, iv, 746ff.

19. Chadwick, *Victorian Church*, ii, 91.

20. Ibid., 96.

21. Ibid., 94.

22. J.H. Newman, *Apologia*, 221.

23. Ibid., 65.

24. Ibid., 137.

25. Ibid., 164.

26. The letter is dated 8 May, 1846.

27. Quoted in Ker, 138.

28. J.H. Newman, *Apologia*, 29.

29. Ibid., 186.

30. Ker, 637.

31. Pattison, *Memoirs*, 236.

32. Ibid., 210.

33. Stanley, i, 182.

34. Ibid., i, 304.

35. Quoted in Chorley, 74.

36. Ibid., 11.

37. J.H. Newman, *Apologia*, 54.

38. Chorley, 83.

39. *DNB*, iv, 584.

40. The biographical details about Jowett in this chapter are nearly all drawn from Geoffrey Faber's magnificent biography.

41. Jowett, 58.

42. McTaggart, *Studies*, 198.

43. Quoted in Geoffrey Thomas, 117.

44. Quinton, 320 and 312.

45. Mrs Humphry Ward, *Robert Elsmere*, 176.

46. Sparrow, *Mark Pattison and the Idea of a University*.

Chapter 7: George Eliot, The Word, and Lives of Jesus

1. Now in the Tate Gallery, London.
2. J. Guille Millais, 36.
3. Quoted in ibid., 37.
4. Ibid., 37.
5. Ibid., 37.
6. Ibid., 127.
7. Dickens, 34.
8. Ibid., 127.
9. Haight, *Eliot Biography*, 57.
10. Strauss, ii, 435–6.
11. Ashton, *Eliot Life*, 52.
12. Froude, *Short Studies*, iv, 286.
13. Duclaux, entry under 'Renan', *Encyclopedia Britannica* (1911).
14. Seeley, *Ecce Homo*, Introduction by J.A.T. Robinson, vii.
15. Renan, 165.
16. Ibid., 179.
17. Asseline, 4.
18. Ibid.
19. Renan, 115.
20. P.A.D.A., 170.
21. Anon, *Le Nouveau Crucifiement* . . .
22. Finlayson, 387.
23. Published by Robert Hardwicke, 192 Piccadilly, London (1864).
24. Christianos, 8.
25. Chadwick, *Victorian Church*, ii, 64.
26. Luke xix.5 (Authorized Version).
27. Seeley, 196.
28. Ibid., 8.
29. Chadwick, op. cit., 64.
30. Gladstone, 5.
31. Schweitzer, 396.
32. Ibid.
33. See Wilson, 1988.
34. Maude, 64.
35. Ibid., 60.
36. Ashton, *Eliot Life*, 125.
37. Feuerbach, 210.
38. Ibid., 268.
39. Quoted in Dollimore, 207.
40. Thesis 8, quoted in Dollimore, 213. See also Bottomore and Rubel, *Marx: Selected Writings*.
41. Thesis 6, in Bottomore and Rubel, 83.

42. Feuerbach, 98–9; Dollimore, 215.
43. Feuerbach, 91.
44. Haight, *Eliot Biography*, 39.
45. Ibid., 42. The account of George Eliot and Chapman which follows derives from Haight, op. cit., and from Ashton, *Eliot Life*.
46. Ashton, *Lewes Life*, 115; an excellent study.
47. Haight, op. cit., 84.
48. Gross, 75.
49. Haight, op. cit., 88; Gross, 68.
50. Haight, op. cit., 93.
51. Ibid.
52. Ibid., 116.
53. Ibid., 115.
54. *Spectator*, 11 June 1983.
55. Ashton, *Lewes Life*, 46.
56. Haight, op. cit., 490.
57. Locker-Lampson, 316.
58. Tennyson, ii, 394.
59. Haight, op. cit., 464.

Chapter 8: A Passion for Generalizing

1. Spencer, *Autobiography*, ii, 203.
2. Copleston, VIII, 121.
3. Spencer, *Autobiography*, i, 6.
4. William James, *Letters*, I, 254.
5. Perry (Abridged), 145.
6. William James, *Pragmatism*, 26.
7. Spencer, *Autobiography*, 173.
8. Tennyson, ii, 373.
9. *DNB*, XII, 320.
10. Haight, *Eliot Biography*, 118.
11. Ibid., 120.
12. Ibid., 121.
13. Webb, *Diary*, i, 7.
14. Ibid., 15 Dec. 1877; 8 Mar. 1878.
15. Ibid., 53.
16. Bede's *Ecclesiastical History*, II, xiii.
17. Quoted in Webb, op. cit., 9.
18. Spencer, *First Principles*, 73.
19. Passmore, 40.
20. Copleston, VIII, 122.
21. *Oxford Companion to Philosophy*, 844.

22. Spencer, *First Principles*, 119.
23. Ibid., 110.
24. Ibid., 127.
25. Ibid., 207.
26. Ibid., 243.
27. Ibid., 112.
28. Ibid., 287.
29. Ibid., 313.
30. Ibid., 315.
31. Ibid., 317.
32. Webb, *Diary*, i, 89.
33. Ibid., 172.
34. Ibid., 209.
35. Spencer, *Facts and Fragments*, 210–13.
36 Morley, *Recollections*, i, 114.
37. Ibid.
38. Ibid., 116.

Chapter 9: Science

1. Kuhn, *Structure of Scientific Revolutions*.
2. Hawking, 274.
3. Dawkins, *Blind Watchmaker*, W.W. Norton, New York (1986), ix.
4. Ibid., 165.
5. Crick, 88.
6. *In Memoriam*, liv; Tennyson, ii, 370.
7. Burgon, 210 for all these anecdotes.
8. *DNB*, XII, 966.
9. Russell, *History*, 740.
10. Lightman, 6.
11. Mansel, *Limits of Demonstrative Science*, 2.
12. Mansel, *Lecture on ... Kant*, 4.
13. Mansel, *Prolegomena Logica*, 72.
14. Mansel, *Limits of Religious Thought*, 45.
15. Ibid., 93.
16. Ibid., 18.
17. Burgon, 185.
18. Browne, 541.
19. Irvine, 85.
20. Ibid.
21. Ibid., 58.
22. Lyell, II, 131.
23. Stephen, i, 161.

24. *DNB*, iv, 24.
25. *Origin of Species*
26. Ibid., 441.
27. Dawkins, *Blind Watchmaker*, 6.
28. *DNB*, xii, 319.
29. Ibid., 968.
30. Moore, *Controversies*, 219.
31. Milton, *Paradise Lost*, vii, 452–9 and 470–4.
32. Willey, 40.
33. Ibid., 38.
34. Quoted in Moore, *Controversies*, 264.
35. Ibid., 260.
36. All the details which follow derive from Desmond, *Devil's Disciple*, 274ff.
37. Newsome, *Parting of Friends*, 306.
38. *DNB*, iv, 538.
39. Desmond, op. cit., 278.
40. Lightman, 136.
41. Ibid., 122.
42. Passmore, 322.
43. Ibid., 95.
44. Chadwick, *Victorian Church*, ii, 21.
45. Desmond, *Evolution's High Priest*, 54.
46. Huxley, 238–9.
47. Lightman, 137.
48. Gosse, 122.
49. Ibid., 107.
50. Ibid., 202.

Chapter 10: Swinburne and the Gods

1. *Swinburne Letters*, 25 Jan. 1904.
2. *Swinburne Letters*, 18 August 1862.
3. Swinburne, *Lesbia Brandon*, 47.
4. Gibson, 100.
5. Ibid., 308.
6. Ibid., 252.
7. Swinburne, *Whippingham Papers*, 62.
8. Ibid., 26.
9. Leith, 31.
10. Newsome, *Godliness*, 86.
11. Ibid., 87.
12. Ibid.
13. See Jenkyns, *The Victorians and Ancient Greece*.

14. Rooksby, *Poet's Life*, 179. The use and abuse of Christian imagery in Swinburne's poetry, and the multiplicity of biblical and liturgical echoes contained therein, is traced in Louis, *Swinburne and His Gods*.
15. *Swinburne Letters*, I, i.
16. Jowett, 53.
17. Ibid., 47.
18. Lafourcade, 85.
19. Quoted in Rooksby, *Poet's Life*, 102.
20. *Swinburne Letters*, VI, 237.
21. Ed. Robert E. Lougy, Ohio University Press, Athens (Ohio), 1982.
22. Wilton and Upstone, 196.
23. Dobree, 10.
24. Rooksby, *Poet's Life*, 117.
25. Waugh, 109.
26. Wilton and Upstone, 156.
27. *Swinburne Letters*, IV, 16.
28. See F.L. Cross, *Oxford Dictionary of the Christian Church*, 1427.
29. *Swinburne Letters*, II, 316.
30. Ibid., II, 312.
31. Friedman, 228.
32. Alan Sandage, quoted in Friedman, 243.
33. Friedman, 245.
34. Swinburne, *William Blake*, 206.
35. See Hughes in *The Nineteenth Century and After*, 237–41.
36. McTaggart, *Some Dogmas*, 3.
37. Darwin, *Origin*, 441.

Chapter 11: In the Name of the Father

1. Gosse, *Father and Son*, 289.
2. Ibid., 290.
3. Ibid., 304.
4. Ibid., 45–6.
5. Ibid., 118–20.
6. Compton-Burnett, *Daughters and Sons*, 272.
7. Compton-Burnett, *A Family and its Fortune*, 176.
8. Compton-Burnett, *Daughters and Sons*, 7.
9. Spurling, *Secrets*, 263.
10. Butler, *Notebooks*, 221.
11. Ibid., 231.
12. Butler, *The Way of All Flesh*, ch. xx.
13. Ibid., ch. v.
14. Ibid.

15. Butler, *Notebooks*, 79.
16. Jones, i, 29.
17. Ibid., i, 60.
18. Quoted in Raby, 58.
19. Ibid., 61.
20. Butler, *Notebooks*, 96.
21. Raby, 88.
22. Ibid., 93, 94 for quotations here and in preceding paragraph.
23. *Nineteenth Century*, Autumn 1878.
24. Yeats, 'Recollections of Samuel Butler', in *Essays*.
25. Quoted in Willey, 74.
26. Ibid., 80.
27. Ibid., 82.
28. Ibid., 106; the short quote preceding from a letter to Mrs Hatherley.
29. Raby, 142.
30. Ibid., 251.
31. Auden, 241.
32. Butler, *Notebooks*, 165.
33. Gay, *Freud: A Life*, 30–1.
34. Gay, *A Godless Jew*, 60.
35. Ibid., 153.
36. Ibid., 112.
37. Ibid., 37.
38. Ibid., 41.
39. Freud, *Civilization*, 199.
40. Gay, *A Godless Jew*, 133.
41. Compton-Burnett, *The Mighty and Their Fall*, 64.

Chapter 12: Two Prophets

1. For biographical details see Murray, *Matthew Arnold*.
2. Arnold, *Essays*, 15.
3. Ibid.
4. Arnold, *Literature and Dogma*, 145.
5. Ibid., 5.
6. Ibid., 15.
7. Ibid., 25.
8. Ibid., 48.
9. Ibid., 135.
10. Ibid., 137.
11. Ibid., 193.
12. Ibid., 127.
13. Ibid., 271.

14. Ibid., 290.
15. Ibid., 145.
16. Ibid., 113.
17. Ibid., 44.
18. Arnold, *The Poems*, 401.
19. Arnold, *Literature and Dogma*, 291.
20. Morley, *On Compromise*, 34.
21. Ibid., 42.
22. Quoted in Leon, 459.
23. Quoted in Evans, 174.
24. Ibid., 196.
25. Collingwood, *Ruskin's Philosophy*, 43.
26. Ruskin, *Praeterita*, opening words.
27. Ruskin, *Ethics of the Dust*, para. 120.
28. Quoted by Yarker in Ruskin, *Unto this Last*, 13.
29. Ruskin, *Ethics of the Dust*, 100.
30. Ibid., 118.
31. Ruskin, *Queen of the Air*, 3.
32. Ruskin, *Praeterita*, II, vi, 73.
33. Ruskin, *Modern Painters*, III, 178, quoted in Leon, 79.
34. The indelicate story of the annulment of Effie's marriage was told for the first time by Admiral Sir William James (not to be confused with the American philosopher) in *The Order of Release* (1947). James was the grandson of Effie and Millais and his account is biased in their favour; a more balanced version is given by Leon, op. cit. But the best biography is that by Joan Evans.
35. Evans, 267.
36. Ibid., 266.
37. Leon, 361.
38. Evans, 353.
39. Ibid., 403.
40. Ruskin, *Praeterita*, II, v, 119.
41. Ruskin, *Queen of the Air*, 1.
42. Ruskin, *Fors Clavigera*, Letter 76.
43. Quoted in Leon, 544, 501.
44. Ruskin, *Praeterita*, I, 181.
45. Evans, 412.
46. Leon, 442.
47. Collingwood, *Ruskin's Philosophy*, 20.
48. Ruskin, *Fors*, Letter 36.
49. Op. cit., Letter 35.
50. E.g. 'Tolstoy by thinking he was upholding the eternal principles of religion was in reality merely maintaining the old feudal order, the way of life of the oriental peoples', etc., etc: quoted in McKown, 107.

51. Payne, *Life and Death of Lenin*, 164.
52. Ibid., 165.

Chapter 13: The Most Inexpressible Calamity

1. Tolstoy, *Anna Karenina*, Part v, ch. ix (Aylmer Maude's translation).
2. Tolstoy, *A Confession*, i (Maude's translation).
3. Chesterton, *Autobiography*, 146.
4. Webb, *Diary*, i, 18.
5. Ibid., 19.
6. Ibid., 12.
7. Ibid., 38.
8. Muggeridge, *Green Stick*, 206.
9. Tsuzuki, 13.
10. Webb, *Diary*, loc. cit.
11. Payne, *Marx*, 501.
12. Ibid., 502.
13. Ibid., 503.
14. Holroyd, i, 154.
15. Arnstein, 176.
16. Ibid., 193.
17. Ibid., 198.
18. Ibid., 278.
19. Webb, *Diary*, i, 107.
20. Ibid., 110.
21. Hyde, *Lord Alfred Douglas*, 55.
22. Roberts, 93.
23. Arnstein, 264.
24. Holroyd, i, 154.
25. Taylor, 39.
26. Ibid., 45.
27. Ibid., 132.
28. Ibid., 223.
29. Ibid., 245.
30. Webb, *Diary*, ii, 322.
31. Chesterton, 27.

Chapter 14: William James

1. R.W.B. Lewis, 476.
2. Perry (Abridged), 269.
3. Perry, op. cit., 292.

4. Simon, xix.
5. Perry, op. cit., 225.
6. Emerson, *Journal*, 1848, Section 10.
7. Ibid., 22.
8. Ibid., 552.
9. Ibid.
10. Henry James senior: following information and quotations from Perry (Abridged), ch. 1.
11. William James, *Letters* (hereafter LWJ), I, 95.
12. Ibid., 64.
13. Ibid., 97.
14. Simon, 47.
15. LWJ, I, 85.
16. Ibid., 126.
17. Ibid., 118–19.
18. Ibid., 130.
19. Quoted in Knight, 70.
20. Knight, 33.
21. Bradley, 450.
22. LWJ, II, 269.
23. Quoted in Ayer, *Origins*, 187.
24. LWJ, I, 265.
25. Ayer, op. cit., 41.
26. Perry, op. cit., 232.
27. Simon, 211.
28. Perry, op. cit., 231.
29. LWJ, II, 127.
30. William James, *Varieties of Religious Experience*, 448.
31. Ibid., 447.
32. Putnam, 99.
33. William James, *A Pluralistic Universe*, 312.
34. Ibid., 125.
35. Ibid., 29.
36. Ayer, op. cit., 223.
37. Perry, op. cit., 256.

Chapter 15: Conclusion: The Modernist Experiment

1. Hardy, *Collected Poems*, 370.
2. Coleridge, 39.
3. D.M. Thomas, 188.
4. Quinton, 320.
5. Petre, *Autobiography ...*, II, 442.

6. Ibid., 444.
7. Leslie, 129.
8. Ibid., 125.
9. Petre, *Von Hügel and Tyrrell*, 9.
10. Reprinted in Reardon, 237–48.
11. Quoted in Vidler, *Variety*, 117.
12. T.S. Eliot, *Collected Poems* (Faber, 1966): *Little Gidding*, i.
13. Vidler, *Varieties*, 67.
14. Ibid., 10.
15. Ibid., 14.
16. Loisy, *Mémoires*, I, 260.
17. Ibid., 276.
18. Ibid., 444.
19. Ibid., 309.
20. Falconi, 10.
21. Ibid., 14.
22. Ibid., 54–5.
23. Ibid., 41.
24. Loisy, *Mémoires*, I, 268.
25. Lagrange: quoted in an undated and unsigned leaflet found in Our Lady of the Rosary and St Dominic Church, Southampton Road, London NW3, in June 1997.
26. Petre, *Autobiography*, II, 366.
27. Loisy, *Mémoires*, I, 151.
28. Ibid., 135.
29. Ibid., 152.
30. Quoted in Inge, 162.
31. Petre, *Autobiography*, II, 444.
32. Ibid., II, 5.
33. Op. cit., I, 223.
34. Op. cit., I, 10.
35. Ibid., 270.
36. Ibid., 337.
37. *Contra Gentiles*, i, 7, quoted in *Programme of Modernism*, published anonymously by Ernesto Buonaiuti, p. 27: see Reardon, 211ff.
38. Crews, 86.
39. Falconi, 37.
40. Weil, 36.
41. Vidler, *A Variety*, 73.
42. Luke iii.17.
43. Apocalypse i.18.

Bibliography

Under each title, the edition listed first is not necessarily the earliest, but rather that which has been consulted. The place of publication is London unless otherwise stated.

Alexander, Edward, *Matthew Arnold, John Ruskin and the Modern Temper,* Columbus: Ohio State University Press, 1973.

Allott, Kenneth, *Matthew Arnold,* Longmans, Green & Co., 1963 (published for the British Council in their Writers and their Work series, no. 60); New York: Longmans, Green & Co., 1955; New York: Viking Penguin, 1985.

Annan, Noel, *Leslie Stephen, The Godless Victorian,* Weidenfeld & Nicolson, 1984; New York: Random House, Inc., 1984; Chicago: Univ. of Chicago Press, 1986.

Anon, *Le Nouveau Crucifiement de N-S Jésus Christ par MM. Ernest Renan, J. Michelet etc.,* Paris: L. Hervé, 1866.

Anstey, F., *Vice Versa,* Smith, Edles & Co., 1882; Boston: W. H. Baker & Co., 1910; New York: Viking Penguin, 1985.

Arnold, Matthew, *Culture and Anarchy,* ed. J. Dover Wilson, Cambridge: Cambridge University Press, 1932; New York: E. Maynard & Co., 1889; Herndon, VA: Books International, Incorporated, 1996.

——. *Essays, Literary and Critical,* Dent, 1906; New York: E. P. Dutton & Co., Inc., 1933.

——. *Literature and Dogma,* Nelson, 1910; New York: The Macmillan Company, 1902; Folcroft, PA: Folcroft Library Editions, 1989.

——. *The Poems,* Oxford University Press, 1930.

Arnstein, Walter Leonard, *The Bradlaugh Case. Studies in Late Victorian Opinion and Politics,* Oxford University Press, 1965; Columbia: University of Missouri Press, 1983; 1984.

Ashton, Rosemary, *G.H. Lewes, A Life,* Oxford: Clarendon Press, 1991; New York: Oxford University Press, 1991.

——. *George Eliot, A Life,* Hamish Hamilton, 1996; New York: Oxford University Press, 1983; New York: Viking Penguin, 1998.

Asseline, Veen, *Preuves de l'existance de Dieu, suivies de quelques réflexions sur a Vie de Jésus de Renan,* Paris, 1864.

Auden, W.H., *The English Auden,* ed. Edward Mandelson, Faber, 1997; New York: Random House, 1977; Winchester, MA: Faber & Faber, Inc., 1988.

Augustine, Saint, *Confessions* (2 vols, Eng. transl. William Watts), Cambridge, MA: Harvard University Press, 1995.

Ayer, A.J., *Hume,* Oxford: Oxford University Press, 1980; New York: Hill and Wang, 1980.

——. *The Origins of Pragmatism,* Macmillan, 1968; San Francisco: Freeman, Cooper, 1968.

Balfour, Arthur James, *The Foundations of Belief,* London and New York: Longmans, Green & Co., 1895.

Barzun, Jacques, *Darwin, Marx, Wagner—Critique of a Heritage,* Secker and Warburg, 1942;

Boston: Little, Brown, and Company, 1941; Chicago: University of Chicago Press, 1981.

Battiscombe, Georgina, *Shaftesbury. A Biography of the Seventh Earl,* Constable, 1974; Boston: Houghton Mifflin, 1975.

Beard, John R., *A Manual of Christian Evidence, Containing as an Antidote to Current Materialistic Tendencies, Particularly as found in the Writings of Ernest Renan, An Outline of the Manifestations of God in the Bible, etc. etc.,* Simpkin, Marshall & Co., 1868.

Bede, the Venerable, *Venerabilis Baedae Opera Historica,* ed. Plummer, Oxford: Clarendon Press, 1975.

Beer, M., *Life and Teaching of Karl Marx,* Eng. transl. T.C. Partington and H.J. Stenning, London, 1934 (reprint).

Behe, Michael J., *Darwin's Black Box. The Biochemical Challenge to Evolution,* New York: The Free Press, 1996.

Benson, A.C., *The Diary of Arthur Christopher Benson,* arranged for publication by Percy Lubbock, Hutchinson, 1927; New York: Longmans, Green, and Co., 1926.

Bentham, Jeremy, *Church-of-Englandism and its Catechism examined,* Effingham Wilson, 1818.

——. *The Works of Jeremy Bentham,* ed. John Bowring, 11 vols, Edinburgh, 1838–43; New York: Russell & Russell, 1962; Herndon, VA: Books International, Incorporated, 1996.

Berlin, Isaiah, *Karl Marx,* Oxford University Press, 3rd ed., 1963; New York: Oxford University Press, 1978; New York: Oxford University Press, 1996.

——. *The Crooked Timber of Humanity,* John Murray, 1990; New York: Alfred A. Knopf Incorporated, 1991; Princeton: Princeton University Press, 1998.

——. *The Sense of Reality,* Chatto and Windus, 1996; New York: Farrar, Straus and Giroux, 1997, 1998.

Biswas, R.K., *Arthur Hugh Clough: Towards a Reconsideration,* Oxford: Clarendon Press, 1972.

Bixler, J.S., *Religion in the Philosophy of William James,* Boston: Boston Marshall Jones Company, 1926; New York: AMS Press, 1979.

Bottomore, T.B. & Rubel, M., eds, *Karl Marx: Selected Writings in Sociology and Social Philosophy,* Harmondsworth: Penguin, 1963; Englewood Cliffs, N.J.: Prentice-Hall, 1973.

Bowne, Borden Parker, *Kant and Spencer,* Boston: Houghton Mifflin, 1912; New York: Associated Faculty Press (no date).

Bradley, F.H., *Appearance and Reality. A Metaphysical Essay,* 2nd edn (revised), New York: Swan, Sonnenschein & Co., 1897; New York: Oxford University Press, 1969.

Broad, C.D., *Five Types of Ethical Theory,* Kegan Paul, 1944; Paterson, N.J.: Littlefield, Adams, 1959.

Browne, Janet, *Charles Darwin. Voyaging,* Princeton, NJ: Princeton University Press, 1995.

Brunhes, H.J., *Ruskin et la Bible,* Paris, 1901.

Buonaiuti, E. and others (Eng. transl. G. Tyrrell), *The Programme of Modernism,* Fisher Unwin, 1908; New York: G. P. Putnam's Sons, 1908—also contains an Eng. transl. of Pius X's Encyclical *Pascendi Gregis.*

Burgon, John William, *Lives of Twelve Good Men,* John Murray, 1889; New York: Scribner and Welford, 1891.

Butler, Samuel, *Erewhon* and *Erewhon Revisited* (Everyman Library), Dent, 1932; New York: The Modern Library, 1933; Lanham, MD: Biblio Distribution Centre, 1979.

——. *Selections from the Notebooks,* Cape, 1930; New York: Dutton, 1951; Murietta, CA: Classic Books, 1999.

——. *The Way of All Flesh,* A.C. Fifield, 1903; New York: E. P. Dutton & Company, 1913; Murietta, CA: Classic Books, 1999.

Cairns, John, *False Christs and the True,* Edinburgh: Edmonston & Douglas, 1864.

Cambridge Companion to Kant: see under Guyer.

Carew-Hunt, R.N., *The Theory and Practice of Communism,* Harmondsworth: Penguin, 1963; New York: Viking Penguin, 1963.

Carlyle, Thomas, *Collected Works: The Centenary Edition of the Works of Thomas Carlyle,* Chapman & Hall, 1896–1899, 30 vols.

Chadwick, Owen, *The Secularization of the European Mind in the Nineteenth Century,* Cambridge and New York; Cambridge University Press, 1975; New York: Cambridge University Press, 1990.

———. *The Victorian Church,* 2 vols, Adam & Charles Black, 1970; Lanham, MD: Barnes & Noble Books–Imports, 1971; Harrisburg, PA: Trinity Press International, 1979.

Chambers, Robert, *Vestiges of the Natural History of Creation,* 12th edn, G. Routledge & Sons, 1887; New York: W. H. Coyler, 1846; Chicago: University of Chicago Press, 1994.

Chesterton, G.K., *Autobiography,* Hutchinson & Co, 1936; Darby, PA: Arden Library, 1978.

Chorley, Katharine, *Arthur Hugh Clough. The Uncommitted Mind,* Oxford: Clarendon Press, 1962; New York: Oxford University Press, 1962.

Christianos (*sic,* send.), *Jesus The King of the Jews. A Letter to his Grace the Lord Archbishop of Canterbury Suggesting an English Life of Jesus,* Robert Hardwicke, 1864.

Clark, Ronald W., *Lenin. The Man behind the Mask,* Faber, 1988; New York: Harper & Row, 1988; San Bernardino, CA: Borgo Press, 1991.

Cockshut, A.O.J., *The Unbelievers,* Collins, 1964; New York: New York University Press, 1966.

Cohen, J., *Les Déicides,* Paris: Michel Lévy, 1864.

Coleridge, S.T., *The Table Talk and Omniana of Samuel Taylor Coleridge,* Oxford University Press, 1917.

Collingwood, R.G., *An Autobiography,* London & New York: Oxford University Press, 1939; New York: Penguin Books, 1944.

———. *Faith and Reason. Essays in the Philosophy of Religion.* Chicago: Quadrangle Books, 1968.

———. *Ruskin's Philosophy,* Chichester, Sussex: Quentin Nelson, 1971.

Compton-Burnett, I., *A Family and a Fortune,* Gollancz, 1939; New York: French, 1976; New York: Viking Penguin, 1983.

———. *Daughters and Sons,* Gollancz, 1937; North Pomfret, VT: Trafalgar Square, 1937.

———. *The Mighty and Their Fall,* Gollancz, 1961; New York: Simon & Schuster, 1962; North Pomfret, VT: Trafalgar Square, 1992.

Comte, Auguste, *The Positive Philosophy,* condensed by Harriet Martineau, 3 vols, W. Reeves, 1896; Chicago: Belford, Clarke & Co., 1880; New York: AMS Press, Incorporated (no date).

———. *The Positivist Calendar and Other Tables,* ed. Frederic Harrison, W. Reeves, 1894.

Cooney, Terry, *The Rise of the New York Intellectuals,* Madison: University of Wisconsin Press, 1986.

Copleston, Frederick, *A History of Philosophy, Vol. VI, Wolf to Kant,* Search Press, 1960; *Vol. VII, Fichte to Nietzsche,* 1963; *Vol. VIII, Bentham to Russell,* 1966; New York: State Mutual Book and Periodical Service, Limited, 1994.

Cotkin, George, *William James: Public Philosopher,* Baltimore: Johns Hopkins University Press, 1990; Champaign, IL: University of Illinois Press, 1994.

Crews, Clyde, F., *English Catholic Modernism. Maude Petre's Way of Faith,* Notre Dame, IN: University of Notre Dame Press, 1984; New York: State Mutual Book & Periodical Service, Limited, 1994.

Crick, Francis, *Life Itself,* New York: Simon & Schuster, 1981.

Crook, Paul, *Darwinism. War and History,* Cambridge: Cambridge University Press, 1994.

Cupitt, Don, 'Mansel, Maurice and The Kingdom of God', *Theology* 73, July, 1970, pp. 301–11.

Cupitt, Don, 'What was Mansel trying to do?' *Journal of Theological Studies,* 22 October 1971, pp. 544–47.

Darmestier, M.J., *Notice sur la vie et l'oeuvre de M. Renar. Extrait du Journal asiatique,* Paris, 1893.

Darwin, Charles, *On the Origin of Species by Means of Natural Selection, or the Preservation of Favoured Races in the Struggle for Life,* John Murray, 1859; New York: D. Appleton & Company, 1860; Cambridge, MA: Harvard University Press, 1964.

——. *The Descent of Man,* 2 vols. Reprint with introduction by J.T. Bonner and R.M. May, Princeton, NJ: Princeton University Press, 1981; Amherst, NY: Prometheus Books, 1998.

——. *The Expression of the Emotions in Man and Animals,* John Murray, 1872; Philadelphia: Richard West, 1873; Westport, CT: Greenwood Publishing Group, Incorporated, 1969.

Dawkins, Richard, *River out of Eden,* Weidenfeld & Nicolson, 1995; New York: HarperCollins Publishers, Incorporated, 1996.

——. *The Blind Watchmaker,* Longman, 1986; New York: W. W. Norton & Company, 1996.

De La Bedoyere, Michael, *The Life of the Baron von Hügel,* J.M. Dent, 1951; New York: Charles Scribner's Sons, 1951; Norwood, PA: Telegraph Books, 1982.

DeLaura, David, J. (ed.), *Victorian Prose. A Guide to Research,* New York: The Modern Language Association of America, 1973.

Desmond, Adrian (with James Moore), *Darwin,* Penguin (new edition), 1982; New York: Warner Books, 1991; New York: W. W. Norton & Company, Inc., 1994.

——. *Huxley, Evolution's High Priest,* Michael Joseph, 1997; Reading, MA: Addison-Wesley, 1997; Reading, MA: Perseus Books, 1999.

——. *Huxley, The Devil's Disciple,* Michael Joseph, 1994; New York: Viking Penguin, 1994.

——. *The Politics of Evolution: Morphology, Medicine and Reform in Radical London,* UCP, 1989, 1992.

Dickens, Charles, *The Life of our Lord,* Associated Newspapers, 1934; New York: Simon & Schuster, 1934; Auburn, CA: Media Bridge Technologies, 1991.

Dollimore, Jonathan, *Death, Desire and Loss in Western Culture,* Allen Lane, Penguin, 1998; New York: Routledge, 1998.

Dobree, Bonamy (ed.), *Swinburne. Poems,* Harmondsworth: Penguin, 1961; Baltimore: Penguin Books, 1961.

Dostoyevsky, F.M., *The Devils* (Eng. transl. David Magarshack), Harmondsworth: Penguin, 1971; Baltimore: Penguin Books, 1953; Evanston, IL: Northwestern University Press, 1999.

——. *The Diary of a Writer,* (Eng. transl. Boris Brasol), Haslemere: Ianmead, 1984; New York: Charles Scribner's Sons, 1949; Layton, VT: Gibbs Smith Publisher, 1985.

Duclaux, Agnes Mary Frances, 'Renan' entry in *Encyclopedia Britannica,* Cambridge: Cambridge University Press, 1911.

Dunn, Waldo Hilary, *James Anthony Froude. A Biography,* Oxford: Clarendon Press, 1961.

Edel, Leon, *Henry James: The Untried Years,* Rupert Hart-Davis, 1953; New York: Avon Books, 1978.

——. *Henry James: The Conquest of London,* Rupert Hart-Davis, 1959; Philadelphia: Lippincott, 1962; New York: Avon Books, 1976.

——. *The Treacherous Years,* Rupert Hart-Davis, 1968; New York: Avon Books, 1976.

——. *Henry James: The Middle Years,* Rupert Hart-Davis, 1963; Philadelphia: Lippincott, 1962; Temecula: Reprint Services Corporation, 1992.

——. *The Master,* Rupert Hart-Davis, 1972; New York: Avon Books, 1978.

Eliade, Mircea (editor-in-chief), *The Encyclopedia of Religion,* New York: Macmillan Publishing Company, 1987, 1995.

Eliot, George, *Middlemarch,* Oxford: Oxford University Press, 1967; New York: Harper & Brothers, 1872; Murietta, CA: Classic Books, 1999.

Emerson, Ralph Waldo, *The Journals and Miscellaneous Notebooks,* ed. Merton M. Sealts, Jr, Cambridge, MA: The Belknap Press, Harvard University Press, 1973, 1982.

Engels, Friedrich, *The Condition of the Working Class in England,* Oxford: Blackwell, 1958; Stanford, CA: Stanford University Press, 1968; New York: Oxford University Press, 1999.

Evans, Joan, *John Ruskin,* Jonathan Cape, 1954; New York: Oxford University Press, 1954; Brooklyn, NY: M.S.G. House, 1970.

Faber, Geoffrey, *Jowett: A Portrait with Background,* Faber & Faber, 1957.

Fabro, Cornelio, *God in Exile. Modern Atheism from its Roots in the Cartesian Cogito to the Present Day,* Eng. transl. Arthur Gibson, Neuman Press, Westminster, MD, 1968; Mahwah, NJ: Paulist Press, 1968.

Falconi, Carlo, *The Popes in the Twentieth Century,* Eng. transl. Weidenfeld & Nicolson, 1967; Boston: Little, Brown, 1968.

Feuerbach, Ludwig, *The Essence of Christianity* (Eng. transl. Marian Evans), John Chapman, 1854; New York: C. Blanchard, 1855; Amherst, NY: Prometheus Books, 1989.

Finlayson, Geoffrey B.A.M., *The Seventh Earl of Shaftesbury,* Eyre Methuen 1981.

Fisher, George, *Essays in the Supernatural Origin of Christianity with Special Reference to the Theories of Renan, Strauss and the Tübingen School,* New York: Charles Scribner & Co., 1866.

Flegg, Columba Graham, *Gathered under Apostles. A Study of the Catholic Apostolic Church,* Oxford: Clarendon Press, 1992; New York: Oxford University Press, 1992.

Freud, Sigmund, *Civilization, Society and Religion,* Harmondsworth: Penguin, 1991.

——. *Introductory Lectures on Psychoanalysis,* Eng. transl. Joan Riviere, George Allen & Unwin, 1949; New York: W. W. Norton & Company, 1965; New York: Liveright Publishing Corporation, 1989.

Friedman, Richard Elliott, *The Disappearance of God,* Boston, New York: Little, Brown, 1995; New York: William Morrow & Company, (date not set).

Froude, J.A., *On Great Subjects,* Longmans, Green & Co., 1894.

——. *Short Studies on Great Subjects,* Longmans, Green & Co., 1894; New York: Charles Scribner & Company, 1868; Ithaca, NY: Cornell University Press, 1967.

——. *The Nemesis of Faith,* 2nd edn, John Chapman, 1849; New York: D. M. Bennett, 1879; Leonia, NJ: Paul & Company Publishers Consortium, Inc., 1991.

——. *Thomas Carlyle, A History of the First Forty Years of his Life, 1795–1835,* Longmans, Green & Co., 1882; New York: G. Munro, 1882; Philadelphia: Richard West, 1973.

——. *Thomas Carlyle, A History of his life in London, 1834–1881,* Longmans, Green & Co., 1885; Philadelphia: Richard West, 1884; Temecula, CA: Reprint Services Co., 1992.

Garrard, L.A., 'The Historical Jesus', The Essex Hall Lecture 1956, The Lindsey Press, 1956.

Gauchet, Marcel, *The Disenchantment of the World. A Political History of Religion,* Eng. transl. Princeton, NJ: Princeton University Press, 1997.

Gay, Peter, *A Godless Jew: Freud, Atheism and the Making of Psychoanalysis,* Yale University Press, New Haven, 1987, 1989.

——. *Freud. A Life for Our Time,* W. W. Norton, New York, 1988, 1998.

——. *The Enlightenment: An Interpretation,* Weidenfeld & Nicolson, 1967; New York: W. W. Norton & Company, 1977, 1996.

Gibbon, Edward, *A Vindication of some Passages in the Fifteenth and Sixteenth Chapters of the History of the Decline and Fall of the Roman Empire,* with a preface by H.R. Tevor-Roper, Oxford University Press, 1961.

——. *Autobiography* (edited Lord Shelfield), Oxford University Press, 1954; New York: Meridian Books, 1961; New York: Routledge, 1970.

——. *The History of the Decline and Fall of the Roman Empire,* 3 vols, ed. David Womersley, Harmondsworth: Allen Lane, 1994: New York: P. N. Nicklin and Isaac Riley, 1816; New York: Routledge, 1997.

——. *Memoirs of My Life and Writing,* Everyman, 1948; Boston: Ginn & Comapny, 1898; New York: Columbia University Press, 1998.

Gibson, Ian, *The English Vice. Beating, Sex and Shame in Victorian England and After,* Duckworth, 1978; Lanham, MD: Biblio Distribution Centre, 1978.

Gladstone, W.E., *'Ecce Homo'* (Review reprinted from *Good Works*) Strahan & Co., 1868.

Gore, Charles, Introduction to the Everyman edition of Renan's *Life of Jesus,* Dent, 1927; New York: E. P. Dutton & Company, Inc., 1934; Amherst, NY: Prometheus Books, 1991.

Gosse, Edmund, *Father and Son. A Study of Two Temperaments,* popular edn, Heinemann, 1925; New York: Oxford University Press, 1934; Temecula, CA: Reprint Services Corporation, 1992.

Gould, F.J., *Auguste Comte,* Watts & Co., 1920.

Grant Duff, *Ernest Renan, in Memoriam,* 1893; Philadelphia: Richard West, 1893; Darby, PA: Darby Books, 1981.

Green, T.H., Works of Thomas Hill Green, ed. R.L. Nettleship, London and New York: Longmans Green & Co., 1888 (Volume III, *Miscellaneous and Memoirs*); New York: AMS Press, 1973.

Gross, John, *The Rise and Fall of the Man of Letters,* Weidenfeld & Nicolson, 1969; New York: Macmillan Company, 1969; Chicago: Ivan R. Dee Publisher, 1992.

Guyer, Paul (ed.), *The Cambridge Companion to Kant,* Cambridge: Cambridge University Press, 1992.

Haight, Gordon S., 'The Carlyles and the Leweses', *Carlyle and His Contemporaries: Essays in Honor of Charles Richard Sanders,* ed. John Clubbe, Durham, NC: Duke University Press, 1976.

——. *George Eliot and John Chapman,* Oxford University Press, 1969; New Haven: Yale University Press, 1940; North Haven, CT: Shoestring Press, Inc., 1969.

——. *George Eliot, A Biography,* Oxford: Clarendon Press, 1968; New York: Oxford University Press, 1968; New York: Viking Penguin, 1985.

Hardy (Mrs Thomas) (in reality, Hardy himself), *The Early Life,* Macmillan, 1928; *The Later Years,* Macmillan, 1930.

Hardy, Thomas, *Jude the Obscure,* Macmillan, 1896; New York: Harper & brothers, 1895; New York: W. W. Norton & Company, 1999.

——. *Tess of the Durbervilles,* Macmillan, 1891; New York: Harper & Brothers, 1892; New York: W. W. Norton & Company, 1965, 1979, 1991; New York: Viking Penguin, 1999.

——. *The Collected Poems of Thomas Hardy,* Macmillan, 1974; New York: Macmillan, 1926.

Hasler, August Bernhard, *How the Pope Became Infallible,* Eng. transl. New York: Doubleday & Company Inc., 1981.

Hawking, Stephen, *A Brief History of Time,* New York: Bantam Books, 1988, 1998.

Hazlitt, William, *The Spirit of the Age,* Everyman Library, Dent, 1967; New York: G. Bell, 1894; Herndon, VA: Cassell Academic, 1989.

Heaney, John J., *The Modernist Crisis,* Geoffrey Chapman, 1969; Washington: Corpus Books, 1968.

Heffer, Simon, *Moral Desperado. A Life of Thomas Carlyle,* Weidenfeld & Nicolson, 1995; North Pomfret, VT: Trafalgar Square, 1996.

Hegel, Georg Wilhelm Friedrich, *Lectures on the Philosophy of Religion,* ed. P. Hodgson, Berkeley: University of California Press, 1984, 1995.

——. *Lectures on the Philosophy of World History* (Eng. transl. H.B. Nisbet), London and New York: Cambridge University Press, Cambridge, 1975, 1981.

Henry, John and Parker, James, eds, *A Lecture on the Philosophy of Kant* by Henry Mansel, Oxford, 1986.

Hilton, Tim, *John Ruskin, The Early Years, 1819–1859,* New Haven: Yale University Press, 1985; Ann Arbor, MI: Books on Demand, 1985.

Holroyd, Michael, *Bernard Shaw. The Search for Love,* Vol. One, Chatto & Windus, 1988; New York: Random House, 1988, 1998.

Honderich, Ted (ed.), *The Oxford Companion to Philosophy,* Oxford: Oxford University Press, 1995.

Hooper, F.J. Bodfield, *Supernatural Religion versus 'Natural Religion'. A Fragment from 'Modern Thought',* To be had only of the author, 1884.

Horgan, John, *The End of Science. Facing the Limits of Knowledge in the Twilight of a Scientific Age,*

Little, Brown, 1997; Reading, MA: Addison-Wesley Publishers, 1996; New York: Broadway Books, 1997.

Hughes, Randolph, 'Algernon Charles Swinburne. A Centenary Survey', *The Nineteenth Century and After,* Volume XXIII, August 1937.

Hume, David, *Dialogues Concerning Natural Religion,* ed. Norman Kemp Smith, Nelson, 1935; New York: T. Nelson, 1997; New York: Routledge, 1991.

——. *Enquiries Concerning the Human Understanding and Concerning the Principles of Morals,* ed. L.A. Selby-Bigge, Oxford: Clarendon Press, 1966; Westport, CT: Greenwood Press, 1980.

——. *Natural History of Religion,* ed. Wayne Gower, Clarendon Press, Oxford, 1976.

Hunt, John Dixon, *The Wider Sea. A Life of John Ruskin,* J.M. Dent & Sons Ltd, 1982; New York: Viking, 1982.

Hutton, R.H., *Essays on Some of the Modern Guides of English Thought in Matters of Faith,* Longmans and Green, 1887; New York: Macmillan, 1887; North Stratford, NH: Ayer Company Publishers, Inc., 1977.

Huxley, T.H., *Science and Christian Tradition,* Macmillan, 1909; New York: D. Appleton, 1894; Philadelphia: Century Bookbindery, 1981.

Hyde, H. Montgomery, *Henry James at Home,* Methuen, 1969; New York: Farrar, Straus & Giroux, 1969.

——. *Lord Alfred Douglas,* Methuen, 1984; New York: Dodd, Mead, 1985; Northbrook, IL: W. Clement Stone, PMA Communications, Inc., 1985.

Inge, William Ralph, *Outspoken Essays* (First Series), Longmans, Green & Co., 1927; New York: Longmans, Green, and Co., 1921; North Stratford, NH: Ayer Company Publishers, Inc., 1977.

Inglis, K.S., *Churches and the Working Classes in Victorian England,* Routledge & Kegan Paul, 1963.

Ironside, Robin, *Pre-Raphaelite Painters,* Phaidon Press, 1948; New York: Oxford University Press, 1948.

Irvine, William, *Apes, Angels and Victorians,* Weidenfeld & Nicolson, 1956; New York: McGraw-Hill, 1955; Lanham, MD: University Press of America, 1983.

James, Henry, *Letters,* 4 vols, Cambridge, MA: Harvard University Press, 1974–84, ed. Leon Edel; Temecula, CA: Reprint Services Corporation, 1992.

——. *Notes of a Son and a Brother,* Macmillan, 1914; New York: Charles Scribner's Sons, 1914; Temecula, CA: Reprint Services Corporation, 1992.

——. *The Princess Casamassima,* Penguin, New York, 1977; New York: Macmillan, 1886; Temecula, CA: Reprint Services Corporation, 1992.

James, William (Admiral Sir William James, GCB), *The Order of Release, The Story of John Ruskin, Effie Gray and John Everett Millais,* John Murray, 1947; Philadelphia: Richard West, 1973.

James, William, *A Pluralistic Universe,* Cambridge, MA: Harvard University Press, 1977; New York: Longmans, Green, and Co., 1909; Lincoln, NE: University of Nebraska Press, 1996.

——. *Essays, Comments and Reviews,* Cambridge, MA: Harvard University Press, 1987.

——. *Essays in Radical Empiricism,* Cambridge, MA: Harvard University Press, 1976; New York: Longmans, Green, and Co., 1912; Lincoln, NE: University of Nebraska Press, 1996.

——. *Memories and Studies,* London and New York: Longmans and Green, 1911; Temecula, CA: Reprint Services Corporation, 1992.

——. *Pragmatism* and *The Meaning of Truth,* bound together, with introduction by A.J. Ayer, Cambridge, MA: Harvard University Press, 1975.

——. *Talks to Teachers,* New York: W. W. Norton, 1958; New York: Henry Holt, 1899; Temecula, CA: Reprint Services Corporation, 1992.

——. *The Will to Believe,* Harvard University Press, Cambridge, MA, 1979; New York: Dover Publications, 1960; Temecula, CA: Reprint Services Corporation, 1992.

——. *The Varieties of Religious Experience,* New York: Penguin, 1982; New York: Longmans, Green, and Co., 1902; New York: Simon & Schuster, 1997.

——. *The Letters,* ed. Henry James III, 2 vols, Boston: Atlantic Monthly Press, 1920; Temecula, CA: Reprint Services Corporation, 1992.

——. *The Principles of Psychology,* Cambridge, MA: Harvard University Press, 1983; New York: Henry Holt and Co., 1890; Temecula, CA: Reprint Services Corporation, 1992.

Jenkyns, Richard, *The Victorians and Ancient Greece,* Oxford: Blackwell, 1980; Cambridge, MA: Harvard University Press, 1980, 1990.

Jones, Henry Festing, *Samuel Butler, Author of 'Erewhon' (1835–1902). A Memoir,* 2 vols, Macmillan, 1919; New York: Octagon Books, 1968; Temecula, CA: Reprint Services Corporation, 1992.

Jowett, Benjamin, *Scripture and Truth,* Henry Frowde, 1907.

Kant, Immanuel, *Critique of Judgment: Including the First Introduction,* Eng. transl. Werner S. Pluhar, New York: The Free Press, 1970; Indianapolis: Hackett, 1987.

——. *Critique of Pure Reason,* Eng. transl. Norman Kemp Smith, 2nd ed, Macmillan, 1933; New York: The Colonial Press, 1899; New York: Cambridge University Press, 1999.

——. *Critique of Practical Reason,* Eng. transl. Lewis White Beck, Indianapolis: 1956; Bobbs-Merrill, Milwaukee, WI: Marquette University Press, 1998.

——. *Foundations of the Metaphysics of Morals,* Eng. transl. Lewis White Beck, Indianapolis: Bobbs-Merrill, 1959; New York: Macmillan, 1969.

——. *Kant Selections,* ed. Theodore Meyer Greene, New York: Charles Scribner's Sons, 1929; Paramus, NJ: Prentice Hall, 1988: the best selection of Kant's writings.

——. *Religion within the Limits of Reason Alone,* Eng. transl. Theodore M. Greene & Hoyt H. Hudson, New York: Harper & Row, 1960.

Karl, Frederick, *George Eliot, A Biography,* HarperCollins, 1995; New York: W. W. Norton & Company, 1995.

Kaufmann, Walter, *Critique of Religion and Philosophy,* Princeton, NJ: Princeton University Press, 1978.

Kemp Smith, Norman, *A Commentary to Kant's Critique of Pure Reason,* 2nd edn, Macmillan, 1918; New York: Humanities Press, 1962; Atlantic Highlands, NJ: Humanities Press International, Inc., 1991.

——. (ed.), Hume's *Dialogues:* see under Hume

Kenny, Anthony, *God and Two Poets,* Sidgwick & Jackson, 1988.

Ker, Ian, *John Henry Newman,* London & New York: Oxford University Press, 1988; Mahwah, NJ: Paulist Press, 1994.

Knickerbocker, Frances Wentworth, *Free Minds. John Morley and his Friends,* Cambridge, MA: Harvard University Press, 1943; Westport, CT: Greenwood Press, 1970.

Knight, Margaret, *William James. A Selection from his Writings on Psychology, Edited with a Commentary,* Harmondsworth: Penguin, 1950.

Kojève, Alexandre, *Introduction to the Reading of Hegel,* assembled by Raymond Queneau, ed. Allan Bloom, Eng. transl. James H. Nichols, Jr, Ithaca: Cornell University Press, 1980.

Kuhn, Thomas, *The Structure of Scientific Revolutions,* Chicago: University of Chicago Press, 1962, 1996.

Lafourcade, Georges, *Swinburne. A Literary Biography,* G. Bell & Sons, 1932; New York: Russell & Russell, 1967; Norwood, PA: Norwood Editions, 1980.

Lavrin, Janko, *Nietzsche: A Biographical Introduction,* Studio Vista, 1971; New York: Scribner, 1971.

Leith, Mrs Disney (Mary Gordon), *The Boyhood of Algernon Charles Swinburne,* Chatto & Windus, 1917; Folcroft, PA: Folcroft Library Editions, 1917.

Lenin (V.I. Ulyanov), *The Lenin Anthology.* Selected by Robert C. Tucker, New York: W. W. Norton, 1975.

——. *On Britain,* Moscow: Progress Publishers, 1959.

——. *British Labour and British Imperialism,* Lawrence & Wishart, 1969; Woodstock, NY: Beekman Publishers, Inc., 1969.

Leon, Derrick, *Ruskin the Great Victorian,* Routledge & Kegan Paul, 1969; Hamden, CT: Archon Books, 1969.

Leslie, Shane, *The Anglo-Catholic,* Chatto & Windus, 1929.

Letwin, Shirley Robin, *The Pursuit of Certainty,* Cambridge: Cambridge University Press, 1969; Indianapolis, IN: Liberty Fund, Inc., 1998.

Lewis, C.S., *Miracles,* Fontana (Collins), 1960; New York: Macmillan, 1947.

Lewis, R.W.B., *The Jameses,* New York: Farrar Straus & Giroux, 1991.

Liddon, H.P., *Life of E.B. Pusey,* 4 vols, London & New York: Macmillan, 1893–7.

Lightman, Bernard, *The Origins of Agnosticism. Victorian Unbelief and the Limits of Knowledge,* Baltimore: The Johns Hopkins University Press, 1987; Ann Arbor, MI: Books on Demand, 1987.

Lockes-Lampson, F., *My Confidences,* Smith, Elder, & Co., 1896.

Loisy, Alfred, *Mémoires,* Paris: émile Nourry, 1930–1 (3 vols).

——. *The Gospel and the Church* (Eng. transl. Sir Isaac Pitman, 1908), introduction by George Tyrrell, Sir Isaac Pitman & Sons, 1908; Philadelphia: Fortress Press, 1976; Amherst, NY: Prometheus Books, 1988.

Louis, Margot, K., *Swinburne and his Gods. The Roots and Growth of an Agnostic Poetry,* Buffalo: McGill-Queen's University Press, 1990; Ithaca, NY: CUP Services, 1990.

Lubbock, Percy (ed.), *The Diary of A.C. Benson,* Hutchinson & Co., 1927; New York: Longmans, Green, and Co., 1926.

Lucretius, *De Rerum Natura,* ed. Cyril Bailey, Oxford: Clarendon Press, 2nd ed, 1921; Chicago: Encyclopedia Britannica, 1955; Baltimore: Johns Hopkins University Press, 1995.

Lyell, Sir Charles, *Principles of Geology,* 4 vols, John Murray, 1834; Pittsburgh, PA: J. I. Kay and Co., 1837; New York: Viking Penguin, 1998.

MacCarthy, Fiona, *William Morris. A Life for our Time,* Faber, 1994; New York: Knopf, 1995.

McKown, Delos B., *The Classical Marxist Critiques of Religion: Marx, Engels, Lenin, Kautsky,* Martinus Nijhoff, The Hague, 1975; Norwell, MA: Kluwer Academic Publishers, 1975.

McTaggart, John McTaggart Ellis, *Studies in the Hegelian Dialectic,* Cambridge: University Press, 1896; New York: Russell and Russell, 1964.

——. *Some Dogmas of Religion,* Edward Arnold, 1906; New York: Greenwood Press, 1968; Herndon, VA: Thoemmes Press, 1997.

——. 'Dare to be Wise': An address delivered before the 'Heretic' Society in Cambridge, 8 December 1909: Watts & Co., 1909.

Mallock, W.H., *Memoirs of Life and Literature,* Chapman & Hall, 1920; New York: Harper & brothers, 1920; Philadelphia: Richard West, 1973.

——. *The New Republic,* Michael Joseph, 1937; New York: Scribner and Welford, 1878; Philadelphia: Richard West, 1989.

Mansel, Henry, *A Lecture on the Philosophy of Kant,* John Henry and James Parker, eds, Oxford, 1956.

——. *Prolegomena Logica. An Inquiry into the Psychological Character of Logical Processes,* Oxford, 1851; Boston: Gould and Lincoln, 1860.

——. *The Limits of Demonstrative Science Considered in a Letter to the Rev. William Whewell, DD,* W. Graham, Oxford, 1853.

——. *The Limits of Religious Thought,* Oxford, 1858; Charlottesville, VA: Lincoln-Rembrandt Publishing, 1986.

Bibliography

Marcuse, Herbert, *Eros and Civilization: A Philosophical Inquiry into Freud,* Boston: Beacon Press, 1966, 1974.

Marx, Karl and Engels, Friedrich, *Werke,* Berlin: Dietz Verlag, 1961– ; Evanston, IL: Adler's Foreign Books, Inc., 1999.

———. *The Communist Manifesto,* Eng. transl. Samuel Moore, with introduction by A.J.P. Taylor, Harmondsworth: Penguin, 1967; New York: New York Labor News Co., 1893; New York: Oxford University Press, Inc., 1998.

Maude, Aylmer, *Tolstoy and his Problems,* Grant Richards, 1901; New York: Haskell House, 1974; Brooklyn, NY: M.S.G. House, 1974.

Mayhew, Henry, *Mayhew's London,* selections from *London Labour and the London Poor* (1851) by Peter Quennell, Spring Books, 1949.

Metzger, Bruce M. and Murphy, Roland, E. (eds), *The New Oxford Annotated Bible,* New York: Oxford University Press, 1989, 1994.

Meyers, Terry L., 'Swinburne, Shelley and Songs before Sunrise', in Rooksby and Shrimpton, 1993.

Mill, John Stuart, *Three Essays on Religion,* Chapman & Hall, 1874; New York: H. Holt and Company, 1874; Amherst, NY: Prometheus Books, 1998.

———. *On Liberty* and *The Subjection of Women,* Oxford University Press, World's Classics, 1986; New York: Cambridge University Press, 1989.

———. *Collected Works,* Toronto, from 1963; New York: Gordon Press Publishers, 1972.

———. *Autobiography,* ed., Cockshut, Halifax: Ryburn Publishing, 1992; New York: Columbia University Press, 1924, 1960.

Millais, John Guille, *The Life and Letters of Sir John Everett Millais,* Abridged edn in 1 vol., Methuen & Co., 1905; New York: Frederick A. Stokes Company, 1899; New York: AMS Press, Inc., (no date).

Miller, J. Hillis, *The Disappearance of God,* The Belknap Press of Cambridge, MA: Harvard University Press, 1963.

Milton, John, *Paradise Lost,* Harmondsworth: Penguin, 1990; Philadelphia: William Young and Joseph James, 1787; New York: W. W. Norton & Co., 1975, 1993; White Plains, NY: Longman Publishing Group, 1998.

Mitford, Nancy, *Frederick the Great,* Hamish Hamilton, 1970; New York: Penguin Books, 1995.

Monk, Ray, *Ludwig Wittgenstein. The Duty of Genius,* New York: The Free Press, 1990; New York: Viking Penguin, 1991.

Moore, J.R., *The Post-Darwinian Controversies: A Study of the Protestant Struggle to come to Terms with Darwin in Great Britain and America, 1870–1900,* Cambridge and New York: Cambridge University Press, 1979, 1981.

Morley, John, *On Compromise,* Macmillan, 1874, revised edn, 1921; Darby, PA: Arden Library, 1979.

———. *Recollections,* 2 vols, Macmillan, 1921; New York: Macmillan, 1917; New York: AMS Press Incorporated, 1978.

———. *The Life of William Ewart Gladstone,* 3 vols, Macmillan, 1912; New York: Macmillan, 1903; Saint Clair Shores, MI: Scholarly Press, Inc., 1972.

———. *Voltaire,* Macmillan, 1900; New York: Appleton and Co., 1872; Philadelphia: Richard West, 1989.

Muggeridge, Malcolm, *The Earnest Atheist. A Study of Samuel Butler,* Eyre & Spottiswood, 1936; New York: G. P. Putnam's Sons, 1937; Philadelphia: Richard West, 1973.

———. *The Green Stick,* Collins, 1972; New York: William Morrow & Company, Inc., 1973, 1982.

Muirhead, John, *The Platonic Tradition in Anglo-Saxon Philosophy,* George Allen & Unwin, 1931; New York: Humanities Press, 1965; Herndon, VA: Books International, Inc., 1996.

Murray, Nicholas, *Matthew Arnold,* Hodder & Stoughton, 1996; New York: St. Martin's Press, 1997; New York: Thomas Dunne Books, 1997.

Newman, Francis, *Phases of Faith,* Leicester: Leicester University Press, 1970; New York: Humanities Press, 1970.

Newman, John Henry, *Apologia Pro Vita Sua,* Dent: Everyman Library, 1955; New York: Longmans, Green, and Co., 1897; New York: Viking Penguin, 1995.

——. *An Essay in Aid of a Grammar of Assent,* Longmans, 1906; New York: Longmans, Green, and Co., 1892; Notre Dame, IN: University of Notre Dame Press, 1979.

Newsome, David, *Godliness and Good Learning,* Cassell, 1961; Albuquerque, NM: Transatlantic Arts, Inc., 1961.

——. *On the Edge of Paradise,* John Murray, 1980; Chicago: University of Chicago Press, 1980; Ann Arbor, MI: Books on Demand, 1980.

——. *The Convert Cardinals,* John Murray, 1993; North Pomfret, VT: Trafalgar Square, 1995.

——. *The Parting of Friends,* John Murray, 1966; Westminster, MD: Newman Press, 1961; Grand Rapids, MI: William B. Eerdmans Publishing Co., 1993.

——. *The Victorian World Picture,* John Murray, 1997; New Brunswick, NJ: Rutgers University Press, 1997.

Nietzsche, Frederich, *The Philosophy of Nietzsche,* New York: The Modern Library, 1927 (contains *Thus Spake Zarathustra, Beyond Good and Evil, The Genealogy of Morals, Ecce Homo, The Birth of Tragedy*); New York: NAL/Dutton, 1984.

Oliphant, Margaret, *The Life of Edward Irving,* Hurst & Blackett, 1862.

Oxford Companion to Philosophy: see under Honderich

P.A.D.A. (*sic*), *Les Erreurs du XIX Siècle,* Paris: Libraire Adrien le Clère, 1865.

Panter-Downes, Molly, *At the Pines,* Hamish Hamilton, 1971; Boston: Gambit, 1971; Boston: Harvard Common Press, 1971.

Passmore, John, *A Hundred Years of Philosophy,* Harmondsworth: Penguin, 1968; New York: Basic Books, 1967; New York: Viking Penguin, 1978.

Pattison, Mark, *Memoirs,* Macmillan, 1885; Brookfield, VT: Gregg International, 1968; Watchung, NJ: Albert Saifer Publisher, 1984.

Payne, Robert, *Marx,* W. H. Allen, 1968; New York: Simon & Schuster, 1968.

——. *The Life and Death of Lenin,* W.H. Allen, 1964; New York: Simon and Schuster, 1964.

Perry, Ralph Burton, *The Thought and Character of William James,* 2 vols, New York: Oxford University Press, 1935; Cambridge, MA: Harvard University Press, 1948; Nashville, TN: Vanderbilt University Press, 1996.

——. Abridged version, Nashville: Vanderbilt University Press, 1996.

Petre, M.D. *Autobiography and Life of George Tyrrell,* 2 vols, Edward Arnold, 1912.

——. *My Way of Faith,* J.M. Dent & Sons, 1937; New York: E.P. Dutton and Company, 1937.

——. *Von Hügel and Tyrrell: The Story of a Friendship,* J.M. Dent & Sons, 1937.

Posnock, Ross, *The Trial of Curiosity. Henry James, William James, and the Challenge of Modernity,* New York: Oxford University Press, 1991.

Pusey, E.B., *An Historical Enquiry into the Probable Causes of the Rationalist Character Lately Predominant in the Theology of Germany,* Oxford: Parker, 1827.

Putnam, Ruth Anna (ed.), *The Cambridge Companion to William James,* Cambridge and New York: Cambridge University Press, 1997.

Quinton, A.M., 'Absolute Idealism', in *Proceedings of the British Academy,* 1971.

Raby, Peter, *Samuel Butler,* Hogarth Press, 1991; Iowa City: University of Iowa Press, 1991.

Reardon, Bernard M.G. (ed.), *Roman Catholic Modernism,* Adam & Charles Black, 1970; Stanford, CA: Stanford University Press, 1970.

Ridler, Anne, *Collected Poems,* Manchester: Carcanet, 1994.

Roberts, Brian, *The Mad, Bad Line,* Hamish Hamilton, 1981.

Rooksby, Rikky, *Algernon Charles Swinburne. A Poet's Life,* Scolar Press, 1997; Brookfield, VT: Ashgate Publishing Co., 1997.

——. and Shrimpton, Nicholas (eds), *The Whole Music of Passion: New Essays on Swinburne,* Scolar

Press, 1993; Brookfield, VT: Ashgate Publishing Co., 1993.

Ruskin, John, *Fors Clavigera* (4 vols, New Edition), Sunnyside, Orpington: George Allen, 1896; New York: J. Wiley & Sons, 1871; Westport, CT: Greenwood Publishing Group, Inc., 1969.

——. *Praeterita,* Rupert Hart-Davis, 1949; New York: J. Wiley & Sons, 1886–7; New York: Oxford University Press, 1990.

——. *The Ethics of the Dust,* George Allen, 1906; New York: John W. Lovell Company, 1885.

——. *The Queen of the Air,* George Allen, 1906; New York: J. Wiley & Sons, 1878; Cheshire, CT: Biblo & Tannen Booksellers & Publishers, Inc., 1969.

——. *Unto This Last,* George Allen, 1906; New York: J. Wiley & Sons, 1866; New York: Viking Penguin, 1986.

Russell, Bertrand, *A History of Western Philosophy,* George Allen & Unwin, 1990; New York: Simon & Schuster, 1990.

——. *Mysticism and Logic,* Harmondsworth: Penguin, 1954; New York: Longmans, Green, and Co., 1918; New York: W. W. Norton & Co., 1929; Albuquerque, NM: Foundation for Classical Reprints, 1991.

——. *Religion and Science,* Home University Library, Oxford University Press, 1935; New York: H. Holt Company, 1935; New York: Oxford University Press, 1997.

——. *The Autobiography of Bertrand Russell, 1872–1914,* George Allen & Unwin, 1967; Boston: Little, Brown, 1967; New York: Routledge, 1998.

Sampson, R.V., *Tolstoy: The Discovery of Peace,* Heineman, 1973.

Schneider, Herbert W., *A History of American Philosophy,* 2nd edn, Columbia University Press, 1963.

Schweitzer, Albert, *The Quest of the Historical Jesus* (Eng. transl. of Van Reimarus Zu Wrede, 1906), 3rd edn, with introduction by Author, Adam & Charles Black, 1954; New York: Macmillan, 1950; Baltimore, MD: Johns Hopkins University Press, 1998.

Scruton, Roger, *A Short History of Modern Philosophy,* 2nd edn, London & New York; Routledge & Kegan Paul, 1995.

——. *An Intelligent Person's Guide to Philosophy,* Duckworth, 1996; New York: A. Lane, 1998; New York: Viking Penguin, 1999.

——. *Kant,* London & New York: Oxford University Press, 1982, 1983.

Seeley, Sir John R., *Ecce Homo,* Dent: Everyman's Library, 1964; New York: E.P. Dutton & Co., 1920; Philadelphia: Richard West, 1978.

Shaw, P.E., *The Catholic Apostolic Church Sometimes Called Irvingite. A Historical Study,* Morningside Heights, New York: King's Crown Press, 1946; North Stratford, NH: Ayer Company Publishers, Inc., 1977.

Simon, Linda, *William James Remembered,* Lincoln & London: University of Nebraska Press, 1996, 1999.

Sparrow, John, *Mark Pattison and the Idea of a University,* Cambridge: Cambridge University Press, 1967.

Spence, Margaret E., 'The Guild of St George: Ruskin's attempt to translate his ideas into practice', in *Bulletin of the John Rylands Library,* Vol. 40, 1957–8.

Spencer, Herbert, *Autobiography,* Williams & Norgate, 1904; New York: D. Appleton & Co., 1904.

——. *First Principles,* Williams & Norgate, 1863; New York: J.A. Hill & Co., 1904; Westport, CT: Greenwood Publishing Group, Inc., 1976.

——. *The Data of Ethics,* Williams & Norgate, 1879; New York: D. Appleton & Co., 1879; Kila, MT: Kessinger Publishing Co., 1998.

——. *The Principles of Biology,* Williams & Norgate, 1894; New York: D. Appleton & Co., 1866, 1897.

——. *The Principles of Ethics,* Williams & Norgate, 1892; New York: D. Appleton & Co., 1892; Indianapolis, IN: Liberty Fund, Inc., 1980.

——. *The Principles of Psychology,* Williams & Norgate, 1890; New York: D. Appleton & Co., 1872; Brookfield, VT: Gregg International, 1971.

——. *The Principles of Sociology,* Williams & Norgate, 1893; New York: D. Appleton & Co., 1880; Westport, CT: Greenwood Publishing Group, Inc., 1975.

Spurling, Hilary, *Ivy when Young,* Gollancz, 1974; New York: Knopf, 1984; New York: Columbia University Press, 1986.

——. *Secrets of a Woman's Heart,* Hodder & Stoughton, 1984.

Stanley, Arthur Penrhyn, *The Life and Correspondence of Thomas Arnold, D.D.,* B. Fellowes, 1844; New York: Scribner, Armstrong, and Co., 1877; New York: AMS Press, Inc., 1978.

Stephen, Leslie, *History of Thought in the Eighteenth Century,* Smith, Elder & Co., 2 vols., 1876.

Stephenson, Alan M.G., *The Rise and Decline of English Modernism,* SPCK, 1984.

Strachey, Lytton, *Eminent Victorians,* Chatto & Windus, 1956; New York: G. P. Putnam's Sons, 1918; New York: Viking Penguin, 1990.

Strauss, David Friedrich, *The Life of Jesus, Critically Examined,* Eng. transl. Marian Evans, John Chapman, 1846; New York: C. Blanchard, 1855; Mifflintown, PA: Sigler Press, 1994.

Strawson, P.F., *The Bounds of Sense,* Routledge, 1975; New York: Routledge, Chapman & Hall, Inc., 1966.

Swinburne, Algernon Charles and Gordon, Mary, *The Children of the Chapel,* ed. Robert E. Lougy, Athens: Ohio University Press, 1982.

——. *A Year's Letters,* ed. Francis James Sypher, Peter Owen, 1976; Portland, ME: T.B. Mosher, 1901; New York: New York University Press, 1974.

——. *Lesbia Brandon. An Historical and Critical Commentary being Largely a Study (and Elevation) of Swinburne as a Novelist by Randolph Hughes,* The Falcon Press, 1952; Westport, CT: Greenwood Publishing Group, Inc., 1978.

——. *The Poems of Algernon Charles Swinburne,* 6 vols, Chatto & Windus, 1904; New York: AMS Press, 1972.

——. *The Swinburne Letters,* ed. Cecil Y. Lang, 6 vols, New Haven: Yale University Press, 1959–1962; Ann Arbor, MI: Books on Demand, 1960.

——. *The Whippingham Papers,* Wordsworth, 1993.

——. *William Blake, A Critical Essay,* J. C. Hotten, 1868; New York: E. P. Dutton & Co., 1906; Ann Arbor, MI: Books on Demand, (no date).

Taylor, Anne, *Annie Besant, A Biography,* London & New York: Oxford University Press, 1992.

Tennyson, Alfred Lord, *The Poems of Tennyson,* 3 vols, ed. Christopher Ricks, Longmans, 1987; Berkeley: University of California Press, 1987.

Thomas, D.M., *Alexander Solzhenitsyn. A Century in his Life,* Little, Brown, 1998; New York: St. Martin's Press, 1998.

Thomas, Geoffrey, *The Moral Philosophy of T.H. Green,* Oxford: Clarendon Press, 1987; New York: Oxford University Press, 1988.

Tolstoy, L.N., *A Confession,* Eng. transl. Aylmer Maude, Oxford University Press, World's Classics, 1963; New York: W. W. Norton & Co., 1996.

——. *Anna Karenina,* Eng. transl. Aylmer Maude, Oxford University Press (World's Classics), 1931; New York: T.Y. Crowell & Co., 1886; New York: W.W. Norton & Co., 1995.

Tsuzuki, Chushichi, *The Life of Eleanor Marx, 1855–1898. A Socialist Tragedy,* Oxford: Clarendon Press, 1967.

Tumarkin, Nina, *LENIN LIVES! The Lenin Cult in Soviet Russia.* Cambridge, MA: Harvard University Press, 1983, 1997.

Tyrrell, George, *Christianity at the Cross-Roads,* London & New York: Longmans, Green & Co., 1909.

Vidler, Alec, *A Variety of Catholic Modernists,* Cambridge: Cambridge University Press, 1970.

——. *The Modernist Movement in the Roman Church,* Cambridge: Cambridge University Press, 1934; New York: Gordon Press Publishers, 1976.

Ward, Mary (Mrs Humphry), *Robert Elsmere,* ed. Rosemary Ashton, Oxford: Oxford University Press, 1987; New York: Macmillan, 1888; Temecula, CA: Reprint Services Corporation, 1992.

Ward, May Alden, *Prophets of the Nineteenth Century, Carlyle, Ruskin, Tolstoy,* Gay & Bird, 1900; Folcroft, PA: Folcroft Library Editions, 1976; Norwood, PA: Norwood Editions, 1980.

Ward, Wilfrid, *William George Ward and the Oxford Movement,* London & New York: Macmillan, 1889; New York: AMS Press, Inc., 1977.

Watson, James D., *The Double Helix* (new edn with introduction by Steve Jones), 1997; New York: W. W. Norton & Co., 1980; New York: Simon & Schuster, 1998.

Waugh, Evelyn, *Rossetti,* Duckworth, 1928; Folcroft, PA: Folcroft Library Editions, 1928.

Webb, Beatrice, *My Apprenticeship,* Harmondsworth: Penguin, 1971; New York: Longmans, Green, and Co., 1926; New York: Cambridge University Press, 1980.

——. *The Diary of Beatrice Webb,* ed. Norman and Jeanne MacKenzie, Virago, vol. i, 1982; vol. ii, 1983; Cambridge, MA: Belknap Press of Harvard University Press, 1982–5, 1990.

Weil, Simone, *Waiting on God,* Fontana Books, Collins, 1969; London: Routledge & K. Paul, 1979.

Wilde, Oscar, *The Letters of Oscar Wilde,* ed. Rupert Hart-Davis, New York: Harcourt, Brace & World Inc., 1962; New York: H. Holt & Company, Inc., 1999.

Willey, Basil, *Darwin and Butler,* Chatto & Windus, 1960; New York: Harcourt, Brace, 1960.

Wilson, A.N., *Tolstoy,* Hamish Hamilton, 1988; New York: W. W. Norton & Co., 1988.

Wilton, Andrew and Upstone, Robert (eds), *The Age of Rossetti, Burne-Jones and Watts. Symbolism in Britain, 1860–1910,* Tate Gallery Publishing, 1997; New York: Flammarion, 1997; New York: Abbeville Press, Inc., 1997.

Wittgenstein, Ludwig, *Philosophical Investigations,* Eng. transl. E. Anscombe, Oxford: Blackwell, 1958; New York: Macmillan, 1953; Malden, MA: Blackwell Publishers, 1998.

——. *Tractatus Logico-Philosophicus,* Eng. transl., Ramsey and Owen, Kegan Paul, 1922; New York: Harcourt, Brace, 1933; Mountain View, CA: Mayfield Publishing Company, 1997.

——. *The Wittgenstein Reader,* ed. Anthony Kenny, Oxford: Blackwell, 1994; Malden, MA: Blackwell Publishers, 1994.

Wollheim, Richard, *F.H. Bradley,* Harmondsworth: Penguin, 1959.

Yeats, John Butler, *Essays Irish and American,* Dublin: Talbot Press, 1918; Freeport, NY: Books for Libraries Press, 1969; North Stratford, NH: Ayer Company Publishers, Inc., 1977.

Young, G.M., *Victorian England, Portrait of an Age,* 2nd edn, London & New York: Oxford University Press, 1953, 1977.

Zeller, E., *Strauss and Renan,* Eng. transl. Trübner & Co., 1866.

Acknowledgements

This book evolved from a series of conversations with Donald Lamm and Starling Lawrence, who read it at various stages of composition, and whose help has been invaluable. Thanks, too, are owing to Linda Lawrence, who kept me supplied with William James material. Others who read all or part of the typescript include John Grigg, Naomi Lewis, Herbert McCabe, David Newsome, Roger Scruton and Francis Wheen. I feel warm gratitude to them for all the trouble they took, and there would have been more mistakes without them. As to mistakes, the usual formula applies: that is, that all those which remain, and all the opinions, are my own.

Much of the book was written or researched in the London Library, the Doctor Williams Library and the magnificent new British Library. In each of these institutions, the staff have been of enormous help.

Thanks, too, to my family and friends, who have allowed me to be a bore about the Doubters, and whose conversation has often stimulated further reading or thoughts.

Amy Boyle typed and retyped. I could not have written the book without her. At a later stage, Gail Pirkis, Caroline Knox, Liz Robinson and Caroline Westmore were the best of midwives, gentle but firm. Douglas Matthews compiled the index.

5 Regent's Park Terrace, London,
December 1998

Index